100 YEARS OF TENNIS
IN THE
WEST OF SCOTLAND

1904 - 2004

Written and compiled by Myra Hunter

ISBN 0-9546588-0-9

THE WEST OF SCOTLAND LAWN TENNIS ASSOCIATION
appreciates that this publication is

Supported by the
Heritage Lottery Fund

CONTENTS

Foreword   7

Committee   8

Acknowledgements   9

The Beginning   11

Developments   14

The Leagues   22

The Championships   29

The Red Hackle Years   38

These That Are   - The Clubs   62

Those That Were   - The Clubs that used to be   182

                          - Public Parks   190

West of Scotland County   196

Personalities   201

The Purple Patch   - The Veterans   228

Memorable Moments   232

Appendices   - The statistics   246

Bibliography   326

FOREWORD

For anyone who has been involved with Tennis in the West of Scotland at any stage over the past 100 years, this book is a fantastic trip down memory lane. It certainly was for me when I first read the early drafts. Now that it is finished it provides, for the first time, an important record of the history of achievement; of development; and of change, which has been seen over the past century.

In particular, 'The Red Hackle Years' brings back fond memories of a time when my interest in tennis administration was being developed. My involvement in The West of Scotland Championships on the Press Relations side, my first and last match (the same one) as an Umpire in a Professional Event and the Thursday nights at Newlands in the Squash court bar after play had finished will always be remembered as some of my best tennis memories.

Pat Cash and Manuel Santana no longer grace the courts at Newlands, many clubs have come and gone but there have always been volunteers to administer the clubs, run the Juniors to their matches, make the match teas and brush the courts.

I take this opportunity to thank them all and although, as in many other walks of life, some of their work is being taken over by paid officials, the game of Tennis will continue to rely on "The Volunteers" for many years to come, perhaps as long as tennis is played.

Finally to Myra Hunter, the epitome of the volunteer, who has laboured long and hard over the past 3 years to produce not only our Centenary Exhibition in the Peoples Palace, but this excellent record of our first 100 years, I take this opportunity to thank her, most sincerely, on behalf of Tennis West of Scotland.

Clive M Thomson
President

TENNIS WEST OF SCOTLAND COMMITTEE

The Committee 2003

Mrs Irene Stewart, John G Beeley, David W Marshall, Eric Dalgetty, Brian Knox, Clive M Thomson, Mrs Elspeth MacLean
John AE Stevenson (Secretary/Treasurer), W Baxter Allan (President), Myra F Hunter

The Committee 1947

Alex Stevenson, Harold Herbert
Jack Hall, R Lightbody, Willie Drummond, R French, Tom Millar, Willie Reid
John Patrick, ?, B Moulding, ?

ACKNOWLEDGEMENTS

Writing and editing this history of the West of Scotland Lawn Tennis Association has involved a great many people who have given time and effort to cover as many aspects as possible.

It all had to start somewhere. Mrs Clara Black neé, Butters provided much memorabilia and four books of cuttings which commenced in 1930. What a wonderful start to get that far back so easily. We have had many conversations and meetings since.

In 1935, at the Jubilee of the Championships, and again in 1954, at the Jubilee of the Association, George B Primrose was the author of the booklets produced to celebrate these milestones. These have been incorporated into this publication celebrating the Centenary of the founding of The West of Scotland Lawn Tennis Association on Thursday 3rd November 1904.

2000 - Clara Black and Myra Hunter at the start of the centenary quest for information and memorabilia

There being no surviving minutes prior to 1962, the booklets and the scrapbooks proved invaluable. Then there was another stroke of luck, Lenzie LTC had League results back to 1933, so another avenue was opened. Minutes from some clubs produced other gems of information and gradually a history was developing, however the story will never be complete since it would take a hundred years to tell it all.

The Clubs have worked hard to produce their potted histories and a few have gone even further and produced a fuller history as well.

The Committee have been supportive and John Stevenson our Secretary has provided much information and help. An enormous number of people have provided written information and or photographs of places and events and have been ever helpful with answers to my questions and among these are Elva Allan, Ann Barr, Mina Brady, Colin Baxter, Max Black, Sandra Cochrane, Eileen Drummond, Eric Flack, Billy Gillespie, Dorothy Gray (widow of James E Gray), Lorna Hamilton, Diane Howie, Marjory Love, Alan McNeilage, Harry and Carole Matheson, Sheila Moodie, Anne Paul, Elaine Robb, Avril Robertson, Maisie Rutherglen, Angus Shaw, Stuart Walker, JB Wilson. Robert Cameron for the cartoons (see Rutherglen and Paisley). Please do not take offence if your name is not here.

The research has reached far and wide and many have provided help and information. George Robertson author of "100 Years of Tennis in Scotland" gave advice on how to put it all together. Tennis Scotland has made available its archive material and photographs. Audrey Snell of the Kenneth Ritchie Library at Wimbledon pointed me in the right direction when on visits to that Library for research.

The staff of the Mitchell Library in Glasgow both in the Glasgow Room and Archives have been of enormous help in aspects of research and information. The Herald and Evening Times Newsquest Media Group and the Scottish Daily Record & Sunday Mail Ltd. have given their permission to reproduce photographs and information from their publications.

John McCormick & Co. Ltd. Printers have provided advice and help and have steered a new author in the right direction.

Finally there are those who have given their time in research, typing and proof reading, some of whom have no connection with tennis Jessie Cross, Irene Dick, Fiona Fyfe, Moira Henderson, Christine Lindsay.

My thanks to everyone who has in any way made a contribution to this publication. It would take a hundred years to write about it all.

The most important is kept to the last and that is the Heritage Lottery Fund. Their contribution has made all of this possible.

It is your history, enjoy it!

Myra Hunter 2004

This book Is dedicated to all those who love the game of Lawn Tennis.

THE BEGINNING

As we are about to celebrate our Centenary, and proud we are too at the achievements of the past hundred years, it should be noted that there was a "Tennis Court" in Glasgow four hundred years ago! Never you might be tempted to say! Read on.

"In 1608 Thomas Forret probably the father of Baillie Forret had lands called "The Caitchpuill" on the other side of which were lands belonging to St Nicholas Hospital (which we know today as Provands Lordship)"

"The Caitchpuill" was A Tennis Court (Jamieson's Dictionary)

Costumed players were playing what we know today as Real Tennis, played by hitting the tennis balls off walls and using a net which was draped across the centre of the playing area. Today you can visit Falkland Palace in Fife to view such a court.

The game as we know it was supposed to have been invented in 1873. Major Walter Clopton Wingfield was the inventor and he called the game Sphairistike (from Greek meaning skill in playing ball). It was played on a lawn court laid out in the garden of his home. The game was a success but not the name of it. Soon it was known as Lawn Tennis and is the game we play today. Should you visit The All England Championships at Wimbledon there is a restaurant called "The Wingfield" named in his honour.

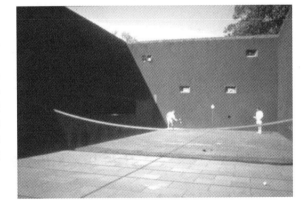

Fresh light on the subject indicates that Lawn Tennis was being played in England before 1870. It is believed first to have been seen in the West of Scotland in the secluded grounds of country houses about 1875. Some information on the position of the game in the district before the West of Scotland Championships were established is given in a paragraph appearing in the newly-founded weekly sports paper "The Scottish Umpire" in August 1884, as follows:

"Lawn Tennis continues to make rapid strides in popular favour. It is not so long since all the clubs in Glasgow could easily be numbered in one hand, when, indeed, the West (West of Scotland Cricket Club) and the Academy had the courts all to themselves. How things have changed since then! Now we have the Glasgow Tennis Club, 1st L.R.V., Albany, Clydesdale, Pollokshields Athletic, Langside, Golfhill, Bellahouston, United Northern, Poloc and Grosvenor, all open membership, not to mention the hundred and one semi-private affairs throughout the city."

Sir John Lavery the painter lived at Cartbank, Cathcart, where he had a tennis court in his garden and it is where, in 1885, he painted q watercolour named "A Rally" showing Miss Alix MacBride playing tennis. He painted several pictures with a tennis theme.

The earliest Club Courts in the district are those believed to have been laid down in the West of Scotland Cricket Club's enclosure before 1878.   It is said that tennis was played on the turf of Hampden! What a fabulous Centre Court that would have been. Pollokshields Athletic Club founded about 1870 for the playing of cricket and football, introduced Lawn Tennis as one of its recreations in its old enclosure known as Pollok Park, near Haggs Castle, in 1878. In April 1886, the Club, which was devoting itself more and more to tennis and less and less to other pastimes, opened its enclosure in Maxwell Drive, and a month later the first West of Scotland Championships were held there. The event was then known as the Pollokshields Athletic Club Tournament. Nearly twenty years elapsed before the West of Scotland Lawn Tennis Association was formed and took over from the Club running the Championship meeting.

Hamilton Lawn Tennis Club has a minute of 1884 mentioning the proposed formation of The West of Scotland Tennis Association. This is the only mention so far of this proposal but no indication of why it was not carried out.

During the late 1890s Lawn Tennis suffered something of a slump owing to the rivalry of cycling, but there was a recovery after the new century began. With the formation of several new clubs and the revival of several that had closed down, the feeling prevailed among the growing number of players in the West that an Association should be formed and be responsible for the tournament, the promotion of other competitions and the general control of the game in the district.

A meeting was accordingly called in Glasgow for the evening of Thursday the 3rd of November 1904 and was attended by representatives of Kelvinside, Partick, Johnstone, Cathcart, Bellahouston, Queen's Park, Cartha, Pollokshields and Bothwell. On the motion of Mr. AJ Smellie, Pollokshields, member of a well-known tennis playing family, seconded by Mr. GA Paterson, Partick, a future West Singles Champion, it was unanimously decided to form the West of Scotland Lawn Tennis Association with the following objectives :-

1) To take over the running of the Championships from the West of Scotland Tournament Committee,

2) To Institute a West of Scotland Inter-Club team competition (the League),

3) To send a separate West team to compete in the British Inter-County Cup competition (in which hitherto a team representing all Scotland had taken part,

4) Stimulate and promote the game and place it on an organised basis in the district.

The meeting agreed that an application should be made for the affiliation of the new body to the Scottish Lawn Tennis Association, which had been founded in 1895. The annual subscription was fixed at 10s 6d for city and 5s. for country clubs. A total of twenty three clubs joined the Association in its first year. They included the newly founded Newlands Club, the revived Titwood Club and also Ayr Club as the separate Ayrshire LTA was not formed until many years later. Mr. Smellie was elected President and Mr JT Rankin, CA, Honorary Secretary.

Application was also made at this time to affiliate to the Lawn Tennis Association as recorded in the minute of the LTA meeting on Wednesday 9th November 1904
"Affiliation:- The following was elected to membership of the LTA without representation:- The West of Scotland Association", The newly formed WSLTA certainly were quick off the mark once they were inaugurated!

The League programme for 1905 was arranged and was for the gentlemen only!

The Committee made arrangements for the annual tournament, which it was decided, should be held in the enclosures of the leading city clubs in rotation, Bellahouston being the first choice.

Each of the aspects of the Association has a chapter devoted to it therefore no further comment is required except to say that "Play was suspended during the two World Wars".

George Primrose wrote some of these details in his writings of 1935 and 1954. No minutes of the Association survive prior to October 1962 the Committee of the day gave their permission for the destruction of old papers! They were most surely not archivists!

Over the years the Association has developed and evolved with the introduction of many competitions, coaching, team selection, development, and the professional input of County Coaches, a Development Officer and a Performance Officer (both funded by Tennis Scotland).

We have appointed a full time County Tennis Executive in John Stevenson who has served as Secretary for some years and have opened a County Office within the premises of the David Lloyd Club in Renfrew.

In 2003 The West of Scotland Lawn Tennis Association incorporated as a company limited by guarantee and renamed itself Tennis West of Scotland.

HOW COACHING DEVELOPED
By W. J. Moss

Bill Low and Jimmy Wilson Vice President of the SLTA came to Edgbaston Birmingham, where I was coaching in 1958, with a proposal - would I be prepared to come to Scotland and run a weeks coaching course for selected juniors at the New National Sports Centre, Inverclyde, Largs?

So began a long association with the SLTA and that I should reside in the West of Scotland. It was not surprising that I was in contact with so many players, young and old, in the West who were in the forefront of tennis in Scotland.

An early coaching weekend at Inverclyde for promising Juniors, 1958/9

The courses at Inverclyde in 1958 and 1959 produced a group of very talented West juniors who gave impetus to SLTA's vision of getting more competitive play and widening their tournament play in England, with Junior Wimbledon play the ultimate target.

We must remember that at the time tennis was still an amateur game. School, University and a working career were still the main priority for many of the young players, so their tennis was still of a recreational nature, but structured coaching was beginning to broaden young players' approach to the game, becoming much more competitive. Entering more tournaments was now strong on their agenda.

West players were now making great progress towards International recognition, bringing about a period of domination in Home Internationals. More success was to follow with West players being selected for Great Britain teams.

Harry Matheson playing in the Kings Cup was leading the way towards the Championships at Wimbledon. Frances McLennan was also giving the girls a boost by playing more in England with great success, followed by Winnie Shaw, later to become Winnie Wooldridge, who was to achieve great things. A winner of Junior Wimbledon set her on the road to a successful career at the higher level in the game; a Wimbledon and Wightman Cup player of distinction.

Being on court with Winnie was something very special for me. We were to remain great friends throughout her short life.

The success of West players continued. Marjory Love who so many players found hard to beat, along with Shiela Moodie were International players of real quality. Ken Revie winning Junior Wimbledon and under 21's Champion led to Great Britain honours. Other players along with Ken Revie were making an impact on the international scene. All these players and those before them achieved their standing in the game through dedication and hard work on court. Certainly a week at Inverclyde gave them a good start, but continuous coaching for them was still in its infancy.

There were many more West juniors who were at Inverclyde over the years who were competing strongly in home-based tournaments and travelling to England for more competition, but to push towards a career in tennis was not for everyone. So many players, even the star performers were giving more thought to their education and working careers, taking a step back from the higher tennis arena.

Clubs were now being encouraged to run their own junior programmes. To help those who were prepared to work with juniors the Elementary Coaches Award was introduced. While I ran courses around Scotland Ken Selbie LTA Professional Coach was the instructor for these courses in the West of Scotland. Good venues for these courses were difficult to find, but Ken Selbie's enthusiasm ensured their success.

The Elementary Course itself was a simple basic coaching instruction giving guidance to many candidates taking part, and so began a more constructive coaching programme to develop a better understanding of the game and how to play more efficiently.

Clubs put forward their most promising juniors for the West County Development Programme. Squads were formed covering an age range from 10 years old through to their final year of junior tennis. The main base for these squads was to be at Scotstoun originally in a small hall just big enough for one tennis court. The luxury of the eight indoor courts was still some way off, but to be ready for the new facility, coaches needed to be trained to a higher coaching standard so the Intermediate Coaching award came into being.

Competition for all these young players would be the best way of measuring their improvement. Individual team competitions at club and county level were now well established, which kept officials, parents and coaches extremely busy in organising so many events.

The success of Heather Lockhart and Malcolm Watt through all their junior events, junior Internationals at home and abroad gave them the experience to become amongst the best senior players in Scotland. For Heather tennis was never a life or death affair. She enjoyed other sports in equal measure, but when called on for County and Country she was the most reliable of players. Likewise Malcolm's improving play was making him the most consistant tournament player since the days of Colin Baxter. So it was not surprising that full Senior International honours were a formality for these two fine players. Their reliability and continued enthusiasm played a major part in the success of the Four Nations Senior Team.

For sometime now open tennis was bringing about a new way of life for coaches and the talented juniors. More money was becoming available to suport the juniors in their desire to play on the world stage of "professional" tennis, which also meant a change in coaches approach to their pupils' demands.

Maximising the full potential of these young players was now in the hands of coaches giving the juniors controlled individual lessons. This was the only way forward. This coaching and sustained practice was now vital. Certainly over the last decade West juniors have benefitted from this individual attention.

Ross Matheson wanted a career as a playing professional. He had all the technical requirements to suceed, a powerful game that todays game requires. I became involved with his coaching and training over a few years. His improvement was to bring about tournament successes that impressed selectors in the south. He was now part of the LTA's elite group of players. Playing at Wimbledon on two occasions was a just reward for all his efforts.

Alan Mackin followed, coached by John Howie, Whitecraigs Club Professional Coach. His game from a very early age until his middle teens under John's coaching and hard practice was improving fast, and was now recognised as one of the leading juniors, but to sustain his high level of play moving south was necessary, mixing with players with the same ambitions to join the professional ranks. He now receives coaching in Spain to broaden his experience.

Young David Brewer is treading the same path. Like Alan he was coached individually by John Howie who gave him a sound grounding in all departments of the game. With his technique and understanding more secure he is proving to be a very fine prospect, joining the World Junior Circuit with great success. His coaching and training is now in the hands of the LTA's programme for selected players.

Elena Baltacha when she moved to the West of Scotland was a very young, talented junior. Jim Mackechnie, Club Coach at Newlands LTC, began to take her for individual lessons. He soon realised that he had a young player who was that little bit special, but her powerful aggressive game needed to be more consistant. Jim's enthusiasm and hard practice with her over the next few years saw her game becoming more secure. Her tournament successes and growing stature in the game was to take her to England joining the LTA's training programme. Playing at Wimbledon in 2002 she played with great authority to reach the third round, a wonderful performance. She has now secured the top spot in the British Ladies ranking list.

These coaches reward is to know that for all their time and effort during their juniors' early years, preparing them for the difficult years ahead has borne fruit. There is no doubt that John Howie and Jim Mackechnie have played a major role in what these young players have achieved to date.

Now another young player is making headway in the game, joining this band of West players bidding for World International honours. Like the players already mentioned Jamie Baker is in the south , but his early coaching was here in the West of Scotland being developed by West training programme, proving that its scheme can produce players of real quality.

Finally, not about todays juniors, but "yesterdays" juniors - juniors of my time in the West of Scotland. Now they are part of that happy band of over 35s and veterans. Although a "wee" bit slower than in the past, they remain as competitive as ever, their enthusiasm and skills still intact, and still with the knack of winning matches at County and International level.

I have no wish to rush towards my 50 years in the West of Scotland but a few years short does not really matter. They have been enjoyable and rewarding years and to be a part of West's development for so long has been a great experience.

WEST OF SCOTLAND LAWN TENNIS AMATEUR COACHES ASSOCIATION 1967

The letter indcates that this Association pre-dates the present one. There is no other information. Can anyone add to this information?

CITy 4061 : Ext. 23

55 Blythswood Street,
Glasgow, C.2.

26.10.67

Dear Sir/Madam,

W.S.L.T. AMATEUR COACHES ASSOCIATION

At a meeting on the 24th October, 1967, attended by Mr. J.B. Wilson, Mrs. A.H. Stevenson and Mr. W.J. Moss, a steering committee was formed to arrange the first meeting of the association to be held at the new Bellahouston Recreation Centre in mid-December.

Programme

Viewing the Centre and facilities.

Half hour in Conference Room

On Court with Mr. Moss

The date proposed was December 12th and will be confirmed later.

It is hoped that you will make every effort to attend the first monthly meeting.

Yours sincerely,

JOHN R. BROWN

WEST OF SCOTLAND TENNIS COACHES ASSOCIATION 1985

With the development of the Elementary Coaches Courses, and the growing number of certified coaches in the West of Scotland, it was a natural progression to form a Coaches Association. So in 1985 a committee including Jimmy Bell, John Lavery, Ken Selbie, Stewart Simpson and Derek Stewart were elected and The West of Scotland Coaches Association became a reality.

It was extremely important that the Association had someone that coaches could identify and look for guidance from and therefore Bill Moss was the most obvious choice given the breadth of experience he had.

The aim of the Association under the guidance of Bill Moss was to encourage coaches to expand their coaching knowledge by attending regular coaching seminars and to exchange coaches ideas on working with young players at club level.

1970s Coaching session

Ian Woodcraft taking a session at Stirling with Coaches

From the coaching seminars, the Association also wanted Elementary coaches to take the then Intermediate Coaching Award. This level of coaching was important for developing juniors for more competitive play, at club level, preparing them for teams, tournaments and for the then National Sifts.

There is no question that the Association in the early days aroused great enthusiasm from the coaches. They in turn passed on their enthusiasm to the junior players, many of them being selected for West of Scotland and National Training.

Coaching activities in the West of Scotland were growing and many more coaches were required to assist in the training sessions.

Many things have changed over the years, but the Association still has a role to play in the West of Scotland development. The Coaches of the Association know the standard of their players better than anyone.

John Lavery.

DEVELOPMENT

The People/ Staff – Nicola Kerr, West of Scotland County Development Officer

The modern day development story begins in 1996 with the appointment of a full - time County Development Officer (CDO) for the West of Scotland. Twenty-three year old Nicola Kerr had become the youngest CDO in the UK, but nevertheless had all the credentials for the job. Originally from a background of swimming and ski-ing, Nicola had been encouraged into tennis by her grandmother, a County player for the North of Scotland. She progressed so quickly that she became an LTA coach at the age of eighteen. She added a degree in Leisure Management to her ever-growing CV and the rest, as they say, is history. Increased activity has meant that Nicola now works as part of a team in a County Office alongside County Executive John Stevenson, National Performance Officer covering the West County Karen Ross, two County Mini Tennis Coaches Julie Gordon and more latterly Shona Ross, and she works closely with Glasgow's Tennis Development Officer Andrew Raitt.

Partnerships and Facilities

The new CDO had arrived in a county that already had a progressive structure in place and was home to almost half of the overall number of players in the country. However there was work to be done. All counties had been encouraged to produce a "Strategy for Change", with the aim of forging strong partnerships between tennis clubs, key sporting agencies and local communities. The key word in this equation was to become 'partnership' especially with Local Authorities, education and grant-aid bodies, sport brands, sponsors and the media.

The purpose of partnerships was two-fold – to produce more accessible tennis facilities and quality coaching development programmes but also to promote the game to a wider audience than before. This resulted in many 'firsts' for the West of Scotland.

Several commercial facilities sprang up to serve this densely-populated county. The upsurge of these indoor tennis clubs throughout the West - David Lloyd, Renfrew, Esporta (Milngavie and Hamilton), Next Generation, Anniesland – was a testament to the growing popularity of tennis and the work that has been done to promote the sport in the West of Scotland. Strathgryffe Tennis Club saw the importance of indoor tennis courts and in 1996 became Scotland's first non-commercial club to build an indoor facility. Subsequently Glasgow City Council acquired funding for the Gorbals Leisure Centre, this time on the southside making Glasgow the only city in Britain to have two pay – and – play facilities.

In the late 1990s, tennis was the second-highest recipient of Sports Scotland Lottery Funding. Twenty-seven West of Scotland clubs have received grants towards court, clubhouse upgrades and clubhouse developments.

Community Tennis Partnerships and the Cliff Richard Tennis Trail

Another kind of partnership between clubs, local authorities and the LTA gave birth to a concept called the Community Tennis Partnership. The West of Scotland LTA acted as trailblazers again, endorsing the first Community Tennis Partnership (CTP) in Scotland. This CTP in Inverclyde inspired two tennis clubs in Bearsden who were also successful in acquiring funding to develop tennis in their community. Both areas became particularly

Announcing the third Cliff Richard Trail to Inverclyde

pro-active in establishing school - club links and more non - members were given the opportunity to play tennis at clubs. Strong relationships were forged with public tennis providers, and tennis has generally become more accessible to all in these sectors of the West of Scotland.

Strong and successful school - club links have also been established in many areas of the county where the Cliff Richard Tennis Trail have visited. They have visited Inverclyde three times, the city of Glasgow three times and the Trail we hope will return to the West of Scotland again in the future. Each visit involves the Cliff Richard Tennis team spending a week in ten primary schools in an area that has not previously been exposed to tennis. The Trail team introduces tennis to approximately 2000 children in that week who are then offered a chance to follow up this experience with a free taster session at the local club or community centre. A variety of follow-on coaching sessions and tennis playing opportunities are organised from this point onwards at affordable prices to ensure that any child who has been attracted to the game is retained.

Coaches

Increased activity in the county over the past decade has meant that driving a comprehensive Coach Education Programme was to become vital. The West of Scotland Tennis Coaches Association takes an active role in recruiting and supporting new and existing coaches and providing an annual programme of Coach Education in addition to the LTA and Tennis Scotland. The governing body have worked hard to make the profession more respected and the coaches it trains more professional. There is now a clear pathway in place from the introductory two day Tennis Assistant Award, to the Development Coach Award, Club Coach Award and Performance Coach Award. More "development" orientated coaches are now able to move up the Coach Education ladder reaching the Tennis Development Award, recognising high standards of practice and knowledge in development. This new system accommodates the range of people opting for tennis coaching as a career. Working as a tennis coach in the 21st century is a role that has developed considerably. The job title, 'tennis coach', used to refer to someone who taught technique and tactics but now encompasses a wider range of skills including running a business, marketing and organising and administering a club programme successfully. The essential role of the tennis coach is also strongly reflected in the respect and reliance shown to this breed in tennis clubs throughout the county and in Britain as a whole. The West now has over 30 full-time coaches in the County, whereas back in 1995 there were only 5 in Scotland.

Club Vision / Mini Tennis

Further to the launch of Club Vision in 2000, which aimed to bring together all initiatives under one umbrella, and put clubs at the heart of the game, Mini Tennis was then launched in 2001. Although Short Tennis and Starter Tennis were very successful throughout the County, many players didn't progress to full tennis at the appropriate time and short tennis became almost a game in itself. Starter Tennis was then introduced as a transition between short tennis and the full game. This was reasonably successful, but confused the marketplace, and a rethink brought the introduction of Mini Tennis. Since her appointment in 2001, Julie Gordon the West of Scotland County Mini Tennis Coach has been working hard to support clubs in Mini Tennis and deliver the best competition programme within the County for our players.

Although still in its early days, Mini Tennis has been probably one of the most successful of the LTA's initiatives. Based on Red, Orange and Green progressions of size of court and equipment, players have more success and the marketing is very strong and attractive to children. Awards have been introduced, and have been extremely well received

Participants in Mini Tennis with Nicola Kerr, County Development Officer

by coaches, providing a scheme that focuses on skill developement. Club Accreditation has been introduced to ensure clubs aspire to deliver a quality programme to set criteria, and there is consistency across the country. To build on Mini Tennis activity and encourage growth in this area and age group, clubs are now encouraged to build a "kidzone", a dedicated purpose-built area where young members can learn tennis in an innovative, colourful environment. They can also double up as a fitness, social and training area for other members.

The Future?

As to the future, Nicola Kerr believes that clubs that strive to provide a quality service for all types of members and are prepared to help themselves will flourish. The governing body will continue to provide resources and financially support clubs who are committed to further development and raising the profile of tennis in the community. There has been a huge change in the tennis club culture over the last ten years, and through the successful Club Vision Strategy, clubs are adopting a more progressive and welcoming approach to juniors. Hopefully in ten years time, club coaches will be the rule rather than the exception. Finally, in the words of John McEnroe, "let the racquet do the talking".

PERFORMANCE TENNIS – WEST OF SCOTLAND

Rover Coaches, Rover Squads, National Coaches, County Coaches, District Coaches, Performance Officers, County Performance Officers, National Futures, County Futures, Performance Clubs, Regional Centres, Academies, Intermediate Squads National Championships, Grand Prix's, Regional Challenges, Bisham Abbey.

All terms associated with Performance Tennis over the years that I have been involved in a coaching capacity with juniors. Since I joined the West in the role of Performance Officer a year ago even more opportunities are becoming available to our young players to become the best they can be.

I was lucky enough to be involved on a national training programme as a junior under the watchful eye of Bill Moss and trained at Largs. Towards the end of my training years Terry Mabbitt was in charge and we trained mainly at the Allander Centre.

Karen Ross, Performance Offficer

How times have changed, infinitely more indoor facilities, many more full time coaches, better structures within the clubs and more recently funding becoming available for those clubs with a performance structure and a commitment to helping young players improve.

Through time tennis has become more than just hitting tennis balls. Players need to be strong, fast and able to last the pace (the physical component). They need to be focussed, committed, make good decisions on the court (the mental component), be able to outsmart their opponent, impose their own strengths and expose their opponents weaknesses(the tactical component), be able to attack and defend when required and maintain good shape and technique from the start to the finish of a match (the technical component).

It is imperative therefore that to give our young players the best chance in tennis we need to build these components at an early age, but without burning them out!

2003 - 10 and Under "County Cup"
L-R Bradley Halsman, Kenneth Campbell,
Matthew Monaghan

Many more tournaments are now available to players. The growth of the indoor centres means that tennis is now an all-year-round sport. Players have the opportunity to play in individual tournaments throughout the UK and also in team competitions – County Cups at U11, U13, U18 levels. It is our job as coaches to guide our players, and make sure they have a balance between training/competition and **REST**

We have many quality coaches involved with the West of Scotland Programme, many of them former players themselves. Our training programme encompasses all the performance components. To produce a player is a long-term process and we need to ensure that during the journey we hone into the windows of opportunity at the prime learning times. The time between 6 yrs and 16 yrs is key. Tennis development and child development go hand in hand and we as coaches need to understand these principles. If we use this information well every young player stands a chance of reaching his or her potential whether that may be at club, county, national or even international level.

It is a long journey, which requires commitment, sacrifice, drive, determination, self motivation, from the player. Communication between the coaches/parents/players is key! Who knows what may happen in the future but all of us involved in the coaching and development of our young West tennis players are committed to making the development process professional but at the same time fun. After all tennis is a sport that can be enjoyed for life, whatever level you reach.

Coaching at Giffnock
Colin Hanbidge, Coach

1995
Newlands U12 Tournament

THE WEST OF SCOTLAND LEAGUE COMPETITION

For the season 1905, the newly instituted League competition was confined to Men's teams. An entry from Newton Stewart was regretfully refused owing to the distance opposing players would have to travel, but Ayr was among the accepted teams, who numbered twenty-four and were arranged in three Divisions. Each Division consisted of eight teams, and as they played their opponents home and away, fourteen matches were involved per team, an exacting total that caused frequent complaints, especially among ordinary club members. Not until 1920 did the system of only one League match against each opponent in a Division help to solve the vexed problem of court congestion.

EARLIEST WEST OF SCOTLAND LEAGUE TABLES

Men's First Division, 1905

						Played	Won	Points
Pollokshields	-	-	-	-	-	14	14	28
Partick	-	-	-	-	-	14	12	24
Bellahouston	-	-	-	-	-	14	8	16
Uddingston	-	-	-	-	-	14	7	14
Ayr	-	-	-	-	-	14	5	10
Kelvinside	-	-	-	-	-	14	4	8
Crookston	-	-	-	-	-	14	3	6
Lenzie	-	-	-	-	-	14	3	6

Ladies' First Division, 1906

						Played	Won	Points
Pollokshields	-	-	-	-	-	8	7	14
Partick	-	-	-	-	-	8	6	12
Uddingston	-	-	-	-	-	8	5	10
Lenzie	-	-	-	-	-	8	2	4
Bellahouston	-	-	-	-	-	8	0	0

Permission to form a Ladies' League section was granted by the committee for the year 1906, on condition that all matches were played in the afternoon. This stipulation remained in force for many years until the increasing number of girls entering business induced the committee to allow evening play for Ladies' matches. In the opening year of the Ladies' League Victorian ideas still prevailed regarding feminine staying powers in tennis, and the first match played between Pollokshields and Bellahouston was restricted to three short sets. On the question being referred to the Association a proposal that matches should consist of two short sets and one advantage set failed to find a seconder, and the committee boldly decided that in future three advantage sets should be played in the Ladies' League.

The League tables of 1908 published in the Glasgow Herald show four Divisions of seven teams each, there being twenty-four clubs four of which fielded two teams. The Ayr club was not in the League, perhaps the travelling proved to be too difficult or time consuming, Pollokshields already showing dominance with their second team winning Division two. The Ladies entered with nine clubs in two Divisions. Over the years more clubs joined in the Leagues competition and the number of Leagues increased.

The First World War saw the Leagues being suspended from 1915-1919. In 1919 there was a Victory competition and then the Leagues resumed in 1920.

Many new clubs established themselves in the early 1920s and there were thirteen Divisions in the Men's League with 125 teams from 98 clubs and with Pollokshields having three teams. The Ladies had twelve Divisions with 103 teams from 85 clubs.

The Juniors had to wait until 1937 for a League of their own.

JUNIOR MIXED DOUBLES LEAGUE.

		Matches				Sets		
	No.	Won	Drn.	Aw.	Lost	Won	Lost	Pts.
Newlands ...	6	4	1	0	1	29	25	9
Clarkston ...	6	3	2	0	1	35	19	8
Broomhill ...	6	3	1	0	2	27	27	7
Pollokshields ...	6	2	2	0	2	26	28	6
Burnside ...	6	2	1	0	3	28	26	5
Giffnock ...	6	2	1	0	3	26	28	5
Springboig ...	6	1	0	0	5	18	36	2

There was a major shake up of the Leagues in 1939 when all the second teams were placed in "Reserve Leagues" (there were 6 Divisions of the Reserves). There were twelve Divisions of the full Leagues making each Division smaller with either seven or eight clubs in them. This showed there were 89 clubs with Ladies' teams and 88 clubs with Men's teams. The Reserve Leagues were smaller with either five or six teams in each Division showing there were 32 Ladies' clubs and 31 Men's clubs with second teams. This format must have proved unpopular since after the Second World War the Leagues resumed their former pattern in 1947. The Junior League had increased to 9 teams in 1939 with the addition of Woodend, Titwood and Cambuslang with Springboig not entering that year.

During the Second World War "Charity Leagues" were run on a very local basis. Glasgow University was known to have organised at least one of them.

When the Leagues resumed in 1947 not every club was ready to enter and it was a year or two before the clubs re-established themselves. There was however a notable absentee who was never to return. In 1939 Partick Ladies won Division 1 and the Men's team were second in Division 1. They both had second teams yet they never again featured in any competition.

LAWN TENNIS.

WEST OF SCOTLAND ASSOCIATION.
FINAL RESULTS IN LEAGUE COMPETITION.
SEASON 1908.
GENTLEMEN'S DOUBLES.

1st League.
Pollokshields beat Partick, 6-3; and Bellahouston, 6-2.

	Pld.	Won.	Lost.	For.	Agst.	Pts.
Pollokshields	12	12	—	89	17	24
Partick	12	9	3	64	43	18
Bellahouston	12	7	5	63	45	14
Partickhill	12	5	7	47	58	10
Kelvinside	12	5	7	43	64	10
Newlands	12	3	9	38	68	6
Crookston	12	1	11	27	78	2

2nd League.
Pollokshields 2nd beat Partick 2nd, 9-0; Bellahouston 2nd beat Partick 2nd, 8-1.

	Pld.	Won.	Lost.	For.	Agst.	Pts.
Pollokshields 2nd	12	11	1	86	20	22
Titwood	12	7	5	60	48	14
Hamilton	12	7	5	55	52	14
Mount Vernon	12	6	6	44	64	12
Bellahouston 2nd	12	5	7	53	55	10
Thorntonhall	12	3	9	39	69	6
Partick 2nd	12	3	9	38	69	6

3rd League.

	Pld.	Won.	Lost.	For.	Agst.	Pts.
Queen's Park	12	11	1	85	25	22
Bearsden	12	10	2	72	36	20
Cartha	12	7	5	56	48	14
Cambuslang	12	6	6	59	46	12
Lenzie	12	5	7	38	61	10
Airdrie	12	3	9	38	62	6
Cathcart	12	0	12	18	90	0

4th League.

	Pld.	Won.	Lost.	For.	Agst.	Pts.
Newlands 2nd	12	11	1	85	22	22
Hillhead	12	9	3	57	51	18
Johnstone	12	8	4	53	49	16
Scotstounhill	12	5	7	53	55	10
Maryhill	12	4	8	53	54	8
St Vincent	12	4	8	40	68	8
Springboig	12	1	11	30	77	2

LADIES' DOUBLES.
1st League.
Bellahouston beat Titwood, 6-3; Uddingston scratched to Titwood.

	Pld.	Won.	Lost.	For.	Agst.	Pts.
Pollokshields	10	10	0	74	16	20
Bellahouston	10	8	2	57	33	16
Partickhill	10	5	5	42	48	10
Partick	10	4	6	38	52	8
Titwood	10	2	8	37	53	4
Uddingston	10	1	9	22	68	2

2nd League.
Cambuslang beat Titwood 2nd, 6-3.

	Pld.	Won.	Lost.	For.	Agst.	Pts.
Pollokshields 2nd	12	10	2	70	38	20
Hamilton	12	9	3	67	41	18
Newlands	12	8	4	72	36	16
Airdrie	12	7	5	60	47	14
Cambuslang	12	5	7	47	61	10
Titwood 2nd	12	3	9	39	69	6
Hillhead	12	0	12	22	95	0

By 1959 there were 17 Ladies' Divisions with 158 teams and 21 Men's Divisions with 166 teams. This number of Divisions made it virtually impossible for a new team entering Division 21 to get to Division 1 during the playing career of the team members and so it was introduced that if a team won all the matches in their Division to win it then promotion would be by two Divisions. A number of clubs were promoted more rapidly due to this factor.

In December 1965 Mr J.I. Smith raised the question of promotion and proposed

"That a scheme similar to the Badminton Association would be of speedier advantage to clubs fighting for promotion through the Divisions the meeting did not appear to share this view but agreed that if Mr Smith cared he could raise this point in the future."

The Matter was raised again at the committee meeting on 5th May 1966 and Mr Smith produced tables with a proposed structure. After discussion the vote was for the "status quo". It was not until season 1970 that this rapid progression was introduced and promotion was by one division.

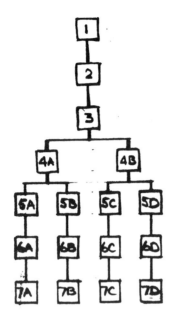

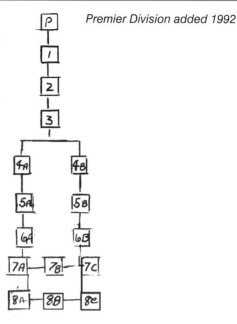

Premier Division added 1992

Proposed structure 1965

Structure adopted 1970

The Leagues have followed this pattern ever since. In 1971 it was decided to have the Leagues fixtures for Divisions 1 and 2 played on specific nights. A fixture list was therefore provided for these two Divisions with the Ladies' playing their matches on Tuesday evenings and the Men's matches being played on Friday evenings. This "fixed" evening match procedure eliminated any dispute about when matches should be played. The arrangement of the fixtures ensures that they are evenly spread out during the season.

The last major alteration to the League structure was the introductions in 1992 of the Premier Divisions. This re-introduced home and away fixtures and applied to the new Premier Division and to the First Division. This allowed for these two Divisions to be smaller in number, there being six teams in each of them. Also introduced was 3 singles of one set at the beginning of the match, then the doubles. This applied to all Premier, First Divisions and to the Men's Division 2. This last introduction was not popular with ordinary club members as it meant that matches could then occupy the club courts all evening. It was eventually withdrawn and the Leagues are once more Doubles only.

Around this time the scoring of points was altered. Previously only the rubber counted and two points awarded to the winner of rubbers and one point for a draw, however it allowed clubs who could only win matches 5-4 to be ahead or equal on points of a club who might be winning their matches by a much greater margin. Therefore the points system was changed to being a point for each set won and two bonus points for the winning team. This allowed for clubs who had a good all round team to benefit.

Mens and Womens Premier League Champions 2002 - Newlands
Captains - Malcom Watt and Christine Lockhart
Winners Men's Spring Singles League

JUNIOR LEAGUES - 1937

At last in 1937 a Junior League was formed. There was one Division and there were seven clubs.

The format was Mixed Doubles and there were three couples in the team, each playing three sets against the couple equal in order. Thus nine sets in all were played in the same manner as the Ladies' and Men's Leagues.

It was after the war before there was a second Division and in the 1950s there were regularly three Divisions. There were six divisions by 1959 and eight by 1989.

Between 1982 and 1987 each of the Leagues was divided into A and B. The A Divisions were north of the River Clyde and the B Divisions South of the Clyde. This was introduced to reduce the distances travelled by Junior teams since six players needed to travel in 2 cars no more was public transport the usual method of travel. It was dispensed with for season 1988 and the Leagues reintegrated.

The need to change was important as these Junior Leagues really provided for the older Juniors (although the lower Leagues with second teams tended to be younger). Therefore in 1992 Girls and Boys Leagues for under 16s were introduced. This time the team was to be 4 players enabling them to travel in one car. The format for play in a three court club was 2 singles and a double, then the reverse with the doubles couple playing the singles and the singles players joining together for a further doubles. Scoring was first to nine games with a tie-break at eight all. This could make for a lengthy match but provided both singles and doubles play for each player.

In 1994 the under 12 Leagues were introduced to be played in the same way as the under 16s but to be played in the Autumn from about mid August. These U12 Leagues had one unusual feature. There was a Girls League and an Open League. The Open League allowed for Boys and/or Girls to be in the team. The WSLTA reckoned that with players of this age, there was not much difference between the play of Boys and Girls. Many clubs were very short of Girl players and this would allow for play where a club might only have one Girl in the age group to play in a team.

NJCL Boys 13 & Under Champions 2002
with coach Colin Hanbidge - Giffnock

NJCL Girls 11 & Under Champions 2002 - Mount Vernon

This asset had to be dispensed with 2001 when the West of Scotland Leagues joined the National Junior Club Leagues (Clubs could play on an individual entry prior to this). The National Junior Club Leagues that were provided at that stage were Girls U17, U13, U11 and Boys U17, U13, U11. The West of Scotland is the administrator of 195 teams in these Leagues, the highest number in the UK at these age groups. For the season 2004 the U15 age group will be introduced.

This large provision of age group and Boys and Girls separate events has seen the decline and conclusion of the Mixed Doubles Leagues. In 2000 the last League was played. It is now a knock out event and re-named "The Junior Clydesdale Cup". So far Thorn Park has had exclusive wins in this event.

VETERANS LEAGUES - 1994

These Leagues were introduced to provide further play for the over 40 Ladies and over 45 Men. 25 Men's teams played in 4 Divisions and 34 Ladies teams played in 5 Divisions. This has been a huge success and is played from mid August till October.

In 1999 a Spring Knock-out Competition was introduced for the Veterans and is played in March and has a playback for first round losers. For 2004 the Spring Knock-out will be split into two age groups as pilot for future development.

Vets KO Winners & Division 1 Champions 2002 - Whitecraigs Ladies

Vets KO Winners 2002 - Whitecraigs Men

WEST OF SCOTLAND CUP SPRING SINGLES LEAGUE

Harry Matheson said at a committee meeting on 6 October 1970 *"the great lack was competitive singles events and wished to see promising players having more opportunity of meeting County players at singles. The general feeling was that players did not seem to develop after they were past the stage of participating in the Junior County Club."*

Ian Graham proposed that the clubs represented in the First and Second Divisions should be asked if they would be willing to participate in an Inter-club Tournament Singles and it was agreed to approach the clubs concerned. In the first competition in 1971 played in the Autumn Whitecraigs men beat Craighelen and in the Ladies competition Newlands beat Hillpark. In 1998 this competition became the Spring Singles Leagues of which there are 3 Ladies and 3 Men's Divisions.

WINTER KNOCK OUT INTER-CLUB SHIELD

There have been Winter Leagues / Knock Out Competitions for many years organised in the West of Scotland but run in conjunction with various sponsors throughout the UK eg. En-tout-cas and Evian competitions.

When the sponsorship ceased WSLTA continued with a KO competition, and the newly formed Strathgryffe Lawn Tennis and Squash Club donated a Shield for this event.

This competition consists of two men and two women. A match consists of four rubbers: Men's Doubles, Ladies Doubles and two Mixed Doubles. Rubbers will be the best of three sets with a tie-break in the first two. Clubs may enter only one team.

WINTER LEAGUES

In Winter 1997/98 our own Winter Leagues were taking place with Monday and Wednesday evening Floodlit Leagues, and Sunday afternoon Leagues the team of three couples consisting of Ladies' and Men's Doubles and Mixed Doubles. The dates for play are fixed by WSLTA and take place every fortnight with a break over Christmas and New Year. The fortnightly slot allows for any inclement weather postponements to be played in the intervening week.

Strathgryffe Shield Winter KO Winners 2002
- Bearsden

CALCUTTA CUP 1907

An extract from the minutes of Hamilton LTC on 31 July 1907 shows how the Association came to have the Calcutta Cup Competition.

To this day the rules remain almost the same.

The Cup is for teams from affliliated clubs excluding the Premier Division. Originally prior to the formation of the Premier Division it excluded teams from the First Division

In 1931 the WSLTA decided to introduce the Junior Calcutta Cup. This was not for Junior players but for Men's teams from affiliated clubs except teams in the Premier to 4th Divisions.

Teams in this competition consist of 4 players and each fixture shall consist of three singles matches (to be played first) and four doubles - seven matches in all. Each match shall be determined by the best of three sets with tie breaks operating at six all in each set.

In the Junior Calcutta Cup there is a further proviso that no player who has played in two league matches in the 4th or higher Divisions during the season in which the match is played shall be eligible to take part in the competition.

Over the years this has been a very popular competition and there have been four clubs who have won both cups in the same year, this shows the strength of these clubs at that particular time.

| 1965 | Hillpark and Hillpark II | 1989 | Burnside and Burnside II |
| 1991 | Hamilton and Hamilton II | 1990 and 2003 | Mount Vernon and Mount Vernon II |

Calcutta Cup 1907

CLYDESDALE CUP 1920

This competition is a knock out one and played in two Divisions. Division 1 consists of 16 clubs who play in the highest of the Leagues ie. when the League placings of the Ladies and Men are added together the lowest 16 totals form Division 1, and the remaining teams form Division 2.

The team consists of three Mixed Doubles couples playing three sets each and the winner is the club who wins the majority of sets

There was only the title of Mixed Doubles until two cups were presented by the Clydesdale Lawn Tennis Club for this competition in 1934. This was the year that the Tennis Section of the club closed. They were part of the Clydesdale Cricket Club.

Bearsden winners of Clydesdale Cup Division 2. Match played against Lenzie (1996)

FIXTURES

A phenomenon each March is the "Match Secretaries" meeting where the Match Secretaries of each team in every Club meet to arrange or confirm all the summer matches and around 2,200 matches are fixed in the space of just over an hour!

All these developments are a far cry from the start with 23 clubs in 1905. Thousands of matches are played each year and enjoyed by all, whether the weather be wet or fine, whether winning or losing everyone is playing tennis 52 weeks of the year!

Match Secretaries meeting - over 2000 matches arranged in an hour!

THE CHAMPIONSHIPS

In the early years of the Championships play was always carried through at the Pollokshields enclosure. The opening Tournament of 1886 gave the Championships a flying start. As a newspaper report of the period observed *"The success marking the Tournament has been equal to the best anticipations and it is more than likely that it will result in the institution of an annual gathering".* The prophetic nature of these words has been fully realised. Except in the years of the two World Wars the Tournament has been played in every season, and, while some seasons have naturally provided higher standards and greater excitement than others, no season has passed without its own special interest and keen contests for the chief honours. Play in the early years of the Tournament was confined to three days. Competitors were attracted from the then leading Scottish tennis centres such as Edinburgh and Alloa. The events were divided into two classes - those open to all comers and one event confined to West of Scotland competitors. Late in April 1886 an advertisement in the following terms appeared in the Sports weekly papers of the period:

POLLOKSHIELDS   ATHLETIC   CLUB.
LAWN   TENNIS   TOURNAMENT.

A TOURNAMENT under the auspices of the above Club will be held on the Club grounds, Maxwell Drive, Pollokshields, on

THURSDAY, FRIDAY, AND SATURDAY,
20th, 21st, and 22nd MAY
Commencing each day at 11 o'clock.

EVENTS.
(LADIES' MATCHES).
No. 1.   Single-handed match.
No. 2.   Ladies' and Gentleman's double-handed match.
(GENTLEMEN'S MATCHES).
No. 3.   Single-handed match.
No. 4.   Double-handed match.
No. 5.   Gentlemen's singles, confined to players in Counties of Lanark, Renfrew, Ayr, Dumbarton and Argyll.

For particulars apply to the Hon. Secretary, Mr. J. B. GRAY, Nithsdale Lodge, Pollokshields, or the Argyll Rubber Company, 60 Buchanan Street, Glasgow.

TENNIS—SONS AND DAUGHTERS.—*(Tournament at Pollokshields.)* 1886

The opening of the Tournament was awaited with keen expectancy. Unfortunately the weather was unkind. As a newspaper writer of the period said, *"rain poured down in one incessant stream, but in spite of the watery elements play continued all day."* The players of that day were of the spartan mould. (In 2003 players are of the same mould and frequently have to finish matches in the rain nothing is new!). On the second day of that first Tournament the weather was much better, while the third and last day was marked by glorious sunshine, and there was an attendance of nearly 1000 spectators. To quote the newspaper writer again:

"Ladies were in the ascendant, and the sight that met the eye - fair women and brave men, in the gayest of gay costumes - was calculated to win many recruits to this fascinating game."

From black and white sketches made in the enclosure we are left with a pictorial record of this first West Tournament final day. There was a Brass Band to encourage the players to better effort. The conductor is depicted waving his baton in one hand and a

With permission from Mitchell Library

trumpet to his lips with the other. The costumes of the ladies playing in the Mixed Doubles final include sailor hats, tight bodice and long black skirts with bustles. A supercilious young blood in flannels, straw hat and eyeglass, smoking a cigar between sets is probably now some tennis player's great-great-grandfather who would have regaled to that generation that he could have taught them something about the game! Seated at a table with wine glasses and a large decanter (empty) a youth in a bowler hat and tailored suit is gazing meltingly at a demure female dressed in the Victorian fashions of the period. Above them is the motto "Far from the madding crowd." And finally an important figure pushing a roller is a venerable groundsman with chin whiskers.

(The description above and the cartoon printed here suggests that there were two sketches. I have been unable to trace the one described, but since it creates its own word picture I have included it.)

Each of the four Open events was won by players from the East of Scotland. A Thomson (Alloa) won the Men's Open Singles, defeating JG Horn, a former Scottish Champion, in the final by 6/4 4/6 6/1, while Miss Jane Meikle, the leading Scottish Lady player, won the Ladies singles and shared the Mixed Doubles with WW Chamberlain, of Edinburgh University and Whitehouse. Chamberlain and ANJ Storey carried off the Men's Doubles. There was no Women's Doubles event.

Of special interest was the result of the Confined Singles Championship because for a long period it was the only singles level event and was regarded as the chief feature of the Tournament. The first winner was Leigh Maclachlan, Glasgow University, later to become Sir Leigh Maclachlan. (From 1930 the Confined Singles became an Open event and the two events merged.) For this first West Confined Singles there were 22 entrants and L Maclachlan won his various rounds as follows :- beat GS Jackson 3/6 6/1 6/2; beat PMW Murdoch 8/6 6/3; beat CA Gairdner 6/2 8/6; beat EM Shand 6/1 6/2; in the final beat 6/1 6/3 6/3. The winner had played the previous year in the Scottish Championships and in the East of Scotland Championships, in which he was defeated by by the ultimate winner, the Hon. H Bowes Lyon.

Sir Leigh Maclachlan

For a number of years leading Edinburgh players continued to compete in the Tournament. The winner of the Men's Open Singles in 1887 was JG Horn, who had been the Scottish Champion in 1881, 1882 and 1883. Horn had been described by Mr. Kenneth Sanderson as an outstanding tennis personality. The "Horn drive" had become famous. He drove harder, both fore and backhand, than any man of the time and he must have had a wonderful eye because he could smash overhead from the back of the court.

The Jubilee spirit was abroad in the land since this second West Championships were in the year of the Golden Jubilee of Queen Victoria's reign.

Though no special steps were taken to associate the Tournament with the national rejoicings the final day's play was notable for the presence of a queen of the stage. Miss Mary Anderson, then appearing in Glasgow in "Romeo and Juliet", "Lady of Lyons", "Pygmalion and Galatea", and other plays, was invited to visit Pollokshields. At that time most playgoers were metaphorically at the feet of this lovely young actress, and tremendous excitement was caused among spectators and players alike when she appeared in the enclosure. Writing of the event one enthusiastic scribe says :-

"Miss Mary Anderson graced the Tournament with her charming presence during the progress of the Men's Doubles final and evinced the most lively interest in the game. The stewards are indeed lucky fellows in being thus honoured."

The match was between RM Watson and JT Conyers on the one side and JG Horn and G Kerr on the other and was won by the former couple after a fast and exciting encounter. Miss J MacKenzie won the Women's Singles and shared the Mixed Doubles with Horn. Apparently Mary Anderson did not wait to present the prizes, this, no doubt, owing to the fact that she was due at the theatre. While the weather was cold, of Arctic chilliness, everything seems to have passed off well, for a newspaper report of the 24th May 1887 says :-

"The courts were in fine playing trim, balls were plentiful, the umpiring was most capably done, the String Band played capitally, the purveying was in good hands, and, over all, the stewards (with Mr JB Gray, the Hon Secretary at their head) were most assiduous in thier efforts to keep the ball rolling steadily and smoothly."

The winner of the Open Singles in 1888 was RM Watson (Edinburgh), who was destined to win the Scottish Singles in 1894, and was chiefly responsible for the formation of The Scottish Lawn Tennis Association in 1895. To quote Mr. Sanderson again, *"he had a very fast service and always ran up on it. After getting position he see-sawed from side to side, and when the opening came the kill followed swift and sure. His game off the ground was a cut with the ball at the highest part of the bound, and, although less suitable for grass, was exceedingly effective on the cinder courts."*

It was in 1888 that JB Gray, who took so large a part in the running of the Tournament in its early years, gained his sole victory in the Confined Singles. GS Jackson, who was winner in the previous year and the two following years, was a young Englishman studying at Glasgow University. He had a delightful tennis style and the game was the poorer when he left our midst.

During the Tournament of 1888 play was interrupted on one of the opening days by thunder and lightning, and rain fell so heavily that planks had to be laid from the pavilion to the refreshment tent! But despite this drawback the meeting was brought to a successful close, and in their lavish tributes the press forgot about the temporary storms. One criticism was made however. Here is what the press reporter of that time said:-

There was only one week spot in the whole proceedings of Thursday, Friday and Saturday, and that was the Band. To those who did not hear it no description could do it justice, while to those who did no description is necessary."

Despite this stricture, the Band either String or Brass, remained a feature of the final day for several years until the practice was finally ended after an infuriated competitor had driven a ball through the big drum.

After a few years There was some widening of the Tournament's management which was carried out by a Committee of Eight, representing at the start, four clubs north of the Clyde - Glasgow University, Golfhill, Kelvinside and Helensburgh - and four on the south of the river - Pollokshields, Nithsdale, Hamilton and Paisley.

The Tournament of 1890, had the distinction, although none knew of it then, of including a competitor who was to become British Prime Minister. Among the entrants for the Confined Singles was AB Law, who had been doing rather well as a member of the Helensburgh Club's team. Described in the press as "an Helensburgh player possessed of a somewhat pronounced but rather effective style," the late Mr Bonar Law was unlucky enough to meet in the first round the 1888 winner of ther title, JB Gray, but to the surprise of everybody he carried off the first set 6/2. The two remaining sets were comfortably won by Gray who passed on to the final. In those days the holder did not require to play through. GS Jackson, who had won the event in 1889, defeated Gray in the Challenge round.

Some of the Tournaments in the early nineties met with unkind weather condititons. During play in 1891 snow fell at intervals, although the period was late May. On the day fixed for the finals the courts were flooded, and play was postponed for a week, when pleasant summer conditions prevailed. In the final of the Ladies Singles Championship, Miss Jones (London), *"a little lady with no end of grit and a capital service"*, beat Miss Prain (Pentland Club) 6/3 6/1. Archie Thomson (Alloa) won the Men's Open Singles, while the winner of the Confined singles was TL Hendry (Langside). The Men's Doubles was described at the time as " the finest match ever witnessed on Pollokshields courts", and this can well be understood when it is stated that both couples HG Nadin and HE Caldecott (who won) and RM Watson and EB Fuller subsequently as couples each won the Scottish Doubles Championship.

A cold nipping wind marked the final day of 1892, but a String Band and a convenient refreshment tent (we are told) helped one to forhet that inconvenience. This was the first year of the West of Scotland Ladies Doubles Championship (which was substituted in place of the Ladies Singles), and the winners were Miss B Watson and Miss Playfair, who defeated Miss Simpson and Miss Bowman in a stern protracted struggle by 6/3 5/7 10/8. JH Conyers, a master of the drop shot, won the Men's Open Singles, while TL Hendry retained the Confined Singles. An entrant that year was JH Neil. Conyers partnered RM Watson in the Men's Doubles final had the satisfaction of defeating the holders Caldecott and Nadin.

The Tournament was now reaching years when tennis experienced a severe slump and when the enthusiastic band of competitors from the East of Scotland was beginning to dwindle. The 1893 entry was disappointing, and a report of the proceedings pays the following somewhat grudging tribute to the feminine spectators -
"The girls, while not so pretty as in past years, made a tolerably fine picture. The spectators were soothed by the delightful strains of Cole's String Band. Those bored by the tennis found relief in listening to the Band."

The feature of the finals was the sensational result of the Men's Confined Singles. TL Hendry, holder for the previous two years, led AW Scott (Partickhill) by 2 sets to 0, 5 games to 4 and 40/30, and yet lost the match by 2 sets to 3 and thus failed to win the cup as his own property. Later in the season Titwood, which was in its third year and then possessed eight courts, held an Open Tournament and in the Men's Singles Hendry and Scott were again the finalists. Hendry had set his heart on reversing the previous decision, and presently there was a thrill of excitement among the onlookers when he again stood 2 sets to 0, 5 games to 4 and 40/30. This time he made no mistake. In the course of the next hot rally Scott netted the ball and victory was with Hendry.

Glasgow University provided the winner of the Confined Singles in 1894 in the person of JF Barker, and then came a long series of years when the main interest of the Tournament by the Singles skill of Hendry, JH Neil and R Baird. In winning the event five times between 1895 and 1902, Neil set up a new record.

1900

This was in due course exceeded by Baird who won the event six times, the first in 1900 and the last in 1912.

For a number of years at the end of the nineteenth century and the beginning of the twentieth Handicaps were substituted for some of the Championships. It was in 1911, after an interval of 16 years that the Women's Singles Championship was restored and it has since then been a regular and popular feature of the Tournament. The first winner of the new Cup was a Scottish Champion and Internationalist, Mrs Robin Welsh.

The 1905 Tournament held at Bellahouston was noteable for a singles between R Baird, the holder, and Stanley Doust. The latter led two sets and was within a stroke of victory in the third, but was ultimately defeated.

Stanley Doust

On the formation of the West of Scotland LTA that body took over from Pollokshields Athletic Club the running of the Tournament and for over twenty years it was held by a kind of rough rotation in other enclosures as well as that of Pollokshields Athletic Club. Under an arrangement with the West of Scotland LTA since 1930 Pollokshields, with its eight fine courts and extensive seating accommodation, was again the home of the Tournament, the neighbouring clubs of Bellahouston and Titwood lending their co-operation in alternate years.

It is impossible to deal with all the tournaments in the series and touch upon the singles performances of such Internationalists as A Fraser, A Blair, IG Collins, AW Hill, and D MacPhail. Nor is it possible to tell of all the famous partnerships the West has produced. Some of them are L Maclachlan, and GS Jackson, JH Neil and JG Couper, AJ Smellie and JT Butters, JNM Sykes and GA Paterson, J Fraser and A Wylie, W and A Fraser, HFB Neilson and RB Irons, J Mathie and J Hamilton or R Paul and J Hamilton. Do consult the Appendices to see just how many partnerships there were.

A Blair

1920

A Blair and DL Craig, the brothers Collins and the brothers Hill, JB Fulton and RR Finlay and many more were the players of the 1920s and early 1930s.

A Blair, Pollokshields, had a run of three years as Singles Champion 1920-1922 and won the Doubles with DL Craig twice. DL Craig won the Singles only once in 1924. He won the Doubles twice with A Blair and once with HL Steel and won the Mixed Doubles five times, from 1921-1925, with his sister Mrs Keith Buchanan.

M Thom

DL Craig

AW Hill & JT Hill

AW Hill, Newlands, won the Singles 1928-1932 and with his brother AW Hill had a run of five years as Doubles Champions 1928-1932. And in the Mixed Doubles AW won with Miss J Rankine in 1928 and 1929, while JT won in 1930-1932 with Miss Winnie Mason. Quite a feat! In one final Arthur Hill played Ian Collins and the match went to five sets and 53 games.

The Ladies of the 1920s tended to be Doubles winners in particular since there were eight winners of the Singles. Mrs Keith Buchanan was one of them and while her only singles win was in 1924 ahe won the Ladies Doubles five times in 1920, 1921 and 1923-1925 partneredby Miss AB Macdonald four times and the last time by Mrs Murray. Miss Jean C Rankine, Newlands, won the singles three times 1926 and 1928 1929 and with Miss Phyllis Hengler won the Doubles in 1926 and a further three times with Miss M Langmuir (a Hockey Internationalist). Miss Langmuir won the Doubles a fourth time with Miss AE Middleton.

Phyllis Hengler

1930 Winnie Mason was the predominent player of the 1930s winning the Junior Singles in 1928 and 1929 then moving to the senior ranks and winning the Singles five times between 1930 and 1936 and the Doubles four times with Miss JA Jamieson. The Mixed Doubles Winnie won five times three with JT Hill and two with Donald MacPhail Jr. This Mixed Doubles partnership with Donald MacPhail won many times in other tournaments. Winnie Mason played at Wimbledon and she dominated the game all over Scotland.

Winnie Mason

L-R WAR Collins, JC Rankine,
J Fry & CG Easner

Donald MacPhail Jr was the next player to make his mark on the Singles winning five times between 1933 (four times to 1937) and 1949. He too played several times at Wimbledon and played in the Davis Cup.

Doubles winners at this time Dr JB Fulton and RR Finlay who won in 1933 and 1934. B Butters (nephew of JT Butters who won Singles at the beginning of the century).

Donald MacPhail

1940 / 1950

There were no Championships between 1940 and 1946 during the Second World War.

The first winner of the Men's Singles after the war was Robbie Barr of "Barr's Irn Bru", who was to be a sponsor of the future. He also won the Mixed Doubles with Mrs Clara Black the following year. He won many events in Central District.

Mrs Gwen Simmers, Kelvinside, won the Ladies Singles in 1947 an event she had won previously as Gwen Sterry in 1931. Gwen had played in the Wightman Cup for Great Britain in the 1920s and was the daughter of Mrs Charlotte Sterry (nee Cooper) who had won the Ladies Singles at Wimbledon five times. Gwen won the Doubles with Miss MS Allan and Miss Isobel Vallance. Bu Fulton and Gwen Simmers won the Mixed Doubles three times.

Heather Macfarlane

Now we come to the record breakers Heather Macfarlane (Craighelen) first won the Ladies Singles in 1948 and won

Winnie Mason & Donald MacPhail

eight times in ten Championships losing to Mrs Clara Black in 1949 and Isobel Vallance in 1952. She won the Doubles five times three of them with Mrs Louise Dick who as Louise Anderson won the Singles in 1937. She won the Mixed Doubles with Colin Baxter three times and they both won the triple crown in 1957, she also had triple wins in 1955 and 1956. Heather won many other Championships as well as being an International player and her record of wins has not been broken.

Other noteable Ladies were Isobel Vallance who won the singles once and the Doubles and Mixed Doubles twice each and was an International player who had won the British Junior Doubles at Wimbledon in 1947. Mrs Clara Black who as Clara Butters (daughter of JT Butters) first won the Ladies Doubles in 1938 and is the record holder in that event with eight wins four with Miss May Thomson and three with Miss Cathie Dungliston, who was to win the Doubles twice more making a five year run as a winner.

The other record breaker was Colin Baxter who won the Singles eight times in eleven Championships from 1953 to 1963. The Doubles saw Colin win ten times with six partners and the Mixed Doubles was won for eleven consecutive years with six partners. The last two Mixed Doubles was won with a young Winnie Shaw in 1963 and 1964. He won the triple crown four times 1957 / 59 / 60 / 63. He had many International Caps and played at Wimbledon.

Colin Baxter

Other noteable players at this time were John Rutherglen, who won the Singles twice in 1950 and 1952, Jimmy Wilson who won the Singles in 1955 and the Doubles three times and Ian Campbell who won the Singles in 1962 and the Doubles three times with CV Baxter and the Mixed Doubles twice with Isobel Vallance.

1960
The beginning of this period really began in 1958 with Anne (Walker) Paul, since from this time there are players who are still playing in 2004 Internationally in Veterans Tennis! The Ladies had EA Walker, who became Mrs Anne Paul, who won two Singles and four Doubles including the triple crown in 1958, Frances MacLennan, who became Mrs Roger Taylor, with two Singles. Frances played at Wimbledon and for a time played abroad so visits to the West were curtailed. Frances now Captains the British Veterans 60's Team.

Anne McAlpine who also played abroad won four Singles and two Doubles. Sheila Moodie won the Triple Crown in 1968, the Doubles twice and the Mixed Doubles six times. Mrs Carole Matheson won the Singles in 1969 and the Doubles three times and Mrs Brenda Livingstone (nee McCallum) won the Doubles three times.

Ian Campbell

Meanwhile there were new faces in the Men's events too Ken Gray, Ian Campbell, Gordon Kerr and Billy Gillespie all won the Singles. Harry Matheson won twice in 1966 and 1968 and also the Doubles twice. JR Maguire won the Doubles three times with CV Baxter. In 1965 the East of Scotland partnership of Harry Roulston and Jim Mc Neillage won the Doubles and apart from that foray and a Singles win in 1951 by JM Mehta of India the West players had exclusively won their Championships since 1939.

All that was about to change. Sponsorship had been found and the Championship became an International Tournament with World Champions past present and future taking part. The Chapter entitled "The Red Hackle Years" accounts for these years.

Only The Mixed Doubles remained as a West event. Players from abroad did not usually play this event. However since it was an "Open " event the account of it is with the Red Hackle Years.

1967 saw three players from abroad Kathy Harter, Ray Keldie and Terry Addison. The following year had none and then David Lloyd began his long association with the West in 1969.

1970

The draw from then on had the West players in round one and the visitors started in the second round. From 1973 those who lost in their first match were included in a "Plate" event ensuring them of a second match and the eventual winner being awarded the West of Scotland Shield. However by 1977 this was further changed when the Championship became part of the ATP Tour, and the Men's draw confined to 64 players. The Shield then became a qualifying event.

This then re-created a West Championship for the local players and with four gaining entry to the main even and created some interesting points.

Ken Revie

Ken Revie won the Shield five times and after the end of those years won the Championship a further three times this would have made him have a total of eight wins and would have equalled Colin Baxter's record. In the Doubles Ken won the Shield four times and together with his six Open wins would have had a total of 10 again equalling Colin Baxter.

Similarly Marjory Love won the Shield five times and together with her Open win would have won six in total and would have been the record holder next to Heather Macfarlane. In the Ladies Doubles Marjory Love and Sheila Moodie won five times together and Sheila once with Anne Paul. Marjory would have won a total of six, Sheila eight (equalling Clara Black's record) and Anne five.

1984

When the Red Hackle / Lang's Supreme sponsorship concluded at the end of twelve years in 1983, efforts were made to find another sponsor. However all efforts failed. It had been decided to run the West of Scotland Championships using the Shields in case a last minute sponsor was found, and if none be found by the following year the 1984 names would be engraved on the Open Cups. This means that the 1984 Singles and Doubles winners have their names on both trophies.

Judy Erskine (Dunblane), won the Ladies Singles in 1984 and 1985, followed by Marjory Love, then Suzie Mair, Colinton won three times from 1987. Only Suzie Mair won the doubles twice in this period.

Ken Revie won the first of four Singles titles, Ian Allan, Broomhill and Colin McGill, Colinton saw the decade out. In the Doubles Ken Revie dominated winning with Russell Howat, then with Ian Allan won five times to 1991. Gordon Bell and John Howie winning in 1998.

1990

This decade saw the introduction of new names Heather Lockhart and Malcolm Watt both of Newlands, each to be record holders.

Heather Lockhart won the first of her Singles in 1990 and her fifth in 2003. Michelle Mair, Colinton, won in 1991 and the other winners are all from the West. Jan Walker (now Mrs Oliphant) Newlands, Deirdre Forrest, Broomhill and Newlands two wins, Nicola Burns, Whitecraigs, had her third win at the end of the century. Michelle Whitelaw and Mrs Romana Owen (neé Orsi) were the final new names. Marjory Love played two more finals against Michelle Whitelaw and Romana Owen.

In the Ladies Doubles Heather Lockhart has won seven times just one less than Clara Black. The win in 1998 was special since her mother Mrs Christine Lockhart was her partner. Other names who featured were

Karen Ross, Elizabeth Adams, K Fulton Deirdre Forrest, Elizabeth Stevenson, Anna Brown and Nicola Burns. Jan Oliphant has four wins and Romana Owen three.

Matheson appeared on the winners role in 1990 - this time Ross son of Harry and Carole. Blane Dodds, Broomhill, won in 1991. Malcolm Watt won the first of his record six wins in seven Championships with Michael McGill, Giffnock, breaking the run. Alan MacDonald, Thistle, has three wins and Jordan Gray has two. Malcolm has also been in other finals.

Malcolm Watt has five Doubles wins, three with Ronnie Terras, and two with Calum McKnight. Ronnie Terras has also won with Gordon Bell and Jordan Gray (who also won with M Hendry). Alan MacDonald has now won four Doubles titles his partners being Gary Smith twice, Jason Barnett and Steven McGuckin.

The Mixed Doubles has had many partnerships and Malcolm Watt and Heather Lockhart have each four wins and Alan MacDonald, Deirdre Forrest, Elizabeth Stevenson each with two wins. Reports in the papers are now practically invisible and so the story of the events are lost.

The Championships are the aim of players and to win is special, but only one can win and many very good players take part, do well and are successful in the Club and League programme without their names on a trophy.

Malcom Watt

West of Scotland Open Championships
1999 Winners and Runners Up at Newlands L.T.C.

THE RED HACKLE YEARS 1972 - 1983

Red Hackle and Lang's "Supreme" were the sponsors during this period. The titles were those of Scotch Whisky and each of the titles was used for six years. Hepburn and Ross owned both labels. This era saw the upgrading of the Tournament so that players of the world took part. The enthusiasts on the Committee of the day encouraged by Mr Cochran MacLennan of the Newlands Club together with James E Gray Managing Director of Hepburn and Ross raised the Tournament to World Class and gave the local enthusiasts sight of matches to remember.

Sponsorship had begun earlier with Rothmans of Pall Mall Ltd 1965, followed by Coca-Bottlers (Scotland) Ltd for 1966, 1967 and 1968. A.G. Barr & Co Ltd were the Sponsors for 1969, 1970 and 1971

Players from abroad were introduced in 1967 with Kathy Harter of the USA, Ray Keldie and Terry Addison from Australia. Frances MacLennan was the number one seed and reached the final by beating Anne Paul 6/3 6/2 in the semi-final and Kathy Harter, seeded two, beat Carole Matheson 6/1 6/1. The finals were played at Whitecraigs and Kathy Harter won the Ladies Singles and with Anne Paul won the Ladies Doubles against Carole Matheson and Brenda Livingstone. Kathy completed the triple crown by winning the Mixed Doubles with Ray Keldie. She then went on to Wimbledon where she reached the semi-final of the Ladies Singles losing to Billie Jean King the winner of that event.

Kathy Harter (USA) 1967
West of Scotland Champion

The Men's Singles had Ray Keldie, Alan McNeilage, Harry Matheson and Terry Addison in the Semi-finals with Terry Addison being the winner of the event. Terry won the Men's Doubles partnered by Vic Israel of Hillpark.

The next year however reverted to local players. The Sponsorship was the sum of £250.

David Lloyd (Essex) won the Men's Singles in 1969 1970 and 1971. 1970 saw International players in the draw and Maria Guzman of Equador won the Ladies Singles and the Mixed Doubles with David Lloyd

David Lloyd makes the following comment about his many visits to the West of Scotland Tournament :-
"My experience in playing the West of Scotland Tournament- will stay with me forever. The friendliness of the people, the tremendous enthusiasm of the crowd made the tournament very special to me."

David Lloyd Mens Singles Champion
1969/70/71 and 1977

Jane O'Hara of Canada won the Ladies Singles in 1971 with Miss B Walsh (Australia) and Marilyn Greenwood (Queen's) winning the Ladies Doubles. JF Manderson and Graham Thomson (both Australia) winning the Men's Doubles. Ian Walker and Gwen Armstrong won the Mixed Doubles title.

At the beginning of the Red Hackle Years local players were in the draw with the seeds and from 1970 to 1976 the Doubles events had a "Plate" for those players eliminated in their first match, thus ensuring players had at least two matches in their event.

From 1977 to 1983 there was a qualifying event in both singles and doubles which really meant that the West of Scotland Tournament was played over two weeks. The first week was the qualifying event for week two where four players / couples gained entry to the main draw which gave the local players their tournament. Such was the attraction of the West Tournament that in 1978 there was a pre-qualifying event of 12 players from 9 different countries playing for six places in the qualifying event and where 64 players played for 16 places in the Main Draw which had 64 entrants, a total of 118 players! Scotland had 5 Men in the Main Draw KM Revie, JF Howie, A Chisholm, I Walker and D Watt. Four had to play seeds in round 1 but none got to round 2 that year.

The players are only part of a Tournament, the organisers being the people who make it all happen and during the Red Hackle years there were many who put in hours of work. The following gave service in one or more capacities.

1977 Ladies Doubles Winners with Tournament Officials
L-R Clare Harrison, Robbie Jenkins, James E Gray, Jo Durie,
Alastair Wotherspoon, Pam Jenkins, Scott Allan

Chairman/Tournament Director was the overall chairman of the whole event and frequently it had been the Vice-President of the Association, among them were KB Gray, RA Carswell, RS Allan. However Robbie Jenkins served from 1978-1983 in this post as well as being Secretary 1975-1978 and previously as assistant Secretary/ Treasurer. The amount of work done in this capacity was enormous both before, in co-odinating all aspects of the event, and during the event itself. Mrs Pat Jenkins served as Assistant Secretary/Treasurer for many years, providing support that is greater than the job title. Christine Lindsay was also an assistant Secretary for a time.

The Treasurer for most of these years was BW Watson. CK MacLennan also served as Treasurer.

Referees were DN Graham (2years), GB Holmes (1), CH Hess (1), AJ Wotherspoon (8). Their word was law! The air around Alastair was always tempered with clouds of cigar smoke and he did his job well.

Roy Paterson served in several capacities and from 1979 to 1983 was Secretary of the Tournament and was ever present at the Tournaments.

Clive Thomson served as PRO and saw to press releases before and during the Tournaments.

Ronnie Carswell was Players Convenor for many of these years. Much of the task took place before the event, visiting tournaments to encourage players to enter the West Tournament and co-ordinating the accommodation and hospitality for them at the tournament with club members and friends. In order to attract players of calibre not only required monetary sponsorship but also hospitality sponsorship. Many tennis families volunteered to host players in their homes and as a result lasting friendships were begun during the Championships. Marilyn Tesch still keeps in touch with the family who hosted her when she played in the Tournament.

James E Gray (Red Hackle), Ronnie Carswell, John Y Crawford (WSLTA Secretary), Mrs Dorothy Gray, Tom Boyd (Giffnock) - Finals Day 1973

Some players returned to play again and again because of the friendly atmosphere. Andrew Jarrett makes the following comments *"I remember———*

"Wonderful social evenings in the Squash Court Bar - 2 squash courts given over to extra bar facilities throughout the week, 1 for the sedate and 1 for the wild!;

Mark Farrell leading the community singing in the wild section standing on top of the bar pointing to the words of "Flower of Scotland" for the non Scots;

Achieving honorary Scots status and therefore being included in the bar rota helping to serve in the wild bar. Heavy or whisky or a combination of both - nothing else;

Several years of Aussies going on the daytime trip to the year's sponsoring distillery (Red Hackle and others), and coming back in no fit state to play tennis in the evening. One Classic match featured two Aussies against two local lads who had come straight from work. There was a gulf in class between the pairs but the handicap of alcohol was perfectly judged to give a cliff hanger that ended late at night deep in a final set with a huge appreciative crowd to enjoy the whole situation!

I remember feeling at home on the Centre Court and having some decent wins over the years - even winning the final on two occasions against Mike Myburg and John Fitzgerald. Another year (1977) I lost the final to David Lloyd. I liked the blaes courts and would have liked it to become a recognised international surface.

I remember Alastair Wotherspoon as referee operating out of the little hut by the clubhouse;

Marjory Love driving supposedly "better" players to distraction with her style of play; in similar vein the Armstrong twins Evelyn and Gwen lobbing Jo Durie and Clare Harrison to death on one of the furthest away courts from the clubhouse and Jo and Clare getting so frustrated (semi-final 1977).

I remember staying around the corner from Newlands LTC with John and Moira Watson together with many other players including Pat Cash and Wally Masur. The Watsons have remained as friends ever since and I have seen their children grow up.

The West of Scotland Championships were probably my favourite tournament to revisit each year. I used to get into trouble each year when Paul Hutchins, the Davis Cup Captain, would try to get me to play the French Open Qualifying but I preferred the appeal of "The West" "[sic].

What about the players? After all they were the reason that there were people in the Stands (seated of course!). A great many were stars of the past present and future. It seemed to us like the Wimbledon of the north for those special years, rushing straight from work in order to see as much as possible of the play, sometimes sunbathing other times with thick jumpers and travel rugs trying to keep warm. Raincoats featured too and play was interrupted from time to time. Singles finals were completed in 1974, but the doubles titles were shared due to rain. In 1976 the Tournament was abandoned due to excessive rain over days and in 1983 the semi-finals and finals were a Professional set only .

Rachel McNair (WSLTA President), Marilyn Tesch, John Y Crawford (WSLTA President), Mrs Dorothy Gray, Ken Gray (Tournament Chairman)

1972

Seven Ladies from Australia, England, New Zealand and USA were the visitors, with the number one seed Pat Cody (USA) losing in the third round to Beverley Vircoe(NZ) who in turn lost to Marjory Love (Elderslie) in the semi-final. The other half of the draw saw Sue Mappin (England) winning against Carole Matheson (Whitecraigs) in the third round with Marilyn Tesch (Australia) winning against her fellow country woman R Knoble. The final saw Marilyn Tesch win 6/2 6/4 against Marjory Love. The Ladies Doubles semi-final saw P Cody and B Vircoe, the number one seeds winning over seeded M Love and H Kelly (Blackhall) and C Matheson and S Mappin overcoming the number two seeds M Tesch and R Knoble. The final was won by P Cody and B Vircoe.

The Men's Championship also saw seven visitors from Australia, Bolivia, England, Equador and S Africa. There were 58 entries and Harry Matheson (Whitecraigs) was the only home player to be seeded reaching his allotted place in the last eight and losing to John Clifton the eventual winner. Ian Walker (Western) beat two seeds, T Dawson (Australia) and E Gorostiaga (Bolivia), to reach the semi-final where he also lost to John Clifton. David Lloyd the defending Champion and number one seed reached the final by winning over Graham Notman (Queen's Club) and E Zuleta (Equador) who was on the first of several visits to the Championships and who had overcome G Thomson (Australia) in the fourth round. John Clifton won the Championship 6/2 6/4.

The Men's Doubles was retained by G Thomson partnered by David Lloyd who won over John Clifton and Harry Matheson in the final and had defeated E Gorostiaga and E Zuleta in the semi-final. The other semi finalists were Harry Roulston and Jim McNeilage (Abercorn).

Ian Walker and Marjory Love won the first of their five Mixed Doubles titles.

John Clifton

1973

Marilyn Tesch returned in to defend her title which she did, again meeting Marjory Love in the final with the score of 6/3 6/4. On the way she won over Elizabeth McIntosh (Queen's Park), Sue Smith (Western), Wendy Slaughter (Yorkshire), M Cooper (USA), and Mrs Joyce Williams (Queen's Club) in the semi-final. Marjory had the benefit of a bye to the second round where she defeated Mrs C Craigie (Broomhill), S Arnott (Australia), Lindsey Beaven (Queen's Club) the number two seed and Christine Matison (Australia) also seeded. There was an entry of 48 players.

The Ladies Doubles with 35 couples was won by M Tesch and C Matison who had won over Mrs Hazel Robb and Mrs Elva Allan (Cambuslang), Mrs Christine Lockhart and Mrs FA Roger (Newlands), Annette Coe and RE Pearson (Queen's Club), and the number one seeded pair Mrs Joyce Williams and Mrs Carole Matheson. Their opponents in the final were Sue Mappin and Wendy Slaughter who reached the final by way of Elizabeth Winning (Cambuslang), and Mrs Maureen Stewart (Rutherglen), Mrs P Garland and Jane Brown (Hamilton), JN Connor (NZ) and P Billing (Australia) and the number two seeds Lindsey Beaven and M Cooper.

*Marjory Love
Finalist 1971-73*

Frew McMillan - one of the first players to use the double handed grip

There were 96 players in the Men's Singles and the list of home players was a roll call of well known enthusiasts (many of whom play veterans events thirty years on). Frew McMillan (S Africa) was the number one seed and reached the final by beating A Collins (Giffnock), N Callaghan (Australia), JR Smith (Queen's), G Thomson (Australia) and in the semi-final K Hancock (Australia) 2/6 6/4 6/4. David Lloyd (Essex) beat M McKnight (Newlands), JB Howarth (Yorkshire), L Baraldi (Mexico), Mark Farrell (Queen's) and his brother John Lloyd in the semi-final by 6/3 6/2. In the final Frew McMillan was the winner 6/3 6/2.

With 54 couples in the Men's Doubles some of the earlier matches were very close and should be mentioned E Zuleta (Equador) and L Baraldi (Mexico) who were seeded had a really tough match against GB Kerr and FN Thompson (Newlands) and the seeds only scraped through 5/7 8/6 6/1; seeds K Hancock and W Mason (Australia) had a difficult time against H Drummond (Newlands) and John Howie (Whitecraigs) with a score of 3/6 6/3 6/4 , and in the following round Billy Gillespie (Newlands and DC Braid (Ayr) beat them 7/5 6/3; in the fourth round E Zuleta and L Baraldi beat Harry Matheson and John Clifton, who were also seeded, 6/3 1/6 6/4. Harry Roulston (Abercorn) and Billy Dickson (Newton Stewart) reached the fourth round losing to David and John Lloyd 3/6 3/6, who in turn beat G Thomson (Australia) and J Royappa (India) 6/4 6/1 in the semi-final. Frew McMillan and John Farrell won the final 6/3 6/4.

Diane Fromholtz, Australia

The Mixed Doubles was virtually all West players and Ian Walker and Marjory Love won 7/5 6/4 against Jim Nicol and Sheila Moodie.

1974

17 year old Diane Fromholtz (Australia) headed the seeds and, after winning from Marjory Love in the semi-final, met Jenny Dimond (Australia) in the final and won 6/3 6/1. Corinne Molesworth (England) was seeded number two and other seeds were Mrs P Gregg (Aus) and West players Ruth Allan, Marjory Love, Sheila Moodie.

Ladies Doubles Finalists share the trophy - Miss J Dimond v Miss D Fromholtz, Mrs Dorothy Gray, Miss P Gregg v Mrs C Matheson

The Ladies Doubles title was shared between D Fromholtz and J Dimond, and Mrs P Gregg and Mrs C Matheson.

Preliminary rounds were played in the Men's Singles, with 24 playing for six places and 96 players were in the main draw. Lew Hoad (Australia) was the first seed and John Feaver at second seed. Other seeds were HS Matheson (Whitecraigs), J Clifton (Scotland), G Perkins (Australia), M Farrell (Queen's) T Bardsley (Canada), R Russell (Jamaica), G Thomson (Australia), E Zuleta (Equador), S Meer (Pakistan), L Tomlinson (USA), J Yuill (S. Africa), M Iqbal (Pakistan), N Holmes (USA) and A Segal (S. Africa).

Lew Hoad

Lew Hoad was in the twilight of his career, having won Wimbledon in 1956 and 1957 (aged 21 in 1956), but Pat McCambridge (Dowanhill) was unable to match the skill of such a player. Just the same there will be a tale to tell "when I played Lew Hoad!". Lew Hoad then overcame Ian Walker (Western) followed by Harry Matheson, before losing to G Perkins in the quarter-final. CM Robertson (Queen's) beat G Thomson and continued his way to the semi-final to meet and beat G Perkins. In the bottom half of the draw John Yuill worked his way to the semi-final where he met John Feaver (who had beaten Abe Segal in the fourth round), he then progressed to the final.

Bill McMurtrie of the Glasgow Herald wrote about that final *"John Yuill won the first set 6/2 and when Yuill broke again for 2/1 in the second set it seemed that the young Englishman's last hope had gone. The rain had started by then, Yuill obviously wished play to be suspended, but the referee ordered them to continue. For once Yuill's composure was broken, and he dropped service twice, Robinson going to 4/2.*
Yuill, however, pulled his game together and won the next four games for the match. Not even the interruption at deuce in the ninth game put him off. When play resumed (almost 2 hours later) he finished the match off in ten points."

Lew Hoad and Abe Segal, seeded one, reached the fourth round of the Men's Doubles and were beaten by John Clifton and Harry Matheson. They in turn were beaten by G Perkins and J Yuill. Gordon Kerr and Graeme Downes (Newlands) beat Mark Farrell and John Feaver the second seeds to reach the fourth round where they lost to N Callaghan and R Gary (Australia) who then defeated R Tomlinson and R Holmes (USA). The title was shared between G Perkins and J Yuill and N Callaghan and R Gary.

Likewise the Mixed Doubles was shared between I Walker and Miss MJ Love and J and Mrs Bardsley (Canada). The other semi-finalists were FAS Paul (Titwood) and Mrs Paul (Newlands) and J Nicol (Bridge of Allan) and Miss SEL Moodie (Stepps).

1975

The top seeds were Miss AM Coe and Miss BR Thompson (England) with the other seeds being Miss MJ Love (Elderslie), Mrs P Elliott (NZ), Mrs V Braun (Australia) and Mrs JS Hume (Whitecraigs) with four other visitors from abroad.

Joyce Hume

Annette Coe reached the final by way of Mrs Christine Lockhart (Newlands), Mrs Anne Paul (Elderslie), and Miss P Elliot. Marjory Love lost to Pam Elliott in the third round, having beaten Mrs Elizabeth Severin (Whitecraigs) and C Bastin (England). Judith Erskine (Dunblane) beat Elizabeth Simpson (Whitecraigs) and Mrs V Braun before losing to Mrs Joyce Hume (Whitecraigs). Shiela Moodie (Stepps) reached the third round where she lost to the number two seed Belinda Thompson who in turn lost in the semi-final to Joyce Hume. Joyce won the final 6/0 6/4.

In the Ladies Doubles Sheila Moodie and Anne Paul lost only one game on their way to the third round where it took them three sets to defeat the New Zealand pair S Meachen and P Elliott. In the semi-final they fought well but in the end lost to the number one seeds Annette Coe and Belinda Thomson 6/4 4/6 3/6. Marjory Love and Sue Smith (Western) reached the semi-final where they lost to Joyce Hume and Carole Matheson (Whitecraigs) the number two seeds. In the final Joyce and Carole won 6/0 6/4.

Once more the Men's Singles had an entry of 96 players. None of the home players were seeded though five received byes into the second round Norrie Paterson (Broomhill), Ian Walker (Western), Harry Matheson and John Howie (Whitecraigs) and George Copeland (Hamilton). They all won into the third round but none survived to the fourth though Harry Matheson took Stephen Warboys to three sets.

Noted names from the entries were Bernie Mitton, Byron Bertram, Pat Cramer, Deon Joubert and Willem Prinsloo (S Africa), Eduardo Zuleta (Equador) a regular visitor, M Collins, Mark Farrell, Richard Lewis, Antony Lloyd, David Lloyd, Stephen Warboys and RK (Bobby) Wilson (England). Bobby Wilson reached the last eight at Wimbledon in 1958. The Australians were G Braun, N Callaghan, G Calvin, P Campbell, R Edmonston, E Ewart, Chris Kachel, SR Wright. P Gorostiaga (Bolivia), MM Sikamder (Pakistan) and L Palin (Finland) completed the visitors list.

Deon Joubert won the final against Pat Cramer 4/6 6/4 6/3 with the semi-finalists Chris Kachel losing to Deon Joubert 1/6 5/7 and David Lloyd losing to Pat Cramer 0/6 6/3 4/6.

1975 West of Scotland County Team
L-R Graeme Downes, Neil Paterson, Ken Gray (non playing Captain), Ken Revie, Harry Matheson
Front L-R Ian Walker, Graham Crosbie, Ian Conway, John Howie

West couples John Howie and Harry Matheson, Ian Walker and Ian Conway, Gordon Kerr and Graeme Downes all reached the third round of the Men's Doubles each couple then losing to seeded couples. Deon Joubert and Willem Prinsloo had a really tough match against the number two seeds David Lloyd and Stephen Warboys before coming out the victors by 10/8 3/6 7/5, only to meet Chris Kachel and E Ewart who won the semi-final 2/6 6/2 6/4. In the top half of the draw Bobby Wilson and Mark Farrell beat N Callaghan and P Campbell 6/4 6/4 and went on to win the final 6/3 6/4. The Mixed Doubles was again all local players with G Calvin and Miss C Bastin and FAS Paul and Mrs Anne Paul the losing semi-finalists. The final was won by Ian Walker and Marjory Love from Jim Nicol and Sheila Moodie 6/2 2/6 6/4.

1976

And then the rain came tumbling down! The first round like the finals yet to come was virtually a washout, only one Ladies Doubles tie was played.

Friday 21st May and Saturday saw the first rounds being played, the local players eliminating each other in order to play the visitors from all parts of the world. Who would refuse an opportunity to play Manuel Santana Wimbledon Champion of 1966 or Roger Taylor the great British hope of those days who had not so long before beaten the Rod Laver the defending Wimbledon Champion and number one seed to reach the semi-final of that event. Paul McNamee a name of the future (he was to win the Men's Doubles at Wimbledon in 1980, with Peter McNamara, and is now Referee of the Australian Open), and regular favourites David Lloyd and Andrew Jarrett were all in the draw. It was nice to have Frances and Veronica MacLennan now Mrs Taylor and Mrs Lloyd playing in the Tournament.

On the Monday there was a typical Scottish wind and there were those who could not control their play as a result, and others who were past masters at it. Billy Gillespie was the only West player to move to the fourth round, by beating Australian Ross Shaw. Roger Taylor, Manual Santana, Andrew Jarrett, David Lloyd, John Paish all comfortably progressed. Stephen Warboys did too but not before being taken to three sets by P Langford (NZ), winning through by 3/6 6/1 6/4.

"And the rain came" Frances and Roger Taylor in the rain at Newlands

In the quarter-finals Roger Taylor beat John Paish 6/2 6/4, Mike Wayman Beat Stephen Warboys 6/1 6/1, David Lloyd beat Terry Rocavert (Australia) 6/0 6/3, Andrew Jarrett (who had beaten Paul McNamee in the fourth round 6/2 6/1) played Manuel Santana and the tenacity of the youth against the skill of experience won through 6/3 6/3. In the semi-final Lloyd beat Jarrett 7/5 6/4. And then the rain-.

In the Men's Doubles there were 68 couples the semi-finalists being Taylor and Santana, Callaghan and Rocavert, Wayman and Paish, Farrell and Lloyd and then-

Manuel Santana, Spain

The Ladies had Linda Mottram, Elizabeth Vlotman, Marjory Love, Lindsay Blachford, Clare Harrison, Frances Taylor, Wendy Paish and D Evers as the seeds, all but Lindsay Blachford (who was beaten by Kym Ruddell) coming through. In the quarter-finals Linda Mottram beat D Evers 6/0 6/2, Marjory Love beat Clare Harrison 1/6 6/3 6/2, Kym Ruddell beat Frances Taylor 6/4 6/2 and Wendy Paish beat Elizabeth Vlotman 3/6 8/6 6/3. Wendy Paish beat Kym Ruddell 4/6 6/4 6/2 to reach the final and then-

The Ladies Doubles semi-finals had Linda Mottram and Clare Harrison, Frances Taylor and Wendy Paish, D Evers and Kym Ruddell and Joyce Hume and Carole Matheson neither of whom played in the Singles. And then-

Roger Taylor

The Mixed Doubles fared no better and five couples remained. Ian Walker and Marjory Love and Billy Gillespie and Judy Erskine were in the third round and semi-finalists were George Copeland and Elaine Robb, Frank and Anne Paul, Jim Nicol and Sheila Moodie and-

1977

The First British Grand Prix Circuit for Men was started in 1977, and the Red Hackle West of Scotland Championships was one of the Qualifying Tournaments.

George Hendon, United Kingdom Circuit Director, wrote about it :-

"In an effort to provide support and continuity to the sport of tennis where it is most needed, the European Tennis Association and the Association of Tennis Professionals are together promoting the unification of well established tournaments into circuits thereby bringing them under the umbrella of international tennis and within a structure that is understandable to both players and public alike.

The Lawn Tennis Association are actively supporting this policy which in the U.K. brings together six of the main pre-Wimbledon tournaments as a Grand Prix Qualifying circuit for men. It is hoped that in successive years when a circuit formula can be worked out, women players will also benefit in a similar points related competition"

The "West" was one of six qualifying circuit tournaments played throughout U.K. with points allocated on a weekly basis and the top 16 men would qualify for the Masters event.

Thus the Championship "Main Draw" was as follows:-
A restriction of a 64 draw composed of
40 ATP ranked players
12 at the discretion of the Circuit Committee
8 qualifyers from the Men's Shield
4 Wild Cards.

The schedule for play during the Championships had been very tight and the rain of the last two days of the 1976 event emphasised this point. Therefore the new structure proved

Mrs D Love with Anne Jones

beneficial. The Ladies event remained a draw of 36, but also using a qualifying event.

Anne Jones was the star attraction for the Ladies Singles. She won the Ladies Singles at Wimbledon in 1969 and still regularly played in tournaments. She displayed her skills well and reached the final via Anne Paul (Scotland), K Pratt (Australia) and in the semi-final Claire Harrison (England) 7/5 6/0. Helena Anliot (Swedish no 1) who was seeded two reached her allotted place in the final via Evelyn Armstrong (Kilmacolm), Mrs M Pratt (Australia) and in the semi-final Jo Durie (England) who was in the future to win the Mixed Doubles at Wimbledon partnered by Jeremy Bates. In the final Anne Jones was very much in command and won by 6/1 6/2.

Helena Anliot (Swedish No.1)
Runner Up

Other players that year were Judy Erskine (Dunblane) Marjory Love, Sheila Moodie, Elaine Robb and Frances Taylor.

Roger Taylor (1), David Lloyd (2), Jonathan Smith (3), R Beven (6) all England; W Maher (4), Jonathan Marks (5), Dale Collings (8) all Australia; and G Morreton (7) France, were the seeds. Also in the draw were Andrew Jarrett, AH (Tony) Lloyd, Harry Matheson, John Howie, Ian Walker, Norrie Paterson, Colin Haig, Graham Crosbie and David Woodhouse. 21 players came fron Australia!

Roger Taylor, a firm favourite with the crowd, having his quest for the Singles title frustrated by rain the previous year moved to the fourth round via J Mills (NZ), V Eke (Australia), to meet Andrew Jarrett. Jarrett won through to the semi-final where he met the unseeded Tony Lloyd, who had disposed of two seeds W Maher and Dale Collings, Jarrett won through to the final. There he met David Lloyd who had progressed via G Suyderhoud (USA) a qualifier, U Eriksson (Sweden) G Morreton, and J Marks. David Lloyd won the final 7/5 0/6 7/5.

In the Men's Doubles there were 70 couples. Top seeds were Roger Taylor and David Lloyd who won the final 7/6 6/2 against V Eke and S Wright (Australia) an unseeded pairing and who had beaten seeds J Smith and P Langsford and C Bradman and A Jarrett. In the top half Taylor and Lloyd defeated seeds D Carter and J Soares followed by G Morreton and M Wayman in the semi-final. West couples GB Kerr and and FN Thompson and HS Matheson and D Watt reached the fourth round.

The Mixed Doubles saw John Howie and Judy Erskine win over Jim Nicol and Sheila Moodie.

James E Gray & David Lloyd, Mens Double Cup

Although the Sponsoring firm was the same their title for the sponsorship for 1978 was changed to
Langs "Supreme" Scotch Whisky
It remained with that title until the conclusion of the sponsorship.

The Prize money by this time was £415 for the Winner of the Men's Singles, halving at each level until the losing first round player received £10. In the Ladies event the Winner would receive £200 and the losing quarter-finalist would get £20. Hospitality to the players for accommodation was provided so that enhanced the tournament enormously.

Everyone looked forward to "The West" and the audiences were on the whole very knowledgeable but it was always difficult to get people to remain seated until the "change-over" every two games as is a must at Wimbledon. At Newlands those in the audience were so close to the play movement could and did disturb the players. Education is on going and this courtesy needs practice!

The Ladies with 44 entries had our own Winnie Wooldridge as number one seed, with P Bailey, K Pratt, W Paish (all Australia,) G Sammel (SA), S Chapman (NZ), MJ Love and J Erskine as the other seeds.

Winnie Wooldridge

Charlene Murphy

A total of ten Scots were playing and only Winnie (Shaw) Wooldridge reached the fourth round. Kerryn Pratt the eighteen year-old No 6 seed met Winnie in the semi-final and while Winnie quickly won the first set 6/0 the match was far from over and in a long second set Kerryn came out the winner 7/5 and then took the final set 6/3. So Winnie was not to have her name on the Singles Trophy (her mother, Winnie Mason, had won the Singles 5 times in the 1930s).

Charlene Murphy (USA) unseeded, started out by beating the No 4 seed G Sammel and when she reached the semi-final she beat the No 2 seed Pat Bailey 6/0 6/1. The final saw Charlene Murphy beat Kerryn Pratt by 4/6 6/2 6/4.

The Ladies Doubles Winnie Wooldridge and partner Wendy Paish the No 1 seeds met Kerryn Pratt and Carol Draper in the semi-final with Kerryn and Carol winning 6/4 6/2. In the other semi-final Pat Bailey and Karen Gulley beat Gwynn Sammel and K Somers 6/2 6/3 and went on to win the final 6/2 6/2.

Seventy two players sought to qualify for the sixteen places available in the Men's Singles. It is tough if you wish to play the tournament circuit! The main draw of 64 players saw Roger Taylor as No 1 seed and Dale Collings (Australia) No 2. Other seeds were R Keighery, J Tricky, D Whyte, G Braun, P Smylie, S Myers (all Australia), V Ericsson (Sweden), M Myburgh (SA), J Thamin (France), S Sorenson (Ireland), DA Lloyd and A Jarrett (England), G Slater (NZ). Scots KM Revie and JF Howie were in the draw automatically and qualifyers were A Chisholm, I Walker and D Watt.

How did they fare? Unfortunately they did not survive the first round. They were all at work or study all day then had to make their way to Newlands for their matches, not exactly a level start! Seeded R Keighery beat

Ken Revie 6/1 5/7 6/2; H Larsen beat John Howie 6/3 5/7 6/2; Mike Myburg beat A Chisholm without losing a game; Andrew Jarrett beat Ian Walker 6/1 6/1; R Hancock beat Donald Watt 6/4 7/5.

Roger Taylor comfortably reached the semi-final and had won the first set 7/5, lost the second set 3/6 then at 5/5 in the third set retired due to an injured back. The tournament doctor had already advised him not to play, but he went on court in order not to disappoint the tennis enthusiasts who were there to watch.

In the first round J Royappa (India) beat Tony Lloyd 6/3 6/1 and in the second round he beat David Lloyd, a crowd favourite, 6/4 6/1. However that was his last win, S Sorenson lost only one game in beating him, then John Paish beat Sorenson in a longer match by 0/6 7/6 6/3 only to lose to Andrew Jarrett.

The No 2 seed Dale Collings lost in the first round to H Drzymalski (Poland) who won through to the quarter-final before losing to Jarrett 5/7 1/6. Jarrett then defeated Paish in the semi-final 6/4 6/4. It was Jarrett's year. He won the final 6/3 6/3 *"at a cracking pace"* said the report in the Glasgow Herald.

Andrew Jarrett

Roger Taylor and P Smillie were the top seeds in the Men's Doubles but lost their first match to S Yuille and H Hauptman 4/6 6/2 7/5. Five of the West couples met seeds in their first rounds and of the twelve couples only J Howie and G Crosbie got through a round.

J Thanin and C Gattiker beat S Myers and M Mirza in the semi-final 7/6 6/0. A Jarrett and C Bradnam the No 2 seeds reached the semi-final only to lose to D Lloyd and R Bevan 2/6 4/6. Thanin and Gattiker won the final 7/6 7/5.

The Mixed Doubles was won by Ian Walker and Marjory Love from John Howie and Judy Erskine 6/7 retired.

1979
The prize money reached £1000 for the Men's winner and a mere £200 for the Ladies winner. While the main draw for the Men was 96 and the Ladies draw only 40, the expenses of travel and training and equipment were the same for both and this enormous differential was quite outrageous. No wonder the Ladies draw had fewer players they just could not afford to be on a circuit!

Nina Bland (Canada)
LS Runner Up

Susan Leo, Australia

The seeded Ladies were Florenta Mihai (Romania), Lesley Charles (England), Leanne Harrison (Australia), Nina Bland (Canada), Clare Harrison (England), Cathie Drury (England), Annette Coe (England) and Marjory Love (Scotland). Other players were Anne Paul, Judy Erskine, Sheila Moodie, Barbara Harris, Susan Leo, Helen Luscombe and Sue Chancellor (Australia).

Florenta Mihai duly reached the semi-final where she met and lost 3/6 2/6 to Susan Leo the unseeded Australian. Susan had beaten seed Cathy Drury 6/1 6/3 in the third round. Marjory Love played Lesley Charles the No 2 seed in the quarter-final

and Lesley was taken to three sets before she got through by 6/2 2/6 6/2. In the semi-final Lesley lost to Canada's Nina Bland 4/6 4/6. Susan Leo won the final 6/4 6/2.

In the Ladies Doubles Anne Paul and Judy Erskine reached the third round where they lost to the eventual winners Helen Luscombe and Barbara Harris who beat Nina and Jennifer Bland in the final.

Colin Dibley (Australia)
Mens Singles Runner Up

The Men's Singles seeds were Geoff Masters, Colin Dibley (Australia), Mark Cox (GB) Brad Drewett (Australia), Frew Mc Millan (SA), David Lloyd (GB), Warren Maher and Noel Phillips (Australia), Rohun Beven and John Paish (England) Greg Braun and Tim Clements (Australia). Others players were, Billy Gillespie, John Howie, Ken Revie, Ian Walker and Donald Watt.

The first round saw the departure of the No 1 seed Geoff Masters to Craig Miller (Australia) who lost in the 4th round to Noel Phillips, who in the semi-final lost to Frew McMillan.

James E Gray of Langs Supreme watches 1979
Winner Frew McMillan with Lord Provost David Hodge

David Lloyd played Mark Cox in the quarter-final, with Lloyd winning 6/3 7/5. Lloyd next met Colin Dibley the No 2 seed, with Dibley winning 6/2 6/0. Frew McMillan won the final 6/4 7/6.

In the Men's Doubles Frew McMillan and Geoff Masters the No 1 seeds progressed to the final where they played Colin Dibley and Brad Drewitt who had been the winners over the No 2 Seeds Mark Cox and David Lloyd. McMillan and Masters won 4/6 6/1 6/3.

Frew McMillan was the holder of the Wimbledon Men's Doubles title when he came to Glasgow and his partner Geoff Masters was the winner of the same event at Wimbledon in 1977 and runner up in 1976.

The Mixed Doubles was won by Ian Walker and Marjory Love.

1980

Frew McMillan returned again, this time with his Doubles partner RAJ (Bob) Hewitt. This pairing won the Wimbledon Men's Doubles in 1967, 1972 and 1978 and reached the semi-final in 1968, 69, 70 and 79. Bob Hewitt additionally won the Doubles with Fred Stolle in 1962 and 1964 and they were runners -up in 1961. With Ken Fletcher, Hewitt reached the semi-final in 1965 and the semi-final in 1966. We were privileged to have such players at our Championships and the crowds in the audience each day confirmed this.

Susan Leo returned to defend her title and was seeded No 1 the other seeds were Lesley Charles and Anthea Cooper (England), Sue Saliba, Kerryn Pratt (Australia), Cathy Drury (England), Nina Bland (Canada) and Karen Gulley (Australia). This was the first year that Marjory Love was not seeded, but she made her point when she was the player to take the eventual winner to three sets in the third round Sue Saliba winning by 6/1 5/7 7/5. Four other Scots were included Sheila Moodie (Hamilton), Judy Erskine (Dunblane), Elaine Robb (Hamilton) and Sue McCulloch (Nottingham).

Of the 48 entries 23 were from Australia, 13 from England, 3 from Canada, 3 from South Africa and 1 from USA. Once more the seeding was put to the test and unseeded Anne Minter the 17 year old Australian Junior Champion reached the semi-final where she met the No 1 and defending Champion Sue Leo. The match went to three sets with Anne Minter winning by 7/5 6/7 9/7. Sue Leo was a Junior herself and she went on to Junior Wimbledon where she went on to reach the final and lost to Debbie Freeman a fellow Australian. Debbie Freeman was scheluled to play in the "West" but no result indicates she may not have come.

Mark Cox (photo courtesy of the Glasgow Herald and Evening Times)

In the lower half of the draw the seeding was accurate with all four seeds reaching the last eight. Sue Saliba played Lesley Charles in the semi-final and won 6/2 6/4. The final was won by Sue Saliba 6/0 7/5.

Elaine Robb played the defending Champion in the Ladies Singles and her first tie in the Doubles with Christine Lindsay (Hamilton) as her partner was against the Champion in waiting Sue Saliba and her partner Lesley Charles. Sue and Lesley progressed to meet Sheila Moodie and Marjory Love and progressed again 6/2 6/0/ to the final by beating Anne Minter and Elizabeth Sayers 6/0 6/1.

The No 2 seeds Sue Leo and Karen Dewis progressed to the third round where they were beaten by Kathy Mantle and Brenda Remilton (Australia) 2/6 6/3 6/1 who were beaten in the semi-final by Kerryn Pratt and Karen Gulley 6/1 6/1. Sue Saliba and Lesley Charles won the final 6/4 6/4. Sue Saliba then qualified for Wimbledon reaching the third round.

Ken Revie

John Howie

Mark Cox was the No 1 seed with the others being Brad Drewett (Australia), Frew McMillan (S Africa), John Lloyd (England), RAJ Hewitt (S Africa), Andrew Jarrett (England), Deon Joubert (S Africa), David Lloyd (England), A Gardiner (Australia), Roger Taylor (England), Mike Myburg ((S Africa), Greg Whytecross (Australia), John Fitzgerald (Australia), Willie Davis (England), Chris Johnstone and Craig Miller (both Australia). Others were Jay Evert (USA), Tony Lloyd (England) and the Scots were Ken Revie, Mike Shrigley, Graham Reid, Russell Howat, Eric Dalgetty, Keith Kordula, Donald Watt, Billy Gillespie, Neil Paterson, Harry Matheson, Alan Liddell, Andy Galbraith, David Morton, John Howie and Alan Mulholland, quite a list!

Of the home players Ken Revie beat Adrian Simcox (England) 6/1 6/1 then lost to Mark Cox. Eric Dalgetty met and lost to Roger Taylor in the second round. Donald Watt beat Dave Segal (SA) then lost to Frew McMillan 3/6 1/6. John Howie met David Lloyd in the first round Lloyd winning 6/4 6/2. Neil Paterson lost to No 12 seed Greg Whitecross 6/0 6/1. Alan Mulholland was beaten by Tony Lloyd 6/2 6/2. David Morton lost to Harvey Becker (England). Andy Galbraith lost to Stuart Eichman (England). Alan Liddell lost to Richard Eden (A) and Harry Matheson lost to Carl Limberger (A).

Two seeds were eliminated in the first round Rocky Royer (USA) beat 11th seed Mike Myburg 4/6 6/4 6/4. Royer won the next round against Richard Eden (Australia) 6/0 6/3 before losing to Bob Hewitt who had coasted through so far, thrilling the audiences with his skill. Hewitt met Fitzgerald in the quarter-final. Fitzgerald, seeded 13, had beaten John Lloyd, seeded 4, in the previous round 6/4 7/5 in a match lasting nearly two hours. However Hewitt refused to go without a fight and the tie break in the first set went to Hewitt but the next two sets were to be won by Fitzgerald, the score being 6/7 6/3 6/3.

James E Gray, Director Langs Supreme, Sue Saliba (Australia), Ladies Singles Winner, Mrs Dorothy Gray and Andrew Jarrett, Mens Singles Winner

Mark Holland (England) beat the No 2 Brad Drewett 6/2 3/6 6/3 (Drewett had reached the last sixteen at Wimbledon in 1979, so he was expected to do well). Holland won one more round beating Paul Butcher (England) before losing to Craig Miller 3/6 2/6. Miller then beat David Lloyd 3/6 6/3 6/1 to reach the semi-final where he met John Fitzgerald who won 6/2 5/7 6/4, to reach the final.

Geoff Masters (photo courtesy of the Glasgow Herald and Evening Times)

In the top half of the draw Mark Cox beat Jay Evert, the brother of Chris Evert, 6/2 6/0 then he beat Ken Revie 6/2 6/4. Chris Johnstone the No 15 seed was next 6/4 6/2. The fourth round saw Cox meet Roger Taylor, who had beaten Eric Dalgetty 6/3 6/1, then Deon Joubert, the Champion in 1975, 7/6 6/0. The meeting of Taylor and Cox saw Cox the winner by 6/2 6/2.

Andrew Jarrett brought an end to Frew McMillan's defence of his title, but not without a fight. Bill McMurtrie of the Glasgow Herald wrote *"Andrew Jarrett, with typical Lancastrian tenacity, battled through three hours of gripping tennis to eliminate Frew McMillan, the holder, from the Men's Singles of the Lang's Supreme West of Scotland Championships at Newlands.*

The final score of 6/7, 6/2, 8/6 was an indication of just how tight the match had been. but it does not tell the whole story as Jarrett had to save three match points before winning through to the semi-finals".

Jarrett then played Mark Cox in the semi-final. The match was two sets and the 22-year-old quickly took the first set 6/1, with the second set being more even at 6/4. Jarrett had reached the final again.

With the impetus of his previous two wins Jarrett beat John Fitzgerald 6/2 6/4.

The Men's Doubles showed a wealth of talent West couples Harry Matheson and Ian Walker lost to Mark Cox and Roger Taylor; John Howie and Ken Revie lost to David Lloyd and Andrew Jarrett. Let us look at the last eight couples.

All eight couples were seeded and Frew McMillan and Bob Hewitt as the No1 seeds beat John Fitzgerald and Craig Miller 6/4 6/3 to meet John and Tony Lloyd, who had beaten Chris Johnstone and Greg Whitecross 6/2 3/6 /63, with McMillan and Hewitt comfortably making their way to the final 6/2 6/2.

Cox and Taylor met and lost to Brad Drewitt and Alvin Gardiner 4/6 2/6. The No 2 seeds David Lloyd and Andrew Jarrett beat Mike Myburg and Steve Fine 6/4 6/0, then lost to Drewitt and Gardiner in the semi-final 7/6 7/6. In the final McMillan and Hewitt displayed their talents, even when they were down 4/5 in the second set and were the winners 6/3 7/5.

The Mixed Doubles was won by Ken Revie and Sheila Moodie who beat Ian Walker and Marjory Love 7/4 4/6 6/2.

Wally Masur

1981

The following year saw the return of many old favourites as well as the introduction of new names. The Ladies seeds were Miranda Yates (Australia), Judy Challoner (NZ), Liz Gordon (SA), Maree Booth (Tasmania), Lisa Pennington (England), Marjory Love (Scotland), Cathy Drury (England), Beverly Mould (SA). The Scots were Lorna Brown, Joyce Leach, Judith Hosie, Sue McCulloch, Sheila Moodie, Judy Erskine, Christine Lindsay and Lindsay Reid (North).

Doubles - Frew McMillan and Bob Hewitt

Of the nine Scots only one survived to the second round, Sue McCulloch beat Linda Stewart (NZ) 6/3 6/2 however Sue lost in round 2 to No 5 seed Lisa Pennington. Judy Erskine took her match to three sets before losing to Margaret Redfern (SA) 2/6 6/1 4/6. Unseeded Lisa Bubltz (USA) reached the semi-final by beating the No 1 seed Miranda Yates 6/0 6/1, then beat Lisa Pennington 6/3 6/4 to reach the final.

Liz Gordon beat Cathy Drury in the other semi-final and went on to win the final 7/5 6/3.

West Ladies in Tournament
L-R Lorraine Wall, Judith Hosie, Carol Wilson, Isabel Stadele, Lorna Browne, Shiela Moodie, Laura Boyd, Marjory Love

Christine Lindsay and Elaine Robb (Hamilton) were the only local couple of the 16 entries to reach the second round, they beat Deborah Gale and A Carlson (England) 6/2 6/1 and lost to No 2 seeds Judy Challoner and Linda Stewart (NZ) by the same score. The finalists were the No 3 and 4 seeds. Beverly Mould and Liz Gordon beat Annette Smith and Lisa Bublitz 7/6 6/0.

The Men's Singles had well known names for the enthusiasts to watch, and some who had yet to make their mark.

The seeds were Phil Dent, John Alexander and Brad Drewett (Australia), Frew McMillan (SA), Syd Ball (Australia), Andrew Jarrett (England), Deon Joubert (SA), Wayne Pascoe, Greg Whitecross, Craig Miller (Australia), John Feaver (England) and Warren Maher (Australia).

The Scots were Raymond Stadele, Eric Dalgetty, Martin Kilday, Russell Howatt, Jeff Williams (East), Andy Galbraith, Ian Campbell, Graham Reid, Keith Kordula(East), John Markson, Dave Williamson, Robin Scott (East), Ken Revie, Peter Gillespie, Colin Haig, Graham Crosbie, Donald Watt (East), Alan Dickson. Looking at the seeding it is tough when you have to play a seed in the first round seven of them did and none survived.

Raymond Stadele lost to Pat Cash without winning a game, this youngster from Australia, two days away from his 16th birthday, was indeed a man of the future. Martin Kilday lost to Craig Miller 0/6 1/6, with Mliller only losing eight games in 4 rounds and destined to be the eventual winner.

Craig Miller

Miranda Yates

Andy Galbraith beat Jeff Young (Aus) 7/5 6/3 then lost to Mike Myburg (SA) who then reached the fourth round. Ian Campbell lost to Andrew Jarrett 0/6 0/6, who reached the semi-final by beating Myburg 6/4 6/3.

There were those who won to play another round Donald Watt beat Chris Trousdale (Eng) but then lost to Jeremy Dier (Eng) 3/6 2/6. Dier then beat John Alexander the No 2 seed 6/7 6/3 6/2 before losing to Wayne Pascoe. Ken Revie did best of all reaching the third round beating Clive Johnson (Eng) 6/3 6/3 then Hugo Fubini (Eng) 6/1 6/2.

What about the stars? Pat Cash that unknown youngster from Australia, who in the future would be Wimbledon Champion, was already making his mark in the second round he beat James Boustany (USA) 6/0 7/5 and in the next round his biggest scalp so far the No 1 seed Phil Dent. The report in the Glasgow Herald on Friday 29th May went as follows :-

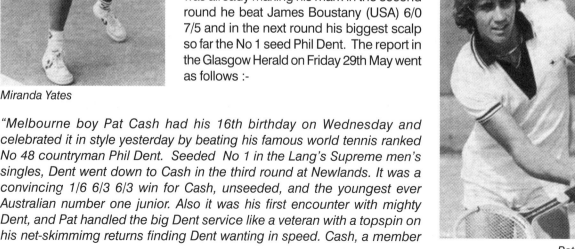

Pat Cash

"Melbourne boy Pat Cash had his 16th birthday on Wednesday and celebrated it in style yesterday by beating his famous world tennis ranked No 48 countryman Phil Dent. Seeded No 1 in the Lang's Supreme men's singles, Dent went down to Cash in the third round at Newlands. It was a convincing 1/6 6/3 6/3 win for Cash, unseeded, and the youngest ever Australian number one junior. Also it was his first encounter with mighty Dent, and Pat handled the big Dent service like a veteran with a topspin on his net-skimmimg returns finding Dent wanting in speed. Cash, a member

of the Ruffels touring team, won the final game of the match from 40-15 and the first match point. Cash's efforts against Dent told their tale three hours later when he lost to the No 10 seed, Craig Miller, in the quarter-finals. He was a spent force and crashed out 0/6 2/6."

There are no reports of there being adverse weather to cause two matches to be played on the same day, however there were several other match results at the same time which indicate that other players also played two matches on the same day. Perhaps a log jam of too many matches for the number of courts at Newlands was the cause.

How did our other favourites get on? Frew McMillan the No 4 seed had a long three set match against Toru Yonezawa (Japan) winning 7/6 0/6 6/2 and perhaps this took its toll for in the second round he lost to Wally Masur (Aus) 2/6 3/6. Andrew Jarrett beat Mike Myburg, unseeded but a former finalist, 6/4 6/3 to reach the semi-final against Craig Miller where Miller won a long three set match 7/6 4/6 6/3.

John Feaver beat Wayne Pascoe 6/4 6/4 to reach the final. Craig Miller became the Champion winning 6/4 7/6.

In the Men's Doubles of the home players only Roderick Coull (Eng) and Keith Kordula (E Scot) got a set when they played Pat Cash and Wally Masur. John Alexander and Phil Dent were the No 1 seeds and beat Cash and Masur 6/2 6/4 in the quarter-final and duly reached the final by beating Wayne Pascoe and Andrew Jarrett 4/6 6/2 6/4.

Frew McMillan and Brad Derwett the No 2 seeds made their way to the final via Alan Dickson and Peter Gillespie 6/1 6/0, Craig Miller and Greg Whitecross 4/6 6/2 6/4 and Warren Maher and Syd Ball 5/7 6/2 6/4. Alexander and Dent won the final 6/3 6/4.

An indication of the high standard of players at the West of Scotland Championships at this time were John Alexander and Phil Dent who were Doubles finalists at Wimbledon in 1977 when they lost to Ross Case and Geoff Masters and semi-finalists in 1978 when they were defeated by Bob Hewitt and Frew McMillan. Of these three doubles pairs only R Case was not at the "West".

The Mixed Doubles was won by Ken Revie and Sheila Moodie.

1982
The prize money was £1000 for the Men's Singles winner and £400 for the Ladies Singles which was an improvement for the Ladies.

The Ladies seeds were Kim Sneddon (SA), Linda Stewart (NZ), Elize Badenhorst (SA), Masako Yanagi (Japan), Joy Tacon (England), Wendy Gilchrist, Elizabeth Minter and Bernadette Randall (all Australia). The Scots were Marjory Love, Sheila Moodie, Lorna Brown, Judith Hosie, Isobel Stadele, Sue McCulloch and Judy Erskine

Only Marjory Love reached the second round, where she met and lost to the eventual winner Bernadette Randall. Sheila Moodie lost to the 7th seed Elizabeth Minter who also reached the final. Judy Erskine lost a three set match against Anne Seidler who in turn lost to E Minter.

As so frequently happened the seeding in the Ladies event was no indication of who would be in the final. The No 1 seed Kim Sneddon lost to Bernadette Randall in the quarter-final and the No 2 seed lost to Vicky Marler (Aus), who in turn lost to Elizabeth Minter. The other semi-finalists were Elize Badenhurst and Masako Yanagi.

The final between the two Australian 16 year olds was a great disappointment as Elizabeth Minter had to retire with an injured ankle when she was leading 4/1 and so Bernadette Randall was the winner.

The Ladies Doubles semi-finals saw Linda Stewart and Masako Yanagi being beaten by Elizabeth Minter and Bernadette Randall 4/6 6/2 6/3. Joy Tacon and Kim Sneddon beat Marjory Love and Sheila Moodie 6/3 6/2. The final was played on the day before the Singles Final and was won by E Minter and B Randall 6/2 7/5.

The Men's seeds were Buster Mottram, Jonathan Smith, Andrew Jarrett (England), Craig Miller, Paul Kronk, Greg Whitecross (Australia), Mike Myburg (SA), Warren Maher (Australia), Frew McMillan Christo Van Rensburg (SA), Wayne Pascoe, John McCurdy, Mike Fancutt (Australia), Barry Moir (SA), Mark Blincow, Martin Robinson (England). Again there was a draw of 64 players.

The Scottish interest had John Markson who lost to No 1 seed Buster Mottram 1/6 0/6. Mike Shrigley won through to the second round and lost to Howard McGuiness (Eng) 6/2 6/2, Donald Anderson beat Brian McNamee then lost in the next round to John McCurdy 6/3 6/4. Robin Scott reached the second round without losing a game then himself lost to Paul Kronk 3/6 1/6. Donald Watt beat Tim Robson (Eng) 6/2 6/1 then met the No 2 seed Johnathan Smith and put up a spirited fight before losing 4/6 5/7.

In the quarter-finals Mottram beat Christo Van Rensberg 6/2 6/2, McCurdy beat Craig Miller, the holder, 3/6 6/0 6/2, then Mottram beat McCurdy 6/3 6/1.

In the bottom half of the draw quarter-finals saw Paul Kronk beat Andrew Jarrett 6/7 7/5 6/4 and Warren Maher beat the No 2 seed Jonathan Smith 6/4 6/2. Kronk beat Maher in the semi-final 6/4 6/4.

For once the sun was shining and Kronk beat Mottram 6/3 6/4.

The Men's Doubles the semi-finalists were Craig Miller and Warren Maher who lost to the No 1 seeds 4/6 4/6 and John McCurdy and Greg Whitecross lost to the No 2 seeds by the same score. The No 1 and 2 seeds duly met in the final. Buster Mottram and Frew McMillan were No 1 seeds over Andrew Jarrett and Jonathan Smith at 2 and Mottram and McMillan comfortably won 6/3 6/4.

It would be good to detail more about the results however space does not allow.

Paul Kronk (Australia)

The Mixed Doubles was won by Ken Revie and Sheila Moodie. No further details of the Mixed Doubles is available since the event was not printed in the programme nor published in the press.

1983

Sheila Moodie, Winner of Mixed Doubles

The Ladies Singles had an entry of 32 with the seeds being Sue Barker (England), Rene Mentz, Kim Seddon (S Africa), Debbie Freeman (Australia), Sarah Sullivan (Engalnd), Miranda Yates (Australia), Monica Reinach (S Africa), Linda Bayly (Australia).

The Scots were Marjory Love, Sheila Moodie, Judy Erskine, Lorna Browne and local players Judith Hosie, Christine Lindsay, Marie Dixon, Carole Wilson, Joyce Leach, Alison Brown, Lorraine Wall, Rona Harvie, Christine Lockhart, Isobel Stadele (local names in the order they appear in the draw).

Everyone was looking forward to watching Sue Barker (Wimbledon semi-finalist 1977 and Doubles semi-finals 1978 and 1981). In the first round Sue played Judith Hosie, who just managed to get one game in the second set. In the next round against Louise Fitzgerald an unseeded Australian, Sue won the first set 7/5 and was leadin 1/0 in the second when an ankle injury flared up and she conceded. Such a disappiontment for the watching enthusiasts.

Sheila Moodie also conceded after winning the first set 6/4 against Anne Gibbons of Australia, Anne Gibbons scratched and Linda Bayly the No 8 seed went through to the third round where she lost to Louise Fitzgerald.

Judy Erskine beat Caroline Clark 7/6 6/3 but then lost to Debbie Freeman the No 4 seed.

Rain interrupted play and ties were postponed for a day. The report in the Glasgow Herald on Saturday 28th May said *"Sarah Sullivan, Essex, the highly ranked British junior, pulled out before the quarter-finals and flew off to Paris to practise on the instruction of her coaching director, Sue Mappin. Sullivan should have played Kim Seddon (SA), the No 3 seed this morning after rain caused the delay (cancellation) of the quarter finals last night"*. Well, well!

Ken Revie wins against Frew McMillan

Because of that rain the semi-finals were a professional set (first to 8 games) Louise Fitzgerald beat Kim Seddon 8/6 and Rene Mentz beat unseeded Lina Jacobs (SA) 8/3, (Lina had beaten D Freeman in the quarter-final 8/6). Rene Mentz won the final 8/5.

The Ladies Doubles was won by Rene Mentz and Monica Reinach who beat Lina Jacobs and Kim Seddon 8/2. It was difficult to report here since the other doubles results were not in print.

The seeding in the Men's Singles was Buster Mottram (England), Jeff Borowiak (USA), Andrew Jarrett, Jonathan Smith (England), David Schneider (Israel), Brent Pirow , Deon Joubert (SA), Ken Barton (Australia), Barry Moir , Arnold Pienaar, Frew McMillan (SA), Mark Harnett Australia).

The Scots were Ken Revie, John Markson, Keith Kordula, Robin Scott, the local players were Graham Reid, Eric Dalgetty, Colin Haig, Colin Hanbidge, Gerry Kelly, Alan Liddell, Mike McKnight, John Fraser, Keith Haig, Martin Kilday, Alan Lackie, Douglas Morrison, Alan Dickson, Eric Riley, Graham Crosbie, Alex Harper, Ronnie Caldwell, Donald McLachlan, Dave Williamson, Mike Robson (E Scot).

Andrew Jarrett withdrew at the last minute with a stomach complaint so Kelly got through. So did Revie, K Haig, Kilday, Markson, Harper and Robson. Only Revie got further. He played perennial favourite Frew Mc Millan in the curtailed quarter -final and won 8/2. Revie then played Mottram in the semi-final with Mottram the winner 8/2.

The No 2 seed Jeff Borowiak came through to the quarter-final where he lost to Pienaar 4/8 then Pienaar lost to Jonathan Smith the No 4 seed 6/8.

Mottram won the final 8/4.

The Doubles as said already were not in print and the programmes that are available have names but not scores. Do fill in your programmes with the scores. Do become archivally conscious!

Ken Revie and Russell Howat reached the third round and were beaten by Barry Moir and Christo Van Rensburg who met and were beaten by the No 1 seeds Buster Mottram and Frew McMillan. Ken Barton and David Felgate reached the final by beating Jeff Borowiak and David Schneider. Mottram and McMillan won 8/5.

The Mixed Doubles was won by Alan Lackie and Judy Erskine who beat Ian Walker and Marjory Love 6/0 6/3.

Rain certainly had a dampening effect in 1983! It was as if it foretold the

Buster Mottram (Great Britain)

future, for here the wonderful sponsorship came to an end. It had reached its allotted span and despite considerable efforts by the Committee and others it could not be replaced, and so the Championship reverted to what it had been before - a Tournament worth winning! To have your name engraved on a cup which bears the names of other famous ones AW Hill, Donald MacPhail, Colin Baxter, Ken Revie, Malcolm Watt, Winnie Mason, Heather Macfarlane, Heather Lockhart and many many more.

But to the Red Hackle and Lang's Supreme years it was a farewell to the stars past and those yet to be stars who had graced the courts of the West of Scotland Championships over the past twelve years. Friendships were made and many families are still in touch with the players whom they hosted.

Roger Taylor comments that he always enjoyed being at the "West" and appreciated the welcome and the support of the audiences of tennis enthusiasts.

Judy (Erskine)Murray Scottish National Coach says of those days :-
" I well remember the halcyon days of the West Tournament. It was one of the biggest in Britain in the 1970s and early 1980s and certainly the major international event in Scotland. It was a huge opportunity for the leading Scots to compete against some of the worlds best. My most vivid memories are of partnering Marjory Love against Helena Alniot (Sweden) and Ann Jones (semi-final 1977); rubbing shoulders with David and John Lloyd, Roger Taylor and Sue Barker; getting an early glimpse of a 16 year old Pat Cash, complete with chequered headband! I also remember getting my first win against a foreigner when I beat Aussie Vicki Braun in the second round in 1975. Those were the days!"

Frew McMillan writes

Much of my decade affair with the W of S stems from the fact that both my maternal grandparents came from the West – Kilmarnock in fact. One a Frew, the other a Mackay.

In the early 60's I had played successfully in Montrose and St. Andrews but had not seen the opportunity of playing in the West. By 1973 I had won two Wimbledon titles, so when the West and the Newlands Club showing enterprise and determination sought a few "foreign names", I jumped at the opportunity to re-visit Scotland and meet up again with friends and relations. Most of whom lived in and around Glasgow.

Sponsorship was obviously a key to the opening up of the W of S tourney and naturally without it (unlike the early 60's visit) I should not have appeared at Newlands. So eternal credit to Langs who at one stage was the longest running sponsor of a British tournament. Ringing applause too to Robbie Jenkins whose untiring efforts, along with his wife Pam's serene assistance, channelled the sponsorship into making the West a real International event.

In 1973 it was a "Clay Court" tourney of course, and I must confess to enjoying those shale courts very much more than the subsequent hard, unresponsive variety even though I recognised why the change had been made. In 1973 I even chose to play the West and not Wimbledon – it was the year of the big player boycott! Part of the fun of that first visit was the trip to the distilleries where Langs and others were able to get their message across. From this and social evenings at Newlands friendships developed, none more so than with John and Judy McKenzie who were my hosts so often for the West. Friends then and I am pleased to say friends to this day. Their's was a home from home for me and my family and that was how I felt about the West. This encouraged me to return as often as I did in the late 70's and early 80's. Success played its role as did my Mother's many cousins with whom reunions were always warm. Along with the Jenkins family, Ronnie Carswell too played a most welcoming role in making Newlands such a good place to go back to.

The late Jimmy Grey of Langs was a supreme host at Newlands and deserves as much credit as anyone for the success that the West undoubtedly was. Sadly I don't have a dram of his nectar left in my cellar to drink to his memory. I do have a McMillan Tam O'Shanter however given me by Tommy McMillan. He did sterling work in the Newlands bar and oversaw the raising of spirits by the downing of spirits.

Just thinking back to many happy days at Newlands for the West is in itself a tonic. Congratulations on your Centenary.

Your sincerely

Frew McMillan

THE JUNIOR CHAMPIONS

A great many of the Junior Champions went on to further successes which are recorded elsewhere. Some photographs have survived and are of interest.

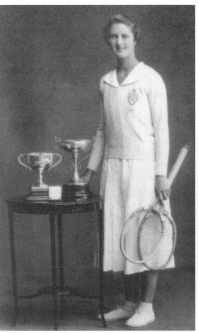

1933 KAS Nicol (Poloc) known as Audrey now Mrs Bell. Was still playing in her club in near Warwick in 1999 and won a Doubles Cup at her Club.

1931/2 Clara H Butters (Pollokshields) (Mrs Black) still playing golf.

KB Gray and A Tankel and M McMillan

1951 EA Walker Singles and Doubles with her sister ML Walker

1953 JD Lillie (Giffnock)

*1954 U15 Champion
George Copeland*

1955 IB Miller (Pollokshields)

*1983 Ian MacAulay
with Lord Provost
David Hodge*

1968 U 15 ECL Robb

*2002 Ian MacAulay, still winning -
Men's 35 Singles Shield with
Baxter Allan, WoS President*

1969 Junior Inter County

1996 The Champions
l-r S Jigajinni, B Saunders, M Gilmour, J Gray, C Lavery
Seated R Maxfield, L Drennan, S McFadyen, P Downes.

The West of Scotland Lawn Tennis Association

Honorary Secretary and Treasurer
JOHN Y CRAWFORD

Blanefield 70742.

26th September 1986.

Gordon Bell,
21, Atholl Drive,
Giffnock,
Glasgow.

Dear Gordon,

On behalf of the Committee, I am writing to congratulate you on your great record in the Prudential junior inter-county championships where, in five years, you have won all twenty-nine rubbers in which you have played. I am sure that very few in Britain can approach your achievment.

I should like to add my congratulations on your other successes this year and send you my best wishes for senior tennis in which you have already made an excellent start.

Yours sincerely,

John Y Crawford.

THESE THAT ARE

Over the century there have been so many clubs, more than a hundred and fifty, and while none of the founding clubs have survived at least fourteen have now celebrated their centenary with several more about to.

These that are the clubs of today have changed enormously in what they provide and how they provide it; upgrading their facilities over the years, adding floodlighting and providing programmes where the Juniors are very much seen and heard.

Anchor	Kirkhill
Ardgowan	Kirktonhill
Arthurlee	Lenzie
Bardowie	Milngavie
Bearsden	Mount Vernon
Bishopbriggs	Newlands
Bishopton	Next Generation - Glasgow West End
Broomhill	Oban
Burnside	Paisley
Busby	Poloc
Cambuslang	Rutherglen
Cardross	Springwells
Clarkston	Stamperland
Cove & Kilcreggan	Stepps
Craighelen	Strathaven
David Lloyd	Strathgryffe
Dowanhill	Thorn Park
Drumchapel	Thorntonhall
Eaglesham	Titwood
East Kilbride	Uddingston
Esporta Glasgow	Uplawmoor
Esporta Hamilton	Weir Recreation
Fort Matilda	Westermains
Giffnock	Western
Glasgow University Staff	Westerton
Hamilton	Whitecraigs
Helensburgh	Wishaw
Hillhead HSFP	Woodend
Hillpark	The West of Scotland Veteran LTC
Kilmacolm	The West of Scotland Tennis Coaches Association

ANCHOR 1923

ANCHOR RECREATION CLUB 1923-1983

The best facility in the South West of Scotland was provided by Clark's Thread Mills to all their employees.

Seven Tennis Courts and pitches for Football ; Cricket ; 3 pitches for Hockey ; 3 Bowling Greens ; Putting Green ; Table Tennis ; Billiards and a hall accommodating two hundred people for Dancing and Socials completed the complex.

Tennis Teams were formed in April 1923. Some of their early successes were in 1927 when two Ladies won the Scottish Welfare Tennis Association open Tournament and in 1929 the team won the Glasgow S.W.T.A. League Championship. Then in 1931 a Mixed Doubles team won the league in S.W.T.A.

Cups were presented to the club in 1951 for a Mixed Doubles Tournament as memorial trophies to R.E.H. Burton and Geoffrey Clark.

Anchor Recreation Clubhouse

Another successful season was in 1954 when the Ladies won the 12th Division winning every match; winning sixty sets and losing only twenty one in nine matches. They moved up two Divisions!

The Teams always had a good entry in the Paisley & District Tournaments and over the years have been promoted in the West of Scotland leagues. In 1979 they had finalists in the Ladies Plate event and in the semi-final of the Gents' Doubles Plate event.

Tennis was played at Anchor Recreation Club till 1983 when due to the closure of both Paisley Thread Mills (J.& P. Coats) the Sports facilities were sold to Pitz Complex.

The Tennis Club (Ladies only) moved to courts at Linwood Sports Centre in 1984 and though very small in numbers continued to field two teams in the West of Scotland League plus, lately, one team in the Veterans' League.

The Gents played from 1984 to 1994 in the league playing from courts at Anniesland before eventually folding.

In 2002 Linwood Sports Centre resurfaced the courts and relaid them as dual purpose tennis and five aside football. We found this an impossible situation for playing tennis matches and after one season Brookfield Tennis Club nearby kindly volunteered the use of their courts for our League matches. To Brookfield we are indeed grateful.

Anchor Ladies on tennis holiday in Tenerife

Due to lack of numbers we now have only one team in the League and one in the Veterans' League but we intend to carry on playing competitive tennis.

Whilst at Linwood we only had two hours tennis weekly and had to pay extra for match bookings. We must be the smallest club in Scotland with twelve members, and will probably merge with Brookfield when we are too old, but the important thing is that we have kept the name Anchor to the fore as an acknowledgement to the Company which gave us such a good start in sport and of the days when Companies had a real care for the welfare of their employees. We thank J.&P. Coats for all the happy hours we have spent on the tennis courts and for the many dear and long-standing friends met through our introduction to tennis.

We are indeed a friendly club and for the past nine years have enjoyed a weeks foreign holiday in the sunshine during the first week in October when eight of us play tennis every day, swim etc. and have a whale of a time. Roll on next year.

ARDGOWAN 1891

"The Game was first played on Ardgowan Club Grounds in 1875"

Ardgowan had a Bowling Green and tennis was within the grounds. The formal formation of the Tennis Club was 7th June 1891.

The first set of Bye-laws were drawn up in 1908, and in 1911 it was considered that 10 dozen tennis balls were sufficient for two courts for the season. In 1947 with four courts 80 dozen were used and today many many more, about thirty five dozen, an increase repeated in every club.

1941 Committee
AB Cockle, WB Jack, JC Young
TH Clark, Raymond K Clark, WE Erskine

The tennis section first entered the West of Scotland League Competitons in 1913, and have taken part since. Over the years the Ladies played in Division one from 1933 to 1938 and from 1947 to 1955, and distinguished players were Mrs Jean Toner and Jean and Muriel Ferguson. Muriel played at Junior Wimbledon and was in the West of Scotland County Team many times in the nineteen sixties. Rhona Harvie, Jean's daughter, became the next generation, and there are now many "next" generations in the club.

The Greenock and District and the Paisley and District tournaments all resulted in successes for the Club. In the past fifty years in the Greenock and District Tournament the Men's Singles has been won by club members forty one times and twenty six times each in the Men's Doubles and Mixed Doubles, with both Ladies' events scoring twenty successes.

The Gentlemen of the club have had their rewards, too, winning the Calcutta Cup in 1922, 1986, 1987 and 1992. The Junior Calcutta Cup was won in 1998 and again in 1999.

The Clydesdale Cup was achieved in 1966 in Division 1 and in 1974, 1998 and 2001 in Division 2.

Overall the club has always tried to encourage tennis in the town of Greenock, where in the nineteen fifties and sixties there were five clubs;

Ardgowan Tennis Club - Easter Camp fun with Inverclyde Leisure's Polo the Bear

Mini tennis is loads of fun at Ardgowan Tennis Club

Ardgowan, Fort Matilda, Greenock High School, Port Glasgow and Rankin Park. Now sadly the choice is only the first two. Both have survived to introduce "All weather" facilities. Ardgowan have also installed floodlights.

In recent years, Ardgowan Tennis Club has greatly expanded its activities amongst the Juniors and Mini members in a number of ways:

The Club has been behind three separate Cliff Richard Tennis Trails to Inverclyde, with all Inverclyde's thirty two primary schools receiving £700 worth of tennis equipment as well as regular coaching in school for their primary three and four pupils. In addition, the Trail set up development squads for a number of pupils with tennis potential. Inverclyde was the first local authority in Scotland to have a Trail visit all its primary schools.

Ardgowan offers regular coaching for Junior and Mini members of all ages and playing standards.

The Club was also first in Scotland to set up a Community Tennis Partnership in conjunction with the LTA and Inverclyde Council. Now known as Tennis Inverclyde this initiative works throughout the year to bring tennis and short tennis to areas of the local community who otherwise might not have the opportunity to take up the sport. Through Tennis Inverclyde, the club runs after-school, short tennis "Wee Smashers" clubs in various primary schools, a Saturday morning club, Easter and Summer tennis camps, regular coaching for primary and secondary school children and adults, "Come and Try" sessions and specific promotions as part of other local community events. Tennis Inverclyde is also involved with the Lawn Tennis Association's(LTA) Mini Tennis programme.

Ardgowan was awarded "Club of the Year" by the West of Scotland LTA in 2001, also receiving that year a special award fron Tennis Scotland for its development and fundraising and sponsorship activities.

Catherine McTavish-Kew is probably the best known member of the last fifty years. Now an Honorary Member, the first Lady to be so honoured by the full Ardgowan Club (Bowling and Tennis). Catherine won the Club Championship and other local events. It was however as an Umpire at the Championships at Wimbledon she went into the record book. She was the first Lady Umpire on Number One Court on Ladies Day (the first Tuesday of the Wimbledon Fortnight) in nineteen seventy nine.

Ardgowan is in good heart and looks forward to the next century.

Ian McShane, Callum Gerrard, Jim Lion, Graham Roberston - Winners of the Junior Calcutta Cup 1999

ARTHURLEE 1950s

Springhill Road, Barrhead is where to find Arthurlee. The courts are in the grounds of Arthurlee House which is now a Community Centre.

There was a tennis court in the grounds (all big houses in the late nineteenth century had the latest fashion - a Tennis Court) and Arthurlee was no exception. It would have been a lawn court.

In the nineteen fifties a group formed themselves into a club and built the blaes surface on the court, adding a second court about ten years later. Then a third court, this time of tarmacadam, was created.

In order to fund a Clubhouse, the Club members broke away from the Community Centre and built their own small clubhouse.

Mhairi and Jill Walton, granddaughters of founder member Jim McLeod. Jill went on to win the Paisley and District Under 14's in 1987

The members are a close unit and they pride themselves on their hospitality, providing Match Teas par excellence!

Douglas Henshall, the actor, was a member and won the Paisley & District Tournament in his youth.

*Back Row L-R: Bill Young, Murray McMillan, Jim Law
Front Row L-R: Marshall Thompson, Adam Grieve, Jim McLeod, Lachlan McDougall*

Prizewinners from Arthurlee Tennis Club in the early Eighties

BEARSDEN LAWN TENNIS CLUB 1887

Bearsden L.T.C. is one of the oldest clubs in Scotland having been founded in 1887. Throughout its history the club has adapted to changing circumstances and the requirements of it membership and today it continues to seek ways to make its future as successful as its past.

MISS ADA YOUNG   HARRY ROBERTSON
ROBERT WALLACE   JAMES BOYNE   HAMILTON WALLACE   MISS ANNIE GRAHAM   MISS LIZZIE BARR   HARRY SEAMAN
MISS MAGGIE PATERSON   MISS ANNIE MEIKLEJOHN   MISS MADGE BARR   MISS JENNY ANDERSON   MISS IDA GALBRAITH   MISS MAGGIE MOIR
W.E GRAHAM   ANDREW LYON   MISS MARY CARRUTHERS   MISS AGGIE MEIKLEJOHN   WILLIAM LYON   JOE McFARLANE   MRS McCALL   McCALL   TULLIS   GEORGE THOMSON
HARRY HEATHERHILL   FORREST   MISS MAGGIE GALBRAITH   JOHN CARRUTHERS   MISS MARY ROBERTSON   HARRY TAYLOR   JAMES HEATHERHILL

The first printed record of the club is a programme for a fund raising concert held on January 23rd 1888. Minutes of meetings were first kept in 1891 and they record the first club match against Mansewood. Complete records have been maintained to the present day. A club history published to celebrate the centenary in 1987 was based on these records and copies can be found in the Mitchell Library.

In its early days the club had two blaes courts and a clubhouse located off Ledcameroch Road. However in 1901, by which time the membership was 61, the club was given two weeks notice to quit as the land had been feued. Eventually an alternative site was found in Jubilee Gardens, where the club remains today, and two new courts were laid by a local builder for £45. A third court costing £20 9s.6p. was added in 1905 with the cost met by donations from members. It was not until 1961 that the fourth court was added, funded by a legacy and a debenture. While all the courts were initially of blaes one court was converted to 'All Weather' porous concrete in 1973 and floodlighting was added. Eventually the remaining blaes courts were converted to artificial grass in 1994 and all courts were fitted with flood lights in 1999 with the help of Lottery funding. The club had a succession of wooden clubhouses until late in its centenary year of 1987 when disaster struck and the structure built in 1965 was destroyed by fire. This setback was turned to advantage as a new brick building was constructed and a practice wall was added in 1997.

Dressed for the game - 'Old Time' tennis match to celebrate the club's 90th anniversary in 1977

Back in 1896 club membership was restricted to 40 men and 20 ladies and it was not until 1910 that ladies had equal membership rights. Still, almost a century later not all golf clubs have yet caught up!

The club affiliated to the Scottish Lawn Tennis Association in 1902. Match fixtures were arranged at a meeting in Edinburgh and Gents and Mixed Doubles games were played. After the club joined the West of Scotland LTA in 1905 men's and ladies' teams were entered into league competitions.

During the 1914-18 war, with many members unable to play because of military service, one court was closed down and the club championships were suspended. Members on active service were excused their subscriptions.

In the period between the wars the club thrived and with attractive grounds and some of the best courts in Scotland it was the venue for many inter district matches and the club played an important part in life in the 'village' of Bearsden. The clubs golden jubilee in 1937 was celebrated by a dinner dance held at the Baillie Nicol Jarvie Hotel in Aberfoyle attended by 70 members. However in the 1939-45 war the club was forced to operate at a lower level. Afternoon teas were a casualty of food rationing, only reconditioned tennis balls were available and the annual retarring of tennis nets was prohibited because of fuel rationing. After the war ended the club recovered rapidly and more ladies' and men's teams were entered into WSLTA leagues.

Junior members were first admitted in 1904 but it was not until 1967 that the first professional coach was appointed and junior teams were entered into leagues in 1970. In 1976 three club members gained Elementary Coaching certificates and weekly small group coaching for 120 of the juniors was set up. An indoor Short Tennis course was started in 1984 and continues today as part of the Mini Tennis programme. As a result of this initial training a number of juniors went on to receive West or Scotland coaching and several players have represented the West of Scotland at Junior or Senior level and a few have represented Scotland. The club is currently LTA Accredited for Mini Tennis and has a thriving Mini Tennis membership.

Throughout it existence the club has established several long standing traditions. One of these

Finalists at the 20th Annual Invitaion Tournament held at Bearsden LTC in June 1996. The men's event was won by the home team (Jordan Gray and Derek McKay) and the women's by Western (Carolyn Morgan and Maggie McLellan)

Club Centennary 1987

is the Saturday afternoon tea which by 1897 had become an integral part of club life and gentlemen members were levied 5 shillings to defray the cost of providing teas 'with the Ladies Committee making the necessary arrangements'. Social tennis and tea on Saturdays remains a feature of the club.

A further tradition from which the club has gained is that several individuals have given unstintingly of their time and energy to support its activities, in several cases over a period of many years. In addition club members have taken part in tennis activities at county and national levels. Among former members of the club three have been West presidents and one SLTA president.

'You are being observed'
Spectators at the 20th Annual Invitation Tournament at Bearsden LTC June 1996

The club celebrated its 90th anniversary in 1977 by starting an Invitation Tournament in which 12 invited clubs played men's and ladies' doubles. This event has been continued and is now in its 27th year. Also well established as an annual event is the Bearsden Summer Series (Ratings) Tournament which was started in 1990 and in 1991 received the SLTA 'Tournament of the Year' award.

Currently the club has some 250 members and 12 senior and 9 junior teams in West summer leagues. It also has strong local links as a member of one of only two LTA Community Tennis Partnerships in the West of Scotland.

Winners of Division 1 of the McRoberts West of Scotland Junior League - 1996. The Bearsden team members were: David Taylor, Gordon Yates, Steven Mills, Colin McCambridge, Jordan Gray and Mark Robertson

BISHOPBRIGGS 1960

In 1958 the Johnston Tennis Club was notified by the then Glasgow Corporation to vacate their courts at Colston Road, Springburn. The members determined to form a new club and contacted the 9th District Council at Bishopbriggs for assistance to find a suitable area for tennis courts in the district.

This was made available on ground behind the Memorial Hall in Bishopbriggs, and was large enough to accommodate four courts. A Committee was then formed consisting of Mr. J Bain, Mr. J Brash, Mr. A Duncan, Mr J Gilchrist and Mr. C Tindal. Due to their hard work and dedication enough money was raised for work to commence on the courts in 1959. All the work was done by the members themselves - the following materials were used.

> 80 tons of clinker
> 40 tons of ash
> 20 tons of blaes

Ladies Doubles Champions - Linda Taylor (left) and Hilary Clews.

Brian Jilks (Club President) and Hilary Clews (Vice-President) who were the winners of the mixed doubles this year.

Three courts were built, thus leaving space to accommodate a clubhouse.

The Club opened for play in 1960 and continued to flourish and expand to enter two Gents and two Ladies Teams and 1 Junior Team in the West of Scotland Leagues. In 1964 after a lot of fund-raising activities enough money was raised to erect a Pavilion.

Fiona Watt (Girls Champion) on the left with cup, Rebecca Cox (Girls Runner-Up) and Brian Jilks (President).

Standard of play continued to improve and both Ladies and Gents Teams managed to reach the then 2nd Division of their respective leagues. On two occassions the Club also contested the finals of the Clydesdale Cup for Mixed Doubles, which they unfortunately lost 4-5 on both occasions.

The Junior section of the club was also proving to be very successful and three of the Juniors managed to achieve higher honours, as follows:

Kenneth Revie won the West Of Scotland Under 18 Singles 4 times from 1971 became Junior and Senior County Player a Scottish Internationalist and won various

British and Scottish Titles
Iain Allan won the West of Scotland under 18 Singles in 1981 become a Junior and Senior County player and a Scottish Internationnalist

Maureen Crawford won the under 18 West of Scotland Singles in 1979. She played in Junior and Senior County Teams.

Although the club has not managed to repeat all the previous achievements, it is still going strong, and has two Ladies and two Ladies Veterans' Teams, two Gents and two Junior Teams in the West of Scotland Leagues.

Bishopbriggs is the only surviving Tennis Club in a district which used to have five clubs Bellview, Cairnview, Johnston, Kenmuir and Springburn North.

BISHOPTON c1920

Founded in the early 1920s and originally known as Erskine Lawn Tennis Club, tennis in the village has been established as an important community facility. It was through the generosity of Miss Ella Winifred Brown and her family leasing the land for the playing of tennis, that the Club was established on its present site.

The earliest records note that the Club played in the West of Scotland Leagues in the early 1930s and entered a team in the Junior Calcutta Cup in 1935 and the Scottish Cup in 1946.

In those early days Dunlpo tennis balls were purchased from the Robertson Rubber Company who were located in Queen Street Glasgow.

In May 1945 a flag was purchased, for 10/6, to hang from the Club flagpole during Victory week. A year later the Club Championships were re-instated with an entry fee of 2/- and the Ladies and Gents Singles winners each receiving a voucher to the value of one guinea and half a guinea(10/6) going to each of the winners of the Mixed Doubles.

The cost of a tennis net purchased in 1950 from Alexander & Son of Paisley was œ5-17-6. The membership at that time was 51 Senior, 25 Junior and 12 Intermediate.

Several Donors gave money to purchase Gents and Ladies Singles Trophies. The first Gents winner was H.I.F. Harper andthe first Lady was M.C. Young. These Trophies are still competed for annually in the Club Championships.

At the A.G.M. in September 1971 the Club name was changed to Bishopton Lawn Tennis Club with the West of Scotland LTA being notified, and the following season teams the Club entered in the Leagues were 2 Ladies 2 Gents and one Junior.

Mr George McGill donated three match scoreboards in 1974 and the following year saw the introduction of Dunlop's yellow tennis balls.

In May 1987 the Club purchased the lease on the land from Miss Brown on the understanding that the land be used for tennis. Two silver plates were purchased and engraved and a Mixed Doubles Tournament called the Miss Brown Tournament is now played for annually.

With assistance from the Sports Council and the LTA three new artificial grass courts were laid to replace the red blaes and were completed in 1992.

Stars of the Future
Junior Coaching

Junior Finals Day 16/8/03

1993 saw the introduction of the Douglas Adam Mixed Doubles Tournament with two Caithness Glass trophies being contested for in memory of the late Douglas Adam who was always keen to to see tennis being played when ever possible during the winter months. This tournament continues to be an important part of the tennis calendar at Bishopton Tennis Club.

A tractor was purchased in 1994, with assistance of money donated by Anne Adam on behalf of her family, to assist with the maintenance of the tennis courts and they are faithfully maintained by this method to this day.

SLTA involvement in the Junior coaching programme took place in 1998 and in 2000 the Robinson's Starter Tournament was hosted by the Club. The following year saw the LTA Club Vision programme being presented to the Club members at the AGM in January and the Club took, part in the National Play Tennis Day, as it did in the following two years.

The Club was accredited for Mini-Tennis in 2002 and a link made with Bishopton Primary School to promote tennis.

Promoting Junior Tennis Summer Camp 2000

The Tennis Club has supported the community over the years on "Bishopton Day". A very active Social Committee arranges special evenings such as Cheese and Wine, Junior and Senior Barbecues, Quiz nights etc. along with an Annual Club Dance

At present the Club is very active with 70 Senior and 100 junior members. A Junior coaching programme incorporating Mini-Tennis takes place throughout the year with the coaching provided by DCA coaches and tennis assistants. Junior and Senior teams participate in the West of Scotland Leagues.

Bishopton Tennis Club looks forward to continuing its long association with the West of Scotland Lawn Tennis Association and within it the promotion and development of tennis and congratulates it in its Centenary Year.

BROOMHILL 1922

Around 1920 two brothers, Tom and John Inglis, members of Drumchapel Lawn Tennis Club decided that as there was an ever growing number of tennis enthusiasts in the West-end of Glasgow and a shortage of courts, they would build a new club at Broomhill. A field of the Scotstoun Estate in Crow Road was bought by them and thereafter four blaes courts were laid by Messrs. Stutts of Paisley, and a basic wooden clubhouse was built. In 1922 Broomhill Lawn Tennis Club was officially formed.

Opening Day 1922

The club was run as a going concern by Tom Inglis until his death in 1947. At that time the members approached Mrs. Inglis with a view to buying the club and she generously offered it at a nominal price of £1,400. The courts by this time had increased to six in number with a membership of nearly two hundred and fifty. During the 1950s on every second Saturday - alternating with Woodend Tennis Club - the Club organised regular dances, with most nights all 200 tickets being sold out. They became so popular, that in 1955 the BBC broadcast the Saturday dances, with bands such as the George Henderson Quartet and the Bunny Holliday Sextet. Also on certain Mondays, Jazz nights were held featuring famous bands such as the Clyde Valley Stompers. Halcyon days!

An amusing story is told of the eccentric Glasgow millionaire A.E. Pickard, a club member, who lived in nearby Mitre Road. During a friendly billiards match with fellow club member Stewart Kilpatrick, it was suggested that they "play for the table" - normally meaning what stakes are on the table. A.E. Pickard lost the match, but took the bet literally, and within a few days had replaced the current dilapidated table with a brand new three quarter size Billiards table!

In 1956 Broomhill introduced the first full-scale floodlighting of a tennis court in the West of Scotland. The lighting, which was a copy of a

Club Stalwarts 1964
Stewart Kilpatrick, Dave McGorum, Jimmy Hunter

scheme built by a London club, was erected at a cost of only £120. The winter of 1956 saw tennis being played at night right into the New Year.

By 1963 the first threats of Compulsory Purchase Order for the approach roads of the Clyde Tunnel were looming. Thereafter it was confirmed that the club would lose a substantial piece of ground, resulting in the loss of two match courts and the re-siting of the remaining four. Following a settlement for this loss being agreed with Glasgow Corporation, gave the Club a chance to think about upgrading the facilities with four new En-Tout-Cas Tennis-Quik courts. The estimated cost for four courts, with two fully floodlit, was the then frightening figure of £8,800.

Scottish Cup Winners 1982 - Ken Revie, Andy Galbraith, Dougie Morrison, Iain Allan, Ronnie Caldwell, Alan Lackie

In 1967 the Men's first team gained promotion to the top Division 1 and won the Senior Calcutta Cup. The Men's second team gained promotion to the Division 3. The new courts were officially opened with an Invitation Floodlit Tournament in January 1968. Following this the Club, headed by the then President Ian Ross, initiated a project to build a new clubhouse. A Management Committee, and also the Building Committee under the Chairmanship of Jimmy Hunter, raised funding of £7,000 from Scottish and Newcastle Brewers, £2,000 from the Lawn Tennis Association, also with internal funds including fire damage settlement for the old clubhouse, found the necessary £17,000 required to build the new clubhouse and two squash courts. The Clubhouse was officially opened at the start of the 1973 Tennis season.

The Club continued to grow, with a new breed of talented young players now overtaking the "old guard". Ken Revie, in 1974, became the first ever Scot to win the coveted Under 18 Boy's Junior Title. He then went on to win the British Under 21 Title in 1977. Ken also played in every one of Broomhill's record breaking Scottish Cup wins. The team won 14 times in 15 years between 1978 and 1993. The year that they did not win was because of a "time out" by their West section opponents when level at three rubbers each. Justice, however, was served to that team, who were defeated in the final! Over all these years, only 12 players were used in the 14 finals. The most honoured players were Ken Revie (14), Andy Galbraith (14), Iain Allan (11), Ronnie Caldwell (11), Alan Lackie (11). The Ladies team won the Scottish Cup in 1983.

Team success continued and in terms of tennis league achievements season 1994/95 was possibly the best,

Tennis	Men's 1st Team	Premier Division	Ladies	1st Team	Premier Division
	2nd Team	1st Divison		2nd Team	4th Division
	3rd Team	2nd Division		3rd Team	6th Division
	4th Team	4th Division			
	5th Team	7th Division			

Juniors 5 Teams at different ages

During 1996 the club had a windfall, following H.M. Customs and Excise legislation allowing retrospective repayment of VAT on members subscriptions for prior years. This gave the Club some £15,000. The then President Stewart Walker, thereafter put forward proposals to use the money towards totally revamping the Clubhouse and Grounds. The Club raised a further £15,000 loan from the Lawn Tennis Association, which together with a £20,000 Grant from the Sports Council Lottery Fund and the Club's own resources of some £20,000 meant that the £70,000 necessary was raised to carry out the work. This included the relaying of Astro Turf on Courts 1 and 2, replacing Tennis fencing, creating a new Short Tennis court, installing and extending double-glazed picture windows overlooking the Tennis Courts, creating a new full length Bar, re-positioning and upgrading the Junior room and providing new curtains, carpets and chairs.

Since the heyday of the Club in the mid 1990s it has, together with others throughout Scotland, seen a general decline in membership - mainly caused by the opening of Sports and Fitness clubs, and other leisure activities being made available to both Senior and Junior members. The age of the members seems to be growing older, with significantly, in 1999, one of the more "mature" gentleman players past President Stewart Walker, becoming Broomhill's first Veteran Scottish Internationalist! One other mature member who has to be mentioned, who was still playing tennis, and squash in 2002, was 80 year old Dave McGorum, well respected throughout the West of Scotland for his superb racquet stringing.

In 2002 the membership totalled 173, made up of Honorary 20, Senior 84, Student, Intermediate and Junior 40 and Social &OAP 29. The Club has settled down to a more comfortable existence of three Men's and three Ladies, and three Squash Teams. The emphasis now being in the "taking part" rather than the winning of titles - a much less stressful environment for all concerned!

LADIES DIVISION 1 CHAMPIONS – 1980

Back row l. to r. Rona Harvie   Isobel Stadele   Maureen Crawford
Front row l. to r. Laura Boyd   Joyce Leach   Mairi McCulloch

The men's side of Iain Allan (capt.), Andy Galbraith, Alan Lackie, Ronnie Caldwell, Ken Revie and Robert Whitesmith beat Giffnock in the Cala Homes Scottish Cup Final. The ladies just failed to make it a double, losing to Cults 5-4.

BURNSIDE 1909

1989 Winners Division 2. L-R Back Derek McKay, Alan Dickson, Stuart Clark. L-R Front Derek Stewart, Gerry Kelly, Alan Fairfield.

Situated alongside the Bowling Club, Burnside Tennis Club has had a long and varied history.

By the thirties the Ladies' teams were doing well and the first team was playing in Division 2. In the same period the Men's team were in Division 7. When a Junior Mixed Doubles League was introduced in 1937 Burnside entered a team and they remained in Division 1 until 1953.

There were two outstanding juniors in the club at that time, Isobel Vallance and Sylvia Litton. They played each other in the final of the West of Scotland Junior Championships of 1946, with Isobel winning by 6-4 6-2. Together they won the Girls Doubles against Cristine Morrison and N Roxburgh (Fort Matilda). Isobel completed the triple by winning the Mixed Doubles with John Baird also of Burnside by defeating G Ferrari (Pollokshields) and Miss N Roxburgh (Fort Matilda) 6-2 6-8 6-4. The two girls successfully defended their titles in 1947.

In 1947 Isobel went on to play at the British Junior Championships at Wimbledon winning the Girls Doubles with Norma Seacy of East of Scotland. This began a career of International play and many representative matches for the West of Scotland.

The Men's teams had to wait some years before they made their mark. In 1980 they won the Junior Calcutta Cup (no not a Junior event just Division 2 of the event). By 1989 the club were playing with a team in each of the Calcutta Cups and won them both.

Sponsored tennis match raised £1000 for charity

From 1990 to 1997 the Men's first team was in the First and Premier Divisions and the Club fielded two other teams. However from 1998 the club had fewer members and participation in the leagues diminished, but like the phoenix rising from the ashes there is now a revival.

Over the years the Burnside Club participated and took its turn in hosting the Cambuslang and Rutherglen District Tournament.

When the courts were upgraded and floodlights installed the Club was active in fundraising for the benefit of others. In 1991 Burnside Tennis Club raised £1,000 for the Chest, Heart and Stroke Association by having a 24 hour sponsored tennis match when about 100 members took part.

BUSBY 1924

A summer barbeque and American Tournament. Participants relax on Busby's crazy-paving 'grandstand' built by members in the mid 80's. (Now demolished to make way for new clubhouse.)

The Tennis Cub at Busby is believed to have been founded in 1924 when the current club premises were gifted by a local landowner, Busby Estates.

Activity later dwindled but the club revived with a merger with Muirend Tennis Club, when Muirend's courts, which were on rented land, were reclaimed for their own use by their owner, a neighbouring nursery, in1948.

The influx of Muirend's active membership of over 100 brought about a successful spell for the Club during which Court Four was built to the east of the present Court Three. By 1960, however, the club had reverted to being called Busby, and the fourth court had fallen into disrepair by the 1970s, with the area being used instead as a practice wall.

Replacement of the Club facilities was planned for a long time. Around 1970 a Fête was held to raise funds for a new Clubhouse with Stanley Baxter as a celebrity guest. A replacement Clubhouse was finally secured in 1981, when the Sports Council made former Chalets available free of charge to clubs who could organise and fund their transport and installation, and during another busy spell at the Club through the 1980s various options were explored for the replacement of the courts, or reinstatement of the fourth court. The Clubhouse had to be rebuilt in 1985 after being damaged by fire. A high point in the life of the Club in this period was the staging of tournaments under the "Volkswagen Ratings" scheme in 1988 and 1989.

'Volkswagn Ratings' Tournament at Busby LTC 1988

By the middle of the 1990s replacement of the courts became imperative, as the original clay surface was becoming harder to keep playable with each passing year, and waning membership resulted in the demise of Junior teams. The opportunity to redevelop came through the National Lottery Sports Fund, which matched funding generated through the sale of land owned by the Club to the east of the courts, allowing the construction of a new Clubhouse and three Savannah sand-filled courts in 1998.

Increased interest generated by the development has placed the club in a healthy position going into the 21st. Century. This has been helped by the differing fortunes of neighbouring clubs Stamperland, whose closure at the end of the 2000 season led to an influx of active Lady members, Eaglesham, which met its fate when the land they tennanted was put up for sale and Weir Recreation, whose loss of funding-support from their parent organisation has also resulted in a struggle to stay afloat.

The new facilities have also appealed to other users. The West of Scotland Veteran Ladies Team has used the club as a venue for home matches in successive recent seasons. The annual "Clarkston Confined" Inter-club Tournament (in which Busby has regularly been a small but active participant) also made use of the facilities for Junior events in 2002.

The Club has never, within recent memory at least, attained a spectacular standard of League tennis, having long made a conscious effort to focus on being friendly and non-intimidating to beginners and "social" players. Currently the Club runs two Men's Teams, the First of which has managed brief flirtations with Division 3 at best. There are two Ladies Teams (having had none at all for some years in the 1980s) and there is perhaps more strength in the Ladies tennis at the Club now than at any time in the preceding quarter century, with the First Team going strongly in Division 5. Veterans' Teams also perform solidly, but keeping a Junior squad running seems to be a persistant struggle. At the time of going to press the Club has a rare chance of some glory having just reached the Final of the 2003 Clydesdale Cup Division 2!

Notwithstanding a healthy level of membership and funds in 2003, Busby is mindful of the struggle many small clubs around the West of Scotland face to survive in the current climate, and shares the problem (no doubt familiar to many clubs) of a chronic shortage of teenage and young adult players staying in the game, and providing a prospect of continuity.

Notes by Gordon Watson (immediate Past President) and recollections of Mrs. Elsie Fry (former member of Muirend & Busby LTC 1940s-70s)

CAMBUSLANG 1891

According to the minutes of the Club, it was founded on the 5th of August 1891 and the first Annual General Meeting took place on the 18th of May 1892. The first (of three) clubhouses was opened on the 16th August 1892.

The Accounts of the newly formed Scottish Lawn Tennis Association show that Cambuslang paid its affiliation fee of 5/-(25p) on the 10th September 1895, although the Club was not represented at the inaugural meeting of the Association on 11th June 1895.

In 1901 friendly matches were played against Mount Vernon and Cathcart, both of which were played home and away. In 1902 Dr. and Mrs. Laird were members.

The Minutes of 1st April 1904 record that "in 1903 usual Committee meetings were held but no minutes were written which in the absence of last season's Secretary I have now to state". What's new?

1904 records that matches were played against Newlands (4 times) Mount Vernon (twice) and Queen's Park (twice), so it is obvious that clubs were aware of the existence of others. The Secretary reported on the Constitution of the West of Scotland Lawn Tennis Association and was instructed to enter one team.

January 1989

Season 1908 saw the Men's Team in the 3rd Division winning 7 matches out of 12 and played against Queen's Park, Bearsden, Cartha, Lenzie, Airdrie and Cathcart. The Ladies played in Division 2 and won 5 of their 12 matches, playing Pollokshields II, Hamilton, Newlands, Airdrie, Titwood II, and Hillhead.

1912 saw the Club win its first trophy, the Calcutta Cup.

During the First World War so many were serving in the Forces that the Club was suspended, and in 1917 two members were killed in the fighting. By 1919 play had resumed and a "Victory Cup" was run by the WSLTA. The Club resumed participation in the Leagues when they restarted the following year.

Cambuslang won its next trophy in 1921. This time it was the Clydesdale Cup Division 2 (Mixed Doubles) and that was repeated in 1966, 1968 and 1975.

The Ladies and Men were both playing in Division 1, but both were relegated after poor results in 1933. By 1939 the Ladies had dropped to Division 5, though the Men remained in Division 2. Again during the War the Leagues were suspended. The Men's team descended while the Ladies consolidated and began their climb to the top. In 1951 they won D5, 1952 second in D4, 1955 second in D3, then playing in Division 2 till winning it in 1961.They played there till 1964 when the results were poor, then played in D2 for two seasons and when the team returned to D1 greater success was yet to come.

The Ladies won Division 1 in 1968 and 1971. In the Scottish Cup there were successes too. In the West section the team reached the Final in 1967 and 1968 losing each time to Newlands. In 1970 they won the West Section final beating Clarkston. In the Scottish Final they lost to Blackhall. In 1971 they beat Elderslie in the West section final and reached the Scottish Final again losing to Dundee West End. In 1973 they lost to Elderslie in the West Section Final. The team stayed in The Premier Division till the end of 1993 season.

Time moved on and the Club continue to flourish with coaching for the Juniors taken by Elva Allan who was also involved with the Grass Roots scheme which covered the West of Scotland involving hundreds of youngsters at many Clubs and Parks. Short Tennis was the next move and Elva was involved with its promotion and the local Burnhill Short Tennis Club was a success story.

Cambuslang LTC West League Champions 1969 -
Back row L-R: Mrs Dorothy Dean, Miss Elizabeth
Winning, Mrs Sylvia Frame
Front row L-R: Mrs Patricia Finlayson, Mrs Elva
Allan (captain), Mrs Hazel Robb

Burnhill Short Tennis

Time marched on and modern ideas need better facilities and the Club Committee got together under the leadership of the President Dan Lavery and with a great deal of effort new Artificial Grass courts were laid in 1992.

That left the matter of the clubhouse. It was well past its sell by date and so once more great efforts were made. Anna (Lavery) Brown was the organiser and grants were made by the Foundation for Sport and the Arts and the Club were the first in Scotland to receive Lottery funding. In 1995-1996 a grand new clubhouse was built to the design of Alasdair MacFarlane and the surveyor was Kevin Brown. It was opened Officially by Graeme Simmers, the Chairman of the Scottish Sports Council, in the presence of The Scottish Lawn Tennis Association President Gordon Kerr, David Marshall President of the West Of Scotland Lawn

Tennis Association and many guests including Jack McLean the Herald writer who played at the Club in his youth.

Coaching continued and Summer schools run by Danny Lavery (son of the above Dan) were highly popular.

Now that the facilities are good the Club is revitalising itself and looks forward to the years to come.

Official opening of new clubhouse

CARDROSS 1951

Cardross Tennis Clubhouse on the official opening day

Cardross Tennis Club sprang from a meeting of Cardross residents in 1949 when an approach was made to the Cardross Trust about the possibility of providing tennis courts for the village. The Cardross Trust on whose land the courts would be built, supported the application and in October 1950 the first committee was formed.

Shiela McGown was appointed Secretary and the other two members of that first committee who still live in the village are Jim Sherriff and Mary Deuchars (née McKinstry). The courts were opened for play in April 1951. At that time the adult subscription was one pound, ten shillings (£1.50). There was also a category of Honorary membership for people who did not play tennis but wished to support the Club and their subscription was one guinea (£1.05).

There were only two courts, which were adequate until the Club entered teams into the West of Scotland League. Matches had to be played in the second half of May and June when there were more hours of daylight. The third couple had to wait until the first or second couple had finished their match. On some occasions Lady Cunningham Graham of Ardoch allowed the third couple to use the tennis court in her garden.

The first Clubhouse was a wooden hut with a veranda. The courts were of a bitumen-type surface with loose covering which resulted at times in nasty grit injuries when players fell.

In its first year the Club was very fortunate to have three silver cups gifted for the Ladies and Gents Singles and Mixed Doubles, all of which are still being used. The first winner of the Ladies' Singles was Shiela McGown with the Rev. A.A. Orrock winning the Men's Singles. Shiela went on to win the Ladies' Singles a total of eleven times.

Other winners in those early days included Helen Killin and Sheena McLeod, Alex Walker, Arthur Mitchell and Junior player Stuart Walker who is still an active player and recently played for the Scottish Veterans. Prominent Juniors in those days included Isobel Brown, Margaret Taylor, Norma Sigsworth, William McPherson and Finlay Colquhoun.

For many years Cardross played competitive matches against other local clubs including Kirktonhill, Helensburgh and Garelochhead. To celebrate the Jubilee of the West of Scotland

2002 Fun Day Activities

Lawn Tennis Association in 1954 a Reception and Dance were held in the City Chambers, Glasgow. Four Cardross members attended, including Shiela McGown who still has the programme.

The Ladies' Team started in the thirteenth Division of the West of Scotland League in 1954 and over the years had its fair share of good years and bad. Very few people had cars in those days to travel to away matches so it was done by public transport.

The thought of travelling by bus to far off places such as Garrowhill in Glasgow's east end for a game of tennis does not bear thinking about nowadays. Many clubs in those days were like Cardross, in that they only had two courts so the matches would last well into the evening.

In the early 1970s the Club was in severe decline. Gordon Hanning was President and there were about six Lady members. A meeting was called in the village to decide the fate of the Club and about twenty people attended. There was much emotion, with everyone determined that the Club would not fold. Margaret Duncan and Sandra Brown agreed to be Treasurer and Secretary and with Gordon staying on as President a committee was formed.

The following year Peter Foster became President and the first of the famous Mid-summer Dances was held. At the first one Peter removed the flooring from his loft to provide the dance floor.

When Brian Duncan became President in 1977 little did he know that he would hold the post for nine years. Brian oversaw the construction of the third court in 1979 by which time the original two courts had also been upgraded.

The main fund-raising event at this time was a jumble sale. On one memorable occasion on a very wet day, the late and much-loved Robin Biggart, who served as Treasurer for a while, collected all the umbrellas that had been donated and went out to the queue to sell them and almost caused a riot as the demand was so great.

The Club went from strength to strength in the 1980s guided by stalwarts Tom Wilson, Brian Duncan, Ian and Sandra Brown, Christine Buchanan and many others. Numbers were increasing and the Junior section was very strong. The Club asked Marie Dixon to coach the Juniors and a wealth of talent was produced -

Allan Adam, Andrew Irving, Jenni and Susie Crumless.

In the first half of the 1990s most tennis clubs saw their membership rise and Cardross saw Junior members reach record levels. Guided by Junior Convenor, Joanna Crumless, the Club boasted four Junior Teams with players in the West of Scotland Training Squad.

2002 Fun Day Activities

The one thing that other clubs had, that Cardross did not, was synthetic grass courts and floodlights. Both Helensburgh clubs had received large Lottery grants and had their facilities upgraded. The concrete courts of Cardross were becoming very unfashionable and membership started to decrease. By the late 1990s the club had no Junior Teams and only one Ladies' and one Men's .

Despite a healthy bank balance the Club could never afford to resurface all three courts by itself. The Club enquired about Lottery funding in 1997 but no action was taken. The Committee then co-opted Bobby Kerr on to the Committee in 1998 with the remit to obtain funding. Becoming President later that year he set about the task. The Club was very unlucky in its timing as the Lottery changed its priorities away from small clubs to funding dual-use projects with schools.

The Cardross Trust gave the Club a £5,000 loan, which coupled with its own funds, allowed the Club to resurface two of its courts. When the floodlights at Helensburgh Tennis Club were installed Cardross Club doubled its fundraising efforts and installed floodlights over two courts. In June 2000 the Foundation for Sport and the Arts awarded the Club £10,000 which allowed the resurfacing of the third court.

2002 Fun Day Activities

The Club is now in a stable financial position, with first class facilities, an increasing membership and there are now two Men's, one Ladies' and two Junior teams.

The success of the Club over the past fifty years has been its members. Even when the membership was almost in single figures, their determination and passion for their sport ensured that Cardross had a tennis facility to pass on to the next generation. Here's to the next 50!

CLARKSTON 1909

The first meeting of gentlemen interested in the formation of a Bowling Green for Clarkston District was held on Friday 2nd October 1908. A site was chosen and the Clarkston Bowling Company Limited was registered. The purpose was to form or assist in the formation of bowling, tennis or other clubs. The original intention was the layout of two greens and one tennis court but such was the demand for tennis that two courts and one green were laid. On Saturday 29th May 1909 the green and courts were opened. The tennis subscription was twelve shillings and sixpence (62p).

In 1912 the name became Clarkston Bowling and Tennis Club. It had cost £1,400 to erect and furnish the Clubhouse and lay the green and courts. In 1914 dressing accommodation for the tennis section was added at a cost of £50. This wooden structure stood for 40 years without alteration.

During the 1914-18 war the clubhouse was used by many charities serving the armed forces and wounded soldiers were entertained.

In 1909 a third court was laid followed by a fourth and fifth in 1922 and a sixth en-tout-cas tarmacadam in 1953.

The club continued to grow and by 1924 there were 60 gents and 109 ladies. It was becoming obvious that the Clubhouse was becoming too small. In 1934 the toilets and kitchen were improved, enlargement at west end and east end carried out and a central heating system and a special oak floor for dancing installed.

During the Second World War all sections tried to operate normally only the Senior Championships being cancelled. The Clubhouse was used as an emergency evacuation centre after the Clydebank Blitz in 1941. Servicemen were entertained and many fund raising events were held. Four tennis members were killed in action serving with the Royal Air Force.

1959 was Jubilee year. Funds had to be raised. This was raised by a levy in 1958 and 1959 of 2/6 (12p). Tournaments were organised and a dinner dance followed.

The club continued to prosper over the years and the six courts were well maintained. However in 1987 Winnie Shaw, whose incredible achievements are listed elsewhere, returned for a special invitation tournament to celebrate the opening of three new all-weather courts and launch the Club's first-ever winter season.

Clarkston Ladies Team won Division 2 in 1962
Back Row L-R: Audrey Scott, Jean Legge, Elizabeth Dron
Front Row L-R: Vi Affleck, Jean Woore, Winnie Shaw

In 1993 a new viewing room constructed from what had been an old hall was unveiled in memory of Winnie who had died so tragically young. Her parents made a special visit to the club to perform the official opening ceremony.

Over the years many tennis players have achieved success in local tournaments and major championships. In the West of Scotland Junior Championships the following results were achieved:-

1932 Under 18 Jack Sayers
1955 Under 18 Boys singles   Robert Seaton
1960 Under 15 Boys singles   William Currie
1962 Under 15 Girls singles   Helen Morton
1963 Under 18 Boys singles   William Currie
1964 Under 15 Boys singles   Johnnie Moore
1980 Under 12 Boys singles   Gordon Bell
1982 Under 14 Boys singles   Gordon Bell
1984 Under 16 Boys singles   Gordon Bell
1986 Under 18 Boys singles   Gordon Bell.

Gordon Bell

Doubles events:
1961 to to 1986 Open Doubles:-
1961 William Currie (N Thomson)
1968 Johnnie Moore (L A Findlay)
1969 Johnnie Moore (C M Duthie)
1983 Gordon and Alistair Bell
1984, 1985 and 1986 Gordon Bell (S Wilson, A Wright, J Woodall)

Open Mixed Doubles
1963 Winnie Shaw and W. Currie
1964 Winnie Shaw (J Edmond)
1984 Gordon Bell   (M Armstrong)

Open Girls Doubles
1961 to 1964 Winnie Shaw, Helen Morton
1995 Romana Orsi (E. Stevenson)

Under 14 Boys Doubles
1982 Gordon Bell (M. Watt)

Ladies Singles
1939 Mrs P Smith
2002 Mrs Romana (Orsi) Owen

Ladies Doubles
1997 Romana Owen (H Lockhart)
2001/2002 Mrs Romana (Orsi) Owen (H Lockhart)

From a very early age the ability of Romana (Orsi) Owen as an outstanding player was recognised and from the age of 11 she became a player in under 12 teams and she has won West of Scotland and Scottish Junior events. In 2002 she won the Ladies Singles and Ladies Doubles and plays in the County Team.

In season 2003 Clarkston has 6 Junior , 3 Ladies, 4 Gents, 2 Ladies Veterans and 2 Gents Veterans teams.

Tennis Committee: Ross Johnstone, Captain; Heather Edwards, Secretary; Dorothy Brown, Treasurer and Junior Match Secretary; Heather Smylie, Ladies Match Secretary; Kenny Bryce, Gents Match Secretary; Tom MacPherson, Junior Match Secretary,; Lyndsay Hood, Minute Secretary; Carol Milne, Coaching Convener; Pat Darge, Invitation/Winter Secretary; Romana Owen, Past Captain; Mark Weir, Tennis Ball Co-ordinator; Graham Hood, Web-site Administrator; Lesley Taylor, Ordinary Member.

COVE & KILCREGGAN 1908

Tennis Court, Cove, and Kilcreggan

The Cove & Kilcreggan Recreational Grounds, which included tennis courts and a bowling green, were officially opened by Provost James Gilchrist in May 1908. The land had been given to the Burgh at the nominal rent of 1 shilling (5p) per acre by the 8th Duke of Argyll 15 years previously. The local newspaper announced that " The appeal locally for subscriptions had been so heartily responded to that the green was opened practically free of debt".

One of the photographs appears to have been taken on the "Opening Day" as indicated by the number of spectators! The other photograph could be slightly more recent as there is the addition of a verandah to the front of the Tennis Pavilion also the length of the Ladies' dresses appears to have shortened somewhat. The flagpole to the rear of the Bowling Clubhouse was donated by Provost James Gilchrist.

Today the two buildings remain relatively unchanged. The Club now pays a nominal rent to the local Council and the blaes courts are regularly maintained by a group of enthusiastic members.

TENNIS COURTS, COVE

CRAIGHELEN c1920

Since the early 1920s Craighelen Lawn Tennis and Squash Club has provided a meeting place for many generations of townsfolk, who enjoy the sports of tennis and in more recent times, squash. From the blaes courts and wooden clubhouse of the Twenties when the season ran from April to October, to the artificial grass courts with floodlights, the three squash courts and clubhouse facilities offering up-graded changing rooms, a club area with a unique friendly atmosphere for social functions and a licensed bar. The club and its members have moved with the times. In the 1930s the affiliation fees to the parent body, The Scottish Lawn Tennis Association cost just £2 and twelve dozen Slazenger Tennis Balls cost around £7! In 1943 there were 35 Junior Members, one notable name recorded being that of Miss E. Stanton.

The Catering Team at Craighelen Tournaments play their vital part

Throughout the fifties and sixties, the Club continued to flourish, with teams participating in West of Scotland Tennis Leagues and many individual members achieving County standard. The late Dr. Tom Miller was a great driving force in the running of the club and along with John Smith had the vision to move the Club forward into its next phase. In 1957 the new Clubhouse was built at a total cost of around £3,500.

With the new clubhouse in place, Craighelen then became the home for many successful Open Tournaments. In the extract below you will read of several local players, who took part in the Craighelen Clyde Coast Championships in the early sixties. Over the decades since, many famous Scottish ranked players have played in the Craighelen Senior and Junior Open Tennis Tournaments. Malcolm Watt, grandson of the late Dr. Tom Miller is just one such player. John Smith masterminded many of the Club developments and Junior initiatives over many years.

In the seventies there was a Squash boom, Craighelen's response to which was to build an additional two Squash Courts, which cost £20,000 and were funded partly with a grant form the Scottish Sports Council, but also with monies raised by club members through various activities such as dances and grand fetes.

As artificial grass courts came on stream, Craighelen was one of the first clubs in the West of Scotland to lay the new surface. The five courts were much envied by players from near and far and competitors at the various open tournaments appreciated the surface which is kind to ageing legs!

In 1981 one of the finest achievements of any Club Team was recognised, when four members won the Scottish final of the En-Tout-Cas Tournament. One of the team was the late Marie Dixon who will long be remembered in the local area for her work in the coaching of hundreds of youngsters.

In the latter years of the twentieth century, two tennis courts were resurfaced, the membership numbers were high, the tennis and squash sections were flourishing and mini squash was arousing a great interest in the game at an early age, just as Short Tennis had previously done.

At present, as the Club enters the Twenty First Century, it is in a healthy position, with membership of 150 Seniors and 180 Juniors and plans for the refurbishment of two Squash Courts for the Spring of 2001. In both Sports, both on the competitive and recreational side, there is a rosy future. None of this would be possible without the dedication and enthusiasm of the large numbers of volunteers, who, as in any Club, are the rocks upon which Craighelen was founded and will continue to flourish in the decades to follow..

DAVID LLOYD RENFREW 1993

September 1993 saw the birth of the first commercial Racquets and Fitness club in Scotland. Its extensive facilities included seven indoor Claytex tennis courts, six floodlit outdoor tennis courts, four squash courts, a sports injury clinic and the biggest gymnasium in the country. Ten years on, this relative newcomer continues to develop and improve its already extensive facilities and reputation. Such was the demand that, in 1995, an additional hall boasting a further three indoor tennis courts and four badminton courts was constructed. In 1996, David Lloyd himself decided to sell his control of his mini empire to Whitbread Plc.

The West of Scotland county office is currently located within the club.

Club achievements

1994 Scottish Cup Final Champions - David Lloyd 5 - 1 Stirling University

Team: Gregg Whitecross, Gary Engleman, Donald Watt, Martin Kilday, Blane Dodds and Derek Lauder

1995 Scottish Cup Final Runners up - Newlands 5-3 David Lloyd

Team: Donald Watt, Martin Kilday, Blane Dodds, Jimmy Wood, Derek Lauder and Sohail Shah.

Junior enthusiasts

1997 Scottish National League Champions
Team: Nick Fulwood, Ross Matheson, Martin Kilday, Stuart Clark, Derek Lauder, Damon Petken and Sohail Shah.

1998 Scottish National League Champions
Team: Gary Smith, Russell Allan, Damon Petken, Graham Martin, Lee Alkureshi, Jamie Baker

Original staff of David Lloyd Club, Renfrew Donald Watt kneeling at front

DOWANHILL 1920

Dowanhill Lawn Tennis Club was formed at a meeting held at 3 Kingsgate Dowanhill on 21st December 1920. Mr Laurence Glen chaired the meeting and was elected as President. The membership was 60 Ladies and 60 Gentlemen, with no-one under 17 years.

West End Inter Club Tournament Shield Winners c1969/70

The Club was officially opened by ex-Provost Stan Brown and Mr Keith Buchanan, President of the West of Scotland LTA, was present. The back shop of Mrs Nicol was used as a temporary pavilion!

The first Annual General Meeting was in Colquhoun Tearooms in Byres Road on 13th January 1922 and membership numbers were increased to 70. Mr and Mrs Laurence Glen were created Honorary Life Members of the Club in recognition of their kindness and generosity in presenting the Club with its grounds and courts.

In 1923 a Ladies Committee was formed and a proposal to enter teams in the West of Scotland Leagues was defeated. Junior members were allowed to play during July and August till 6pm, but only if they belonged to a household who were already members. On Tuesdays and Thursdays after 6pm the courts were reserved for Men only. The courts were used for the West of Scotland Championships in 1925 from 1st to 14th June. Ladies were allowed to play matches in the evenings!

The old Clubhouse

The gift of further ground was made by Mr Glen which allowed a fourth court to be built in 1928 and the Wooden Clubhouse was built. Plans were passed on 28th February 1928 and it was completed and in use six weeks later. It stood the test of time for in the very extreme gales of 1968 when chimney heads and slates from surrounding buildings were blown down the clubhouse stood firm and undamaged.

Mr Glen died in 1938 and Mrs Glen was elected President. However, she died in 1939 and Mr NHC MacPherson, their nephew, was elected President. In 1950 Mr MacPherson sold the ground to the Club for £250.

1989 - Work in progress

By 1947 it was time to consider puting electricity into the clubhouse. The cost put that project back two years.

Play continued and Tom Warden got the Club on its feet again after the war and Colin Snell followed after him. Colin was President of the WSLTA in 1958.
That year of 1958 there was a proposal to floodlight the fourth court. The members turned it down by 12 votes for and 150 against why? Money! The members were not prepared to pay a one off levy of 25/-(£1.25)

One of the Jubilee celebrations in 1970 was a Dinner in Dowanhill House, the very building of the first AGM.

Many years later the courts were upgraded, first to a plastic surface which looked like waffle squares. This proved to be very slippy with the slightest dampness. In the nineties the courts were upgraded yet again with artificial grass and new floodlighting. A splendid new Clubhouse was built.

What about the game of tennis? The teams had been climbing the Leagues and in 1953 the Ladies won Division 3 and the Men won Division 5 and in 1957 the Ladies were in Division 1, a short lived visit. In 1965 they won D 2 and played in Division 1 for the next two years. The Men were in Division 1 in 1968. In 1959 the men's second team won Division 19 without losing a match won D14 in 1961, 2nd in D 8 in 1966, won D5 in 1969.

The new Clubhouse

The club continued to play in upper Divisions and in 2003 the Men were 3rd in D 3; 2 Men's 6th in D 4b; the Ladies 3rd in D 4b (they missed promotion by 2 sets).

Cup successes   Clydesdale Division 1, 1988   Division 2, 1953

For many years Dowanhill hosted a Mixed Doubles Invitation Tournament enjoyed by all the visitors.

DRUMCHAPEL LAWN TENNIS CLUB 1898

Two grass tennis courts were laid out on what was known as "Tennis Square" in 1898. The first proper recorded matches which were friendlies were played in 1904. Because of problems of wear due to excessive play both grass courts were replaced by blaes courts in 1920. In 1928 the club acquired a third court on a separate site backing on to the railway. A fourth court was added in 1949, again on a separate site.

Postcard showing grass courts dated 1916

Prior to 1924 the club used a tent for changing purposes. This was erected in April and dismantled in September. A clubhouse was built in 1924. Before 1939 ladies matches were played in the afternoons. Gents played in the evenings.

During the 1950s the club experienced a boost in membership due to the construction of Drumchapel and Blairdardie. By the mid 1950s Two Gents Teams, Two Ladies Teams and a Junior under 15 mixed doubles team competed in the West Leagues. A third gents team was started.

In September 1966 the Clubhouse which had been extended in 1959 was set on fire by vandals and completely destroyed. Undeterred by this set back the committee rebuilt the clubhouse. A membership drive to attract funds and new members resulted in the Friday and Saturday night discos which could attract up to 200 youngsters. Having fulfilled their purpose they ceased in 1970.

Photo taken at the opening of the season on blaes courts 1920. Mary Smith is at the bottom right hand side looking from left to right.

In June 1989 the clubhouse was again targeted by vandals and set on fire. Again the committee rebuilt the clubhouse. After this setback a few members expressed a fierce determination to improve the club. The blaes courts which had been in place since 1920 were wearing out and giving rise to the infamous "Drummy Bounce" often at a crucial point in a league match ! Not always in Drumchapel's favour.

Thus fundraising took place at an amazing rate. Dances, jumble sales, raffles and even chopping down the trees and having a monster 5th of November fire on the blaes courts raised sufficient cash for work to commence in February 1992 replacing three courts with a porous macadam surface. The courts cost £34,000. To save money all the fencing work was done by club members. Floodlight ducting was installed on two courts. On the 14th June 1992 the late Donald Dewar the local MP formally opened the new courts. Following a successful grant application to the Foundation for Sport and Art floodlights were installed eighteen months later. The new courts resulted in new members and due to excessive wear two of the courts had to be resurfaced in 1999. No lottery or grant money was made available to the club, the entire £12,500 cost being met from club funds.

During the last three years the club has been attempting to introduce more youngsters to the game by active participation in the City Council's Easter, Summer and Autumn play schemes at Blairdardie Sports Pavilion. This year the club were able to link in with the Cliff Richard Tennis Trail in four Drumchapel Primary Schools and offer further out-of-school-hours coaching at the club.

The three Drumchapel youngsters undefeated in all the games they played in from 1997 to 1999 with the silver salver at the West of Scotland presentation 1999.

Recent highlights in the West of Scotland Leagues include winning the Clydesdale Cup in 1967. The clubhouse was a burnt out shell and "West" dignitaries had to be entertained in a local tennis member's house. In 1982 the Gents team won the senior Calcutta Cup and gained promotion for the first time in the club's history to the first division; a cultural shock for some of the elite clubs having to play on Drumchapel's blaes courts. This probably accounted for the club's greatest win beating Whitecraigs 5-4 at home. Unfortunately the team were relegated with five points.

In 1999 the under 11 team won the first division. Having started in Division 3 they played for three years without losing a match.

A sporting legend at the club was the late Mary Smith. She started playing on the grass courts before World War One and was still playing in the first ladies' team, often at first couple, in the 1960s. Well into her 70s she broke her leg and asked a very surprised surgeon if it would possible to play in a tennis match some six weeks later.

March 1992. Tennis members concreting fence posts on the new courts.

1996 - Same view of courts as in 1916.

EAGLESHAM c1920

Eaglesham is a beautiful conservation village in a corner of Renfrewshire and Eaglesham Lawn Tennis Club was founded in the ninteen twenties. It has always been essentially a village club and social play was most important as were the social activities which were a regular occurence.

The Men's team were in Division 11 in 1933 and progressed to Division 7 by 1950 thereafter playing in the lower Divisions again playing in D 8a in 1995. The Ladies were in Division 10 in 1933 progressed to D 9 in 1947 and then descending for a few years. The 1960s saw a gradual climb to D 4, and the 1970s onwards remaining in D 6-8. The Juniors played in the League too and reached D2.

All the while social events took place and the Club took part in the "Eaglesham Fair" a bi-annual event frequently having a float in the Procession and helping in the Stalls.

Buffet meals regularly took place the Club had the use of the Bowling Pavilion which was larger. The meals came from the local Chinese Restaurant and these evenings were well attended.

The local Primary School used the courts during PE lessons.

However the Club was to suffer a lethal blow. Their original lease had been for 50 years extended for a further 25years and then the owning family would only give a month to month lease. In 2002 the Ladies team won D 8 the lease was called in and the Club were homeless. The ground was to be "developed"!!

EAST KILBRIDE 1967

Courts just completed 1999 American Tournament

On Tuesday 8th August 1967 an informal meeting was held in a local factory canteen to inaugurate a tennis club in the town. (There were eighteen people at this meeting).

This club would form the tennis section of the East Kilbride Sports Club which had held its inaugural meeting one month previously. This latter composite club would have cricket, archery, tennis and hockey sections – in fact similar to the Cartha Club in Glasgow. This achievement was largely due to the negotiations and hard work of Dr Hugh Fletcher.

Thereafter the tennis club functioned by interim committee until it was formally constituted at the first Annual General Meeting on Tuesday 28th January 1969. In the intervening period fund-raising was by sale of waste paper to a local processing firm.

Affiliation to the West of Scotland Lawn Tennis Association had been made in 1968 for the season 1969, when the club entered 1 gents' team, 1 ladies' team and a junior team in the league competitions.

The first two Tennisquick courts were not ready until June 1969, so all matches in the first season were played away from home and match practice was held on hired municipal courts at Rutherglen. By the spring of 1970 the parent East Kilbride Sports Club pavilion was completed adjacent to the four porous concrete courts. This pavilion gave members changing facilities, showers, toilets, cloakrooms, a function hall with bar, as well as two lounges and a kitchen.

1999 Clydesdale Cup Division 2 Win

In the first four seasons the gent's team went from 11th Division, via modified divisions to the 3rd division, having lost only one game in the process, also winning the Junior Calcutta Cup in 1971 – this cup success was repeated by the gents' 2nd team in the mid-seventies (1977). The ladies' team meanwhile had remained in division 5.

In 1974 four young members (R Gibson, M McDougall, B Houston & J Morrison) played doubles for 45 hours to establish a record, which at the time was recognised in the 21st edition of the Guinness Book of Records. The sponsorship money raised by this feat went a long way towards the cost of floodlighting 2 courts in 1976.

In 1975 the club's founder President, Harry Faichney died just before he saw completion of the floodlighting project, which had been his venture. His widow, May, was invited to be the first to switch the lights on.

By 1978, the club was running three gents' teams, two ladies' teams and two junior teams.

In 1979, the Ladies were in division 3 and the Gents' 1st team in Division 2. The Mixed Doubles team won the 2nd Division Clydesdale Cup. Further cup success came this year when the gents' 1st team won the Senior Calcutta Cup.

Men's 1st Team 1971 - Winners Junior Calcutta Cup
HK Faichney, T Ross, AD McIntosh, HS Fletcher

1997/98 - Before new courts

By 1983 the Gents' 1st team had reached Division 1 and the Ladies were moving between divisions 3 & 4. The club membership had reached almost 300, with a third of these being Juniors.

Having lost a few of their original team in 1984 the gents' 1st team was relegated to division 2. However in 1985 the juniors were in division 1 with two juniors in national ranking for their age group.

By the end of the 80s the club membership had fallen to approximately 150, but there were still a good number of juniors joining the club.

The 90s was a defining decade for the club as, despite having 2 Ladies and 2 Gents teams competing in the League, towards the end of the 90s membership had fallen to an all time low of less than 50. The tennis courts were over 20 years old and in some disrepair so attracting new members was almost impossible. The committee realised that the only hope for the club was to apply to the Lottery for funding to replace the courts.

Endless hours of writing applications, securing advertising and sponsorship for the club and organising fundraising events was undertaken by a small team co-ordinated by Susan Weanie (President) and Jane Lees (Secretary). Sheer hard work and determination paid off and, with mainly Lottery funding and a loan from the LTA, four new all weather courts (two floodlit) were offcially opened in 1999.

East Kilbride was voted Club of the Year in 2001 both nationally and by the West of Scotland in recognition of this achievement. Membership has steadily increased and is currently over 100 with two ladies' teams, (Division 2 and Division 8) and two gents' teams (Division 4 and Division 7) in the league. In addition we have 6 Junior teams and have a major junior coaching programme running several days a week. We have close links with a few schools in the area, running tennis coaching for pupils and we have annual tennis events with disability groups.

ESPORTA GLASGOW 1999

Esporta Tennis was first launched when the Club opened in August 1999. At that time we entered the West of Scotland Leagues with a Ladies, Gents and Junior Team. We now successfully run 3 Gents Teams, 3 Ladies Teams and also this season one Veteran Ladies and one Veteran Gents Team which we hope to double in the season 2004/2005.

This year, in conjunction with the L.T.A. initiative we started a very extensive mini tennis academy with over 170 Juniors involved in the Red, Orange and Green stages of the weekly programme throughout the year. We also run bronze, silver and gold performance squads and footwork sessions to enable Juniors to progress onto the Performance Journey organised by the L.T.A.

At the present time we have a Racquets Manager, three full time tennis professionals and two assistants on site to provide both Junior and Senior weekly classes which cater for all ages and abilities.

As well as five indoor carpet courts and four outdoor Savanah courts, the Club offers extensive facilities for members that enjoy golf, badminton, swimming, fitness classes, sauna, steam room and spas as well as superb dining and conference facilities.

ESPORTA HAMILTON 1998

Esporta Hamilton boasts excellent tennis and badminton facilities in its Lanarkshire location. Seven indoor tennis courts, four badminton courts and three outdoor tennis courts, recently resurfaced with Savannah grass ensures that the clubs' tennis members have superb surfaces all year round.

Coaching is available from the age of three and a range of classes are on offer for both adults and children of all ages and abilities. As well as classes individual lessons are also available. Led by a strong team of Coaches, Esporta Hamilton has produced a strong team of players including five teams in the West of Scotland Leagues and three Veterans Teams.

After the hard work and commitment of practice and competition is over tennis members have the opportunity to attend the Club's Annual Dinner Dance and Presentation, where the best of the year are presented with their prizes.

The Club offers members the use of their spacious fitness arena, 25m swimming pool with separate baby pool, sauna, steam room and spa, children's club and creche. A bar and restaurant with separate adult lounge is also available at Esporta Hamilton along with a Tranquillity Spa and Maxwell Findlay Hair Salon.

Juniors at Esporta Hamilton

Mini-Tennis at Esporta Hamilton

FORT MATILDA 1922

The Fort Matilda Tennis Club was opened officially in 1922. Before that the Greenock Academy Secondary School used the courts. There were four blaes courts on Newark Street and two blaes courts at Octavia Terrace.

The Club played in the West Leagues but the war (I suppose) stopped that and then restarted again.

GREENOCK ACADEMY TENNIS TEAM–SEASON 1927

M Nicol   M Boyd   Miss McDonald   B Burns   M Urquhart

B Greer   R Neill   F McAuslan   J McIntyre

Captain

Matches played 10,   Won 7 Lost 3 Sets for 60 Against 39

In 1957 Elizabeth Holmes had the honour of playing at Junior Wimbledon by invitation as the Junior West Champion and Junior East Champion were usually accepted. She reached the quarter finals of the doubles the year Christine Truman won it. That year she won also Renfrewshire Senior Singles and Doubles (with her mother), Greenock and District Singles and doubles, Highland Junior Singles and South of Scotland Singles and Ayrshire Singles and North of England Under 21 with Stanley Matthews' daughter.

The Club grew steadily and had a large junior section. Sunday tennis came into play in 1970s.

NICOL KEEPS HIS SOUTH TENNIS TITLE

JIM NICOL, of Laurieston, retained his South of Scotland men's singles tennis title at Moffat yesterday with a 6—2, 6—1 win over George Copeland, of Hamilton, a former West of Scotland junior champion. Nicol's much more accurate and varied play had Copeland in trouble from the start.

There was a big surprise in the women's singles when former title-holder Mrs. A. H. Stevenson, of Hamilton, was beaten in straight sets by Miss E. Holmes, Fort Matilda. The young Greenock player gave an impressive display of forceful and accurate tennis to win by 6—3, 6—4.

In the women's doubles, however, Mrs. Stevenson, partnered by Miss E. Winning, Burnside, beat Miss Holmes and her mother, Mrs. E. Holmes, 6—3, 6—3. The Hamilton pair, J. G. Steele and A. J. Wotherspoon, took the men's doubles title by beating Jim Nicol and J. L. Nicol, of Laurieston.

In the 70s and 80s the Club played in the Greenock and District Tournament with all the clubs in the area - Port Glasgow, Gourock, Ardgowan, Alexandria, Greenock High School.

The end of the 90s saw the four front courts turned into all weather savannah grass, for the three ladies, three gents and junior teams.

Stephanie Norris represented the Senior West Team in 2003 although only 17 years old.

She was Scottish Singles Under 16s Indoors Champion. She won Scottish doubles many times in age group, represented West Junior team from age of 11 and played for Senior team in past four years. She won singles and doubles at Craighelen, East and West Scotland, North East and Ayrshire.

On the administration side mention should be made of John Ewing who ran the tournaments in the Club and also Greenock and District with great flair and individuality. Brian Orange now more recently has taken over as Secretary and general helper in the Greenock and District Tournament.

Raymond Norris Senior has run the Club Championships for the last fifteen years and has given great service to the Club.

2003 sees the mini tennis getting off the ground and the Juniors now start at age 5 years to gain ball skills on Saturday mornings. We can have 50-60 juniors on Saturdays now, a great revival of coaching!

THE LAWN TENNIS ASSOCIATION

PATRON: HER MAJESTY THE QUEEN

RIVER PLATE HOUSE
FINSBURY CIRCUS LONDON EC2

SECRETARY:
S. BASIL REAY, O.B.E.

TELEPHONE:
MONARCH 9051

Miss E.S. Holmes

29th August 1957

Junior Championships of Great Britain 1957

Your entry has been accepted in the following event(s) :-

Singles

In the Academy photograph B. Greer became Mrs Holmes. Her daughter was Elizabeth Holmes who became Mrs Soutar, and her daughters are Gillian and Susan (Mrs Faint). Elizabeth's grandchildren are now playing tennis. Four generations all at Fort Matilda. Rhoda Neill became Mrs Morrison and was the mother of Peter Morrison, the singer.

Top ladies at the Fort

● Finallists in Fort Matilda Tennis Club's Championships this year: back row (from left to right) — Liz Soutar, Susan Faint, Kath Gairns, Fiona Lindsay, Ann Glen, Eleanor Hulme. Front row — Gillian Soutar, Alan Clark, Campbell Skinner, Lewis McShane and Alison Daisley.

GIFFNOCK TENNIS CLUB - FOUNDED 1895

The Marathon team celebrate in 1972

Rob Jenkins and Ann Jones during a Triangular match at Giffnock

From humble beginnings on two ash courts in a Giffnock garden in 1892, Giffnock Recreation Club evolved into Giffnock Bowling and Tennis Club in 1895, at its present location in Percy Drive, Giffnock. A pictorial record of those early days exists in the Club's Golden Jubilee Booklet (1945), where the lady tennis players can be seen wearing their maxi-dresses and the men cut a dashing figure on court with their straw boater hats.

In those early years 'old' Giffnock was one of the most select areas of Glasgow and there was no shortage of funds for club improvements. In the 1920s our far-sighted predecessors bought the land where the present tennis courts are situated. They also built a new clubhouse, which accommodated the bowlers and tennis players until 1969, when the Tennis Club moved into a separate clubhouse.

Giffnock remained one of the top clubs in the West of Scotland throughout the 'forties', dominated by Tom Boyd, surely one of our finest players ever. The future seemed bright in the early 'fifties', particularly when John Lillie and Derek Frenz proved themselves to be among the top juniors in Scotland in 1953-54. Sadly, however, things began to go wrong by 1955. One by one, our top players retired or left the area, and the subsequent decline in membership, to under 80 at one point, was matched only by the decline in playing standards. The 1st Gents team had the dubious distinction of being relegated every year for seven years!

Throughout the lean years, however, our Junior Section remained strong and by 1965 there appeared in the Senior ranks a large group of good tennis players, male and female, who within two years had virtually replaced their Senior counterparts in the teams. As Juniors they had been used to winning (they won the Junior 1st Division in 1965 and again 1967), and they continued to win. In 1971 Giffnock won the Clydesdale Cup, our first ever West of Scotland LTA trophy, and then in 1975 the Men's 1st Team reached the 1st Division after a 25-year absence and the Ladies 1st Team gained promotion to the 1st Division after a 20-year absence.

As the standard of play improved, so did the Club spirit, and successive Committees organised Coffee Mornings, Sponsored Walks, Jumble Sales, Marathon Tennis Matches (see "The Guinness Book of Records, 1972), and countless Fêtes to raise funds to further develop the Club. In 1969 the Tennis Section took on a new identity when the present clubhouse, in its original form, was opened. This was followed by a period of rapid development with the opening of squash courts in 1974 and an extension to the clubhouse the following year to provide a lounge bar and improved changing facilities.

Four international visitors open our new all-weather courts.
L-R: David LLoyd, Mark Cox, Frew McMillan and Brad Drewett.

There have been many dedicated and influential members of Giffnock, but perhaps one of the most dedicated and respected members was Rob Jenkins. Not only was he a President of the Club but he became President of the WSLTA in 1977 and was subsequently recognised for his outstanding contribution to tennis by being made an Honorary Life Member of the SLTA and of Giffnock Tennis Club.

It is not every day that four world-class players take to the courts of Giffnock Tennis Club to play the best of three sets, but the 25 May 1980 was no ordinary day and a crowd of over 700 people were thrilled to watch British Davis Cup stars David Lloyd and Mark Cox battle against South African Frew McMillan and his young Australian partner, Brad Drewett. The occasion was the official opening of our six new all-weather courts with floodlights, and all four players rose to the occasion. Understandably all four players were resting themselves for the West of Scotland Tournament at Newlands that same week, but nevertheless they showed the brilliance that had taken them to their individual rankings and provided a great afternoon's entertainment that was one of the highlights in the history of Giffnock Tennis Club. Tennis had been at a peak for some years at this stage and the Gents proved their superiority by winning the Clydesdale Cup to round off a memorable year.

Another milestone in the Club's growth came in 1982 when the former Whitecraigs Hockey Club joined and we became Giffnock Tennis, Squash and Hockey Club. The following year, 1983, proved to be one of the most successful tennis years for the Club with six of the eight teams consolidating their positions in their Divisions of the West Leagues. Juniors had always been the life-blood of the Club and a new coaching schedule and a sophisticated ball-machine proved to be invaluable. Juniors from three different age groups embarked on a three-stage course, culminating in a weekly tournament and this proved very popular. Four of our more promising youngsters were chosen for various different groups within the WSLTA and joined talented players from other clubs in a winter coaching programme.

Scottish Cup Winners 1999

Around the club 2003

Throughout the 80s the Club continued to flourish with success at all levels for seniors and juniors. In 1985 our Ladies 1st, 2nd and 3rd teams were in WSLTA Divisions 1, 2 and 3, the Gents 1st team was second in Division 1, the Gents 2nd team was promoted to Division 3, the Junior 1st team won Division 1 and the Junior 2nd team was promoted to Division 2.

Membership continued to be strong in all sections and in 1988 the tennis courts were upgraded to artificial grass courts. A further extension to the clubhouse followed.

As in the past, various part-time coaches worked very hard to maintain Giffnock's good reputation, until 1990 when we appointed Colin Hanbidge as our first full-time, professional coach. Colin, or "coach" as he became known, injected a new sense of direction to our coaching programme and became a firm favourite with 'kids' of all ages. With his own inimitable style, Colin played an important part in the development of tennis not only in Giffnock but also as coach for the West of Scotland LTA. Between the years of 1999 and 2000 he worked towards justifying his club logo, **'Best in the West'** and had considerable success when the Gent's 1st team became Scottish Cup Winners, Premier League Champions, the Spring Singles Premier Division Champions and, ably assisted by the ladies, won the Clydesdale Cup. In the same period the Ladies 1st and Gent's 2nd were both in 1st Divisions while the Boy's 1st team and the Boy's under-12 team were champions of their 1st Divisions. The Club as a team won the Inter-Club Shield and International honours went to Owen Hadden and Ryan Maxfield.

The WSLTA has seen many of Giffnock's best players reach a high standard, with some at International standard and many representing the WSLTA. We are confident of the future of tennis at Giffnock because of the commitment of the many players who return to share their talent and expertise by offering coaching to all ages. Giffnock can boast of the only purpose-built Mini-Tennis Courts in Scotland where the very young can experience their first taste of tennis and develop their skills. All ages and abilities are welcome and members are encouraged to sample the coaching with either team tennis in mind or simply to generally improve their game. On a high note we have qualified for the *LTA Initiative of Performance Tennis* - making Giffnock a *Nationally Accredited Performance Club;* a pioneering scheme requiring high standards of ability and dedication from both coach and player.

With seven men's teams, four ladies', six veteran's, thirteen junior teams and numerous social players we are truly following the LTA's vision of *"More players, better players"*.

Giffnock Tennis, Squash and Hockey Club is delighted to congratulate the WSLTA on 100 years of service to tennis.

GLASGOW UNIVERSITY STAFF 1922

"The College Lawn Tennis Club" was formed in 1922 and was for social play.

Originally located on Main Campus Medical Building Boiler House roof, we moved to Garscube in 1960, as the site was to be used for the Biochemical Building.

"The Glasgow University" won the Senior Calcutta Cup in 1954, but this was a Student team with no connection to the Staff Club, though it is known that the Students applied to the Staff to use their courts for practice around that time.

Garscube courts were originally tarmac and were resurfaced in 1994 by artificial grass and at a later date floodlights were a welcome addition.

The Clubs Second Home 1953-1960
(On the roof of the West Medical Building)

The Club affiliated to the West of Scotland in 1996 and entered the Men's League and at a later date also a Ladies team.

2003 saw a Ladies Second Team which saw the revitalisation of the Club which is now going from strength to strength.

The University of Glasgow Staff Tennis Club Ladies participated in the U.K. and Ireland Corporate Games in Aberdeen in 2001 with the Ladies Team Division 1 winners (for teams of 5 members or less). In Limmerick this year, the team consisiting of Josie Beeley, Melanie Mackie, Heather Parton and Veronica Goodard not only won three first and three second place medals in the events in which they competed, they were also Champions of Division 1 of the games overall having won the most games points in their division.

Games points are awarded to the top eight competitors in each event in all sports and teams are divided into Divisions based on their team size. In Division 1 which consists of organisations with teams of one to five competitors, the University Team was overall winners finishing ahead of the 56 other Corporate Teams in their Division.

Team captain Josie Beeley with the Division 1 Champions Trophy at the Corporate Games in Aberdeen.

UK and Ireland Corporate Games at Aberdeen 2000
Back - Gregory La Platre and John Beeley
Front - Heather Parton, Josie Beeley and Melanie
Mackie

The Clubs Third Home 1961-....
Garscube Estate

HAMILTON 1884

Of the clubs still in existence today Hamilton was the third club to be formed in Scotland, the distinction of the first club going to Perth and Helensburgh was founded in the same year also. This predates the Scottish Lawn Tennis Association and is only seven years after the All England Club at Wimbledon.

Various fields were inspected and the first grass courts were rented from a Mr D Naismith at a field in Auchincampbell. The rent for the whole field was £12 per annum or £5 for three quarters of an acre, of which the latter was chosen. In the first year of existence the joining fee was a guinea (£1.05) and 10/6 (52$\frac{1}{2}$p) for Ladies. In 1885 the rent was increased to £10, which was considered too much and the Club decided to move.

Hutton Bank, Hamilton was the new site, where two ash courts were constructed and a five year lease was obtained on the ground. The Lanarkshire weather was also rumoured to have influenced the decision to change to ash! At the Annual General meeting of 30th March 1885, a circular regarding "the proposed West of Scotland Tennis Association" was laid on the table and it was resolved to join the Association as a Club, yet the Association did not actually form till 1904.

Hamilton Ladies Winners Division 1 1976
L-R: Jane Brown, Christine Lindsay, Catherine Jamieson, Christine Maxton
Seated L-R: Elizabeth Tweedlie, Elaine Robb, Sheila Moodie

In 1886 the Club acquired a Clubhouse or Pavilion as it was known in those days and by 1888 two further courts had been laid.

His grace the Duke of Hamilton was President of the Club as is shown in the minutes of March 1898.

The Club wound up in 1902 when the ground was lost due to the construction of a new road, but thankfully resurrection was almost immediate on a new site. There is an entry in the minutes of 20th May 1902 stating that Ballantyne and Jackson's offer to put the new courts in order for £2 prior to the start of the season and keep them in order throughout the season at 4/- per day was accepted. Nets were purchased from the Argyll Rubber Company at 5/- each. The Calcutta Cup was offered in 1907 by George Paterson of Calcutta and accepted and is competed for annually in the West Of Scotland. The Final of the Cup is played at Hamilton if the Club requests it.

The title deeds of the Club show that the courts were purchased in 1922 from the Duke of Hamilton. Between 1942 and 1946 the courts were closed when the courts were covered over to provide a dance floor to entertain the troops during World War II.

The Courts have been upgraded over the years and are floodlit providing all the year round play.

Many have served the Club well over the years as well as Tennis further afield:

JGSteel Treasurer of the Club, West of Scotland President 1961

Mrs Lorna Stevenson first Lady President of West Of Scotland 1964, President SLTA 1975/76

AJ Wotherspoon West of Scotland President 1976 and President SLTA 1981/82

Alastair Prentice, Referee of Tournaments.

Dan G Russell, Secretary for countless years.

What about the Club successes?

Calcutta Cup
1923, 1964, 1969, 1970, 1975, 1991, 2002.

Junior Calcutta
Hamilton II 1991

Clydesdale Cup
Division 1 1971, 1972   Division 2 1929

League Champions
Men 1955   Ladies 1976, 1979, 1982.

Calcutta Cup 2002
Grant Gordon, Alastair Sandilands, I Wilson, D Wilson

Calcutta Cup 1923

HELENSBURGH LAWN TENNIS CLUB 1884

Established 1884

Helensburgh Lawn Tennis Club (HLTC) was established in 1884 at Suffolk Street on a field presented by ex Provost Breingan. In 1911, this property was first conveyed from the Trustees of the late Alexander Breingan to Hew Tennent Young and Peter Lindsay Miller in their capacity as President and Vice-President of HLTC.

HLTC minutes are available from the first half of the 20th century. This summary report, drawn up specifically for the WSLTA centenary records of 2004, does not permit the naming of all individual committee members who have served HLTC throughout the many decades of the club's history. The Wedgwood families and the Steuart – Corry families deserve special mention as does Donald Fullarton, our present Hon. President, as some of the longest serving committee members. Committee members throughout the years will be documented in the full history of HLTC which will be available during the WSLTA centenary.

Common to all tennis clubs, items appearing regularly throughout our minutes see little change and tend to fall into the following categories, communications, social events, tennis, juniors, coaching, development, finance, grounds & building and membership.

Perhaps the earliest record under communications would be a report in the Helensburgh & Gareloch Times of 22nd July 1885, recording a match, played at Helensburgh against Dumbarton. The Helensburgh Advertiser now records our extensive participation in West of Scotland leagues and other match reports in addition to our social programmes.

Social events e.g. annual dances, club tournaments etc. have always featured in the history of HLTC, perhaps culminating in our Centenary week celebrations of June 1984.

President D. Robson (front row) is seen with other committee members in 1984. A full programme of events took place during this week from 23rd to 30th June, 1984. Additional photographs and details of these events will be available for the WSLTA Centenary in 2004.

Tennis, junior and coaching committees have produced a high standard of player throughout the years. The late 1980s saw HLTC junior member Katie Fulton achieve an outstanding record in club, national and international events. Katie was ranked No.1 in the West of Scotland and No. 2 in Scotland in U – 16s in 1989. Katie was a member of the Senior West County team for several years. Details of all Katie's achievements will be documented in the full history of HLTC.

Development, finance/funding, grounds and building issues have all demonstrated progressive results throughout the decades. Our picture shows Graeme Simmer, Chairman of the Scottish Sports Council, opening our new courts in August 1992.

In April 1996 Martin Bowie, Project Officer of the Lottery Sports Fund, presented a cheque to Gordon Whitelaw, one of the team responsible for the major club development and later HLTC President. HLTC having matched the Lottery Sports funding, completed the erection of our present two-storey brick-built clubhouse and the covering of 3 remaining courts with artificial grass.

Our photograph, on next page, taken in November 2000 records members in attendance as Hon. President Donald Fullarton officially switched on the lights after the completion of HLTC's latest development which completed the floodlighting in all seven courts.

Last but not least, HLTC membership status! HLTC record an average of 4 – 500 members in recent decades. Our club operate five men's and five ladies' teams, both 1st teams being in Division 1. In addition we have two men's vets teams, four ladies' vets teams and seven junior teams. The club also have teams in the Mens & Ladies Scottish Cups, the Junior Calcutta Cup, the Clydesdale Cup and the Junior U – 18's Clydesdale

Cup. The first class facilities of our new clubhouse and our seven floodlit, all weather courts makes HLTC one of the largest and progressive tennis clubs in Scotland.

Ex-Provost Alexander Breingan would be justly proud of his original contribution to the game of tennis in Helensburgh.

1953

A. J. T. McDOWALL

COACH IN LAWN TENNIS

Renfrewshire Singles Championship—10 times
Ayrshire Singles Championship
West of Scotland County
West of Scotland Doubles Championship, 1950

Terms on application to—

**I ROSS STREET,
PAISLEY.**

Tel.: Western 65

SCHEDULE OF CHARGES

Course of 12 lessons	£5 12 6
Course of 6 lessons	£2 18 6
Three Lessons	£1 10 0
One Lesson	£0 10 6

(Half Hour Lessons)

SPECIAL CARE AND ATTENTION GIVEN TO BEGINNERS

Match and Tournament Players given First Class Practice
Terms for Groupe Coaching on Application.

HILLHEAD HSFP 1910

In 1910 the Former Pupils Club bought 3 good blaes courts and a well appointed Pavilion for £43 from the Maryhill Tennis Club. The price nearly crippled them at the time, although it became a major source of revenue with both school and FP usage.

During the Great War tennis went on at Maryhill with the school providing maintenance parties.

In 1920 the School Magazine showed a picture of Hilda Rosser, Marjorie Langmuir and Margaret McEwan who were all in the semi-finals in the West of Scotland Championships Girl's Singles. Hilda beat Marjorie in the Final.

Marjorie Langmuir returned to teach in the school and created a record which may never be equalled by representing Scotland a total of 50 times in three sports Hockey, Badminton and Tennis (she captained the only Scottish Hockey side to beat England in England). She was to win the West of Scotland Ladies Doubles 4 times 1928-1931 and played in the County Team many times.

Miss Shiela Moodie was also a pupil at the school and became a Scottish International Player.

In the 1960s the Club ran a Mixed Doubles Tournament in conjunction with the Annual Fête which was highly popular.

There are six new artificial grass courts with floodlighting, and were the venue for WOS confined Tournament and have made their courts available for other events too.

The present day teams play in the West of Scotland Leagues the Ladies being in Division 4b and 5b. The Men play in Division 4a, 6b and 7b. There are two Ladies and one Men's Veterans teams. The Juniors play in Division 3b in the Under 13 League.

Junior coaching is a regular feature of the Club programme.

Miss Marjorie Langmuir

HILLPARK c1924

Hillpark Lawn Tennis Club is situated on a hillside with a beautiful outlook. There were 7 blaes courts.

During the 1930s the Men's team were as high as Division 4 in 1933 and 7 in 1939, and the Ladies from 7 to 9. It was not until after the War that the teams began their climb to the First Divisions. The Men took till 1951 and the Ladies till 1961 thereafter the Club were very successful. Winning the Calcutta Cup in 1949, 1950, 1960 and in 1965 the Club won both the Calcutta Cups Senior and Junior the first Club ever to do so.

Players who were predominant then were Harry and Carole Matheson, Johnnie and Judy McKenzie, Alan McNeilage, Norrie Graham, Hoy Reid, Jimmy Wylde and many more.

Norrie Graham served on the West of Scotland Committee and was closely involved with the Tournament for many years and was President of the WSLTA in 1954.

In the mid 1970s there was a sudden decline and by 1982 the Men's team had dropped to Division 7c and the Ladies to 7b. At this time it became the fashion to join a Squash Club as a means of keeping fit in the winter and perhaps this contributed to the decline.

Later some of the courts were sold and houses are now on that site. The remaining three courts were upgraded to artificial grass and are floodlit.

League Winners
6th Div. - 1947   5th Div. - 1948   3rd Div. - 1949   2nd Div. - 1950

CR Paton, JB McGeachy, HJ Wylde, JC Nicol, CR Irving
RJ Simpson, DH Graham, AH Reid

KILMACOLM 1890

Kilmacolm Tennis Club was founded in 1890. The ground was gifted by the Birkmyre family to be held in trust (the adjacent Bowling Club being the trustees) for use for sporting activities by the inhabitants of Kilmacolm. The Bowling Club was appointed "landlord"to the Tennis Club , a situation which is still in exisence.

The Ladies' team can be found in the West of Scotland League Division 7 in 1933 and since there were 12 Divisions at that time there must have been a team for some years. By 1947 they were playing in Division 4. The Men entered a team in the League in 1934.

Finals Day 13/9/03

The Club tried to lay All-weather courts as early as the 1950s and the firm recommended to carry out the work was the same one which laid Princess Marina's court at her home in Gloucestershire. Unfortunately the weather in Scotland caused this All-weather surface to be a failure and the surface had to be dug up and relaid with blaes. En-Tout-Cas courts were laid in the 1970s.

Finals Day 13/9/03

Kilmacolm was very much a social tennis club - Saturday Afternoon Teas were served and much tennis played.

Evelyn and Gwen Armstrong played in many Tournaments throughout Scotland in the 1970s and in 1979 won the Scottish Hardcourt Doubles. During the 1980s and 1990s Kilmacolm had several successful Junior players. Linzi Clark won the West of Scotland Under 16 Singles in 1986 and represented Scotland. Campbell McCulloch represented the West of Scotland as a Junior in the early 1990s.

The First Ladies' team reached the Premier Division in 1994 and currently plays in Division 2. So many Ladies wished to play in teams that there are now three Ladies' teams in the League. The Men have recently formed a second team and much work is being done to raise the standard of Men's tennis in Kilmacolm although we are hindered by the advent of emerging commercial clubs.

The Club is still very much a village club, with many Juniors now participating. There were about forty youngsters taking part in each of five separate weeks of "Summer Clubs" with coaching. In the past Senior members gave much of their time to encouraging the youngsters but now the Club has a Professional Coach.

In 1988 Artificial Grass courts were laid and in order to finance this a loan was obtained from the L.T.A. and more than thirty members stood surety for this loan, a sign of the local support for Kilmacolm Tennis Club.

Now there has been a complete re-development of the Club with three new courts and a practice court , floodlights and a brand new Clubhouse (no more burst pipes in the winter). There has been a subsequent large rise in membership!

There is great enthusiasm at Kilmacolm and we intend to go on encouraging and facilitating the game of tennis in Kilmacolm.

1960

KIRKHILL 1915

Kirkhill Lawn Tennis Club lies in Cambuslang on the south eastern edge of Glasgow.

In 1910, a fete was held in a filed at the edge of Kirkhill to raise money for the forming of a Kirkhill Lawn Tennis Club. That field, which belonged to one of the club's founder members, is where the club now stands.

In the late nineteenth and early twentieth century, the small village of Cambuslang expanded rapidly due to the growth of coal mining and other heavy industry in the area. A population of 15,000 in 1901 became 25,000 in 1911, and during this period much of the new house building was concentrated in the Kirkhill area, along with roads and railways (Kirkhill Station opened 1904). However, such expansion also created a need for new leisure facilities for local residents, and the founding of Kirkhill Bowling club in 1906 and Kirkhill Golf Club in 1910 was closely followed by the formal creation of Kirkhill Lawn Tennis Club in 1915. It is worthy of note from early records that the ground was to be "used for Tennis Courts and Croquet Green", but there is no evidence that croquet was every played at the Club.

The tennis club lies in a quiet, sheltered area surrounded by the fine, stone houses of the early 1900s on two sides and Cambuslang Public Park to the south and east. This park was opened by the Parish Council in 1913 following the acquisition of some agricultural land, and around the same time the adjacent parcel of land was acquired from the Duke of Hamilton by a group of local residents and the tennis club was born. There is however considerable evidence that tennis was played at this location before 1915. Past members of the Club recall stories of how the local women kept the Club going throughout the first World War, and in one case the cancellation of a match against Hamilton when many of Lanarkshire's finest young men had just fallen in a major battle.

These photographs show club members and players, c. 1918 to 1930.

Kirkhill Lawn Tennis Club's first, small, wooden hut was apparently blown into the nearby park during a storm just after the first World War. The second, much larger Clubhouse, also of timber construction, was built in 1920 and was heated and lit by gas until 1961 when the Electricity Board finally brought power to the Club for the princely sum of £56. In April 1972, however, this Clubhouse was virtually burnt to the ground by vandals, an event which occurred at a time when Club membership and funds were low.

Like most suburban clubs, Kirkhill has experienced the highs and lows of interest and membership one would expect over the years. From the late 1950s to the early 1970s, membership dropped and remained at a low level. In the mid 1960s the Club was running at a loss, the groundsman had become a part-time employee and the luxury of a clubhouse cleaner could no longer be afforded. Of the Club's five blaes courts, the three senior courts continued to be maintained to a high standard, and some upgrading work was carried out in 1970. However, in the same year the two Junior courts were reported to be in a state of some disrepair.

A group of members c. 1948

Over the 18 months following the fire, negotiations were undertaken with a local builder, and the concluding arrangement was that, in exchange for the land occupied by the two Junior courts, a new clubhouse would be built. The work was completed in 1974 and the new clubhouse officially opened at start of the 1975 season. This date effectively marked the beginning of more than a decade of club revitalisation.

Later in the same year, as the club celebrated its Diamond Jubilee, a new all-weather court with floodlights was opened bringing the facilities up to their present level of four courts. The new court cost some £3,000. Grants were obtained from the District Council (£500) and Sports Council (£1250), and topped up by membership loans.

The Club had five red blaes courts from shortly after its founding until 1973 when the two junior courts were exchanged for construction of the new clubhouse. The three "Senior" blaes courts, supplemented by the floodlit "all-weather" court, remain in place today and although the introduction of more modern playing surfaces has been much considered in recent years, the Club for the moment continues to play on the blaes courts which it believes continue to be of the highest standard.

The original Cambuslang Bachelors. The Bachelor's Ball began shortly after the First World War.

Throughout its history, Kirkhill has been very much a "Junior" club. Although the Senior teams have come and gone over the decades, there has almost always been junior representation in the West of Scotland Leagues. This approach continues today with over 50% of the membership under the age of 14, and two Junior teams representing the Club. Kirkhill also offers all Junior members free coaching, a tradition of which it remains very proud and which is certainly not common in other clubs.

As might be expected, the success of the Club's Senior teams has always depended very much on the strength or activity of membership. Occasionally in the past years of low or relatively inactive membership, it has not been possible to enter teams in the West of Scotland Leagues. However, the Club has normally provided both a Ladies and at least one Gents team througout its history and although these teams generally play in the lower West of Scotland Leagues, occasional periods of strength allow forays up to the middle or higher divisions.

In the late 1920s and early 1930s the club appears to have had a particularly strong Gents' First team. In 1931 this team won the Calcutta Cup, the West of Scotland's premier knockout competition and records show that in 1933 they finished fifth in Division 2 (of 13) and reached the semi-final of the Calcutta Cup before losing to the eventual winners, Titwood. In that same year the Ladies' team played in Division 4 (of 12). A similar, relatively successful period occurred in the late 1970s and early 1980s, culminating with a Gents victory in the Junior Calcutta Cup Final (for the lower divisions) in 1984. The Club currently runs a Ladies' team and two Gents' teams - the first of which has been promoted to Division 5 for 2004.

No details are available for membership levels before the second World War, but it seems that club membership has always generally oscillated between 50 and 150. Membership hovered around the low end of the range throughout the 1960s and early 1970s and also for a brief period in the mid 1990s. Conversely however, membership peaked at well over 150 from 1975 to 1984 (aided by a very strong "Afternoon Ladies" section). Membership currently stands at 109 (2003)

The cost of membership has of course changed dramatically over the years. Records do not show what the Senior subscription was in the earliest years but in 1964 the cost of a full season's tennis was £3.10/-. The current subscription is £60 per year, a cost which is beaten by few other clubs.

Throughout its history the Club has always served as one of the focal points for the social life of Kirkhill and indeed has contributed significantly to that of Cambuslang over the same period. For a number of decades, from the post second World War years until the 1980s, the highlight of the season was the Bachelor's Ball, a grand affair which in its heyday was attended by 300 to 400 individuals and often had a waiting list for tickets. The Ball was held in the Cambuslang Institute in its early years and latterly in a variety of hotels in the area.

The Clubhouse was also the regular scene of dances, discos, parties, fêtes, jumble sales, film shows and coffee mornings and it is only in the past twenty years or so that such activity has reduced as other venues and facilities have become available. Nevertheless, although the Bachelor's Ball has not been held for some time, a Ceilidh has concluded the season in recent years.

KIRKTONHILL 1896

The Tennis Club and Club House appear on the Ordinance Survey Map of 1896 and in 1899 it is on the Valuation Roll.   The Kirktonhill Tennis Club had the following comment made by the Rev. M. Stephen, 'It is well supported by the congregation and, as tennis is on the boom in the town, the new Club has secured a firm footing. The membership is open to all.'

On the 12th July 1919 after the First World War the Tennis Courts at Kirktonhill were acquired by the United Free North Church and were declared open for play by Col. John M. Denny CB of Helenslee. The old courts which formerly belonged to the old Kirktonhill Tennis Club had fallen into disrepair during the war but as a result of the enthusiasm of the Rev. W. L. Stephen and the energy and practical help of a number of interested parties two of the four courts were bottomed with tons of material.

By 1922 there had been an entire overhaul of the grounds with structural alterations and additions to the pavilion which are a marked improvement. The Club has joined the League and intimation given for a number of fixtures for inter-Club play.   A flagstaff was presented by Col. J. M. Denny and the flag was raised on 24th June of that year.

The Lennox Herald, 28th June, 1919

NORTH CHURCH (Social & Athletic Club.)

Kirktonhill Tennis Club.

Hon. President, ... COL. J. M. DENNY, C.B.

The above COURTS will be OPENED

On SATURDAY, July 5th,

AT 3 P.M.

By the Hon. President.

TERMS (for this Year):—

A.—For those connected with North Congregation.

	Gentlemen.	Ladies.
Entry-money,	15s	7s 6d
Annual Subscription,	10s	5s

B.—For those not connected with North Congregation.

Entry-money,	£1	10s
Annual Subscription,	15s	7s 6d

Application Forms for Membership can be obtained from Miss M'Gillivray, Glasgow Road; Mr Marshall, Church Officer; Mrs Thomson, Bridgend; Mr J. M'Dougall, Carraig Cottage; Mr Peter Giles, Denny Institute. These Forms to be filled up and returned to any of above before July 2nd.

J. M'DOUGALL, Secy.

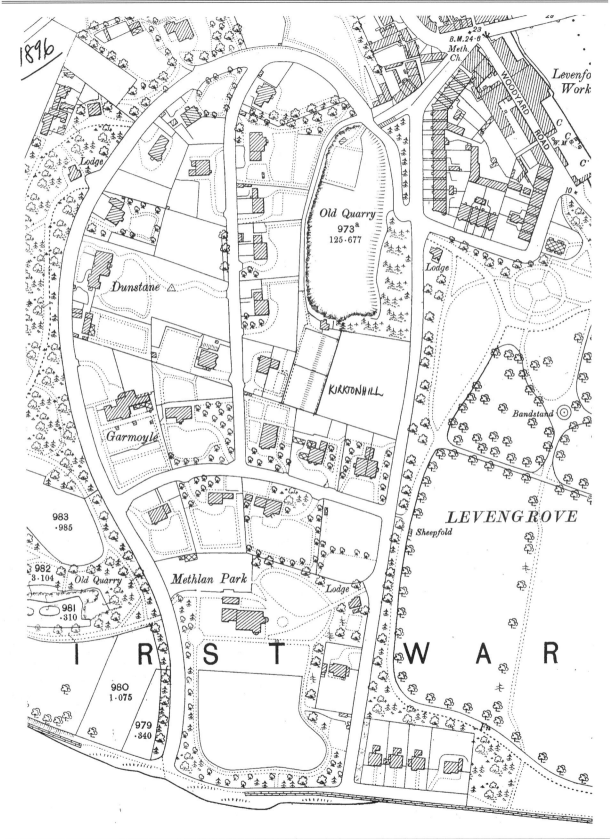

LENZIE TENNIS CLUB 1888

Lenzie Tennis Club was started in 1888 by enthusiastic members of the Cricket Club and became Lenzie Cricket and Tennis Club until 1901, when the flourishing tennis section broke away from the cricket section and has been known ever since as Lenzie Tennis Club.

In 1888, three red ash courts were constructed at Millersneuk at a cost of £120 and were formally opened by the President of the Club, Mr Dempster, on 15th May 1888. It was reported in the local paper The Kirkintilloch Herald, that the courts compared favourably with the best courts in the West of Scotland and that "the game of tennis goes merrily on from early morn till dewy eve"

The first AGM of the Club was held on 12th February 1889 and listed 30 Lady members and 40 Gentlemen members and the funds stood at £27.16.11d. The Committee was all male, but it was decided to form a Ladies' Committee to provide teas at the Club. Six ladies duly consented to this proposal. It is noted that members from Partickhill Club enjoyed a cup of finest Pekoe tea on a visit to the Club!

For many years the courts were reserved every evening for the exclusive use of the Gentlemen members - from the time the 5.07 rain from Glasgow arrived at Lenzie station (about 15 minutes later). If the ladies wished to arrange a match, they had to apply to the Committeee and of course play the match during the day. The ladies, however, were relied upon to organise numerous Sales of Work to raise funds for the Club. A Sale of Work, officially opened by Mr Graeme A. Whitelaw, MP for North West Lanark, was held over two days in October 1894 to raise money for two new clubhouses - one for the Tennis Club and one for the Cricket Clu;b. The sum of £242. 4/- was realised - which was sufficient to pay for both clubhouses.

In 1889 a Junior section was formed - the subscription was 7/6 and play permitted only during weekdays - and never after 5pm.

In 1893 a fourth court was constructed to accommodate an ever-increasing membership. In 1894 there were 100 members in the Club, which meant that every evening and every Saturday afternoon during the season there were a great many players waiting to play. An article in the Kirkintilloch Herald of that year reported "night after night all four courts are going in full swing, until darkness compels the enthusiastic racquet wielders to retire".

During these years matches were being played against other clubs:- Pollokshields, Carlton, Partickhill,

Hillhead, Cathcart, Hamilton, Golfhill, Greenock, Mount Vernon and Newlands are mentioned in the Minutes or in the local paper. In 1894 a Mixed Doubles match at Lenzie was played against Newlands and Hillhead - the results - Lenzie 12 sets, Newlands 0; Lenzie 7 sets, Hillhead 5 sets.

Lenzie was one of the first clubs to affiliate to the West of Scotland LTA in 1905. Matches at this time consisted of all male or mixed doubles. It was not until 1911 that a ladies' team was entered in the West of Scotland League.

Fundraising activities were numerous and varied. In June every year a Garden Party was held with an American (or a Patagonian) Tournament, Junior Tournament, Darts, Miniature Golf, Ping-Pong, Archery, Treasure Hunt, Penny Throwing, Wheel of Fortune and Bulb-Smashing (whatever that is!). During the winter months, there were at least two dances held, Whist Drives (with 40 tables reported - 160 people) and an occasional Bridge Drive. Ticket prices for the dances were twice as much for the gentlemen as those for the ladies.

At the AGM held on 13th March 1915 it was agreed that the Constitution be amended "that any member serving in any capacity in HM Forces shall not be liable for his subscription during the period of the present war." The Club remained open for play throughout the war, but with a shortened season and the members maintained the courts. Ladies and Junior Tournaments were held to play for prizes which had been kindly donated and any surplus money was given to the Hospital at Gartshore House (which was Lord Whitelaw's family estate near neighbouring Kirkintilloch). In 1916 a Patagonian Tournament was held in aid of the Limbless Soldiers and Sailors Fund. A Roll of Honour is noted in the Minutes of the time, with ten members names and the deaths of two members, T Russell and R. Wilson, are minuted in 1915 and 1917.

At a West of Scotland LTA Meeting in 1919 it was decided not to carry on with the pre-war Leagues but that Match Secretaries would arrange friendly matches. Mr J S Richardson of Lenzie Tennis Club was elelcted to serve on the Committee of West of Scotland LTA.

For the season of 1921, the Club entered two Ladies', two Gents' and 1 Mixed Doubles teams in the West of Scotland LTA Leagues and a Gents' team in the Calcutta cup. This format with the addition of Junior teams and Vet teams has continued to the present time.

In 1934 there were 34 lady members, 14 gents and 9 junior members and the Club was suffering from depression like other clubs and chasing outstanding subscriptions. The ladies team was in Division 3 and the gents in Division 5.

In 1935 the subscriptions were:- Gents £1.15/-, ladies £1.10/- and Juniors 12/6d.

The Club records from 1936-1951 are missing - however it is known that the ladies' team played in 3rd Division and the gents' team worked their way up from 9th to 7th Division between 1947 and 1951. A Junior team was formed in 1951. By 1953 the senior members had risen to 51 and the junior members to 50.

Tennis was played only between April and the end of September but throughout the winter months the hardworking Committee was constantly fundraising. In 1957 the annual Scavenger Hunt was postponed until a decision regarding petrol rationing became clear.

In 1957 the Ladies' 1 team was promoted to 1st Division and have played in Division 1 on several occasions since.

A new clubhouse was opened in 1966 when the membership numbers were 80 Seniors and 89 Juniors. Both Ladies 1 and Gents 1 teams were promoted to 1st Division between this time and 1972 and in 1983 the Junior 1 team was promoted to 1st Division.

In 1989 the Juniors were doing extremely well. Carolyn Morgan was ranked 6th in Under 18 Girls and 3rd in Under 16 girls. Elaine Kerr ranked 4th in Under 14 girls. Julia Taylor ranked 1st in Under 12 girls. Mandy Thompson ranked 7th in Under 12 girls. Raymond McNeil ranked 9th in Under 16 Boys.

This was also the year that new all-weather tennis courts were constructed - and what a disaster that was! After years of fundraising and planning, dreams were shattered when the all-weather playing surface was in fact not what it should have been. Either the Club had to accept a very bad job or insist that it was done properly and the latter option was, of course, unanimously decided upon. It took another nine years before the Club had tennis courts which it deserved. During this time, the Club was indebted to the LTA Consultant, Donald Paterson, whose knowledge on tennis court construction was second to none and who supported the Club through years of disputes and legal proceedings which were hugely expensive. It must be mentioned that the Club is also indebted to those members who continued to support the Club throughout those years when playing tennis on an uneven, slippy and bumpy surface was sometimes risky or impossible. Without them the Club would not have survived.

In July 1990, Ronnie Morgan organised the first very successful Lenzie Open Junior Tournament which had an entry of between 94 and 134 Juniors from as far afield as Carlisle. In this tournament, Elaine Kerr (Lenzie) won the Under 16 girls. The following year Carolyn Morgan (Lenzie) won the Under 18 girls. Sadly Ronnie died suddenly and it was decided to discontinue the Tournament. Ronnie, who also served on the West of Scotland LTA Committee, was such an enthusiastic and valued member of Lenzie Tennis Club and contributed so much to the Club he was sorely missed. In 1990 our Junior 1 team won all their matches in West of Scotland LTA Leagues and were promoted to 1st Division. The Junior Leagues were restructured by West of Scotland LTA for 1992 and by 1993 our juniors had been relegated to Division 2. In 1994 Vets ladies and Vets Gents teams were taking part in West of Scotland LTA Leagues.

Since the new all-weather courts had been constructed so badly in 1989 and despite three unsuccessful attempts at resurfacing by the contractor, it was agreed that somehow the situation had to be brought to a conclusion, so that the Club could move forward. Therefore a settlement was reached and in 1996 an application for Lottery Funding was submitted for a new, artificial grass surface and floodlights. This application was granted.

The new courts were opened in the summer of 1998 - exactly 100 years after the very first courts were constructed in Lenzie.

In 2002 tennis is played all year round, under floodlights in the dark evenings and there are some enthusiastic members who are constantly at the Club in all weathers. The Ladies 1 team and Junior teams especially are doing well in the League matches with the Under 13 boys playing this season in the Premier Division. A new, professional coach has just started. The membership stands at around 76 Seniors, 70 Juniors, 13 Minis and 10 Associates.

The on-going business of the Club has not changed much in the last century - repairs to the clubhouse, subscriptions, courts, balls, nets, fencing, fund-raising, matches, open days, coaching, committee meetings, club championships, tournaments - are some of the topics which have been mentioned in the Minutes of almost every meeting since 1888.

Having read through all the Minute Books of the Club from 1888 to the present day (with the exception of the missing ones for years 1936-1951, which hopefully will eventually turn up) - members of the Club throughout the last century have all played a part in the history of the Club. There have been some outstanding players, coaches, organisers and experts in a variety of skills and many, many others who have all given their time freely and willingly to ensure that Lenzie Tennis Club exists today. I hope this will be the same for the next hundred years.

1957

MILNGAVIE LAWN TENNIS CLUB 1912

Milngavie Lawn Tennis Club, originally named Milngavie and Bearsden Cricket and Tennis Club was founded in 1912 at Auchenhowie, Milngavie. The Cricket Club had been formed in 1904 and in 1912 three tennis courts were laid down and a pavilion erected at a total cost of £380. Hockey was introduced in 1926 but did not last for long and was wound up in 1937. The Club operated continuously until the AGM of March 1941 after which there was a break in activity during the war years and the Club was reconstituted in May 1945. In the late 1960s Western Hockey Club amalgamated with the Club and the name of the Club was changed yet again to Milngavie and Bearsden Sports Club. In the 70s two squash courts and a fourth tennis court were built and significant improvements were made to the pavilion buildings. This was enabled by a generous legacy left by one of the most colourful and dedicated cricket members of the club, Roy Barrowman. In 1983 an artificial hockey pitch was built on the cricket pitch, bringing to a sad end the playing of cricket that had lasted for some eighty years. In the late 1980s, Mike Shrigley, a member of the tennis section, purchased the freehold of the Club through a company pension fund. This allowed the development of hockey facilities and the building and floodlighting of a further two tennis courts together with the resurfacing of the existing courts in tarmac. An archery and junior shinty section were formed in the late 1980s and in 2000 the Tennis Club changed its name to Milngavie Lawn Tennis Club. During 2002/2003 negotiations have been taking place between the Club, its landlords and Vida, a company in which David Murray, a director of Rangers Football Club, has an interest. Vida propose developing five-a-side football pitches next to the hockey pitch and rebuilding most of the facilities at Auchenhowie and floodlighting and landscaping around the tennis courts. As yet, a deal has not been concluded.

Over the years, the tennis section has perhaps been the backbone of the Club and has usually had the largest playing membership of any section. The Club has always managed to maintain a healthy balance between social and competitive tennis but it has not been until the late 1990s that the competitive side of the Club has blossomed.

The Gents 1st team won the Calcutta Cup four times around this time and also have been holding their own in the premier division of the West of Scotland Spring Singles League. The best team performance in the history of the Club has been in the year 2002 when the gents 1st team, led by Club Coach John Wilson, won the second division of the National Club League and gained promotion to division one for 2003/4.

There have been many good players at the Club over the years. The player who has had most recognition in terms of international honours is Russell Howat. Russell learned to play tennis at Milngavie and now plays at the Cumberland Club in London. He continues to perform impressively for Scotland at Veterans 45 level and has in 2002 and 2003 performed a unique feat by twice beating the no 1 singles players from England, Ireland and Wales in the Four Nations' International Tournament.

Milngavie Players participate in the Glasgow Wide Boys
match against Vicopellago, Lucca,
during the 2003 tour of Italy
(left to right) Ian Swann, Alistair Dickson, Scott Wilson,
John Bennett, Russell Howat, Jim Hastie, David Sillars,
Hunter Reid.

Another memorable and perhaps the hardest hitting player ever to play at Milngavie is Australian, John Bennett. John, from New South Wales, played at the Club in season 2001 and 2003 and undoubtedly has been the most powerful server ever to play at Auchenhowie. The lady player, who has had the most success in tournaments, particularly at junior level, is Muriel Bannerman. In the 1960s Muriel (Brocket) had some fine performances in West of Scotland junior tournaments and also competed in other tournaments throughout Scotland.

In 2001, 2002 and 2003, gents from the Milngavie Club have formed the majority of the Glasgow Wide Boys team that has played competitive matches in Tuscany in Italy. Although not formally connected with Milngavie Tennis Club, the tour is organised by Milngavie Chair and long-standing member, Hunter Reid. As far as is known, this is the first regular foreign tour to be undertaken by a team from Scotland. Western Coach Ian Campbell arranges the tour. In 2003, the team included both Russell Howat and John Bennett and secured victories against clubs in Florence and Lucca while drawing with Montecatini and losing to Pisa.

At present the Club is thriving. This is mainly due to the hard work put in over a number of years by Club Coach John Wilson. Throughout this period, John has been supported by committee members and parents of juniors. In season 2003 the club will field over 40 junior and senior teams in league and cup competitions. In addition there is an extensive coaching programme with 9 coaches operating at the Club.

Perhaps the last words should be in recognition of our longest-standing, playing-member, Jack Wood. Jack joined the club in 1946 and is now in his seventies. He has been an inspiration to countless members with his boundless enthusiasm, advice and encouragement. He still runs individual coaching sessions several days each week, in between doing running repairs around the grounds. He is a role model for any tennis player. This is the essence of what really makes a club successful.

Prepared by Hunter Reid, August 2003.

MOUNT VERNON TENNIS CLUB -1886

Mount Vernon Tennis Club was founded in 1886 but it was thought not to be on the original site in Bowling Green Road. The original site is suggested to be on a plot of land behind what is now Carrick Drive, Mount Vernon being a farming and green belt area during the late 19th and early 20th Century.

There are existing records which show Mount Vernon Tennis Club played Lenzie Tennis Club in 1890. Another match registered was against Cambuslang Tennis Club in 1901.

An illustrious figure in Mount Vernon's history, Sir David Carrick Buchanan, KCB agreed favourable terms for the feu of the land on which the Club was built, apparently insisting it had to be 'used for sporting facilities' only. 1894 saw the Bowling Green housed on part of the land and the existing tennis courts in the Carrick Drive area closed and new tennis courts built adjacent to the Bowling Green a short time later.

The club then became known as Mount Vernon Bowling and Tennis Club and participated in the West of Scotland Leagues.

Over the years the members of the Tennis Section were involved in organising Dances, Fêtes and many other social occasions to raise funds for the upkeep of the blaes courts.

2003 Mount Vernon Winners Junior Calcutta Cup. L-R Neil McClure, Alan Wilson, Neil Haig, Hugh Weir and Roy Dalgetty

During the 1950s Dora Kerr played for the West of Scotland District Mixed Doubles Team.

The Club was host to the Eastern Districts of Glasgow Tournament for many years, in which local clubs (Springboig, Garrowhill, Uddingston, Whifflet, Springwells, Sandyhills) all participated. Sadly neither Springboig Garrowhill, Whifflet or Sandyhills are now in existence although Mount Vernon were fortunate to boost their membership from the above clubs' demise. This tournament ran for many years with Mount Vernon members being successful in many events but unfortunately with the closure of so many clubs the Tournament had to be abandoned.

During the 1970s Eric Dalgetty and Christine Lindsay represented the West of Scotland at both District and County level the latter also serving on the West of Scotland Committee in varying roles.

During this time Olwyn Budge Jnr. sat her British Association of Umpires qualification and is now the top Umpire in Scotland.

In approximately 1986 the Club sold off land and with some of the profit, a levy placed on tennis members, and the Tennis Development Fund 1988 saw the erection of our new, all-weather tennis courts thus increasing our membership yet again.

The club continued to flourish with American Tournaments, barbecues, dances all well attended by members and friends.

Up until this point the Club Championships had only included singles events, but with generous members donating trophies we were able to introduce doubles, mixed and handicap events at both senior and junior level.

Early 1990s saw the Club introducing an Annual Dinner Dance which was a huge success enjoyed by all.

In the mid 1990s we were able to secure a lottery grant to upgrade our courts and also secure finances to employ Club Coaches for junior and senior members. This also included a 5-8 year old age group for mini tennis.

Our membership again increased and with the addition of floodlights, thus enabled us to participate in the Winter Leagues. Our membership reached its maximum with a waiting list being introduced for the first time, therefore our club nights, tournaments and social events were a great success and always well-attended.

2003 Mount Vernon Winners Calcutta Cup. L-R Eric Dalgetty, Keith Haig, Derek Lauder, Andy McMenamin and Joe Mullen

Mount Vernon won the Clydesdale Cup Division 2 on numerous occasions and our Gents have won both the Senior and Junior Calcutta Cups twice in the same year, the only Club in the history of the West of Scotland to accomplish this.

All teams, Junior and Senior, continue to be both competitive and highly successful in the West of Scotland Leagues and Cup Competitions.

Members who brought honours to the Club at National and County level –

Dora Kerr	Christine Lindsay
Colin Haig	Eric Dalgetty
Keith Haig	Esther Haig
Robert Dalgetty	Neil Haig
Aimee Black	Julie Dalgetty

NEWLANDS 1904

The members of Newlands owe an enormous amount to the founders of the Club for their initiative, hard work and foresight in creating the Club in a period of 10 months in which they acquired land, levelled the ground and laid 5 courts, built an exceedingly attractive clubhouse and canvassed the families in the developing suburb for members so successfully that the courts were opened for play on 16th April 1904 and the total cost of £700 was cleared within 3 years.

There were a number of clubs in the West which had been established for many years before this and the Polokshields Club readily agreed to send some of their top players to the Newlands Opening Day to give an exhibition and show the novices how the game could be played. This was one of many friendly gestures between those clubs which also became great rivals over the next 60 years especially in hotly-contested Scottish Cup matches in the late evening just before the bell was rung to stop play at the agreed dusk time limit. Then the players as well as most of the supporters were adding up the scores to see if the last unfinished match in the second round could be conceded and still win on a count of rubbers, sets and games where the rules permitted a result after two completed rounds before the time limit, thus avoiding subsequent nights play to complete 3 rounds.

Ladies of Newlands Lawn Tennis Club winners of Division 1 in the West of Scotland League 1913. Standing L-R: Miss Cunningham, Miss J Walker. Seated L-R: Miss Hendry, Miss McKenzie, Miss Ritchie, Miss M Cockburn.

The main developments at Newlands were to add two all-weather courts with floodlighting in 1950 for all-year-round play. In 1967 additional land was acquired and two more blaes courts were constructed with the earth banked up on all four sides to accommodate 1000 spectators at future, sponsored West finals. The Club, at the same time, decided to build a new clubhouse when tennis memberships were generally declining. The new building would offer much better facilities of 2 Squash Courts, Games Room, Lounge and Bar, Kitchen and Changing rooms at a total cost of £20,000 - a major sum in those days when the subscription was only £4.

Thanks to the Physical Training and Recreation Act a grant of £9,000 was received and the Club with £2500 in funds required to raise a further £8500, which it did in 4 years by means of Life Memberships, Levies, Fêtes, Barbecues, Entry Fees, 21 Mile Walk, Jumble Sales, Coffee Mornings, 200 Club Draws, Tournaments and Dances. The Club spirit was never higher than when these efforts were made by so many members.

In 1979 an extension incorporated a third squash court and all-weather tennis courts were laid replacing the blaes courts in 1982. Then, in 1985/86, heavy expenditure was incurred on changing rooms and bar and lounge refurbishments.

The next major development took place in 1999 when the Club applied to Scottish Squash to be a Regional Squash Centre of Excellence and a massive extension was added to the clubhouse with four back-to-back glass backed squash courts with viewing and with a new entrance, stairway, pro shop and toilets costing the Club over £300,000 after grants had been deducted.

The additional ground acquired at this time from Glasgow City Council under a long lease will be available for future development of sporting facilities.

With regard to the high standard of tennis at Newlands throughout its 100 years a few pointers should be given:- Within a few years of starting in 1904 the men's 1st team reached Division 1 in the West leagues and has a treasured record of never having been relegated since, although some of the teams have occasionally suffered real pressure when they felt that they were in danger of becoming the first to be responsible for ending such a record. In 2002 the Club entered 21 teams in the West leagues in the age groups from Under 11 to Veterans.

In Scottish Cup competitions the Club has had 16 wins in the men's and 6 wins in the ladies' with the double being achieved in 1929, 1997 and 1998. Many players have been selected to represent the West at British County Week and in a number of years 5 or 6 out of a team of 7 or 8 were Newlands players.

When mentioning prominent players one hopes not to overlook anyone and the following list has been limited to players who as Seniors (thus not counting age-restricted events for Juniors and Veterans) have done at least one of the following:- won West titles or won Scottish titles or represented West at County Week or represented Scotland or played in the Wimbledon championships. In alphabetical order they are:-

Ladies
Elena Baltacha, Anne (McAlpine) Barrow, Eileen Christie, Kathleen (Gillespie) Dingwall, Deirdre Forrest, Eileen Hendry, Lorraine (Wall) Kerr, Brenda (McCallum) Livingstone, Claire Lavery, Veronica (MacLennan) Lloyd, Abbe (Lockhart) Brown, Christine Lockhart, Heather Lockhart, Marjory Love, Irene McCready, Jan (Walker) Oliphant, Anne (Walker) Paul, Jean Rankine, Frances (MacLennan) Taylor.

Newlands Scottish Cup Winners 2002 - Ronnie Terras, Gary Smith, David Culshaw, Jordan Gray, Malcolm Watt, Russell Allan

Men
Russell Allan, David Culshaw, Blane Dodds, Graham Downes, Roy Finlay, Buchanan Fulton, John Fulton, Billy Gillespie, Jordan Gray, Kenneth Gray, Gordon Hendry, Arthur Hill, Jack Hill, Gordon Kerr, Ian McAuley, Johnny Mackenzie, Callum McKnight, Graham Reid, John Robertson, John Rutherglen, Andy Smith, Gary Smith, Toby Smith, Ronnie Terras, Norman Thompson, Malcolm Watt, Archie Young.

The above players won over 100 West Titles and over 50 Scottish Titles and 2 Ladies and 3 Men played in the Wimbledon Championships.

The following 7 members have been Presidents of the West:- Hugh Wright, Billy Fulton, John Rutherglen, Aikman Thomson, Billy Gillespie, Kenneth Gray and Gordon Kerr and 2 of these, namely Hugh Wright and Gordon Kerr, were also Presidents of the Scottish LTA.

If Newlands were given 25 D.S.O. Medals to award out of a very large number of deserving candidates it is likely that the following would be recipients in date order:-

Home Club Winners - West of Scotland Championships Jordan Gray and Heather Lockhart

John Reid, Hugh Wright, Billy Fulton, John Rutherglen, Tommy Sellar, Cochrane MacLennan, Billy Laird, Kenneth Gray, Hunter Frew, Billy Gillespie, Ken McCready, Gordon Kerr, Mel Cummock, Stewart Dingwall, Michael McKnight, Gordon Kent, Lindsey Davidson, Allan Turnbull, Brown McMaster, Alan Pearson, Christine Lockhart, Douglas Cumine, Jimmy McKechnie, Malcolm Watt.

Note the successful Squash Section has not been included.

NEW MEMBERS WELCOME

NEXT GENERATION 2000

Since opening Next Generation Club has grown from strength to strength. Our current coaching team is as follows :-

Karen MacPherson DCA: Part-time Pro
Gary Smith DCA: Pro
Jonny Woodall DCA: Pro
Jordan Gray DCA: Head Pro
Toby Smith CCA: Director of Tennis

Our Club has developed in many areas. Firstly our Junior programme has now over 200 players each week. It is structured in line with the LTA's new mini-tennis iniative, for players aged 3-10 years and our own structure for 11-16 year olds.

The adult coaching set-up now looks after 100 Players a week from beginners to team training level. As a Club we believe in providing players with competitive opportunities to play. This takes place in the form of mini-box leagues and regular tournaments throughout the year (some fun ones too!!).

Due to the success of our Junior tennis, an academy was set up for talented players aged between 10-16 years. More recently a mini-tennis academy has been put in place for our younger players (8 under 5s, 8 under 7s & 8 under 8s). With the hard work of the parents, players and the coaching team alike, there are now a substantial number of Next Generation players who are also receiving training from Tennis West of Scotland.

A final area that is planned for 2004 is allowing our coaches to travel with players to a variety of tournaments. The highlight is planned trips to the Republic of Ireland and a further trip to France. By providing these trips players have a real initiative to be motivated to play more tennis.

Finally having begun a club from scratch, it is now very pleasing to have a thriving club, with a highly motivated coaching team. Next Generation Club is now producing strong young players, providing a great environment for all ages to improve / compete and generally ensuring tennis is a fun game for life!

Toby Smith, Director of Tennis.

OBAN TENNIS AND SQUASH CLUB

In the early years Oban was able to boast of eight very fine tennis courts which came under the control of the then Town Council. Indeed in those days tennis was so popular that you had to arrive very early in the evening to be sure of being able to secure a court. Generally there was great enthusiasm amongst players.

As with all sports there came a time when the popularity of tennis waned and the town council who had problems with space were forced to the conclusion that the increasing demand for more parking space for visitors who were flocking into the town in the summer meant that they needed some of the tennis courts for parking. As a result the Town Council appropriated four of the tennis courts for this purpose and as a direct result of this action some resident tennis enthusiasts were of the opinion that the apparent apathy among players was due to the lack of a club to bring them together. A meeting was called to try to establish a club which had been in existence previously until 1964 and was reconstituted on 16th June 1969.

Club nights were organised which brought together players who had not been aware of each other's existence. The result was a general improvement of standards of play among the young and not so young players. From then on the club went from strength to strength.

Anna Lavery,
West Highlands Championships, Oban

The West Highland Tournament was re-established in 1971. It was held from 11th-16th September and the Gents Singles was won by none other than David Lloyd who beat Graeme Notman in the final. The prize money for the winner was the princely sum of £5 and the runner up received £2.50.

Many changes have been experienced by the tennis-playing public in Oban. The change in the set up of local Government was a major factor because this resulted in the new council going ahead with their original plans to build a much-needed new swimming pool in Oban and yes - you've guessed right - the site they wanted was the tennis courts. For five years the courts were temporarily housed at Lochavullin on 5 uneven blaes courts.

Ladies Doubles,
West Highlands Championships, Oban

In the meantime Oban Tennis Club was kept busy raising funds to match grants in order to build the new all-weather tennis courts. Further fund raising was required to raise funds to build a clubhouse and 2 squash courts. Yet still fund raising was required when it was decided to change to artificial grass courts.

Tennis in the Oban area has gone through many changes, some not for the better but there is still a strong tennis-playing membership.

Nigel Beedham, West Highlands Championships, Oban

1960

PAISLEY 1909

Paisley Lawn Tennis and Squash club started its life as Park Tennis Club with a Pavilion costing £180. It had 24 members.

The first Honorary President of the club was Mr Greenlees Jr. and the first President Mr. Alexander McMillan with Vice-President Mr. JM Lang , Hon. Secretary Mr. H Cook and Hon. Treasurer Mr. John McRobert. Among the early Committee members were Mr. Stewart Coats, Mr. WR Cook, Mr. AD Fulton, Mr. JM Greenlees, Mr. AA Gardner, Dr. JD Holmes, Mr. W Hutchison, Mr. W Muir, McKean, Mr. DW McLennan, Mr. N Mc Lennan, Mr. J Spence, and Mr. T Whyte.

The Minutes of 29th January 1909 show the proposed costs of the new club.

Clubhouse	£179: 4:10
Courts	£141: 4: 8
Fencing	£66: 13: 6
Water pipe connection	£18: 10: -
Steps	£2: 15: -
7 cwt roller	£3: 13: -
Hose pipe 90 feet	£2: 4: -
Marker	-: 17: 6
4 sets of posts with	£15: 2: 9
best nets	£430: 5: 3

Another interesting item from the Accounts of 11 February 1909 is a payment of 3d for Marbles. (what they were for is not explained).

Committee meetings were very formal at this time :-

22 March 1909 "Mr H Cook that the Club supply not more than six balls per court per week to be issued on Saturdays at 1 o'clock. Mr McLennan seconded ————Mr Cook's motion was carried.

The question of League membership was then discussed and the Interim Secretary was instructed to fill up and send in the form of entry which had been sent to him by the League Secretary entering the Club for those fixtures which were open to first-class teams.
The Interim Secretary reported that he had insured the club-house and courts against fire (£250) and the Committee approved of this being done"

Extract from the accounts show the payment.   NB "Fire Brigade Guarantee!"

'SORRY SIR, ITS GAME, SET AND MATCH!'CAUSE YOU AINT GOT A FIRE MARK!!...

The Club had still not joined the West of Scotland Leagues by 1908. However the Club allowed their facilities to be used for important games eg. the Coronation Match on 19th July 1911 (see Memorable Moments). In 1912 the accounts record 15/- being paid to West of Scotland League.

Mr. DW McLennan served on the West of Scotland LTA Committee and was President of the Association in 1926.

The Ladies team were in Division 1 in 1933 and they were runners up in 1939. The Men meanwhile were in Division 3

After the War the Ladies played in Division 2 from 1948 to 1953 then returned to Division 1 for two years. Over the years they have played in several Divisions The Men were in Division 1 in 1950 -1952 and 1959-1960, 1963-1964 and various Divisions since.

Exhibition Match 1953

Among the successes of the club are the 1938 1957, 1958, 1962 wins in the Calcutta Cup Clydesdale Cup Division 2 in 1961

Saturday teas were a feature of the Club and were looked forward to.

60 years on in 1969 after three years in planning the Pavilion was replaced with a more modern Clubhouse costing £8,000. Financial help was provided by Paisley Town Council, the Scottish Education Department and the National Playing Fields Association as well as members and friends.

Saturday afternoon tea, 1950s

Scottish and Whiteman Cup tennis player, Miss Winnie Shaw performed the opening ceremony of Paisley Lawn Tennis Club's new £8000 clubhouse. Here she receives a presentation from Barbara Bannatyne, of Potterhill Avenue. Looking on is club president, Mr G.R. Anderson

The Official Opening was made by Winnie Shaw the Scottish International and Wightman Cup player, who had once played on the courts as a Junior in a tournament.

Two squash courts were built in 1979 with support from Renfrew District Council and the Scottish Sports Council.

Play continued at the Club and declining membership and with competition from the local Commercial Club taking its toll they were financially stretched.

Paisley University now own and maintain the property as part of their Sports Campus while the membership of Paisley Lawn Tennis and Squash Club are still using the facilities.

David Brewer hit his first tennis balls at the Club when aged about 5 years while his father was Treasurer of the Club. Alan Mackin also hit balls at the Club.

1959 Paisley Lawn Tennis Club celebrate their Golden Jubilee

POLOC TENNIS CLUB

—We play the game we enjoy so much at our club on the south side of Glasgow in the beautiful setting of Shawholm in Pollok Country Park, formerly known as Pollok Estate. Although always referred to by its members as 'Poloc Tennis Club', it is believed that Poloc is unique in that it is, and always has been, a section of a cricket club, rather than a tennis club in its own right. Over the years there have been regular proposals to make the two separate entities, but they have always foundered because such a move would be detrimental to the ethos of the Club as a whole. Poloc Cricket Club was established in 1878, and a lawn tennis section was introduced in 1883, along with the admission of the first lady members. It really was lawn tennis until 1924. Ironically, the year the club joined the West of Scotland Lawn Tennis Association, the six grass courts were converted to blaes!

Minutes of meetings from 1895 onwards exist and this means that there is information on almost all of the Club's tennis history, with the older details being much more comprehensive than the modern ones! The high standard of those early secretaries' minutes and the general organisation described give the reader the impression of a well-run and well-loved club. In the old days, as illustrated by framed photographs on the Clubhouse walls, long skirts/hats, long trousers/striped blazers and caps were the standard court attire, and membership of Poloc had much to offer Southsiders. In 1911, for instance, for an annual playing subscription of 25/- for gentlemen and 15/- for ladies, bowls, putting, and social events such as a Garden Party, a Sports Day, concerts, and dances could be enjoyed in addition to tennis and cricket.

The inaugural meeting of the West of Scotland Lawn Tennis Association was held in November 1904. Pre-dating this, a minute of a Poloc meeting of 18 April 1904 states: "It was arranged to grant the Tennis Association the use of the courts to play the Inter-city Match with Edinburgh on Saturday 14 May". An application was again granted for the Inter-Association Match between East and West on 20 May 1905, for which "it was decided that a sixpenny gate be taken", and in advance of the East/West encounter at Poloc on 10 June 1911 "it was agreed that the match first be advertised in evening papers on Friday and 'The Herald' on Saturday and that a sandwich man be engaged for Saturday forenoon." However, the minute of the Poloc meeting of 15 April 1914 states:

An application from the West of Scotland Lawn Tennis Association for the use of the Tennis Courts was submitted but it was resolved that this be not granted as in previous years the courts had been a good deal cut up on the occasion of these matches

So popular was tennis among the ladies of Pollokshaws and Shawlands that year that the membership list had to be closed, except to the wives and sisters of members. At this time the courts were available to ladies only on certain days although, as the end of each season drew near, they were allowed to attend every day - except Sundays, of course (Sunday play was not permitted until the autumn of 1949).

Once Sir John Stirling-Maxwell, whose tenants the Club were, gave his approval at the end of the 1923 season to the plan to build a new pavilion and install six hard tennis courts, a sub-committee made site visits to blaes courts laid by two potential contractors, after which it was decided to proceed with J R Stutt's tender of £534.10.8d. Although the new pavilion was not completed until 1930, the new courts were opened on 3 May 1924 by Mr Campbell Murray, the Estate factor, who was presented with a silver highland quaich by the Club as a token of appreciation. This quaich was, in fact, presented back to the Club 50 years later by his grandson for annual competition as a mixed doubles trophy.

Despite being approached to become affiliated to the WSLTA in 1920, around the same time as the first murmurings about blaes courts were heard in the Club, it was not until these courts were in place that Poloc took up this membership, at a cost of approximately £4.00, and were represented in the West of Scotland doubles leagues for the first time in 1925 — by the ladies in Division 7, and the gents in Division 5. It was not until the 1931 season, however, that tennis fixtures were printed in Club membership cards. Both teams did well in their inaugural competitive season and gained promotion for 1926, with the ladies winning all eight matches and being promoted two divisions. In 1926 the ladies entered the Scottish Cup competition for the first time and a team was also entered for the Mixed Doubles competition. A second ladies' team and a second gents' team began competing in 1928, both being placed in Division 10 of their respective leagues, and in 1936 a third ladies' team started playing in Division 11, although this team was not re-instated after the war and did not compete again until 1974-1987. The Ladies' 1st team continued to climb steadily and, in a relatively short time, achieved the ultimate goal of playing in the West of Scotland 1st Division in 1936, 1937 and 1938, whereas the Gents' 1st team had to wait until 1960 before emulating the ladies' success.

In June 1928 Thomas Leask, a former Club Champion/Tennis Convener, became the first Poloc member to win an event in the West of Scotland Tournament - the 1st Class Singles Handicap. Miss K A S (Audrey) Nicol, a member of the small Junior tennis section (3 girls and 3 boys!) formed in 1930, brought further distinction to the Club in 1933 with her achievements of winning both the Scottish Junior Lawn Tennis and the West of Scotland Junior Championships, and being runner-up in the East of Scotland Junior Championship.

The total Club membership in 1935 was 470, of whom 165 were tennis section members — 43 gentlemen and 122 ladies. This was the year that Mr John G Brown kindly presented the Canada Cup for the Ladies Singles Championship. The first winner was Jean Knox, who was also the beaten finalist the next year. The photograph below shows some early winners of this trophy and of the Jubilee Cup for the Gents Singles Championship, which was also first presented in 1935 and won by Johnny Mitchell. Other multiple winners of this trophy in later years were John McCaffer and Jimmy Duncan, who were also great servants of the Club in the Gents' 1st teams and in official capacities over a long period. Other more recent multiple winners of the Canada Cup are Irene Brown - seven occasions between 1958 and 1966; Sheila Robson, Club champion from 1968 to 1975; and Barbara Scorgie, another seven times winner through the 1980s/early 1990s.

From 1942 to the end of the war the cricket and tennis facilities were shared by around 80 members of the Rolls Royce Club, which gave Poloc some valuable extra income and plugged the gap left by members who were on active service. The wartime tennis committees imposed rationing on tennis balls (only two per court), with a fine of 2/- for each ball lost, and old balls were taken to the Sportsman's Emporium for re-

*Back Row: J Burnfield, 1948, 1950 :
M Waterson, 1948 : R Lipsett, 1949,
1951 : J Smith, 1952 : J Mitchell, 1935,
1937-39, 1953, 1954
Front Row: M Wallace, 1950 : E Smellie,
1947, 1951, 1953 : M Allan, 1949*

inflation! Although some friendly games were played, no official matches were arranged during the war years, and there were no Club championships. It was 1947 before things got under way again, after some court reconstruction.

Cricket and Tennis - Poloc Garden Fete - 19 June 1897

Early in 1952 one bitumen all-weather court was erected in what is now the car park area (despite the tennis committee's recommendation that two or even three courts were desirable!) and the tennis playing membership again had to be closed, except for juniors. A winter tennis section was formed over 1952/53, paying an extra £1 on top of the respective annual subscriptions of £3.31- (gents) and £2.10I- (ladies). In May 1954 Mr & Mrs William Walker and Mr & Mrs

Frank McPherson represented the Club at the WSLTA Golden Jubilee Dance. From the 1950s onwards permission was regularly granted to the WSLTA to use some of our courts for their Junior and Senior Championships and for Inter-district matches, e.g. on 1st October 1955 the West defeated Durham 2-1 at Shawholm.

The 1955 season was a significant one in that it was when Mrs Jean McNair and her son Terry, aged 12, joined Poloc. Both won their respective Club Championships that summer at the first attempt and, with her partner, Mrs McNair won the Scottish Ladies' Hard Court Handicap Championship in 1955. She won several representative honours during the 1960s with another Poloc member, Irene Brown -together they formed a very successful league/West partnership - and acted as both formal and informal club coach from 1965. Naturally, her great interest was encouraging the many junior members and during the 1960s the Mixed Doubles team played for several successive seasons in their 1st Division. Competition to get into that team was fierce, and a number of these juniors went on to make their mark in senior teams in later years. In recognition of her many years of dedication to tennis at Poloc, Jean was made an honorary life member in 1979. Terry McNair had a distinguished tennis career as a junior and young senior representing Poloc and the West District, along with fellow club member John McCaffer. In 1959, Terry

Poloc Gents' 1st Team – 1952 – Winners of WSLTA 4th Division

Back Row (left to right):   H H Sheppard (President) : G A Milne : R J Lipsett : Dr E Bloch (Tennis Convener)

Front Row (left to right):   J G Burnfield : J D Budge : J A Mitchell : J Bruce won a string of titles, including the Central District and the Ayrshire Junior Championships, the 18 and Under Boys' Doubles at the Scottish Grass Court Championships, and was beaten finalist in the Singles of the Scottish. He won the West Junior Tournament in 1960 and also played at Junior Wimbledon. Progressing to the Gents' 1st team and playing consistently in the 1st Division, Terry won the Gents' Club Championship for the first time in 1962 and was a member of the team which won the Calcutta Cup in 1963 and 1968 and lost in the 1966 final. In 1964 he won the Glasgow University Championship and was ranked as 6th Scottish seed, so when he left Glasgow to live and work in Oban around 1969 it was a great loss to the Club.

Probably the most notable of several other Poloc members who gained representative honours is Alison Douglas. She won the Scottish Under 18 Doubles Championship with her partner in 1971, was a junior internationalist against England and Ireland, and reached the Junior Wimbledon Singles final. Unfortunately, she only briefly shared her talent with us before leaving to train for PE down south.

The 1950s/60s were very successful for Poloc as a club, both on the cricket field and on the courts. It is no coincidence that during this period extremely active tennis committees were in place, for a number of years under the convenership of Dr Bloch, to whom the Club is also indebted for his work as a photographic archivist. Total membership of the Club reached an all-time high of 752 in 1957, the year in which the Pollok & District Tournament was contested for the first time. Participating clubs were Bellahouston, Cartha, Pollokshields, Poloc, Titwood, Scottish Gas Board — with Poloc's Eddie Craig acting as Tournament Secretary and Club Patron Dr Albert Sharman presenting trophies for the Ladies and Gents Singles Championships. Poloc won this Interclub Tournament frequently during its lifetime, often for several years in succession. Jack Budge, one of the driving forces in the tennis section during these boom years, was the first Poloc member to be elected on to the WSLTA committee in 1961, becoming President in 1966, and was followed to the Chair in 1971 by another Club member, Jimmy McAlpine. All five tennis teams were promoted for the 1962 season — the men to Divisions I and 5, the Ladies to Divisions I and 8, and the Juniors to Division 2 - a unique record, never again equalled.

In 1967, Poloc as we had known it changed for ever. With the gifting of Pollok Estate to Glasgow Corporation, the Club suddenly found itself in the middle of a public park, the close links with the Maxwell family were severed, and money became tight(er!) following recent Clubhouse upgrading and extension. The timing of members' proposals that Poloc should build squash courts/all-weather tennis courts could not have been

worse, as the Club could not consider embarking on the heavy investment which these schemes would involve. While the winter (men only) golf section established in 1889 continues to be very popular to this day, by the end of the 1960s/early '70s many of the activities peripheral to tennis and cricket previously enjoyed had been replaced by other sections, such as table tennis, darts, curling, and bridge. In 1971 the squash project surfaced again and rumbled on for a few years, being on the brink of success in 1975, when a number of inexplicable delays caused the loss of important grants. It was finally abandoned in 1976, much to the disappointment of those who had worked hard on it over a long period.

Poloc Ladies' 1st Team – 1967 – Promoted to WSLTA 1st Division

Back Row (left to right):   Mrs Margaret Howie : Mrs Sheila Robson : Ernie Donaldson (Tennis Convener) : Miss Dorothy Stewart

Front Row (left to right):   Mrs Margaret Ross : Miss Irene Brown

Absent: Mrs Jean McNair

With hindsight, due to the marked drop in popularity of the game of squash, this decision proved to be a blessing in disguise.

1978 saw the centenary of Poloc Cricket Club and an Invitation Mixed Doubles Tournament for annual competition was instituted in honour of this, with Whitecraigs being the first winners of the Centenary Trophy. At the AGM in this special year in the Club's history adult lady members were finally granted full voting rights "in recognition of the fact that a large number of ladies had made considerable contributions

to the Club over many years". They now became eligible to participate in the management of the Club for the first time, but the downside was that they had to pay the same subscriptions as the men from 1979 onwards!

With the old bitumen hard court having finally bitten the dust in 1974 and Courts 1, 2 and 3 having been adversely affected in 1979 by the laying of a new sewer in connection with the construction of the Burrell Collection building, the way was clear for the re-emergence of the lobby for all-weather courts. Like the squash project, this one also rumbled on for a number of years as fund-raising and a drive for new members got underway, and grants were again pursued. Although assisted by an LTA loan and a Scottish Sports Council Loan, vital income anticipated from major schemes failed to materialise and a substantial levy per member and increased subscriptions were required to finance the shortfall when En-Tout-Gas finally began work in September 1987 to provide the third different surface in the section's history for the three front courts, Courts 4, 5, and 6 remaining as blaes. It was twenty years since Jack Budge had made the first suggestion of changing to 'tennis quick' at the 1967 AGM! The new courts were christened by a Mixed

Doubles American Tournament on 3 January 1988, and this event continued to be held for several seasons on the first Sunday of the month for the Bobby Blair Trophy, donated by Jean Sloan in memory of her father.

In 1984, Sheena Sim, who was a member of the Ladies' 1st team, and a former Tennis Convener/ Club Champion, was elected to the WSLTA committee. She went on to become Chairman of the West in 1992 before moving on to the SLTA, where she represented the West on the Council, on the Management Committee, and was Convener of the Tournament and Events committee. She was Vice President in 1995/96, then Scottish President in 1997/98 (only the second lady to hold this office), in 1999 Immediate Past President, and is now an Honorary Vice President — an honour indeed, by association, for our Club.

From 1961 until 1987 the Ladies' 1st team played in either the 1st or the 2nd Division, while the 2nd team settled around Division 4 in the 1970s until the mid-80s, on three occasions achieving Division 3 status in pursuit of the Ladies' 1st, who happened to be in Division 2 each time! Throughout the 1960s and '70s the Gents' 1st team also did the yo-yo act between the 1st and the 2nd Division, regaining 1st Division status for several successive seasons in the early 1990s after a few seasons in the 3rd/4th in the late '80s. Over the same period the Gents' 2nd team played for the most part in the 4th/5th Division. When the West Vets' Leagues were formed in 1995, both a ladies' and a gents' team were entered and this extension of the competitive season has been much enjoyed by all who have participated. Tennis at Polcc was not all serious stuff, however. Club nights and mixed doubles tournaments were always popular, and the ladies have played the cricketers at their game (the gents having to use the opposite hand from normal for batting and bowling) and also at (normal handed) tennis. Over the years the section has been involved in many fund raising/social events such as fêtes, whist drives, quizzes, barbecues, discos, ceilidhs, and fashion shows to name but a few.

Poloc continued to have regular success at the Interclub Tournament during the 1980s, although the participating clubs had changed, as had the name of the Tournament. It is now no longer contested at all. Simon Coom for many years very ably and almost single-handedly ran an annual Junior Ratings Competition at the start of the season and a Ratings Tournament in July. He worked hard for Poloc on and off court for many years before ending his 30 year involvement with the Club a couple of seasons ago. Jim Wightman put in a lot of work with the Junior Section over a long period, assisted latterly by Tom Allan, and coaches Steve Moodie and Graeme MacLean. Not so many years ago Poloc was bursting at the seams with juniors (predominantly male), many of them very talented, but, unfortunately, as competitive interest waned, the teams were withdrawn from the leagues in 1999 and the boys have all now moved elsewhere. It is difficult to imagine how the Club can grow without them.

In common with other private clubs, we are facing an uphill struggle to compete with the attractions of multi-sports centres for members and the tennis membership has fallen away badly of late. From 1982 until 1997 four gents' teams competed in various divisions, reducing to two in 1999, but anyone who was a member of the section ten years ago would find it hard to believe that in 2002 Poloc was forced to withdraw from gents' league competition for the first time since 1925, as almost all the team players had departed. The reasons for this were many and varied, not least of them being the fact that the courts are past their "sell-by" date (when they were opened in December 1987 the life expectancy prior to resurfacing being required was given as 10 years). The Foot and Mouth epidemic of February 2001 hit the Club hard. It was something totally outwith our control, from which we have never really recovered. Pollok Park was closed to the public to safeguard the valuable herd of highland cattle on the Estate and, although we had access to the Clubhouse, outside activities were banned — so no winter tennis, and no winter golf. The restrictions were lifted at the beginning of May, just in time to allow the league tennis/cricket programme to start, but by then the damage was done. A substantial number of people did not renew their memberships because of the uncertainty of the playing situation, and a couple of poor summers have done nothing to improve matters.

Thus, in the 2002 season, it has fallen to the two ladies' teams to keep the Poloc flag flying (fluttering?) in the WSLTA Summer and Vets' Leagues. It goes without saying that there is sadness felt within the Club that where once there was a thriving section, there is now a moribund one. At least I have an advantage over a lot of others — having joined as a youngster in 1958, I can remember the Club as it was in its heyday. 2003 sees Poloc Cricket Club celebrate its 125th Anniversary and the tennis section its 120th Anniversary, which we plan to mark in various ways. Throughout all these years Poloc has remained essentially a family club which has meant a lot to a lot of people from the southside of Glasgow and far beyond. On a lovely summer afternoon or evening, more attractive surroundings in which to play our chosen sport would be hard to find.

RUTHERGLEN 1920

Rutherglen Lawn Tennis Club came to be formed when some keen Public Parks Players decided they would prefer their own "exclusive" Tennis Club. So says the article in Scottish Tennis . It goes on "these enthusiasts raised a considerable amount of money through whist drives and dances the latter evidently held in their own homes, with the doors of some of the rooms removed! By these means the princely sum of £2,000 was raised, which in the immediate post World War One period was a considerable achievement."

From this beginning the club went from strength to strength, the Men winning the Senior Calcutta Cup in 1932. In 1935 they again reached the final losing to Cathcart, while the Second Team reached the semi-final of the Junior Calcutta Cup, losing to Hallside who were the eventual winners. That same year the Men's Team were second in the Second Division and gained promotion to the First Division. The Second Team were also promoted being second in Division Seven. The Ladies were already in the Second Division and were fifth of nine. In the Clydesdale Cup Division 1 the Club were defeated by Pollokshields the eventual winners. 1935 was a good year!

In this era Johnny Woodburn played in the West of Scotland Tournament, was found to have played professional football and was debarred from playing Lawn Tennis for five years. For many years he carried a certificate to prove he was an amateur. He later became President of the Club in 1940.

In 1939 there were 97 Seniors paying a fee of £1-12-6 (£1.62p), 21 Juniors paying 15/-(75p) and 16 Honorary members.

Play at the Club continued during the Second World War even although the West of Scotland Leagues were suspended

'NORMALLY I'M A MAN OF FEW WORDS, BUT IN YOUR CASE I'LL MANAGE A LONG SENTENCE!!...

Balls were very scarce during the War and for some time afterwards. There was a small allocation and they had to be returned for refurbishment!

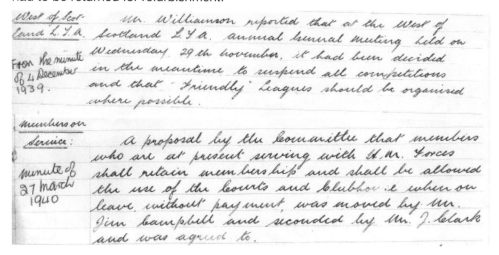

In 1951 and 1953 the Men's Team reached the final of the Calcutta Cup losing to Woodend and Pollokshields II. Bert Muir was a leading light in the Club in the early 1950s overseeing the building of an all weather court on the spare ground which had been let out for

horticulture during the war. There were also plans to build a new clubhouse on the site of the car park. However these plans did not materialise and eventually these areas were sold and a bungalow stands on the site.

Bert Muir was secretary of the Club for a time and also of the Cambuslang and Rutherglen District Tournament and was meticulous in his work. Bert served on the West of Scotland Lawn Tennis Association Committee, was its Secretary from 1963 - 1966 and served also on the Scottish LTA.

The contentious point about Sunday play had the neighbourhood up in arms about the destruction of the Sabbath and furthermore about the noise it would create.

> Rutherglen
> 5th March 1953.
>
> The Secretary,
> Rutherglen Tennis Club,
>
> Dear Sir,
>
> (I am sorry to be so formal but I do not know your name.)
>
> First of all let me thank you and your committee, for the courtesy and consideration shown in your communication of 2nd inst.
>
> I regret that I cannot give this project my sincere approval because, while there is no harm in your playing tennis, you cannot, with the best will in
>
> the world, preserve the peace which we have so far enjoyed.
>
> You propose to open the courts at 2 p.m. When will the club-house be opened? How long will it remain open and how will it be used? These things affect us because we are so near.
>
> However, we have been interested in the club since its inception and we believe that, if you decide to treat this as a purely legal matter, you will use the privilege with discretion.
>
> I am,
> Yours sincerely

There is no record of exactly when this was finally resolved. Sunday play is now accepted and Junior matches are often played on a Sunday since school rugby, football and hockey demand their presence for the school teams on Saturday mornings which used to be the Junior match time.

Over the years amalgamation with the other local clubs to form a "Super Club" in the locality has been discussed several times in the 1960s and in the 1990s. It could have provided for a large complex since between Burnside, Cambuslang, Kirkhill and Rutherglen there were 14 courts and a further 6 at Templeton. However there were good reasons each time why this never happened and each club progressed in its own way.

In the 1970s the Club suffered a decline since many of the team members decided to retire or take up golf. Veterans tennis was not even considered then.

During this period Strathclyde Universtiy had use of the courts in the afternoons during term time and this continued till the University obtained facilities of their own some considerable time later. The local school also had access to the courts. Coaching still takes place with Burnside Primary having a series of lessons in the Summer and Autumn Terms.

The annual preparation of the courts was a serious task. Blaes required constant attention. The Juniors were an enormous help, raking and rolling the courts. They all knew that 56 feet 1 inch was the diagonal of the court, 79 feet was the length and 36 feet was the width. They could use a hammer to put in the nails and were quite an authority on court laying!

However the story continues :- It was not long till there was a revival. In the early 1980s under the Presidency of Evelyn Morris, when the clubhouse showed terminal rot in the foundations, the members got together and saved and saved to achieve a new one. Mrs Jean

Spring 1996 - Last rolling of the blaes courts

Low the Club's Honorary President arranged the first Fashion Show which had Sports Wear from Greaves and the local Ladies Dress Shop. Coffee Mornings, Jumble sales and Fêtes were held and £1,000 was

raised by selling hand and bath towels. Along with a small grant from the Playing Fields Association there was a loan for £2,000 from the L.T.A. which horrified the Treasurer and put shockwaves through the Club. It was an enormous amount to borrow in the early 1980s. The sum of over £14,000 was raised and so was the new Clubhouse. All through the summer of building, matches took place on the courts and friendly neighbours who were members took it in turn to allow their homes to be used as changing facilities. Their dining rooms or lounges provided upmarket tea venues.

All was completed and the Official Opening was performed by Andy Cameron who grew up and lived locally.

The new clubhouse added a new enthusiasm to the members and Junior coaching became a focus of the club, with Flora McCormack taking a major role which she has continued for many years. Junior teams began to be successful. Moira Henderson, the Club Secretary, assists Flora on the Junior coaching evening.

September 1996 - machinery everywhere

In the late 1980s Myra Hunter was elected President and a member rose to speak at the AGM and said "what are you going to do about the courts?"

What indeed! - Discussions started and the first estimate was for £3,000 for a quick tar job. That was quickly abandoned and the serious investigations and the fund-raising began again.

Advice was taken from Ian Woodcraft Development Officer at S.L.T.A. and he advised that one phase was preferable. The advice was taken.

1997 Opening Day - Mrs Jean Low, Honorary President of the Club

Once more Coffee Mornings, Fêtes, Fashion Shows, Jumble Sales and Burns Suppers were the order of the day and funds began to accumulate but the Club needed additional funding. Where was it to come from? Each funder would provide funds only if the others did too, who would say yes first? It was not a race that any of them were over-willing to start!! With a few hiccups the package was eventually put together and we were on our way.

Funding came from Sport and the Arts; the Lottery Sports Fund; Glasgow City Council (the Club was in Glasgow at that time); and a loan of £25,000 from the L.T.A. Ina Leslie the Treasurer, who over the years has husbanded our funds well and "who will not spend a penny if a ha'penny will do", was not overly phased by this borrowing and found the guarantors required from the members. A budget of £128,000 saw the club have four "Elastosol" all weather courts, all floodlit with new power lines to provide sufficient electricity, all fenced and with a "Tarmac" entrance.

The official opening party

In the Spring of 1997 the courts were Officially Opened by Mrs Jean Low, Honorary President of the Club. What did the club have to do in return for the funding? The Club had to promise to raise the fees annually and create a sinking fund to the value of £1,000 per court per year (inflated). This is because having had funding it is up to each club to prepare for future improvements without further funding. Rutherglen L.T.C. tries to fulfil that commitment.

As a result of our development the Club was awarded Runner Up in The Lawn Tennis Assciation awards for Outdoor Facilities 1997.

Playing under the lights was a grand experience and on the first light-up night over fifty players had time on court. The neighbours too were delighted with the facilities; no more pink furniture when the courts were too dry and dusty. The added security to our neighbours when our courts were lit also pleased them.

The Club is for playing tennis so new achievements were sought. Professional Coaching was introduced to enhance that already provided. Juniors and Adults had their game improved and some Juniors moved to West squads for outdoor and indoor coaching over the winter. Gavin Weanie played in a British Futures programme. The Juniors climbed the Leagues and in 2000 won the First Division of the Mixed Doubles League. Currently the U 17 and U13 teams play in the First Division, and a total of eight Junior teams are entered in the Leagues.

The Men's First team won the Junior Calcutta Cup in 2001 and 2002 and in 2003 won Division 2 of the Spring Singles and Division 4a in the Summer Leagues. The Second team plays in D 7c and the Ladies in D 4b and 8b. The Veterans Ladies team plays in D 5b.

The Rutherglen Ratings Tournament takes place in August with Peter Weanie as Referee.

What of the future? Rutherglen Lawn Tennis Club looks forward with confidence to its continued development and evolution.

2000 Winners of the Junior Mixed Doubles 1st Division
L-R: Jennifer Hutchison, Brett Fox, Julie Weanie, Ryan Fox,
Joanna McGregor, John Hutchison, Lyndsay Hayworth

SPRINGWELLS c1910

It is not known when Springwells joined the West of Scotland Leagues but in 1933 the Ladies were in the 12th Division and the Men's team were 2nd in the 10th Division, the latter suggesting several years progress since at that time there were 12 Divisions of Ladies' and 13 Divisions of Men's Leagues.

The Club was socially-minded in that American Tournaments featured in the Club calendar and still do.

The Eastern District Tournament, with Garrowhill, Mount Vernon, Sandyhills, Springboig, Uddingston, Whifflet, Wishaw taking part, was organised for many years by Jack Mort along with members from the other clubs.

Springwells has two courts which were upgraded to porous asphalt with the help of Lottery funding and loans given by the members themselves. These loans were paid back to them within two years.

By 1969 the Men's team was playing in the 3rd Division moving to the 2nd in 1974. They even managed a year in Division 1. Stalwarts of the team in those days were David Woodhouse, David Morton, Dougal Henderson, Billy Gardner.

The courts are to be used by the local schools during school hours for play as part of their timetable.

STAMPERLAND c1960

The first appearance of Stamperland in the West of Scotland Leagues was probably 1960 and in 1961 the Ladies won Division 15. The Men were in Division 18 and were third. In those days if you won a Division without losing a match the team moved up two Divisions, otherwise it would take 14 years to get from D.15 to D.1. In that length of time players may have stopped playing!

Stamperland teams rose through the Divisions with regularity:-

Year		Ladies			Men			
1961	Ladies	D 15	1st		Men	D 18	3rd	
1963		D11	1st			D 16	3rd	
1965		D 5	5th			D 15	3rd	
1969		D 8	6th			D 11	3rd	
1971		D 5a	1st			D 6b	4th	NB 1970 Leagues divided
1973		D 3	10th			D 5a	3rd	to sections a,b, c to help
1982		D 4a	6th			D 4a	7th	teams progress quicker.
1994		D 3	6th			D 8b	6th	Junior U16B D2b
2000		D4a	2nd					no team

The Club had declined in numbers and the competition from surrounding clubs who had upgraded their courts caused the members to disperse at the end of 2000.

The good news is that the Club has been reformed with Juniors at its heart and a programme of coaching has been initiated so much so that the Club was awarded West of Scotland Club of the Year in 2002.

STEPPS 1907

The decision to form a Stepps Lawn Tennis Club was taken at a public meeting in the Hall, Edward Place. on 18th September 1907. The Chairman was Mr A.H.Dunlop and there were 32 persons present. It was reported that Col. Alexander Sprot had offered half an acre of ground on the north-east side of Lenzie Road at a nominal rent of one shilling per annum. The site offered was on ground offered earlier to the Parish Council as a public park, but declined at that time (though taken up later). Col. Sprot had also offered to advance an interest-free loan towards the cost of setting up the club, estimated at around £150 for laying down two courts and erection of a clubhouse. (it was later confirmed that a loan of £100.00 had been granted). A Constitution. Rules and Bye-laws were drawn up and approved. Subscriptions were fixed at 17s 6d for gentlemen and IOs for ladies, with an entrance fee of 5 shillings. Provision was also made for summer visitor tickets of varying duration.

1965

2001 Finals Day - "In the Clubhouse"

Over the following months events were held to raise funds towards the Club's formation. Two courts were laid down, at cost of about £120.00 and a clubhouse erected for an outlay of £16. A third court was laid some years later. The courts were officially opened on Saturday 16th May 1905, by Miss Sprot. daughter of the Colonel, at what was her first public ceremony. She was deputising for her mother. who was unable to be present. Councillor Robert T. Dunlop welcomed the large gathering and referred to the magnificent courts, which he was sure met the wishes of all who had been involved in

the undertaking. He mentioned that the membership then stood at 42 ladies. 12 gentlemen and four honorary members. On his invitation, Miss Sprot played the first ball across the courts and declared them open. Councillor Dunlop then presented Miss Sprot with a silver ball, suitably inscribed to mark the occasion. Col. Sprot, in returning thanks, congratulated the Management Committee and Secretary William McEwan on their work towards the success of the venture. Councillor Dunlop announced that gifts to the club

included a flag pole. and a flag in the club colours of blue and white, with "S.L.T.C" embroidered on it made and gifted by Miss Isa Barclay). Col. Sprot then unfurled the flag. An exhibition match followed, after which tea was served in a large marque.

Five years later the club ran into financial difficulties. At a meeting held on 17th April 1913 it was decided to form a new club on fresh financial lines, with a new Constitution. On the basis of a financial statement prepared by Mr Peter Anderson of "Hollydene" annual subscriptions were set at 15s. for gentlemen. 10s. 6d. for ladies, and 5s for juniors (14—16 years of age), with varying rates for visitors, depending on their number of days on court. At a further meeting (a week later) office bearers were elected. The courts were re-opened for play on Saturday 17th May 1913, with the first ball played by Mrs Watson. wife of the President, Councillor Watson. A large gathering of people was present, including representatives of other village sports clubs — golf, cricket and bowls. Councillor Watson intimated that membership of the Club was 50. Over the following years the Club was able to maintain its affairs in good order. The Courts and Clubhouse were kept in good condition, thanks to the efforts of the members during the close seasons in holding events such as whist drives, sales of work and concerts, to raise funds for maintenance and repairs. The membership varied in number.

By the 1930s the Club had joined the West of Scotland Lawn Tennis Association and was participating in its Leagues. A Junior Section provided a steady flow of talent to the Seniors

In February 1943, during the war years, the Clubhouse was requisitioned for use by the Home Guard. (At the same time difficulties in obtaining a supply of new balls led to a curtailment of play. This was partly met in 1944 by a door-to-door appeal for unwanted balls which succeeded in accumulating a considerable number. Those too far gone for immediate use were sent away to be recovered and reinflated.) Play resumed at this time but with a shortened season. After the war membership picked up again. During the 1950s the number of seniors varied between 58 and 82 and the juniors between 49 and 60. In this period both the Men's and Ladies' teams fared well in the West of Scotland leagues and in local tournaments and other matches.

JUNIOR aces line up for the new season at Stepps Tennis club.

To celebrate the Jubilee of the original founding of the Club a dinner was held in Crowwood Golf Club House on 1st June 1957 attended by 68 members and friends. On the same afternoon a Former Members Day had attracted 50 Seniors, some of whom had enjoyed a game.

Over the years the Club had endeavoured to raise enough funds to erect a new Clubhouse but had found this task difficult to fulfill. In 1964 the Ninth District Council, Lanarkshire offered to build one for the Club and asked for a donation of £500 towards its cost. This was agreed upon and the new building was formally opened on 3rd April 1965 by Councillor Gray in the presence of other Council Members.

The following year the Council granted permission for Sunday play to take place but withdrew this shortly afterwards following protests from local residents.

In 1967 the Stepps Table Tennis Club was given permission to use the Clubhouse on three evenings per week. This continued until 1971 when the Club was disbanded.

In 1969 Club Member Sheila Moodie won the Scottish Grass Court Singles Championship, gained a Scottish International Cap and enjoyed success in other tournaments. She continued her triumphs by representing Scotland on many other occasions. In 1970 she won the East of Scotland and South of Scotland Singles, Doubles and Mixed Doubles and repeated this triple at Grantown-on-Spey. Her achievements brought wider prominence to the Club. Today, she represents Scotland in Veterans Events.

Miss Margaret Stevenson won the Girls Singles and Doubles titles at Hamilton and the Singles title at Elgin. In the following year she played at Junior Wimbledon and the Junior Inter-Counties Week at Inverclyde and was successful in winning Singles titles at Nairn and at Perth.

In 1972 James Nicol had wins in East and South of Scotland tournaments and Grantown-on-Spey.

At this time the Ladies' team reached the second division. Sometimes afterwards this 'Purple Patch' seemed to wane. Membership levels fell and attendances at AGMs were poor, so much so that the continued existence of the Club was questioned. However, a nucleus of members successfully determined to keep it going.

A veterans sections has recently been reformed and competes in August and September in the West of Scotland Veterans' League.

Members represent the Club in the annual Kirkintilloch tournament and other events which are well enjoyed. Coaching is carried out at all levels including the Junior Section where, in due time, some may emulate the 'greats' of the 69-70 era and may be around when the Club celebrates its centenary in 2007.

STRATHAVEN 1893

Strathaven Tennis Club in Crosshill Road opened on 13th May 1893 and comprised of a small clubhouse and two blaes courts.

The Club was well supported by its members who played in various competitions with success over the years. It was recorded that subscriptions in 1920 were Ladies 12/6 (62p) and the Gentlemen 15/- (75p) and Family 40/- (£2).

The Clubhouse was renewed in 1925 and the courts re-laid in 1936 at a cost of £115.

1901

In 1931 the Club entered the Lanarkshire Leagues with many successes, particularly in the 1950s when the Gents' Doubles team won the League on a number of occasions. At that time there were some 16 flourishing Lanarkshire Clubs, most of which, sadly, have now closed. Following the demise of the Lanarkshire Leagues the Club has participated in the West of Scotland Leagues.

Soldiers stationed in the town in 1941 were invited to join the Club at a small fee, but the Club closed in 1943 and was used by the Home Guard. The remaining members were given the courtesy of the Public Tennis Courts in Holm Street when a Mixed Doubles team competed successfully in the Sheeran League.

At considerable cost the courts re-opened on the 8th May 1948. Basket Whist Drives, dances and other social events were held to raise funds.

Saturday American Tournaments and Teas were regular features of the Club in the ensuing years and enthusiasm for the game was so great that one might only be able to play one set during a whole evening.

Season 1955 -
Bert Allingham, Jimmy McRae, Bill Prentice, Guy Park, George Moffat, Alistair Prentice
John Summers, Bill Mason, Bill Summers, Alistair Wotherspoon

Sadly now Club membership has fallen to a rather low level, especially since the courts closed a few years ago to make way for a car park for the new Swimming Pool and the Club has again been re-located to the Public Courts in Holm Street. Indications are that the club now faces an uncertain future.

Members of Strathaven have served tennis beyond the Club. Alistair Wotherspoon was President of the West of Scotland LTA in 1976 and SLTA in 1981-82 and represented them at the LTA. He was also a Referee at the West of Scotland Championships and along with Alistair Prentice refereed the Nairn Tournament.

1920 Ladies Team

Alistair Prentice refereed many Tournaments also (including Nairn for 25 years). Ian Allingham now referees the Nairn Event. Many others have served the club well.

1893 Founding Day

STRATHGRYFFE 1991

BRIDGE OF WEIR c1930

The club originated with only 1 court on the terrace of the local hotel , then purchased the ground on Gryffe Road in Bridge of Weir in the early 1930s. Two grass courts were laid then later changed to blaes.

Membership fluctated but at the club's height there were 40 senior members. Lack of funds made maintenance of clubhouse and grounds very difficult and the opportunity to merge with Elderslie to form the new club which became Strathgryffe Tennis & Squash Club was appealing. Bridge of Weir subsequently sold their ground for £125,000 which was injected into the Houston project, justifying the original move to buy the club land. Bridge of Weir club was closed in 1991 and the members moved to Strathgryffe.

ELDERSLIE LAWN TENNIS CLUB

Elderslie Tennis Club and members

The club was established in 1926 with the assistance of the major local Landowner, Elderslie Estates who leased the ground and built the courts. Further help came from the main employer in Elderslie, A F Stoddard (Carpetmakers) who assisted with the clubhouse. The club had 4 blaes courts and was adjacent to the 18th hole of Elderslie Golf Club. This was very much a community club with membership priority given to Elderslie residents. This continued well into the 1950s.

In 1977 the club formed an association with Neilsonians amateur football club and a squash court and bar facilities were added giving members more facilities and more all year activity.

In the pre war years the ladies & gents teams played in the lower divisions but after the war with an influx of members from Johnstone municipal courts the gents 1st team gained promotion for 6 consecutive years moving up to the 4th division.

In the early 70s again the club experienced a further step change in playing standard with both the gents and ladies team being promoted to the 1st leagues. While the gents maintained this or 2nd division status until merger, the ladies achievements were remarkable for a provincial club not only winning the West League and Cup on numerous occasions but also winning The Scottish Cup in 1974,1976 &1980.

One of the successful members of this team was Marjory Love whose success at both Junior and Senior levels in winning numerous competitions including Scottish Junior & Senior, ensured Elderslie's name figured regularly in the press. She won the Elderslie Ladies Club Championship for 25 consecutive years from 1963 to 1988.

In the 80s there were marketing drives in the local school with the result that junior membership was high. Coaching was organised through voluntary coaches to the extent that on merger, the club had produced 3 of the top under 14 girls in the West of Scotland (Elizabeth Stevenson, Yvonne Hutton and Marion Barclay). They all won Scottish junior titles as Strathgryffe members along with numerous West of Scotland girls and mixed leagues.

Season 1991 was the last competitive season before the merger with Bridge of Weir. The sale of the ground for private housing helped to fund the move to a new site in Houston to form Strathgryffe Tennis & Squash Club.

1976 Ladies Cup winning team. Back row, L-R: Anne Judge, Ann Paul, Gill Lockett, Joyce Bell
Sitting, L-R: Mary Jack, Marjory Love, Moira Hogg

STRATHGRYFFE TENNIS & SQUASH CLUB

Strathgryffe Tennis & Squash Club was constituted in 1991 as the result of a merger between Elderslie and Bridge of Weir tennis clubs. Elderslie was declining in terms of membership and struggling financially when the opportunity arose through the local landowner, Elderslie Estates, to sell the existing ground to builders and move the club to a new site in Houston. After much discussion with members and local residents as to possible alternatives it was decided that, as the future for Elderslie T.C. looked fairly bleak, this golden opportunity to create a new club from the legacy of the old was an opportunity not to be missed. At this stage Elderslie committee members were approached by Bridge of Weir Tennis Club which was now a small struggling village club situated about a mile from Houston where the new club was to be situated. Again after a great deal of discussion between the clubs the members of Bridge of Weir T.C. agreed to join the project and to contribute financially by investing money from the sale of their land, thereby considerably increasing available funds and thus the opportunity to enhance the proposed facilities.

An eventual site was found on the outskirts of Houston which was acceptable to planning and local residents and, with the proceeds from the sale of club grounds at Elderslie and Bridge of Weir, an L.T.A. loan and Sports Council grant , the new club was built comprising a modern well appointed clubhouse with lounge and bar area , 2 glass backed squash courts, 6 outdoor all weather courts (3 floodlit artificial grass and 3 porous tarmac). The facility was officially opened by the Chairman of the Sports Council in May 1992. Naming of the new club was delegated to the joint committee from Elderslie and Bridge of Weir clubs and was derived from the local area name "Gryffe".

Despite the initial success of the new club the committee felt that there was still scope for development and, encouraged by the setting up of the Lottery Sports Fund in the 1990s, began to investigate the viability of building indoor courts, embarking on correspondence and subsequent discussions with the appropriate funding bodies. Consideration was also given to other changes / additions to the club in the form of extra rooms to accommodate a gym and resurfacing of the outdoor hard courts. Presentations of the proposed project were prepared for the Lottery Sports Fund and L.T.A. including detailed budget costs. After nearly 2 years of planning, discussion with funding bodies, architects and town planners etc, the project was given the go ahead at a total cost of around £750,000 to construct 2 indoor tennis courts, additional rooms to accommodate a gym and resurfacing of existing hard courts.

In order to assist the funding of the additional facilities the L.T.A. provided an interest free loan of £220,000 and the Lottery Sports Fund a grant of £350,000. The new facilities were officially opened in 1997. The club has won "Scottish Club of the Year" on 2 separate occasions, 1992 and 1997 and also "L.T.A Facility of the Year" for best outdoor facility in the UK in 1993 .

Strathgryffe now in 2003 has over 800 members, and the facilities comprise clubhouse and bar, 2 indoor

Strathgryffe Ladies' Team Scottish Cup Finalists 2000

carpeted courts, 6 outdoor artificial grass courts, 2 glass backed squash courts and gym with modern resistance and aerobic equipment. It currently has 5 Gents' and 4 Ladies' teams, Veterans' teams and numerous Junior teams playing in West of Scotland Leagues. The Club has reception /administration staff, a full time professional coach, and now a tennis manager whose main tasks are to specifically market the Club, prepare and implement development programmes for all members with special emphasis on mini tennis and to help the Club achieve its target of 1000 members by 2005.

Since moving to Houston, Strathgryffe Gents have won Premier Division and are delighted to record that one of our long standing members Alex Culloch won the British Veterans Over 60s Championship and went on to represent Britain in the World Over 60s Championship. John Stevenson a Past President of Elderslie is West of Scotland Secretary and has recently served as President of Tennis Scotland 2001-2002.

THORN PARK 1925

In 1924 it became clear to the Bearsden community that the demand for good tennis facilities had outgrown the existing supply. Meetings were held in the local public hall at which it was noted that the existing tennis club could not expand on its existing site. Two other options were considered - that the existing club move to a bigger site or that an additional club be formed. After full discussion the latter option was chosen and the name Thorn Park LTC was adopted for the new Club.

In 1925 the local landowner transferred to the new club a plot of land big enough to accommodate six tennis courts, a good clubhouse and a pleasant area of amenity ground. The landowner required only a modest financial return from the club but he did impose various conditions including a restriction on the use of the land to tennis, putting and bowling and a prohibition on the sale of spirituous liquors! As it turned out bowling and putting have never been developed but excellent tennis facilities were provided and, subject to a break during the second world war, have been developed and improved on ever since.

Records indicate that between 1933 and 1939 Thorn Park Ladies' team fluctuated between the fifth and ninth Divisions and the Men's team fluctuated between the sixth and ninth Divisions of the West of Scotland Leagues.

Thorn Park rejoined the West of Scotland leagues in 1949 - each of the Ladies' and Men's teams being admitted into the lowest Division - respectively the twelfth and the thirteenth. By 1955 both teams had risen to Division ten; a second Men's team and a Junior team had been created - the second Men being in Division sixteen and the Juniors in Division three.

By 1953 the Club had five blaes courts, three excellent and two poor. In 1966 a sixth blaes court was added but it was of poor quality and of little use. Shortly after that the club decided that they had to make major improvements and very quickly instituted their " Moneyquick for Tennisquick" campaign (Tennisquick being the then new type of playing surface which had many advantages over the then all-prevalent blaes). At about the same time one member obtained his Scottish LTA elementary coaching qualification and introduced coaching classes for Junior members, which was a concept almost unheard of in these days. He was soon joined as a qualified coach by others and these coaches along with many other Senior members started the regular Saturday morning coaching classes which have been a feature of the Club and have been enjoyed by a huge number of Junior members ever since - but which have become in the last few years just one small part of the comprehensive professional coaching now provided to Junior and Senior members of the Club.

Just when it appeared that the campaign to raise the funds required to build Tennisquick courts might fall short of its target an anonymous donor came forward from outwith the Club. He explained that he was so impressed by the combination of the facilities and the coaching being offered to the young people in the community that he was willing to donate a very generous sum if the members among them would contribute the balance required to fund the project. Happily the members did rise to this challenge and the target was achieved, the donation from the anonymous donor was accepted with much gratitude and Thorn Park became one of the first Clubs in the West of Scotland to have three fully floodlit, instantly draining, playable on all the year round Tennisquick courts.

The combination of the greatly improved facilities and the coaching was accompanied by a quick rise in the playing standards at the club and both the Men's and the Ladies' teams achieved top Division status shortly after that. The 1st Junior team won the 1st Divisions in 1973, 1974 and 1976, the Club produced three West of Scotland under 15 Girls Champions in a row and the Club won the local Inter Club autumn competition ("The Drumchapel Tournament") 16 years in a row. Thorn Park also won an award for being the best club in the area.

Since then there have been two further major improvements in the courts and facilities. In 1987 the three Tennisquick courts were replaced by good quality Astroturf. These were a great success but by 2000 they were no longer of good quality. Another major effort to improve the club's facilities was therefore launched. Again this was highly successful and all six courts were laid out in top specification Astroturf and the 1971 floodlights were replaced. This along with a major refurbishment of the clubhouse has provided Thorn Park with outstandingly good facilities which are now being enjoyed by a large and ever increasing membership. These improvements also led to great achievements in 2001 when the club was awarded

"WEST OF SCOTLAND CLUB OF THE YEAR and TENNIS SCOTLAND CLUB OF THE YEAR".

The awards were in recognition of the many successes of the club during that year but in particular the Junior Section. The Junior players succeeded not only in Scottish events but also in British events with the Girls U 13 team coming third in Britain in the National Junior Club League Finals. Thorn Park also became one of the founding participants in the Bearsden Community Tennis Partnership taking tennis into the local schools and the local community. The major improvement in facilities has been paralleled by a major increase in coaching activity. Although the summer Saturday morning coaching, which still involves amateur volunteers, still happens and is still appreciated by its many participants a huge expansion of coaching led by two professional coaches throughout the week and throughout the year has been put in place. This excellent coaching is bearing further fruit - earlier this year six out of twelve members of two age group teams selected to play for the West of Scotland were from Thorn Park. At the same time the Club is maintaining a very strong family connection. Many of our excellent Juniors are the sons and daughters of active senior members, some of whom have joined recently but others of whom have been mainstays of the Club for decades.

With these facilities, the strong coaching and continuing family involvement the Club is now looking forward with confidence to its Senior teams returning to the highest levels of competition and an altogether positive future.

Some of the past champions who attended the West of Scotland Junior Centenary Championships held at Thorn Park in June 2004

THORNTONHALL c1880

Thorntonhall tennis courts were laid out by Robert Osborne in the early 1880s. Robert Osborne, who was born in Braehead, bought the "Hall" in 1847. He was a farmer, lime manufacturer and merchant of Kilbride Cheese in Glasgow's Candleriggs.

In 1880, Osborne's attention turned to property speculation. He published his feuing plan of part of the Thorntonhall Estate. There were to be 107 feus, although only 8 houses were built by Glasgow businessmen. His tennis courts were laid out and he died in 1884.

The tennis courts are seen in very early maps and still stand in the same position today.

It would appear that Thorntonhall Tennis Club was built up from the mid 1890s as there are records from the results of the 1908 league, where Thorntonhall Ladies, came in second, in Division 2. From here Thorntonhall were successful and from the 1939 results, the Men finished top of Division 3 and the Ladies were 2nd in Division 3 as well. After the war Thorntonhall did not participate in the Leagues untill 1950. By 1958 there were no teams in the Leagues.

Now in 2003 just over 100 years later, Thorntonhall is making a come back. It will take a good number of years to build the Club up to the level that they will have enough members to be able to compete in the Tennis Leagues, however with great support and encouragement from Nicola Kerr, the County Development Officer, they are making progress to upgrade the courts and facilities.

We have to start at the bottom and build on enthusiasm and encourage the Juniors, Intermediates and Seniors, which we re doing with the help of our coach Steve Moodie. We hope it will not be too long till we are back working our way up the Leagues.

Keith Buchanan who was President of the West of Scotland LTA in 1921 and presented the West Of Scotland Ladies Singles Championship Cup in 1920 was a member of Thorntonhall. Mrs Keith Buchanan won the West Singles in 1925, and with her brother DL Craig won the Mixed Doubles 5 times from 1921 to 1926 and the Ladies Doubles with Miss AB Macdonald in 1920, 1921, 1923,1924, 1925.

In 1934 RB White was President of the West of Scotland LTA, as was JC Marshall in 1947.

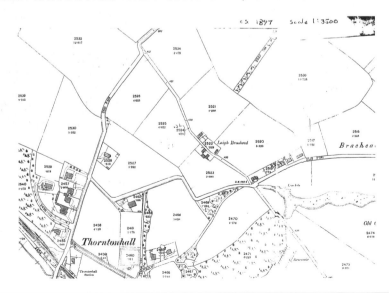

TITWOOD LAWN TENNIS CLUB 1890

As the garden suburb of Pollokshields developed in the southside of Glasgow in the late nineteenth century, the demand for sports facilities grew and following a meeting in 1889 a decision was taken by local gentlemen to form a bowling and tennis club. The Club opened in 1890 on the site of a local nursery at Titwood, close to the Clydesdale Cricket Ground. The inauguration ceremony in August 1890 was well covered in the local press and the cartoon opposite featured in the "Bailie", a weekly magazine.

The tennis section began with an initial membership of 211 but soon went into decline as the new craze of cycling took over. In 1903 tennis began again and since then play has been continuous including during the period of the two world wars.

The original blaes courts remained virtually unchanged until 1989 when two new all-weather courts were built behind the original pavilion. The money to buy the court was raised by a combination of tennis club funds, grants and loans raised by the Development Committee. The new courts were opened by the centenary President Miranda McLean and the practice of all-year-round tennis began at Titwood. Since then a further three courts have been converted to all-weather with a floodlighting system to enable evening play.

Members of Titwood's Men's first Team with the 1965 Scottish Cup & Rowan Cup

When the tennis club reformed in 1903 there were 75 gentlemen and 85 ladies and no junior section. Seventeen year olds were allowed to play from 1913 and 10-15 year olds were allowed to play during the war in 1914-1918. During the 1920s and 30s tennis was very popular but during the Second World War membership declined to 8-10. The Club, however, was held together by prominent figures such as George B. Primrose and by the late 1950s the Club had 200 members. By the late 70s and mid 1980s the membership was strong with around 400 members.

In the period since the centenary the membership has consolidated and family membership and the junior section form an important part of the Club.

Over the years Titwood has provided not only a sports facility for its members but also a great deal of social activity from flannel dances, Cinderella Balls of the early period to discos, car treasure hunts, barbecues and dances.

As far as success in tennis in Scotland is concerned Titwood topped the Men's First Division in 1912 and 1913 and won the Calcutta Cup in 1956. In the 1950s and 1960s the men's team consistently led the First Division League and in 1965 won the Scottish Cup with the help of such outstanding players as Colin V. Baxter.

Opening Tournament, April 1990

In the last quarter of the century, the main emphasis at Titwood was to provide a sporting facility for local families and especially for children to develop an interest in the game. Both the men's and ladies' teams continue to contribute to competitive tennis supported by a coaching regime which encourages success.

Titwood celebrates special occasions by holding dinner dances for their Scottish Cup wins and for individuals who have given outstanding service to the Club. One such occasion was a Dinner to honour George B. Primrose who gave outstanding service to tennis and became Vice-President of the Lawn Tennis Association.

Successful Juniors

UDDINGSTON 1883

As Uddingston Bowling Club the Club was formed in 1863. The original cash books from 1863 are held by the Club. The Minutes exist from 1897 onwards but very brief and the early entries contain little information beyond new tennis members and when the courts opened for the particular season.

However, consideration of the Cash Book shows a "Tennis Court" account from 1883 onwards. In 1883 several dozen balls were purchased from the Argyle Rubber Co and others. The account shows 21 people having paid membership fees, probably all Ladies.

The accounts for early 1883 show payments of reasonably substantial sums to various people to account for their estimates. Unfortunately no detail is provided and it is not clear whether these estimates related to construction of a tennis court or courts.

By 1894 the printed abstract of the accounts show the Club as "Uddingston Bowling and Tennis Club".

By 1889 the membership had reached 67, consisting of 40 Ladies and 27 Gentlemen. This compares more than favourably with 1999 when the adult membership of the Club numbered 48 although admittedly there were approximately 100 Juniors.

Uddingston Gents played in Division 1 of the first West of Scotland League in 1905, playing fourteen matches and winning seven of them.

Uddingston Ladies played in the first Ladies League in 1906 playing eight games and winning five.

In 1921 the men won the Calcutta Cup.

The Club continued to participate in the Leagues and in 1933 the Gents team were in Division 6 and the Ladies in D 7 and 11. Over the years the teams meandered within a Division or two however the Junior team fared better. A team was first entered in 1947, when there were only two Divisions, and in 1950 they were second and gained promotion and went on to win Division 1 in 1951.

The Mens teams settled in to a climb during the late 1950s and reached D 2 in 1962 thereafter settling in about D 4. The Ladies were mostly about D 4 and commenced a move up by winning D 4a in 1974. By the early 1980s they had reached D 1 and apart from 1990/91 have remained in D1 or 2 ever since. (The Premier Division was created in season 1992). The Men's team have maintained position in D 4 or 5 except 1990 when they were in D 3 for a season. Throughout this time both the teams have been supported by second teams. For much of this era there were also two Junior teams.

There were also some Cup successes in the Clydesdale Cup Division 2, winning in 1981, 1984, 1989 and 1991.

The Club has recently upgraded the courts to four artificial grass with floodlights as well as superior clubhouse facilities.

UPLAWMOOR 1963

The Tennis Club was instituted at a public meeting in the Muir Hall, Uplawmoor in November 1963. An interim committee was formed to investigate costs and possible sources of financial assistance and when they reported the results of their investigations to a general meeting in 1964 a Club Committee was elected with Mr. Jack Walker as President.

The District Council gave the Club a site, rent free, in the Playing Fields as well as a substantial grant. This, added to the financial help given by the Scottish Education Department and the Playing Field Association, subscriptions of founder members and funds raised from functions and various donations, allowed the Club to have two courts laid.

Play began in August 1964 only nine months after the first public meeting.

In 1966 the Club succeeded in having a third court made and entered two teams in the West of Scotland Leagues.

Uplawmoor remains a small village Club with the three original blaes courts which are standing the test of time. We now have two ladies teams, one in Division 4 and one in Division 7. The Gents Team is in Division 7 and the Junior Boys Team in Division 3 but Junior Girls have no team at the moment, sharing a difficulty with many Clubs of keeping the interest of girls in the game of tennis.

This Club has produced two County players of note; Keith Walker in the 1970s who played at Junior Wimbledon and more recently in the 90s Nicola Burns who became Scottish Ladies Champion. They both started playing in Uplawmoor later moving to larger Clubs in their teens.

Elizabeth Scott, Alison Todd, Jack Walker, lady unknown, John Pollock, Sandy McIlwham

WEIR RECREATION 1919

The Club was officially opened in 1919 mainly for employees of Weir Pumps Ltd. On 10th April 1920 the Club held its first match practice starting at 6.00 pm. This was the first season we competed against other Tennis Clubs in the West of Scotland League.

The Club have four honorary members. Agnes Dinse joined in 1948 when the Associate Membership was 12s. 6d. and celebrated 46 years as a member. Josephine Costley has been in the Tennis Club for a mere 36 years, 32 of them playing in the Ladies' Team. She also served as Tennis Convenor for many years. Tom Rae was the driving force in the preparation and line-laying of the courts each season and was Tennis Convenor over many years. Amanda Gray was created an honorary member for her fundraising efforts to upgrade the courts and improve the Clubhouse.

Leading lights in Weirs Opening Day 1980
3rd left - Lindsay McKendrick, 4th left - Tom Rae, 6th left - Anna Robertson,
8th left - Carol Costley, 9th left - Joey Costley

Weir Recreation Club has been well served over the years by some excellent Tennis Convenors. The Committees have also kept the Club going through some difficult times when membership was low. During the 75th anniversary celebrations the members of the Club thanked their Honorary Members as well as past and present Tennis Convenors for their excellent work.

Throughout the years the blaes courts were regarded as the best in the West of Scotland and were regularly used for ties in the Junior and Senior West of Scotland Championships. The Club has always been friendly but competitive and we hope that this continues for many years to come.

The successes of the Club are considerable. The highest division the Ladies and Gents Teams have played in is the Second Division. Currently there are three Gents and one Ladies Teams.

Year	Event	Result	Players
1975	Junior Calcutta Cup Winner	Team	T. Rae, C. Jaap, R. Bhalla, B. Stoddart.
1976	West of Scotland Plate Gents Doubles	Runner Ups	C. Jaap, B. Stoddart
1986	Prestwick Tournament	Ladies Doubles Winners	L. Conroy, J. Costley
1986	Poloc Centeneray Tournament	Mixed Doubles Runner Up	C. Jaap, I. Jaap
1987	West of Scotland President		T. Rae, C. Jaap, R. Bhalla, B. Stoddart.
1988	Senior Calcutta Cup Semi-Finalists		C. Jaap, A. Andrew, S. Gray, L. McKendrick
1991	West of Scotland Plate Gents Singles	Winner	C. Jaap
1991	Whitecraigs Volkswagen Ratings Tournament	Gents Singles Winner	C. Jaap
1991	Craigholm Volkswagen Ratings Tournament	Gents Singles Winner	C. Jaap
1991	Bearsden Volkswagen Ratings Tournament	Gents Singles Winner	S. Gray
1993	Bearsden Volkswagen Ratings Tournament	Gents Singles Winner	S. Gray
1992	Clarkston Volkswagen Ratings Tournament	Gents Singles Winner	S. Gray
1993	Poloc Volkswagen Ratings Tournament	Gents Singles Winner	S. Gray
1971	Weirs Jubilee Cup	Winners	
1972	Weirs Jubilee Cup	Winners	
1973	Weirs Jubilee Cup	Winners	
1975	Weirs Jubilee Cup	Winners	
1976	Weirs Jubilee Cup	Winners	
1977	Weirs Jubilee Cup	Winners	
1978	Weirs Jubilee Cup	Winners	
1994	Weirs Jubilee Cup	Winners	
	Clydesdale Cup	Runners Up	Twice
1994 - Date	West of Scotland Veterans Team	Player	Lindsay McKendrick
1997 - Date	Four Nations Veterans Internationals	Player	Lindsay McKendrick

WESTERMAINS 1965

Situated in Kirkintilloch the Westermains Club quickly established itself.

'The Club's first appeared in the Leagues in 1972, just after the Leagues Divisions had been divided into a,b, and c sections which allowed clubs to progress faster when they were successful. The Ladies were in Division 7c and were second winning six out of their seven matches, while the Men won seven out of eight matches to win Division 7a.

In 1974 the Ladies were in D 4b won D 4b, again winning seven out of eight matches. The Ladies won D 3 in 1983 winning eight out of nine matches, while the Men were in the middle of D 2. The Ladies were promoted to Division 1 in 1988 and played there for three seasons. In 1992 the Premier Division, which was smaller than the old Division 1 and teams would play home and away, was created altering the numbering of the remaining Divisions starting with a Division 1 etc. Westermains Ladies won the new Division 1 in 1992 and played in the Premier and were there for the next four seasons, then decline saw them move down till they played in D4a in 2001. The men played in Division 4b in 2002.

The people most involved with the Club have been Tom and Tilly Adams and their daughters Ruth, Sally and Shirley who took the Club to the top.

WESTERN 1924

Western Lawn Tennis and Squash Club was opened in 1924 having been promoted by a group of individuals who founded the Western Lawn Tennis Company which purchased the ground.

The original Clubhouse was a standard wooden type pavilion with balconies, toilets and wash hand basins but with no shower facilities or heating and the playing facilities consisted of 6 Blaes doubles courts and 1 singles court which was reserved primarily for coaching.

The Club continued with these facilities until the early sixties at which time 3 of the Blaes courts were upgraded to all weather Tennisquik and floodlit. This was a welcome initiative which allowed, for the first time, all-year-round play. However, the absence of heating and showering facilities in the Clubhouse had the consequence that only the more enthusiastic members availed themselves of this additional facility.

During the 1950s the Club amalgamated with the Kelvinside Tennis Club who had a four court set up on Beaconsfield Road. This Club had suffered from falling membership and its facilities were utilised by Western for the benefit of their Junior Members.

The condition of the Beaconsfield site deteriorated due to lack of use and demand and the site was sold in the late 1960s to the Nuffield Organisation for the development of a Nursing Home. The price realised was £15,000.

This sum was sufficient to develop a new brick-built Clubhouse complete with all facilities including showers, two Squash Courts and a Bar.

Due to the demand for Squash the Clubhouse was later extended to provide a third Squash Court and additional social space.

The limitations of the Tennisquik courts eventually became apparent and these courts were upgraded in the early 80s with improved floodlighting with assistance from the L.T.A. The chosen finish was artificial sand-filled grass which proved to be an outstanding success.

These courts highlighted the limitations of the remaining Blaes courts and the Club eventually obtained assistance from Sport Scotland and the L.T.A. which enabled them to create a further 3 grass courts complete with floodlights.

Western was one of the first Clubs to follow the lead set by Whitecraigs in employing a full-time professional Coach. This development allowed the Club to promote a very popular Junior coaching regime in addition to adult lessons. The success of the initiative has resulted in the need for several part-time coaches to assist the head coach who also effectively manages the day-to-day running of the Club.

For many years during the 70s and early 80s the Club ran regular Discos and similar functions to supplement its income as the sport subscriptions were not sufficient to maintain the Club's facilities. These eventually became too popular with the result that neighbouring proprietors became restive and these were eventually discontinued.

This resulted in a substantial floor area being available for other purposes and the Club developed a Gymnasium with modern exercise machines which has proved to be extremely popular and has attracted a very considerable number of additional members. This initiative has also helped to meet the competition from the new commercial sports facilities at Anniesland and Milngavie (Next Generation and Esporta)

International Club of Great Britain v. Scottish Select played at Western L.T.C. 14th May 1954
Miss Doris Hart (USA) & Mrs Heather Brewer (Bermuda)

In the early 90s the Club entered into an arrangement with the Western Bath Club which allows for reciprocal use of facilities within defined limits.

In the early 1950s the Club was privileged to host several exhibition matches under the auspices of the Scottish Lawn Tennis Association. They featured a Scottish Select team versus the International Club of Great Britain and Exhibition Matches and were open to the public. They involved the following distinguished players:

14th May 1954

Doris Hart	Wimbledon Singles Winner 1951, Wimbledon Runner Up 1947, 48, 53. In addition she won 3 Doubles and 5 Mixed Titles.
Heather Brewer	Bermuda, Now Mrs Abe Segal. She won the Welsh Ladies Singles and the Midlands Counties
GP(Pat) Hughes	Wimbledon Men's Doubles Winner 1936 and Wimbledon Men's Doubles Runner Up 1937. With Fred Perry and Austin Hughes won the Davis Cup for Great Britain, 1933-1936.
J.A.T. Horn	Junior Champion of Great Britain in 1948 and 1949.

The following well known Scottish and West of Scotland Players represented Western

Ian Walker	Tommy Walker	Graham Downes	Ian Conway
Russell Howat	Seamus Donald	Pat Dorman	Ian Campbell

The Club has participated in all of the Scottish and West of Scotland Competitions with successes as follows

Gents 1st Team
West of Scotland League Division 1.

Scottish Cup 1952, 74, 76, 77, 78
1947, 68, 71, 73, 74, 75, 76, 85

Clydesdale Cup Mixed Doubles Division 1 Winners

1965, 67, 70, 73, 76, 77

Ladies 1st Team

West of Scotland League Division 1 1967, 70

West End District Shield

The Club has been regular Winners.

Apart from participating in the Leagues at various levels the following members served as Presidents of the West of Scotland   1952 H. Herbert   1972 Rachael McNair.

1976 Division 1 Champions
L-R P Gregory, I Conway, P Dorman, I Walker (Captain)
T Walker, R Howat, C Donald

WESTERTON 1914

The Garden City Suburb Recreation Club was formed on 5th June 1914 when fifteen people attended an inaugural meeting. There was one grass tennis court which required to be carefully rolled each night after play. In 1919 the name was changed to Westerton Tennis Club. A second court was added in 1922 at the cost of £190 and a third court added in 1938 at a cost of £327. About this time George Whitelaw donated a medal to mark the birth of his daughter Moira Whitelaw (now Mrs. Fruish). This was used for competition. George Whitelaw has a grandchild presently a playing member.

Some fun at the 24 hour Tennisathon

A hut was built with donations from local people on ground granted by the local council. Later, a two storey building was erected on the site. During the war there was no play and afterwards it resumed with as much vigour as before. Hard courts were eventually laid on the surface and one was floodlit.

The Club still functions with approximately 40 Seniors and 20 Juniors fielding one Ladies and one Gents team. Coaching is available to members and to Juniors.

Junior winners 1999

Mrs. Mina Brady is the Club's Honorary President. She was honoured because of her many years' work with the Club, raising funds, being Match Secretary and providing coaching.

Some fun at the 24 hour Tennisathon

The Saturday am coaching class

WHITECRAIGS LAWN TENNIS & SPORTS CLUB 1927

Whitecraigs Lawn Tennis and Sports Club has played a tremendous part in the South Side and the society that resides there. It still remains very much part of the social fabric of Whitecraigs and Newton Mearns. Having recently celebrated the 75th Birthday, it is touching that over 20 past presidents are still active members.

Past Presidents

Since the grand opening by the Hon Laurence and Mrs Methuen on a summer's day on 18th June 1927, the club has played host to various sporting and social events, and been the heart of tennis culture in the south side of Glasgow.

Prior to the opening of the Club, several committees were formed, which brought about the basis of the club, with many of them still standing today although many of the original features of the Club that were original fixtures have progressed.

For instance, when the telephone was introduced to the club, the charge was 1d for each call. This charge has increased considerably since. Then there was the piano, which had to be purchased to enable the club to have permission to let the pavilion.

It would be a novel sight to see the juniors gathered round the piano singing in this day and age, or for the main source of entertainment to comprise of dances with the piano in the background.

Whilst mentioning Juniors, it was in 1928 that the Junior Associates petitioned for greater rights within the Club, but it was not until 1963 that it was proposed that the junior playing hours should be altered to give them equal rights with senior members.

As it reached the 1930s, the actual Tennis-playing in the Club was building up to success. The league competitions for both ladies and gentlemen reaped success, with the Ladies' team winning all their matches and getting promoted from the 7th to the 5th Division. The Gentleman also managed to retain their position in the 8th Division.

1932 was a year of reward for the Ladies' team, which was unfortunately not shared by the Gents. The Ladies' managed to be promoted to the 4th Division, yet for the Gents, it was thought that they, 'might, with more intensive practice, gain a higher position in the competition.'

The Club itself has gone through some major and some minor transformations over the years. In 1933, following ongoing complaints from the public about parking on Roddinghead Road, a car park was finally completed.

The 1960s also saw Whitecraigs receive more support for improvement. The club was awarded a Capital Grant of £5,750 from the Scottish Education Department under the Physical Training and Recreation Act 1937.

This was part of an £11,500 scheme to build two squash courts and a viewing lounge connected to the far side of the existing clubhouse together with a complete renovation of the changing and kitchen facilities.

As the 60s started swinging, the Whitecraigs Juniors began to feel the effects when in 1963 they saw the proposal to alter the Junior playing hours to give them equal rights with Senior members. This was perhaps a move resulting from the formation of the Junior Committee in 1958. In 1966 the Club was going from strength to strength, with the membership standing at 300 seniors and 200 juniors, a vast difference from the 57 'ordinary members', 79 'lady associates' 33 juniors and 26 honorary members of 1928.

Chris Hart

That year also saw the club acting as Host-Club to the West of Scotland Lawn Tennis Association for their 73rd Annual Tournament, and again in 1967 for the 74th Annual Tournament, which this time, was covered by Scottish Television.

The Club also saw an extra success in 1967 with squash making an appearance, with Whitecraigs joining the West of Scotland Squash Rackets League Division "B".

Socially, the 60s saw the introduction of plans to provide the Club with a bar and lounge in 1967. This would be a welcome addition following in the Club's tradition of "dances". They were very successful with the support of stars such as Lulu, Aker Bilk and Lonnie Donnegan performing. The Clyde Valley Stompers, too, were often a fixture at the Club.

As the 1980s approached it was time for the juniors to stamp their mark in Whitecraigs Tennis Club. In 1980, for the third year running, the Junior Team won the 1st Division. Then in 1981 both the junior teams excelled in their games and won their respective leagues, with the second team finding themselves promoted to Division 2b.

Throughout the years Whitecraigs has played host to many events, and 1981 was no different. Although this time it was not only for fellow-Scottish clubs, this year was more national and extended to teams from Wales and Ireland as well as Scotland, for the 'Triangular Tennis International', sponsored by En-Tous-Cas.

In regard to Whitecraigs other prominent sport, the squash teams were reaping success in the 1980s. The Gents 1st team managed to retain their position in the 2nd Division of the highly acclaimed Scottish League.

Graham Neill

The interest in squash improved in the 1980s, with a great amount of enthusiasm in the area, with the mini leagues and tournaments being greatly supported.

Along with tennis and squash, Whitecraigs has also supported a diverse range of sporting activities throughout the years, curling, ski-ing and darts to name but a few, with curling being the most jubilant. The Curling section had a successful season in 1981, with around 70 members playing in club leagues, Provincial competitions and friendly matches.

INTERNATIONAL EVENTS...

Whitecraigs featured in the growth of World Veterans' Team Competitions during the 1990s. In 1995 the ITF (International Tennis Federation) invited the club to host the Britannia Cup - the Official ITF World Team Championship for Veteran Male players of 65 Years and over.

14 Countries sent teams to Glasgow for the week-long event including Austria, South Africa, Israel, Finland and Canada. The USA team won the event and Heinz Funhoff, the ITF representative at the Championships, reported that the players had an enjoyable and memorable stay in Glasgow.

In 1998, the club was invited to host the Fred Perry Cup Men's 50 ITF Veteran Team competition in which 15 Countries sent teams of 3 or 4 players plus a non-playing captain. During the week the club hosted a 'Welcome party' and a 'Ceilidh' in the clubhouse and a Gala Dinner was held in The Trades House of Glasgow.

Both events were organised by a committee of members and friends and their week involved organising accommodation, driving courtesy cars and buses and taking the teams on sightseeing trips when the players and guests had a day off.

The Great Britiain Davis Cup Team 2003
Alan Mackin back row 3rd from left, Miles McLagan 5th from left
Front row, David Brewer 5th from left

Austin Smith, the ITF representative congratulated the club on the welcome it gave to players from Australia, Sweden, Turkey, Costa Rica, USA and Spain amongst others. He had travelled around the world to many similar events and felt that this event was the friendliest and the best-organised event he had been at.

The Whitecraigs club also had the pleasure of hosting the Official Dinner in October 1995 for the Maureen Connolly International Ladies Match between Great Britain and the USA. The event was played at the Scotstoun Indoor Tennis Centre and the lavish Dinner, which was sponsored by Ecosse à la Carte, was held in the newly-refurbished Whitecraigs clubhouse. Amongst those attending was a former President of the US Tennis Association and Anne Jones, the former Wimbledon Champion.

Finally, it goes without saying that Whitecraigs Lawn Tennis and Sports Club would not be here today for the West of Scotland Tennis Centenary 2004, without the dedication and support through the years from the various Committees, and above all, the members who are, without a doubt the vital ingredients of the Club.

From the very beginning there has been growing support, and it is a warming feeling that even after many years past presidents are still supporting the Club as active members. The number of members is still growing from the opening in 1927, with it standing at 963 today.

Alan Mackin and David Brewer

Two of the best players to emerge from Scotland, ALAN MACKIN and DAVID BREWER spent their formative tennis years in the West of Scotland.

Indeed there are a number of parallels in the way Alan and David developed their prodigious talents. Both were brought up in Paisley and are from families with a strong sporting pedigree. They became junior members at Whitecraigs Lawn Tennis & Sports Club at a very young age where they worked exceptionally hard under the tutelage of Club Coach, John Howie and former President, Alastair Smith.

In their early teens both reached the top of the junior game not just in Scotland but in Britain and beyond. As their tennis travels began to take them worldwide, both Alan and David moved from Scotland to advance their professional tennis careers. In 2003, their paths crossed in a way which brought much pride, not least to their home club of Whitecraigs and to the West of Scotland L.T.A.

Both were in Australia in January 2003 for the Davis Cup-tie between Great Britain and Australia played at the Olympic Arena in Sydney.

Alan opened the tie for the Great Britain team playing creditably in his singles match against Mark Philippousis who was to become runner-up later in the year at Wimbledon. David was one of the two junior players given the experience of being attached to the G.B. squad. A great achievement then for the two young players from the West of Scotland.

WISHAW 1898

In 1898 the master of Bellhaven and Stenton of Wishaw House gave permission for two courts and a clubhouse to be built on the field near to Wishaw West Cross known as Flemington Park. Around 1922, following the war, two more courts were added and a much larger Clubhouse built. In the late 1950s Wishaw Estate was broken up and the Tennis Club bought the land at an auction sale. The Clubhouse was finally pulled down in 1990 following constant vandalism.

The Club started negotiations with North Lanarkshire Council in 1995 and was provided with three all weather courts for a payment of £36,000 and an annual rent. This facility was at Wishaw Sports Centre and the Club found that having no Clubhouse of their own was a big disadvantage.

WOODEND TENNIS AND BOWLING CLUB 1908

Woodend Bowling and Tennis Club was founded in 1909 after a meeting was convened of around one hundred ladies and gentlemen and took place in the United Free Church, Woodend Drive on the 5th December 1908. The meeting was the result of a discussion by a disgruntled section of Jordanhill Bowling Club and took place underneath the railway bridge at Jordanhill. They decided to ascertain what support could be found from the neighbourhood for the formation of a new club, given that their club had turned down the proposal of moving to a new site at Woodend. Two bowling greens, four tennis courts and a pavilion were estimated to cost £1300- £1500 pounds, raised by donations and loans. The meeting carried this unanimously and agreed that the club be called Woodend Bowling and Tennis Club, Jordanhill.

The first general meeting of the club was held on the 2nd March 1909 with 150 members present. Office Bearers and Directors were elected and the annual subscriptions were set at 25s. for gents, 15s. for ladies and 10s. for Juniors.

By the end of the month additional ground had been acquired and the committee had agreed to construct a further three tennis courts. Exactly 6 months after the inception of the club, the opening ceremony took place on the 5th July 1909. Mrs Watson, wife of the Vice-President performed the opening ceremony of the tennis courts by serving the first ball across the net. Thereafter an exhibition of tennis was played on the courts and all the proceedings were reported in the Glasgow Herald.

In July 1909 the Ladies and Gents Tennis Championships were instituted. In 1912, the West of Scotland Lawn Tennis Association was granted use of the tennis courts for their tournaments, a courtesy frequently extended in later years.

During the Great War of 1914, 11 members were killed in action.

The club held the first Annual Dinner on the 15th January 1920 and the last of these 4 years later.

Our coach Ross MacDonald with Juniors

Having fun at one of our fundraising days

The official opening of the 'new' clubhouse took place on the 12 Nov 1928 regarded as one of the finest in the West of Scotland. The clubhouse cost £2900 11s. 4d.!!

The West of Scotland introduced Junior Leagues in 1938 and a year later Woodend entered a team and won the First division. Over the years the Club consistently had two teams in the Leagues when other Clubs had only one and that policy continues today.

In 1939 the north tennis courts were relaid. During the war years inter-club matches were played but the club had real difficulty in procuring new tennis balls and in getting assistance to keep the courts in playing condition. A lot of their concerns were to raise funds for the war-effort.

In the post-war era tennis was back on a high profile and the club flourished over the next few decades. A proposal that Sunday tennis be permitted between the hours of 2 pm – 6 pm was defeated. This decision was reached after consulting householders in the immediate vicinity of the Club who found the proposal unfavourable (democracy has its disadvantages).

The club membership was healthy and vibrant. Many competitions were hosted at Woodend during the sixties and seventies, the most notable of these being the Stella Artois tournmament.

Four new, hard-surface tennis courts were laid during the eighties, but unfortunately the lifespan of these courts was only fifteen years. It was now clearly evident that the tennis facilities needed upgrading.

Most tennis clubs were now offering their members astro-turf tennis courts and Woodend needed to move with the times. The committee decided to apply to the National Lottery for funding and after much hard work by the committee, led by Mr Miles Baigent, the club was rewarded with a grant to construct four new astro-turf courts. This meant that tennis members could now play on a total of seven courts, three upgraded blaes courts and four brand new astro-turf courts.

This project provided fresh impetus for the club who had already introduced a comprehensive tennis coaching programme for both junior and senior members under the direction of a professional coach.

Under 14 Boys Team 2003

The fruits of this programme are becoming evident through the raising of the standard of play of the senior members and club tennis teams and the quality and quantity of the junior tennis players. There is no doubt that this highly successful programme has been greatly enhanced by the new courts.

Club competitions continue to be very successful and cater for a wide range of members. All tennis players, no matter their ability, can always find a tournament suitable to their needs.

The club continues to thrive off the courts where a succession of hard-working committees ensure that the tennis members enjoy a variety of social functions and the feeling of being a member of Woodend Tennis Club is greatly encouraged.

Club successes include reaching the final of the Calcutta Cup in 1934 when they were narrowly beaten by Clarkston. In 1935 they reached the final of the Mixed Doubles Clydesdale Cup and again lost in the finals to Clarkston Club. In 1952 Woodend II reached the final of the Junior Calcutta Cup and lost to Clyde Paper.

WEST OF SCOTLAND VETERANS' LAWN TENNIS CLUB 1982

The West of Scotland Veterans' Lawn Tennis Club was formed in 1982 for Ladies of 40 or over and Men of 45 or over.

JB Wilson was instrumental in its foundation and he explains here what the Club is all about.

The Club was asked to represent Scotland in the British Inter-County Cup Competition and managed to reach the quarter-final stage, being defeated by Warwickshire at Newlands Lawn Tennis Club. We were delighted to welcome on that day quite a number of spectators and hope they enjoyed the tennis played in a rather sedate but competitive manner. It was interesting to see the reaction of some of the younger spectators to what must have seemed strange behaviour:

> ***Calling out the Score!***
> ***Saying "Good shot" to an opponent!***
> ***Serving from behind the baseline!!!***
> ***Positioning the singles sticks in the correct place!***

Much effort has been expended in the last twenty years by dedicated tennis officials to assist and encourage our Junior players, but it is disturbing to find that many do not continue to participate later in life. Is it the lure of the warm, comfortable golf clubhouse, or the deceptive belief that a stationary ball will be easier to hit that loses them to our game?

We are well accustomed to travel Jim Wood travelled 1200 miles to compete in two away matches.

Ferguslie Tournament - 'waiting to play'

Veterans' tennis is thriving. There are now 45 teams in 8 Divisions for Men and 77 teams in 13 Divisions for Ladies in the West of Scotland Veterans' Leagues played in August to October. There are Veterans' tournaments indoor as well as outdoor throughout Great Britain.

The "West Vets" have 4 or 5 "Meets" usually on a Sunday and mostly at Inverclyde, Sport Scotland's National Training Centre. They also have a weekend in January or February usually at at Stirling's Gannochy Centre. It is a very active group.

Veterans meet at Inverclyde

THOSE THAT WERE

Many Clubs existed only for a short time others like Partickhill and Ferguslie only ceased in the past year or so. The Domestic Science College and University were Student Clubs. A great many were recreational Clubs whose grounds were provided by employers for the benefit of their employees and as the firms sold the land or ceased business and sometimes the membership from employees dropped so that there were more associate members than workers, so in turn did these clubs fold.

This list has only as much information as is possible from the League tables which the Association has available and therefore may not be complete.

Airdrie	Craigton
Albion Motors	Crookston
Alexandra	Dalmuir
Alexandria	Drumpellier
Anchor Line	Drysdale Recreation
Babcox & Wilcox	Domestic Science College
Baillieston	Dumbarton
Barclay Curle	Elderslie (became Strathgryffe)
Barr & Stroud	Erskine (became Bishopton)
Bellahouston	Fairfield Works
Bridge of Weir (became Strathgryffe)	Falcon
Brookfield Still exists not affiliated	Ferguslie
Brown & Polson (became CPC)	Ferguslie Mills
Cardonald	Foxley
Cathcart	Garrowhill
Cathcart OPC	Glasgow HSFP
Cartha	Glenfield
Chryston District	Golfhill
City Bakeries	Gourock
Civil Service	Greenock HSFP
Civil Service Riddrie	Halfway
Clyde Paper	Hallside
Clydesdale	Harland & Wolff
Coatbridge	Hawthorn
Coats Staff Club	Hillhead
Cowan Park	Hillington Estate
CPC	Hyndland School FP

India of Inchinnan

Jewish Athletic

Johnston COS (became Bishopbriggs)

Johnstone

Kelvindale

Kelvinside (joined with Western)

Kenmuir

Killermont

King's Park

Kingswood

Kirkintilloch MW

Kirktonfield

Knightswood

Langside Hill Church

Linthouse

Manswood

Maryhill

Mearns

Mechans

M.E.R.L.

Millbrae

Mosspark

Motherwell

Netherlee Church

Old Kilpatrick

Partick

Partickhill

Pollokshields

Port Glasgow

Possilpark

Pressed Steel

Public Parks

Queen's Park

Ralston

Rankin Park

Renfrew

Riddrie

Rolls Royce Hillington

Rolls Royce Lanarkshire

Rootes Motors

Rothley

Ruchill Ch

St Vincent

Sandyhills

Scotstounhill

Scottish Gas Board

Singer

Springboig

Stephen Rec

Templeton

University (Students)

Victoria Drive FP

Walsco

Weir

Wellhall

Whittinghame

Yarrow

BELLAHOUSTON before 1895

This was a founding club of the WSLTA and was highly successful in the Leagues and Cups. The Club reached the final of the West section of the Scottish Cup in 1896.

The McAlpine family were prominent players in the 1950s and 1960s. Anne McAlpine won the West of Scotland Ladies Singles four times 1960/61 and 1965/66. She played in many County matches. Brothers J and K McAlpine presented two pairs of cups for Confined Ladies and Men's Doubles(now called the West of Scotland Shield).

The property was owned by the Bellahouston Bequest and was rented to the club. The club ceased in 1969 at the time of M 8 roadworks

CARDONALD LAWN TENNIS CLUB 1926

Jenny Reid, Muriel Gilmour, Jean Colville, Joan Neil

Founded in 1926, the club managed to survive the difficulties of World War 2 with its three blaes courts and wooden clubhouse from the 1914-18 war intact.

Very much a club for local residents, its facilities were overwhelmed by returning servicemen and women. Social functions, fetes etc. were held and sufficient funds raised to construct the first two all-weather courts in Glasgow – though many said nobody would play tennis in winter in Scotland!

With improved playing conditions, the men's' team gained promotion from the 4th Division and eventually to the 1st. The ladies also gained promotion.

The club never produced a Davis Cup player but both the father and grandfather of Miles Maclagan were prominent team players.

Then disaster struck – the clubhouse was destroyed by fire. For three seasons, the match teas were held in the local café. It was back to fund raising and loans from members. Possibly the most difficult task of all was in obtaining a building licence. The new clubhouse was built with dressing rooms and hot showers and a large hall with hardwood floor suitable for dances. This was to enable the club to repay the loans from members.

The club had a thriving junior membership in 1973 but too few seniors to continue and sadly had to close.

Willie Perry, John Reid, Tom Masson,
David Brown, Louis Wiseman, Jas McLagan

COATS STAFF CLUB 1948

Reports in the Newsreel the firms Staff magazine in 1948 state that the teams have been doing well in the Leagues and that the Men's team were first in Division 10. Training films were shown in the Clubhouse and it was hoped that training would continue so that the staff would improve their game for the following season.

The Courts were at Crossmyloof and from time to time the WSLTA used the courts for some County Matches. The Men's team withdrew in 1964 and the Ladies had two more seasons.

GARROWHILL CIRCA 1936

Mr. George Kirk was the first President of the Club and ran the Club for many years. There were two tarmacadam courts and a wooden shed for storing equipment. During the war many members were called up to the forces and the Club was kept going by the yong teenage members. The courts were deteriorating and, on the advice of Mr. Kirk, they were relaid in red blaes and a groundsman was appointed to maintain them.

1946-1949 American T.
In front of Bowling Club and Tennis Pavilion.

It is an interesting point to note that the Tennis Club helped to found the Bowling Club when it opened a few years later.

After the war the Tennis Club managed to procure a wooden hut as a Clubhouse instead of sharing the Bowling Club House. Here they entertained their visitors.

Outing to Barrassie, June 1961.

The Club were members of the Airdrie and Coatbridge League for Mixed Doubles prior to joining the West of Scotland League. The Gents' team rapidly gained promotion from Division 16 and for several years running won divisions, ending up in Division 5A in 1973. The Club eventually entered a second Gents' Team and a Junior Team.

In 1976 Garrowhill won the Junior Calcutta Cup and a second time in 1983.

During the mid 1950s a third court was laid with the work being carried out by the members themselves under the direction of President Mr. Robert Sherry.

Garrowhill Juniors - Alan Wilson and Alan Lackie.

Garrowhill was well known for its summer outing to the seaside. This annual event was looked forward to by the members and their families and much enjoyed by all.

People who have made a success in Garrowhill Club include Mrs. Mathers, wife of the minister of Muir Memorial Church. She was an Irish Ladies Singles Champion. Syvia Ingles came from England and was a former County Champion. On the male side there was Eddie Stein who was Glasgow Parks Champion in the 1930s as well as Lindsey McKendrick and Alan Lackie who both began their tennis careers as junior members.

A disastrous fire due to vandalism finally closed the Club.

Outing to St. Andrews.

Lindsay McKendrick and I Ross

George Aitken and Lindsay McKendrick

GOLFHILL c1880s

There was mention of the existence of the club in "The Scottish Umpire in August 1884". The club was an early one in the development of tennis and was located in Dennistoun in Marne Street. There were courts on either side of the street. Dennistoun was being built with tenaments in the 1890s, with a suburban railway nearby.

There was an entry for the Scottish Cup in 1896.

Representatives from the club helped to run the West of Scotland Championships (there were four on the Committee from the north side of the City and four from the south).

The club disappeared after the second world war and Council houses were built on the site.

HILLHEAD prior to 1896

This Club is not to be confused with Hillhead High School FP and was located on ground now occupied by the BBC in Hamilton Drive. They had a good reputation for standard of play and their members played in the West of Scotland Leagues.

Tom Eastop was a member of this Club for many years from the 1940s and became a Club Champion at aged 18. The Club survived until the 1970s when the BBC expanded to build on the site. He now plays for Scotland in Veterans events.

Tom Eastop circa 1950

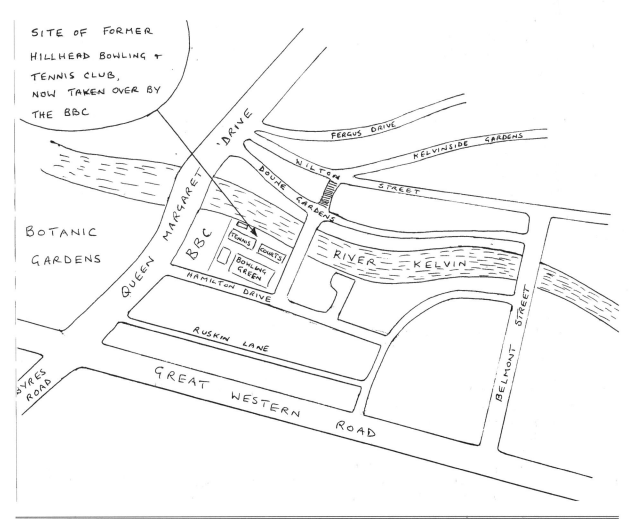

POLLOKSHIELDS c1870

The Pollokshields Athletic Club was founded about 1870 for the playing of football and cricket. It introduced tennis around 1878 in its old enclosure known as Pollok Park near Haggs Castle. In April 1886 the Club, which was devoting itself more and more to tennis and less and less to other pastimes, opened its enclosure in Maxwell Drive in 1886 with eight courts. A month later the first West of Scotland Championships were held there. The event was then known as the Pollokshields Athletic Club Tournament. More is written in the Chapter about the Championships.

From the outset this club dominated in the West of Scotland, gathering to itself the best of players. When the WSLTA commenced the Leagues in 1905 the club entered and won Division 1 without losing a match - played 14 won 14! This was an indication of the future dominance.

1906 saw the introduction of Ladies Leagues, where they won 7 out of 8 matches. The men fielding two teams won Divisions 1 and 2 without losing a match. The Men won Division 1 every year to 1911 and the Ladies to 1910.

In all Pollokshields Men won 21 times to 1954 and as results for 1956 and 1957 are not available it could be more. Newlands have won 27 times to 2003. Only five clubs had won Division 1 in the first fifty years , only seven to 1996 and nine to 2003!

The Ladies won Division 1 at least 23 times to 1963 (with 3 years where results are not known) and with Newlands Ladies winning 19 times to 2003

Other successes were Senior Calcutta Cup, Men's Singles and Doubles, (teams in Division 1 excluded) Pollokshields II ten wins to 1953 (Hamilton 7 wins to 2002) and the Clydesdale Cup, Mixed Doubles, 19 wins to 1962 (Newlands 19 wins to 2003)

There was dominance too in the Scottish Cup 11 wins to 1953 for the Men surpassed by Broomhill who won 14 years out of 15 years between 1979 and 1993, and Newlands who have 15 wins scattered between 1927 and 2003.

The Ladies too had a record of 10 wins to 1961, now surpassed by Dunfermline who had a run of 9 wins between 1988 and 1996 and have added three more since to take the record.

1899 Pollokshields Winners Scottish Cup

Many well known players played for Pollokshields Margaret Allan, Louise Anderson (Mrs Dick), Amy Baird, Clara Butters (Mrs Black), Cathie Dungliston, Heather Macfarlane(Mrs Harvey), Winnie Mason (Mrs Shaw), Irene Miller (Mrs McCready), May Thomson, Isobel Vallance (Mrs Kempsall).

Among the Men there were R Baird, R Barr, A Blair, JT Butters, Donald MacPhail Jr, Archie McVie, JH Neil, Eric Rayner, EH Taylor, JB Wilson, to 1949 there were 31 Champions recorded as having played for the Club.

The Championships had settled in to be played at Pollokshields, however, by the mid 1960s, the courts were in a poor state and the tournament moved to Whitecraigs. There have been several venues since and currently the venue has been Newlands for a few years.

The end had come and the decline continued and the courts finally closed. Flats have been built on the site. Had it survived it would have made a superb County Centre.

1954 Pollokshields Winners of Scottish Cup
(on right, Bulletin Cup is on left)
L-R Amy Baird, Magaret Allan, Rhona Hope
Front - Isobel Vallance, Clara Black, Heather MacFarlane

SCOTSTOUNHILL c1900

Scotstounhill Lawn Tennis Club was located at 633 Anniesland Road. The Club played in the fourth Division in 1906.

The most successful season was in 1938 when a young veterinary student called Alf Wight was playing in the team. You all know Alf Wight much better by his pen name James Herriot.

Jim Wight in his biography of his father entitled "The Real James Herriot" writes :-

Scotstounhill - Alf Wight on left

From the age of twenty he began to play tennis more regularly, joining the nearby Scotstounhill Tennis Club. Although tennis acted as a great antidote to his hours of study, he took the game very seriously and won a number of key matches in the West of Scotland Championships. His partner in these matches, and one with whom he practised for hours, was a young man called Colin Kesson, a fine player who taught Alf a great deal about the game. Alf could never get the better of him and would joke with his college chums that, apart from qualifying as a veterinary surgeon, his other ambition was to be able to say that he had - just once - managed to beat Colin Kesson."

N.B. The Championship was the Calcutta Cup where Scotstounhill reached the Final which they lost to Paisley. The Club also reached the Semi-final of the Clydesdale Cup Division 2.

Colin Kesson was the father of Colin Kesson who is a member of Dowanhill and a Past President of WSLTA.

After the war the club continued to the mid 1950s when they were no longer in the Leagues.

SPRINGBOIG 1895 - 1977

Opening Day 1974 - Myra Hunter, President. Dr Walter Caldwell opened courts

The Club was in the fourth Division in 1906 winning six of their twelve matches, and they progressed as a club over the years.

In 1926 Springboig won the Calcutta Cup and in 1934 lost in the Final of the West section of the Scottish Cup.

In 1927 EH Taylor won the West of Scotland Junior Singles and HC Macmillan won it in 1931.

In the early 1930s the Mens team were in the First Division being second in 1934 and RW Blakey and EH Taylor were selected to play for the West of Scotland County Team at Scarborough and the following year EH Taylor played in the team at Paignton. Thereafter the Pollokshields factor came into play and Taylor played for and represented Pollokshields in the County team 1936-1938. RW Blakey moved to another part of the country. Springboig were in D4 in 1937 and D 5 in 1939!

EH Taylor reached the Final of the WoS Championships in 1938 and lost to L Shaffi (London) in the Final. The following year he won the Final by beating HC Macmillan 6/4 4/6 6/3 6/0

There was a Junior team from the outset in 1937 and they won Division 1 in 1971.

The Ladies team were never higher than Division 4 in the 1930s and were as low as D7 in 1939. In the 1960s they had moved up to D 3 and even had a year in D2.

1939 H MacMillan and EH Taylor

Players and administrators who were noteable were Denise Donnachie, Doris Graham Club Champion 18 times, Susie Marshall (neé, Deans), George Deans, Rob Grassom, Ian Gibson, Evelyn Winkworth, Myra Hunter.

The Club declined in the 1970s and finally closed in 1977

THE GLASGOW PUBLIC PARKS LAWN TENNIS ASSOCIATION 1926

Public Parks as they were fondly called provided a huge amount of tennis in the city. The Parks frequently had many more courts than private clubs and were full most of the time. There were twelve courts at Alexandra Park and ten at both Tollcross and Glasgow Green and others had six. Apart from these three other Parks in the Leagues were Auldhouse, Cecil, Cowlairs, Elder, Ibroxhill, Kelvingrove, Knightswood, Maryhill, Radnor, Springburn, Victoria,

There was a League structure with at least three Ladies and three Men's Divisions. No park could have more than two Ladies and two Men's teams. Matches were home and away and were on fixed dates. The Home team paid for the match courts and since there were no facilities for entertaining hospitality was not a feature. There was however a feature that was unique to the Parks - there was an audience. Dozens of people would line the outside fence to watch play and if it were a match they would stay throughout. That was how youngsters learned how to play the game - watching others play.

Deerpark Ladies Team - League Winners 1947

In 1951 the Public Parks LTA celebrated their Silver Jubilee with a Ball in the City Chambers Glasgow, at which there was the Annual Awards of trophies

The Public Parks were affiliated to the WSLTA and selected teams to play in both the Ladies and Men's Leagues. The first West League entry was 1952 and they were placed in Division 7 and the second teams were in Ladies D 14 and Men in D16. Home games were played at Newlands Park as that was the only Park with a room in the Pavilion to provide match teas. Both Ladies and Men progressed to D 4. By 1961 the Ladies withdrew. It was a time when many Parks players went "Private" ie. they went to private clubs perhaps because it was cheaper.

In the latter days the Men's team played at Alexandra Park and the match teas were in the Nauld Café.

Tommy Flowerday was Secretary for a time and J Rankine Brown also gave service to the PPLTA and did coaching.

The Singles Championship was called the Rowan Trophy. Entry was at the club you played at and the competition played until there was a Park winner who then went on to play all the other Park winners. The entry could be enormous. The Finals were played at Newlands Park.

The Doubles were the Daily Record Cup for Men's Doubles, The Sunday Mail Cup for Women's Doubles and The Evening News Cup for Mixed Doubles. In 1931 there were 128 couples in the Men's Doubles and it was played during the Month of August at various Parks until the Finals which were at Newlands Park. Newspapers of the time record that the Parks were really flourishing where the Private clubs were not doing so well.

Alexandra Park had a groundsman called Mr Diamond who was very strict but fair in organising play. You had to stand in a queue to buy a ticket and the time allowed was 40 minutes of play he would go outside and call time eg Number five. You had to leave the court promptly. Dress was important and you had to wear

'Record' Doubles

Chance For Public Parks Tennis Players.

Public parks players are again given the opportunity of entering for the annual Doubles Championships promoted by the *Evening News, Daily Record, Sunday Mail* and the Glasgow Public Parks Lawn Tennis Association.

Matches will be decided over the best of three full sets.

The competitions will be played during the month of August as follows:—

MEN'S DOUBLES for "Daily Record" Cup.

WOMEN'S DOUBLES for "Sunday Mail" Cup.

MIXED DOUBLES for "Evening News" Cup.

What you have to do.

Fill in the entry form, marking in the first vacant space the public courts on which you play, and post it to:—

TENNIS COMPETITION,
Daily Record,
67 Hope Street,
Glasgow.

Use block letters.
Courts ....
Competition ....
(State whether Men's, Women's or Mixed Doubles.)
Name ....
Address ....
....
Name ....
Address ....
D.R.

tennis clothing and the proper shoes. If you could play reasonably well you might get a "Front" court where the audience were otherwise it was the back courts. The back courts were in fact better courts with a greater run back.

Players of note were Rankine Brown, Eddie Stein, Eric Duffus, Jackie O'Callaghan, Jinty Smith.

Glasgow Public Parks Lawn Tennis Association 1926-1951
Jubilee Ball, City Chambers, Glasgow (members of Alexandra Park Club)

Radnor Park (now called Kelvingrove) were also a succesful Club and won Division 1 several times. a leading player was Mrs Mina Brady.

Tollcross Park Club called themselves Deer Park Club since at one time there were deer in that Park. This club was a very social one and had a Choir and a concert party, both of which performed regularly. The tennis was of a high standard too the teams did well and frequently won Division 1 with players like Mrs Nan Neilson, Mrs Jean Leighton, Mrs Margaret Meiklejohn, Ina McNair.

1949 Radnor Park Winners Division 1, Crowley Shield

In 1951 Fred Perry Came to Tollcross Park at the invitation of Jim and Rena Houston and gave a demonstration match. He came because he heard that the Club gave coaching for youngsters. Rena Comments " He was such a charming gentleman. We felt that it was a bit much to expect him to change at the public park courts, so they came up to our flat and changed in the bay window of our sitting room, overlooking the courts". There were representatives from other parks Glasgow Green, Alexandra, Elder, Radnor. Afterwards there was tea at the flat. Fred signed one of the Balls and gave it to Jim, Rena's nephew.

1951 Tollcross Winners Division 1, Crowley Shield
Margaret Robertson, Margaret Meiklejohn, Jean Leighton, Ina McNair, Cathie Fern, Betty Condie

In the 1960's the bubble burst, some retired others went to private clubs at the end of 1973 it was all over.

DRUMCHAPEL INTER-CLUB

This inter-club tennis tournament was founded in 1948 by Drumchapel Tennis Club as a means of introducing some competition between local clubs at the end of what was considered to be the "Tennis Season". The tournament is held during the last week of August and the first week of September. Originally it consisted of Ladies and Gents singles, doubles and mixed doubles. It has been expanded to include junior singles and now has thirteen events held on the courts of the participating clubs.

It has provided a low-cost competition where ordinary club players can take part in a friendly competition against other local club members of a similar standard.

In the early days the tournament was for senior members only but junior under 15s girls and boys singles were introduced in 1974.

The tournament was further expanded in 1990 to include under 18s and under 14s Junior events and an under 10s singles competition was added in 2000.

A Tournament shield is awarded using a points system for both Senior and Junior events to the club with the greatest number of winners in each event. Individual trophies are also awarded to winners and finalists in each event.

The following clubs and number of times they have won the senior tournament is as follows. Millbrae 2, Bearsden 2, Yarrow 3, Westerton 4, Milngavie 5, Drumchapel 13 and Thorn Park 25. Since its inception in 1990 the junior tournament has been dominated by Thorn Park. They have won it nine times. Milngavie have had two wins and Bearsden one.

The competition is restricted to members of the clubs taking part.

Currently invitations are sent to the following clubs. Bearsden, Drumchapel, Glasgow University Staff, Milngavie, Thorn Park, Westerton and Yarrow.

Bearsden Ratings Tournament Winners 2001

PAISLEY & DISTRICT TENNIS TOURNAMENT

This confined tournament was inaugurated in 1936 for members of clubs within Paisley & District. Currently, players from 10 clubs compete – Anchor, Ardgowan, Arthurlee, Bishopton, David Lloyd Renfrew, Fort Matilda, Kilmacolm, Paisley, Strathgryffe and Uplawmoor. 12 events are oganised annually which provide competition for junior, senior and veteran players.

Throughout the years, the standard of play has been exceptionally high with many national and county players appearing on the championship roll. With 10 mens singles championship wins spanning 1959 – 1976, Alex Culloch of Cardonald and latterly Elderslie has been the most successful player.

Traditionally, the tournament has taken place at the end of the summer and is a climax to the district clubs' annual competition programmes. The P. & D.s, as the tournament is affectionately known, has moved from club to club throughout its history with Anchor, Ferguslie, Elderslie, Strathgryffe and most recently the David Lloyd Club at Renfrew acting as host club.

The tournament has always been well supported by local players and regularly attracts well over 100 entrants. Played during a week in the calendar when many other West of Scotland districts hold similar events, confined tournaments provide competition for players who may not wish to participate in tournaments far afield but do want the chance of playing against players from other clubs. As with many tournaments with a long history, the solid silver trophies, all donated by local dignitaries of the day, are quite magnificent. These have been supplemented with trophies for 'new' events provided by a number of sponsors which the tournament has been fortunate to attract in recent times.

The photograph shows the winners of the 2003 tournament, played at the David Lloyd Club in Renfrew and sponsored by Kier Homes Ltd.

THE SOUTH-SIDE INTER-CLUB TOURNAMENT

In 1932, Ian D McIntyre the Clarkston Tennis Captain organised a tournament named Clarkston and District Inter-Club Tournament. In 1998 the name was changed to "The Inter-Club Tournament" and in 2004 it changed its name yet again to "The South-side Inter-Club Tournament."

The original clubs involved were Clarkston, Giffnock, Hillpark and Whitecraigs. Hillpark has now withdrawn and Busby and Newlands are included.

Many beautiful trophies have been donated. In 1932 Gents and Ladies Singles were played and there is a shield for the club with the most points. In 1934 Gents and Ladies Doubles were introduced. Juniors were added in ever growing age categories.

The Winnie Bell Memorial Quaich was presented in 1958, to be awarded to the club where Ladies and Girls had achieved the most points. A further introduction was Veterans Doubles - Ladies, Gents and Mixed.

In earlier years each club took its turn in running the tournament and supplying tea and sandwiches. There were few club bars then. Dances and discos were also run. However as the entrants grew and grew, it became an impossible undertaking for any one club and so the courts from all the clubs are now utilised.

For the majority of Juniors this is the first tournament they enter and it does encourage them to move on.

The names of many well known West of Scotland players appear on the trophies - Ladies and Gents whose names have become renowned in the whole of the UK. Although one of the bigger Scottish Tournaments we hope it will continue to grow and the tournament is indebted to all who give so much of their time.

Prize winners at the 2002 West of Scotland Open Championship at Newlands

WEST OF SCOTLAND COUNTY

To represent your County must surely be the ambition of all players and because there is such a comprehensive League and Cup programme only a few achieve this honour, so it is all the more precious.

In the Appendix is to be found the list of those who have played and where and in which Division. Many excellent players have represented the "West".

Hunstanton - County Week, 1948 (Group 6)
Margaret S Allan, Isobel M Clark, Melanie Leslie Carter, Isobel S Vallance
Front - Clara H Black, Janet B Harvey, Heather M Macfarlane

West of Scotland County Team 1933 at Scarborough - May Thomson, Clara Butters, Jessie Riddick, Annie Brown, Jeanette Weir, Jean Jamieson, Janet Harvey

In the early days from 1905 to the early 1960s the West was half of the Scottish entry and the East was the other half thus players from Ayrshire, IG and WAR Collins, and from Perthshire, M Thom, were from the WEST part of Scotland.

The distinction of playing in the County team was indicated by the "Association Colours". The Badge was a red Lion Rampant with W S embroidered underneath, which was in use in the 1930s, which was altered to W S C (West of Scotland County). These badges were on the Blazer (navy blue with pale blue stripes) and on the pullover or cardigan. To play for the West of Scotland within our own boundaries there was awarded the "Representative Badge" which was a shield with the red lion rampant imposed on a background of navy and pale blue diagonal stripes and a crown on top. Players might get one or both at the same time as appropriate.

West of Scotland County Badge on blazer. Same badge would be on pullover or cardigan.

West of Scotland Representative Badge

1951 Paignton - Back L-R B Fulton, JB Wilson, IM Campbell, A Murray, T Boyd. Seated L-R - CV Baxter, Dr JB Fulton, JG Rutherglen

1969 Minehead West of Scotland County Team
L-R GT Downes, J McKenzie, FN Thompson, I Walker
Seated L-R GB Kerr, HS Matheson, WC Gillespie (C), KB Gray

West of Scotland County Team Bournemouth 1956
K Gillespie, M Walker, A Walker, K Horne,
L Dick, J Harvey, C Black, H Macfarlane

Extract from the Minute of 8th November 1962:-

1. Association Colours
   Miss WM Shaw (Clarkston)   Miss SEL Moodie (Stepps)   Mr HS Matheson (Hillpark)
   Mr GT Downes (Pollokshields) Mr JR Coulter (Pollokshields).

2. Representative Badges
   Mrs LB Stevenson (Hamilton)   Mrs E Veitch (Hamilton)   Mrs JF McNair (Poloc)
   Miss I Brown (Poloc)   Miss WM Shaw (Clarkston)   Miss SEL Moodie (Stepps)
   Mr J McCaffer (Poloc)   Mr AAP Summers (Poloc)   Mr IJ Davison (Bellahouston)
   Mr HS Matheson (Hillpark)   MR JR McAlpine (Bellahouston)

1974 Eastbourne - only one set short of winning
Division 1. Inter-Counties Grass Court Championships
Ruth Allan, Carole Matheson, Elaine Robb, Winnie
Shaw, Frances Taylor, Sheila Moodie, Anne Paul,
Marjory Love

1972 West of Scotland Lawn Tennis Association
Standing L-R Graeme Downes, Ken Revie, Tommy Walker,
Ian Walker, Russell Howat, George Copeland
Seated Harry Matheson, Ken Gray, Billy Gillespie

Anne Paul writes about her experiences in "County Week" as it was affectionately called.

1979 Cheltenham - L Boyd, M Stevenson, C Lindsay, M Crawford, E Tweedlie, M Love, S Moodie, E Robb

"It was a great honour to be selected for the West County Team. The memory of my first County week at Bournemouth (Group 2) remains with me to this day. It was a heatwave every day and to play three matches every day was quite an effort.

To play in the same team as Heather Macfarlane and Louise Dick was very exciting as they were the top Doubles pair at that time. I can remember Christine Truman's partner had her legs covered in bandages because of the intense heat in 1956.

My sister Marion and I played at third couple every day and we were told to make sure we beat the opposing third couple each day. We managed to do that even if it went to 14/12 in the third set - no tie-breaks then!

We stayed at the four star Carlton Hotel (the food was wonderful). A superb hotel, a high standard of competitive tennis for 5 days, what more could a tennis enthusist want? It made you want to improve and practise so that you ould be selected the following year.

In the 1950s and 60s there was much competition to gain a place. You had to do well in the west tournament. I cannot remember anyone refusing a place because of other commitments. Everyone kept County week free.

I think the LTA helped with the train fares and the West County were generous with their financial help towards hotel expenses.

1984 Worthing - Back row L-R Anna Lavery, Lorna Browne, Sheila Moodie, Judith Hosie Front Row L-R Marjory Love, Eileen Ure, Carol Wilson

We usually travelled to the south of England by sleeper on Saturday night to arrive on Sunday morning and practise on the grass courts all afternoon. We could not practise on grass except at Craiglockhart (now no longer grass), although I remember Norrie Graham and Jack Budge organising a grass court near Craigholm playing fields.

Team Captains 1958 Scarborough - Mr Dunham, Mrs Kemp (Essex), Mrs Bartram (Notts). Front - Mrs Black (West of Scot.), Miss Mortimer (Devon), Miss Buxton (Middlesex), Mrs Mackay (East of Scot.)

I have special memories of Cromer where we played several times in Group 2. the courts were excellent and the ladies of the Cromer Club made such an effort to produce mouthwatering afternoon teas. Other lovely venues were Exmouth, Budleigh Salterton, Frinton and Scarborough.

At Cromer in 1965 it was very exciting playing in the last match which decided whether or not we gained promotion to Group 1. We succeeded and i can remember Captain Clara Black opening a bottle in the car park to celebrate.

Group 1 at Eastbourne was special. All the teams 6 Ladies teams and 6 Men's teams all stayed at the 5 star Grand Hotel which was magnificent and within walking distance of Devonshire Park.

1962 L-R - C Dungliston, S Moodie, A Paul, W Shaw, M Ferguson
Front - F MacLennan, CH Black (C), A McAlpine

Being Captain of the team was made easy when you had such talented players as Winnie Wooldridge, Frances Taylor, Marjory Love, Sheila Moodie, Carole Matheson, Anne Barrow and Ruth Allan and others who put the needs of the team before personal success - this is what County Weekmis all about!

The Highlight of my time as Captain must be the 1974 result where we just missed being the winners by 2 games. In the final match against Devon the score stood at 4 rubbers all and in the deciding rubber our second couple lost 5/7 to Devon second couple. But that is tennis!"

1948 Bedford County Team
L-R - Archie Murray, Nick Smith, Jack Watson
Seated - Tom Boyd, JG Rutherglen, Dr JB Fulton, BU Fulton, Bill Reid

There are many other tales of this great week and it would take forever to tell all. The ethos remains and the desire for success is constant.

1980 Worthing
Rhona Harvie, Sheila Moodie, Maureen Crawford, Laura Boyd, ?, Marjorie Love, Chris Lindsay, Joyce Leach

1980 Cromer
T Walker, K Revie, H Matheson, J Howie, R Howat
A Galbraith, N Paterson, Ross Matheson (mascot), G Reid

1983 Exmouth - West Ladies in the Tournament
Isabel Stadele, Carol Wilson, Judith Hosie, Lorraine Wall
Marjory Love, Laura Boyd, Sheila Moodie (capt.), Lorna Browne

2000 Ilkley
Ladies County Team
Claire Lavery, Elizabeth Stevenson, Romana Orsi,
Anna Brown, Nicola
Heather Lockhart, Stephanie, Eileen Christie (NPC)

2000 County Team at Cambridge
Russell Allan, Calum McKnight, Jordan Gray, Ryan
Manfield, Gary Smith
Malcolm Watt, Harry Matheson (captain), Ronnie
Terras

PERSONALITIES OF THE GAME

There have been so many personalities of the game over the years. Many have been distinguished players and some have been Champions. Only one can be the winner and if there is an entry of one hundred and eighteen, as there was in 1978, then one hundred and seventeen will be disappointed.

Many too have served the Association in other capacities such as President or Secretary or Committee member, others have served the game further afield at SLTA (now Tennis Scotland) and the LTA. No amount of effort can include everyone and this list therefore cannot be exhaustive.

Emphasis here has been restricted to West of Scotland and Scottish successes. Many of the players in this chapter have won much elsewhere and unless the player has made the information available no reference is made.

SIR LEIGH MACLACHLAN

Leigh Maclachlan was the first Champion in 1886 and fifty years later was still able to enjoy a game of tennis and he became an Honorary President of the WSLTA.

J H NEIL

J H Neil won the Championship five times. His first win was 1895 and he won the championship three years running and, as was the custom in those far off days, when a player won three consecutive years that player "won the cup outright". The trophy became his. Many years later it was donated to his club Pollokshields they in turn donated it to the WSLTA and it is in use as the cup for the most successful club in the West of Scotland Championships. It is known as the Neil Trophy. J H Neil also won the Doubles in 1901 and 1902.

*The Cup won outright by
JH Neill in 1897*

A J SMELLIE

A J Smellie was the man who proposed the founding of the West of Scotland Lawn Tennis Association on that memorable day of 3rd November 1904. He became the first President and served for two years in the post. He was a good player and won the West of Scotland Doubles with JT Butters in 1905 1906 and 1907. His niece Winnie Mason would achieve much in the future as would his great niece (and Winnie Mason's daughter) Winnie Shaw.

J T BUTTERS

James T Butters was a member at Pollokshields and won the Singles of the West of Scotland Championships in 1906, 1907 and 1910 and the Doubles with A J Smellie in 1905, 1906 and 1907. William Fraser presented a Cup for Men's Singles to the Pollokshields Club in 1904 and JT Butters won it for the third successive year in 1909 thus winning the cup outright as was the custom in those days.

His daughters were Jean who won the Junior Girls Singles in 1924 and Clara who won the Junior Girls Singles in 1931 and 1932 (see Clara Butters Black). His nephew B Butters won the Men's Doubles in 1936 and 1937.

*The Cup won by
JT Butters in 1908*

STANLEY N DOUST (AUSTRALIA)

Stanley Doust presented a pair of silver cups for the "Gentlemen's Doubles" of the West of Scotland Championships in 1923.

He was an Australian who played at Wimbledon from 1907-1919. Reaching the "all-comers" final in 1913 when he lost to ME McLoughlin (USA). ME McLoughlin then lost in the Challenge Round to A F Wilding (NZ) the holder. In those far off days the holder only required to play the winner of the "All Comers" final.

In 1905 Doust played in the West of Scotland Championships and played R Baird in a singles match. He led 2 sets and was within a stroke of victory in the third but was ultimately defeated.

As captain of the 1913 Australasian team Doust was on the winning side against McLoughlin in the Davis Cup match with the United States. He was Wimbledon doubles finalist in 1909 and won his last major title, the British covered courts mixed championship with Joan Ridley in 1926.

Stanley Doust was the Tennis Correspondent of the Daily Mail 1920-1951. He died aged 83 in 1961.

ARTHUR HILL AND JACK HILL

AW Hill and JT Hill were brothers who had a successful record in the West of Scotland and for Scotland. Members of Newlands they played their tennis in the 1920s and 1930s

Arthur & Jack Hill

John (known as Jack) won the Junior West of Scotland Singles in 1932. Arthur followed on by winning the Junior Singles in 1923 and 1924.

Hill was to be the name on the West of Scotland Singles, Doubles and Mixed Doubles for five consecutive years 1928-1932. Arthur Won the West Men's Singles in each of the five years and the brothers won the Men's Doubles in each of these years. The Mixed Doubles were shared. Arthur won the Mixed in 1928 and 1929 with Miss Jean Rankine (Newlands) and Jack won the Mixed in 1930, 1931 and 1932 with Miss Winnie Mason (Pollokshields). Jack was to win a fourth Mixed title in 1938 with Mrs Lesley Fulton.

At the Scottish Hardcourts Arthur won the Men's Singles in 1929, 1930 and 1931. The Doubles the brothers won in 1929 and Jack won the Doubles again in 1935 with Donald MacPhail

Both played in Inter-Counties Championships and represented Scotland in International matches. Arthur played at Wimbledon.

Jack's great grand-daughter Caroline McCulloch, at fourteen years of age and playing at Newlands, is keeping up the family tradition of tennis playing by competing in Junior Championships, and in the Club Championships reached the final.

MRS CLARA H BLACK neé BUTTERS

Clara Butters played at the Pollokshields and was to win many Club Championships. She won the West of Scotland Girls Singles in 1931 and 1932, and the Scottish Girls Singles in 1932. This was the beginning of many championship wins in tournaments all over the country particularly in Doubles. She made her debut in the West of Scotland Inter-Counties team at Scarborough in

Eastbourne 1970
"Skipper" seated centre with her team
L-R - Veronica MacLennan, Muriel Ferguson,
Ruth Allan, Anne Paul
Marjory Love, Winnie Shaw, Clara Black (NPC),
Sheila Moodie, Brenda Livingstone

1933 and continued her association with the team, latterly as non-plating Captain, until 1972.

Winning her only West Singles title in 1949, Clara is still holds the record with her eight Ladies Doubles wins (the first in 1938 and the last in 1961). Four of the wins were with M Thomson, three were with CE Dungliston and one was with KA Gillespie. She also won the Mixed Doubles in 1948 with R Barr and the Scottish Mixed Doubles with Alan McNeilage in 1960.

Many representative matches were played with considerable success. Clara Black was the first Lady to serve on the West of Scotland Committee. Clara still plays golf.

1950 Wimbledon
John Rutherglen and Torben Ulrich

JOHN G RUTHERGLEN

John Rutherglen was a member of Newlands Lawn Tennis Club and was a member of the Inter-Counties team from 1948 to 1961 (there is no list of team members for 1947).

He won the West of Scotland Singles in 1950 and 1952 and the Mixed Doubles with Mrs L Dick in 1952. He qualified to play at Wimbledon in 1950 and played Torben Ulrich of Denmark who won 6/4 6/4 7/5.

John gave service on the West of Scotland Committee and was President in 1962.

GEORGE B PRIMROSE, J.P. 1881-1969

Extract from a David Beaton article in Scottish Tennis.

George Primrose was a member of Titwood Lawn Tennis Club. He played in matches for the club and played tennis well into the 1950s when he was in his seventies.

He will always be remembered for his Committee work, not only in Scotland, but throughout Britain, over a period of 60 years

This representation started in 1904 when he was the Titwood delegate at the inaugural meeting of the West of Scotland Lawn Tennis Association. The following year he was elected to the Management Committee of the Association. Three years later he became Honorary Secretary of the West of Scotland Championships.

George B Primrose

In 1910 George Primrose became President of Titwood Lawn Tennis Club and the next year he also became President of the West of Scotland Lawn Tennis Association.

During the first World War he held a Commission in the First Volunteer Battalion Cameronians (Scottish Rifles). When competitive tennis was resumed in 1919, GBP, played a leading role in the foundation of the West Junior Championships, the first regular junior tournament to be held in Scotland.

Elected to represent the West on the Scottish Lawn Tennis Association Council in 1920, he became President of the Scottish Lawn Tennis Association in 1924 and one of Scotland's representatives to the Council of the Lawn Tennis Association in London from 1925 to 1928 and again from 1934 to 1959.

"Volley" was the pseudonym he used when writing about tennis in The Bulletin newspaper

In 1936 as a stimulus to singles play he presented two challenge shields for annual competition in the West of Scotland Championships (entries were confined to players who had not previously won the event or an open championship).

George Primrose was elected a Vice-President of the Lawn Tennis Association in 1946. He succeeded the late Lord Mackay, as Honorary President of the Scottish Lawn Tennis Association in 1956, and three years later he was elected a Life Vice-President of the LTA. When he received the latter honour at the AGM of the Association the then President, the Duke of Devonshire, moving Mr Primrose's election, said: *"It is my very great privilege to propose that Mr G B Primrose be elected Honorary Life Vice-President of the Association. Many of you here will know as well as, if not better than I do, the work Mr Primrose has done on behalf of the Association for many years past, and particularly what he has done for tennis in Scotland. I understand that in Scotland he is not known as Mr Primrose but as "Mr Lawn Tennis".*

MRS GWEN SIMMERS neé STERRY

Gwen Sterry 5th from left at Ulster v WoS match 1950

Gwen Sterry was the daughter of a famous mother Charlotte Cooper. Charlotte Cooper won the Singles at Wimbledon five times 1895, 1896 and 1898 then after her marriage in 1901 as Mrs Sterry was to win again in 1901 and 1908.

Gwen was herself a very competent player and played at Wimbledon between 1925 and 1932, reaching the third round on four occasions. She also played in the British Wightman Cup team in 1927 winning the Doubles.

Gwen was in Scotland in 1931 and won the Scottish Grasscourts Singles, Doubles and Mixed Doubles and the West Ladies Singles.

At her marriage she became Mrs Simmers and played for many years at Kelvinside. Mrs Simmers won the West Singles a second time in 1947 and this time the Ladies Doubles with MS Allan and the Mixed with Bu Fulton the first of their three wins (also 1949/50). Her last win at the West was Ladies Doubles in 1951 with Isobel Vallance.

Kelvinside Lawn Tennis Club Ladies played in the First Division from 1934 and won Division 1 in 1938 and 1947 with one year in D 2 in 1952 and then back to D1 the following year. That was short lived and by 1954 the Club was bottom of D1, and 1955 bottom of D2, and by 1958 were in D5. This would seem to indicate that the very good players must have left the club somewhere around 1953/4. The Club did not enter the League in 1967 and amalgamated with Western LTC.

WINNIE A MASON 1910-1994

Winnie Mason played tennis at Titwood, where she won the Club Championship from 1928 to 1931 and then at Pollokshields.

Winnie won the West of Scotland Junior Singles in 1927 and 1928. She played in many tournaments successfully and the emphasis here is the West and Scottish events where she was the dominant figure in the 1930s

She won the West of Scotland Singles in 1930 / 32 / 33 / 34 / 36. The five times record only surpassed by Heather Macfarlane in times yet to come. The Ladies Doubles along with Mrs J Jamieson was won in 1932 / 33 / 34 / 36 and the Mixed Doubles first with JT Hill in 1930 / 31 / 32 and then with Donald MacPhail in 1934 / 36. The East of Scotland Singles was won in 1931 / 32 / 35 and many others in this period.

In the Scottish Championships Winnie won the Singles in 1930 and the Ladies Doubles in 1934 and 36 and the Mixed with Donald MacPhail in 1935. The Scottish Hardcourts in 1933 saw triple wins in Singles Doubles and Mixed Doubles.

The first Scottish Lady to be coached by Dan Maskell, Winnie Mason played at Wimbledon in 1933.

As a Member of the Pollokshields Club she played in Leagues and Cup matches. Representing the West of Scotland many times, Winnie represented Scotland eleven times.

Winnie Mason married Angus Shaw in 1938 and retired from competitive play but living in the south side of Glasgow she then joined Clarkston Lawn Tennis Club where her son Angus and daughter Winifred learned to play the game.

Winnie A Mason

DONALD MACPHAIL Jr

Donald MacPhail Jr played in tournaments in the 1930s and 1940s. He won the West of Scotland Singles in 1933/34 1936/37 and 1949, the Doubles with B Butters in 1937 and the Mixed Doubles with Winnie Mason in 1934 and 1936.

Donald won the Scottish Championships Singles in 1933, 1936, 1939 and 1946 just how many more might he have won if there had not been a break for the second World War. In Doubles he was a winner four times, in 1935 with VA Wood Hawks, in 1936/7 with IG Collins and 1946 with FM Davidson. He won the Mixed Doubles with Winnie Mason in 1935

In 1937/38 he won the Scottish Hardcourt Singles, the Doubles with JT Hill in 1935, and the Mixed with Winnie Mason in 1933 and with Mrs A Robertson in 1937.

There were many other tournament successes, and he played at Wimbledon.

Donald MacPhail Played in the Davis Cup in 1946.

He then coached for a number of years frequently on his own court in his garden.

DR JOHN B FULTON

Dr John B Fulton, along with his brothers Billy and Buchanan (Bu), and his wife Lesley and their daughters Evelyn and Joyce have made major and remarkable contributions to tennis in the West of Scotland, Scotland, Yorkshire and Canada.

Billy was a President of Newlands and also the West and a sound player. John and Bu were members of the Newlands teams which won the Scottish Cup and 1st Division on a number of occasions and both represented the West at County level for many years. Bu won a West Junior Boys Doubles title in 1936 along with Senior West Mixed titles with Mrs Gwen Simmers in 1947, 1949 and 1950. John had a West Junior Boys Singles title in 1921 and West Senior Doubles titles with R R Finlay in 1933 and 1934. John also won the Scottish Boys Singles in 1922 and represented Scotland in an International in 1932 and competed at Wimbledon in 1939 and 1947 to 1950 (in his forties) where he played with John Rutherglen in 1950. John further increased his contribution to the West by acting as non-playing captain of the West Teams at County Week from 1953 to 1965 after he stopped playing.

From the 1930s John and his family lived in Yorkshire and while Lesley and their daughters Evelyn and Joyce played for Yorkshire and England they did visit Scotland as evidenced by Lesley winning the Scottish Ladies Singles title in 1947 and Evelyn and Joyce winning the Scottish Junior Doubles in 1953. Joyce had a good record of appearances at Wimbledon and has contributed as President of Yorkshire LTA, while Evelyn, now living in Ottawa, represents Canada in Veterans tennis. A wonderful family with a remarkable contribution to tennis.

BU & JB Fulton in 1948 County Team Bedford
L-R - Archie Murray, Nick Smith, Jack Watson
Seated L-R - Tom Boyd, JG Rutherglen, JB Fulton, BU Fulton, Bill Reid

J.B.WILSON O.B.E.

James Burns Wilson has played tennis and served the game of tennis over many years. His home Club was Cardonald and he also played at Pollokshields

Jimmy won the West Singles in 1955 and the Doubles three times, twice with Ron Harris. He also won Doubles in Central, East and Scottish. He played at Wimbledon three times 1954/56/57. There were fourteen appearances in the West of Scotland County team and he was capped for Scotland.

Over the years Jimmy continued to play and in the 1980s it was he who was the driving force behind the formation of the Veterans Club in the West of Scotland and he played in the teams in the Vets Inter-County matches.

Administration was part of his service to tennis first of all on the West Committee followed by being President in 1957. Representation on the SLTA Council followed and he became President of the SLTA in 1967/68. Service to tennis continued with representation on the Council of the Lawn Tennis Association from 1965 to 1983.

Other involvements with sport have been undertaken such as the Chairmanship of the Glasgow and District Games and Sports Committee and being on the Management Committee of Bellahouston Sports Centre. Jimmy was Vice-Chairman of the Scottish Sports Council. The O.B.E. was awarded for services to Scottish Sport.

JB Wilson, Vice Chairman Scottish Sports Council with Prime Minister James Callaghan at Inverclyde National Sports Centre

COLIN V BAXTER

Colin was born in Glencairn Drive in Pollokshields in 1931 where Titwood Lawn Tennis Club was and that was probably why he went there in 1942. He had an interview before he was accepted and promised to help to keep up the five blaes courts. One of the Committee Mr Primrose helped him to get to the British Junior Championships at Wimbledon in 1947 and 1948. In 1948 Colin reached three Finals, losing to JAP Horn in the Singles but winning the boys Doubles with JAP Horn and the Mixed Doubles with Norma Seacy. He played at Men's Single at Wimbledon three times.

C V Baxter is an all time record holder in the West of Scotland Championships. He began with the U18 which he won in 1946/47/48.

Moving on to Senior tennis he won the Men's Singles eight times between 1953 and 1963 his run being interrupted by JB Wilson, KB Gray and IM Campbell. He lost in the fourth round to R Munro of Western in 1955 4/6 3/6, and to Billy Gillespie in the fourth round in 1961 6/4 4/6 4/6, and in the final in 1962 to Ian Campbell 6/4 6/8 3/6.

The Men's Doubles Colin won 10 times between 1951 and 1963 (with partners IM Campbell 3, JR Maguire 3, ADL Hunter, MA MacDonald, KB Gray and JT Wood). The Mixed he won in eleven consecutive Championships from 1955 to 1965 (with HM Macfarlane 3, EA Walker 1, AV Paterson 2, JS Barclay 2, WM Shaw 2, BJ McCallum 1.)

Colin Baxter

He had many Scottish successes too in 1947 U18 Grass and Hard, and Grass in 1948 as well as Doubles on Grass in 1947 and 1948 with AR MacWilliam and WK McCandlish. In Senior events Singles and Doubles on Grass in 1958/59/60 with JR Maguire and Mixed Doubles in 1964/65. The Hardcourts saw wins in Singles in 1959, Doubles 1953/54 with JM Campbell, and 1955/56 with AR Mills, and 1957/58 with JR Maguire (shared titles in 57/8).

There have been many West representative matches and International Caps. In the Inter-Counties team Colin first played in 1949 and played in the team until 1966.

HEATHER MACFARLANE

Heather Macfarlane played at Craighelen and Pollokshields and is the record holder in the West of Scotland Ladies Singles winning eight times between 1948 and 1957, with Clara Black in 1949 and Isobel Vallance in 1952 interrupting the run (she was in the final in 1947/48/52, making 11 consecutive finals and creating another record in that she only entered the tournament on those eleven occasions). She first won the Ladies Doubles in 1950 with Mrs Janet Harvey as partner, then again in 1952 with Isobel Vallance and in 1955/56/57 with Mrs Loiuse Dick (neé Anderson the 1937 Singles winner). Heather played in and won the Mixed doubles with Colin Baxter in 1955/56/57.

Heather says of those days *"My parents were the most loyal and enthusiastic supporters and drove me many miles to matches and tournaments. They enjoyed meeting the players and officials and very much felt part of whatever event I was playing in. I remember happy days at the "West" with Jack Hill, Norrie Graham and the Learmonths during the Cental District Tournament. I also recall Bob French of of Pollokshields.*

I am sure my tennis in the late forties and fifties was influenced by Janet Harvey and Gwen Simmers. We were members of Craighelen in Helensburgh and we fought many hard battles in the League.

Yes I played a few times at Wimbledon. I those days, with no International rankings, one was accepted or had to qualify depending on ones tournament results. I was lucky enough to be accepted and enjoyed every minute - alway as a wonderful experience."

Winning the Scottish Grasscourt Ladies Doubles in 1954 with Miss A Bilse and again in 1957 with Mrs CM MacKay, she shared the Mixed Doubles in 1950 partnered by AK Quist. In the Scottish Hardcourts Heather won the Singles in 1954 and the Ladies Doubles in 1948S/50/53/55/57S (S=shared), partnered by Miss JFB Wilson, Mrs HM Proudfoot (2), Mrs RT Ellis (2).

Playing for Pollokshields in successful Scottish Cup teams, Heather played for the West of Scotland County team in the Inter-Counties Championships from 1949 to 1957 (West records are not available for 1947/48). Heather played many other representative matches and had several International Caps. She also played at Wimbledon three times.

ISOBEL VALLANCE

Isobel Vallance was talented in more than one sport. She played hockey at Glasgow High School and for the FP's. In 1948 she played trials for West District Hockey. Isobel from Burnside Lawn Tennis Club won the West of Scotland U18 Singles, Doubles and Mixed Doubles in both 1946 and 1947. She then played at the Junior Championships of Great Britain at Wimbledon in 1947 where she won the the Girls Doubles with Norma Seacy (East of Scotland).

Now playing for Pollokshields Isobel won the West of Scotland Ladies Doubles in 1951 with Mrs Simmers and in 1952 reached three finals, won the Singles by beating Heather Macfarlane 2/6 7/5 6/4, and went on to win the Doubles with Heather against Mrs L Dick and Mrs C Black 6/2 6/3 but lost the Mixed. Shortly Isobel received her first International Cap against Ireland. That same year Isobel went on to win the Singles and Ladies Doubles at the Granton-on-Spey Tournament. In 1953 and 1954 Isobel won the West Mixed Doubles with Ian Campbell. Isobel played in the West Inter-Counties team from 1949 to 1954.

Not content with Tennis there were Badminton successes too in 1952/53 season, winning the West of Scotland Ladies Singles and Doubles, the East of Scotland Doubles, then had International Caps against Ireland England and Sweden, and won the Glasgow Tournament Singles.

She became Mrs Kempsall then took up golf and reached a Handicap of 4 and is still playing.

HARRY S MATHESON

Harry Matheson showed early skills at tennis and played at Hillpark LTC. He had the talent which took him far afield from his native Scotland. Because of travels elswhere playing in the West of Scotland Championships was curtailed.

Harry's successes in the West of Scotland and Scottish Championships are as follows
1960	Scottish Grasscourt U18 Singles, U18 Doubles with RB Low. Hardcourt U18 Singles
1962	Scottish Grasscourt Men's Doubles with RB Low, 1962/63 Mixed Doubles with WM Shaw
1962	British Nestlé U21 Singles
1963	Scottish Hardcourt Men's Doubles with W Jaques
1964	Scottish Hardcourt Men's Singles, Doubles with I Prouse, Mixed Doubles with WM Shaw
1965	Scottish Grasscourt Mixed Doubles with WM Shaw shared with CV Baxter/Mrs GM Williams
1966	West of Scotland Men's Singles, Doubles with FN Thomson
1966/67	Scottish Indoor Men's Singles 1966 Doubles with SGJ Meaking
1968	West of Scotland Mixed Doubles with SEL Moodie
1969	Scottish Grasscourt Mixed Doubles with Mrs Carole Matheson
1970	West of Scotland Men's Doubles with GT Downes

In November 1962 it was minuted that Harry had been invited to join the LTA training group at Queen's Club. Harry played at Wimbledon, played in many other tournaments and in 1964/5 toured abroad. He served for a time on the West of Scotland Committee.

Playing in Inter-County matches from 1962 to 1980 and many International matches throughout his tennis career he then took part in Veterans tennis winning the Scottish National Veterans Indoor Doubles in 1990 and 1991 with GT Downes and in 1994 with G Copeland, British Veterans Men's 45 Doubles in 1991 with RA James and 55 Doubles in 1999 with G Copeland. He now has been Non-playing Captain in the West of Scotland Inter-County team since 1998.

1963 Southsea - a young Harry in the County Team
L-R - Alex Culloch, Graeme Downes, Harry Matheson,
Gordon Kerr, Ronnie Low.
Seated - Billy Gillespie, Colin Baxter, Dr JB Fulton, Ken Gray

FRANCES TAYLOR neé MACLENNAN

Frances writes of her career in tennis:- "45 Years of Tennis in the West of Scotland"

"Without the early practising and matches at Newlands, with Ken Gray and Billy Gillespie and John Coulter and Gordon Kerr and Ken McCready, I would not be the player I am. Do to-day's young male teenagers have time for 11-15 year old girls on a tennis court? I hope so.

World Team Championships Brazil 2000
Frances Taylor & Marjory Love

The highlights of my tennis career began with County Week at Ilkley with Kathleen Gillespie and Anne Paul when I was 14 in 1959 - sunshine, excitement, grass! I went through my first big Senior win at the "West" in 1959 amongst 4 other event titles (she won U15 Singles in 1958 and U18 in 1959, Ladies Singles again in 1964 and the Doubles with Anne Paul also in 1964).

I played in every successful County Week until 1969 with Anne McAlpine whether in Cromer or Bournemouth or wherever with Marjory, Sheila and Anne Paul and Winnie and we never went down. What a great team we were. But it was Norrie (Graham) who really gave us our sense of worth and pride. Each year we would be in the best hotel and have a wonderful experience never to be forgotten or repeated.

I still belong to the West of Scotland - take more pride in our whole group of elegant vintage players who still compete as Veterans, than any others - make more effort in the Four Nations Veteran events when playing at Renfrew or Scotstoun now without conscious reasoning. Highlights of of my UK Cup career as Captain of the 50's, 55's and now 60's were a Visit to Anne McAlpine in Johannesburg in 1997; a 14 strong group of so familiar West Ladies who, on a tennis holiday at the same venue in La Manga in 1999 turned up in support. Fellow team members were Marjory Love 1999-2002; Christine Lockhart in 2000."

Frances played successfully in Scottish Championships Winner of the U18 Hardcourts in 1960 and 1961, joint winner of Singles on Grass and winner of the Hardcourts 1961 and joint winner of Mixed Doubles with RJ Wilson in 1969. She played many tournaments in England and abroad and played at Wimbledon seven times. In 1965 in the round of the last 16 Frances played and lost to Margaret Smith, the eventual winner,

2/6 1/6 (in the semi C Truman only got 1 more game). The following year she reached the third round before losing to the No 3 seed Anne Jones.

In the Veteran era Frances has won many titles (see the Purple Patch) and enjoys the game as much as ever.

MRS LORNA STEVENSON / MRS HAMILTON

Lorna Stevenson was the second Lady on the West of Scotland Committee. She was a member of Hamilton LTC and played in the team very successfully.

She is noted for many firsts in Committee work being the first Lady to be President of her Club in the 1950s followed by being the the first Lady President of the West of Scotland LTA in 1964 followed by being the first Lady on the SLTA Council and then President of the SLTA in 1975/76. Serving tennis on many Committees over the years Lorna (now Mrs Hamilton) still takes an interest in tennis at her club.

CATH McTAVISH-KEW

First Lady Umpire on Centre Court: - from Greenock to Wimbledon.

Why you?"   Well, I could play a number of sports to a reasonable high standard including tennis and therefore knew the rules. My mother, a champion player in both Hong Kong and India, pre-World War 2, took me to Wimbledon (where my grandfather lived in retirement), I saw a notice which read "Have you ever thought of becoming an umpire?" I looked at it again and thought "No, but that's not a bad idea to put something back into another game in which I play". At that time, in the late 1950s, I had started umpiring hockey as well as still playing. The seed was sown. I got an application form and joined the then BTUA. I started umpiring, and continued playing, at the Belfast Championships where overseas players came before going on to England and ultimately Wimbledon although in the Umpires Association. I could not apply for Wimbledon because you required to go there for the first week of the Championships and that was the last week in June and I was still teaching. I had to wait a few years until the first week of Wimbledon started at the end of June. The next year I was accepted for the two weeks and luckily the new Principal of the College had come from being Vice Principal at Jordanhill so from then onwards he would just say "See you at Wimbledon".

In 1979 I made the breakthrough for ladies by umpiring on Court No1 and the media and press, even the "Glasgow Herald" had an article and made quite a thing about it taking 102 years. At this stage I was also given some men's matches on the outside courts and had a long five setter of nearly 3 hours after which the Supervisor's only comment was *"you could have implemented the new 30 second rule more (between serves)"*. At last, in 1981, who would believe now that the first lady to umpire on the Centre Court would be over 50 years old and actually the youngest of the four to be considered. Why me? I truly believe that I had two advantages over the other ladies, all English. It saved the All England Committee having to decide between them and so I was told my Scottish articulation was clearer - "thirty, forty". Also I had umpired a televised match from Wembley Stadium in front of 60,000 screaming schoolgirls, England v Ireland Hockey International (for the curious Ireland won 2-1after I had given a Penalty Bully missed by England). The only lady to have umpired at the two big "Ws". Very satisfactory memories. This achievement then led on to umpiring in Australia - Adelaide (men), Brisbane (women) and Melbourne (Australian Open) for 4 years.

MARGARET AND WILL STEUART-CORRY

Margaret (1915-2002) and Will (1908-2001) Steuart-Corry were honoured by the Scottish Lawn Tennis Association and the Scottish Sports Council (now Sport Scotland) for their services to tennis.

They were members of Helensburgh Lawn Tennis Club from 1935. They were both in the teams for the Club and won many titles in championships.

It was their encouragement of young players and their coaching of them that was so outstanding. Hundreds learnt first the rules and the rudiments and then the skills and the etiquette of the sport. When "Short Tennis" was first introduced, using small rackets and soft tennis balls, Margaret began classes for the under fives at a local Community Centre which she and Will ran for a number of years.

One of their proudest moments was when young pupils of theirs demonstrated short tennis at Wimbledon during the Championships there.

William and Margaret Steuart-Corry with their award from the Scottish Sports Council (now Sport Scotland)

Margaret and Will Steuart-Corry served their Club in many capacities. Both served as President and played a prominent part in the Helensburgh Club's Centenary in 1984. Will also had a role in the major developments at the Club with the building of their new two-story clubhouse and the provision of seven artificial grass courts.

WINIFRED M WOOLDRIDGE neé SHAW 1947-1992

Who better to write about Winnie than Angus Shaw her proud Dad (his choice of title) and the following was written by him, in 1971:

" What makes an International tennis player?

An eye for the ball, physical fitness and dedication to the perfection of stroke production.

These are the fundamentals admittedly but there is much more than that as Winnie Shaw, No 2 in the British tennis rankings, is ready to admit.

Winnie who has won her way into the last eight at Wimbledon on successive years and gained nation-wide acclaim in so doing   acknowledges that defeats are just as valuable to a player as victories.

With a grin that brings crinkles to her steady blue eyes she philosophise's *"Success can come too early and stay for too short a time".*

1964 Winifred M Shaw

She added seriously *"It is all too easy to accept a succession of victories ; they lull one into a false sense of security. Defeats on the other hand, if you school yourself into self analysis, are sign-posts to a more stable background. They are something you can build on for the future*

A player has an instinctive sense of personal weaknesses in stroke production. Unless these things are faced up to and eradicated they can build up into a nagging sense of insecurity which will inevitably affect a player's prformance."

If a word can adequately sum up Winnie's attitude to the game it is **DEDICATION**.

Even before she went to school Winnie was swinging a miniature tennis racket in the back garden of her Clarkston (Renfrewshire) home, under the watchful patient eye of her mother (Winnie Mason), a former Scottish tennis Champion and Wimbledon player.

Inculcated in the basic techniques, she began to regard her tennis racket as essential as her school satchel and even play periods at Hutcheson's Girls' Grammar School, Glasgow, were given over to hitting a ball against a convenient wall.

And although her Hebridean holiday isle, Seil Argyll had no tennis court , her tennis racket continued to form an important part of her luggage. Indulgently the then proprietor of Dunmore Farm, Easdale, Mr Bill Ferguson - now an Oban business man - allowed Winnie to practice on his concrete walled barn. With a good natured smile, he used to contend that the rhythmic thumping of the tennis balls caused the electrically milked cows, in an adjoining byre, to give a better yield!

In winning the Junior Championships of Great Britain   the only Scot to do so in 21 years   Winnie soon established herself as a player of outstanding potential.

Virtually in her first senior season she met the redoubtable Maria Bueno, then holder of the Wimbledon Singles title, on the famous Centre Court at Wimbledon. It was a baptism that conditioned her to the big time tennis and introduced her for the first time to T.V. coverage.

Constant experience in Junior Tournaments all over the country paid dividends. As a schoolgirl she played for Scotland in Junior and Senior Internationals.

While 17, and still at school, Winnie faced a major decision   a tennis career or something more in keeping with the scholastic achievements of her school?

Winning the Nestlé Championship, open to all players under the age of 21, virtually decided the matter, providing as it did the opportunity of competing in Continental tournaments.

In the view of Dan Maskell, the then Lawn Tennis Association Coach and T.V. Commentator, she was possibly the best junior player to emerge in Britain in the post-war period.

Selection for the British Wightman Cup Team and the Federation Cup Team over the past few years she was the first Scot ever to be selected for such an honour opened the way to fresh fields all over the World.

She has competed at all the major American tournaments and the magic carpet of global competitive tennis has taken her all over the World. She finds it easier to mention the countries she hasn't visited rather than those in which she has competed. Some of the countries she has played in are France, Germany, Russia, Finland, Sweden, Norway, Australia, Tasmania, New Zealand, Canada and various countries in the Middle East.

Winnie is magnanimous in her appreciation of the many kindness's she has received in her travels as Scotland's tennis ambassador. She remarks :- "*In most places we are given the Royal treatment, from specially allocated cars for the duration of our stay, entertainment and accommodation in luxury hotels, to private hospitality in the homes of millionaires.*"

The tedium of hundreds of hours spent in jet travel around the World she spends in keeping abreast of her voluminous correspondence.

But Winnie admits with a smile :- "It's nice to get back home to have running repairs attended to and get re-orientated to a more normal mode of life."

Some strange, and at times emotional encounters, with "exiles" have occurred. Their one aim is to identify themselves with some part of the old country.

Winnie at the old No. 1 Court, Wimbledon

New favourite country? Possibly New Zealand where the tempo of life and general atmosphere approximate to those in Scotland.

After this year's Wightman Cup tussle Winnie will return to Scotland to have a tennis / golf holiday at Pitlochry, a reunion with many of her relations on the Island of Seil and then a winter of preparation for next year's tournaments.

A Wimbledon title? Winnie makes no secret of her ambition and those who know her almost fanatical dedication consider that her aim may well be achieved. But no-one knows better than Winnie that all her plans are conditional on continued good health, a blessing which she acknowledges with humility.

Here ended the writing of her Dad at that time.

Winnie married Keith Wooldridge (a Davis Cup player) in 1972 and she continued competing for some years. A Wimbledon title eluded her, though she won many titles on her World tours. On retirement from competitive play she took up golf and represented Scotland. Her sporting skills were repeated at golf.

It was at golf she took ill with a brain tumor and after a battle to survive bravely fought Winnie died in 1992.

SHEILA MOODIE

1963 Sheila Moodie, Stepps

Sheila started playing tennis at Stepps when she was about ten years old. Her very first competition was the West of Scotland U15 girls Singles in 1959 and she won it. This was followed in 1961 and 62 with the U18

The Scottish Grasscourt U18 Singles was won in 1961 and shared with Winnie Shaw in 1962. In 1964 and 1965 Sheila won the U21 Singles.

In 1962 at the British Junior Indoor at Queen's Club, playing with Robin Blakelock, Sheila reached the semi-final of the Girls Doubles

In the Scottish Indoor Championships Sheila won the Singles in 1963 and the Doubles with Marjory Love in 1975 and in 1985 that partnership won the Scottish National Championships.

In her first Senior year in 1964 Sheila won the Scottish Covered Court Championship, and a trip to Cannes to play was her prize.

In 1962 she first played in the West County team and she played each year for 25 years. Sheila's makes the following comment comment about playing :-

"This was hard work but very enjoyable, very competitive and encouraged team spirit, and to be a succseeful team we all had to accept the decision of the Captain."

Highlights in County Week play was playing with Winnie Shaw as first couple two years running and winning 13 out of 15 matches the first year and the following year 14 out of 15.

Many Championship titles came Sheila's way including the West of Scotland Triple Crown in 1968, a Further Ladies Doubles and a further five Mixed Doubles titles. During the Red Hackle years Sheila with partners Anne Paul (1) and Marjory Love (5) won the Qualifying Ladies Doubles six times and without that event it would have seen Sheila equal Clara Black's record of eight wins.

In the Scottish Hardcourts Sheila won the U18 Singles in 1962, and the Ladies Singles in 1967 and 1968. Between 1967 and 1983 she won the Ladies Doubles ten times five of which were with Marjory Love as partner. The Mixed Doubles was won in 1970 and 1978 with Jim Nicol.

Other tournaments had successes too at Pitlochry, North Brewick, Granton-on-Spey and many others.

At 37 years old Sheila had her first Scottish Cap (Winnie Shaw and Joyce Williams had been the Scottish representatives for many years) and she, partnered by Andy Galbraith, won the decisive doubles to give Scotland a win by 13-11. More Caps followed.

Sheila plays Veterans tennis and was a member of the Ladies 50 team who won Division 1 of the British Inter-Counties Championship in 2000 and 2001.

CHRISTINE LOCKHART neé CLARK

Christine Lockhart played her early tennis in Ayrshire and represented the South of Scotland County in the Inter-County Championships over many years.

She has been a long standing member of Newlands Lawn Tennis Club and plays in their Premier Division team and has been a member of their successful National League team as well as Scottish Cup teams.

In her own words has won various Scottish and GB Veteran titles over the past few years (an understatement). Among these successes in 2003 were wins in The Scottish Indoor Championships Ladies 55 Singles and Ladies 50 Doubles (with Marjory Love), the British Veterans 50 Ladies Singles at Wimbledon in 1998 and 1999 and in 2002 runner-up in the 55 Ladies Singles at the same event.

The World Veteran Team Championships in 2000 saw Christine in the Great Britain team with Frances Taylor as the Captain.

Mrs Christine Lockhart 2003 Captain of British 55 Team in Turkey

In 2003 Christine was the Captain of the British 55 Veterans team at the World Team Championships in Turkey when teams from all over the World competed for the Maureen Connolly Cup.

MARJORY LOVE

Marjory Love writes;-

I started playing tennis at the age of 9 at Brookfield, a small village club with one court and about fifteen junior members ranging in age from 9 to 16 years. From the age of 13 I received regular coaching from Arthur McDowall at Western Tennis Club and, with his help, I won my first title, the West of Scotland under 15 in 1962. This enabled me to be occasionally selected for the senior West of Scotland Inter District team - usually at third couple with some long suffering senior. In 1965 I won the Scottish under 18 Girls Championships at Craiglockhart and following from that win I was selected for the Junior Scottish team to play England at Manchester in the same year.

In 1966 I was selected for the first time for the West of Scotland Ladies at Counties Week but with a team comprising of mainly Scottish Internationlists / Scottish Champions I was told that there would be little chance of me playing. However it was a great experience for me as the team was participating in Group 1 at Eastbourne where the best of British tennis was on display, both men and ladies. It was not until the following year that I first played for the County in Group 2 at Cromer but not until the second last day of the week. I was thrilled when the Captain, Mrs Black, told me that I was to play. After that I played every day of every year of Counties Week until 1985.

In 1968 I was awarded my first Scottish senior cap, against Ireland, another big occasion for me.

1969 was probably my best year when I won the third of my Scottish and British University titles, the Scottish under 21 event and both the Scottish Grass Court and Hard Court Championships.

1969 also saw my graduation from Edinburgh University and the start of my law apprenticeship. With shorter holidays there was less opportunity to compete in tournaments. I did however manage to keep playing at a reasonable standard I was Scottish number one lady player between 1976 and 1980. It became more difficult to keep up a standard as I got older and worked long hours and of course there were young talented players coming along.

Just as I was beginning to feel that I no longer wanted to play competitive tennis I heard about veterans tennis which had become very popular in England. A whole new world has opened up to me since I became forty. I have represented Great Britain all over the world in the World Team Championships both at over 45 and over 50 as well as being awarded various Scottish veterans caps and winning Scottish Veterans Singles and Doubles titles. My first trip for the Great Britiain team was in 1994 to Perth, Western Australia for the inaugural Margaret Court Cup. I again played for Great Britiain in this event in Austria 1996, South Africa 1997 and Warwick, England in 1998. From 1999 to 2003 I have played in the Great Britiain team competing for the Maria Esther Bueno Cup which has been held in Holland 1999, Brazil 2000, Austria 2001, Florida 2002 and Germany 2003. In addition in 1997 I won the British over 45 title and in 2000 the British over 50 title. There are also Inter-County Veterans Championships and it was yet another thrill for me to captain the West of Scotland Ladies team which won Division 1 in both 2000 and 2001.

Little did I think that when I won my first title in 1963 I would be fortunate enough to be able to play and enjoy competitive tennis both at County and International levels in my fifties.

ELAINE ROBB

Elaine's first win in the West of Scotland was the U15 Singles in 1968 followed by the U18 in 1971. Also in 1968 she won the West of Scotland Ladies Singles Shield (for players who have not won an Open Singles event).

She made her mark further afield in the Nestlé Schools Tournament winning the Scottish event in 1970 and 1971. This allowed her to compete at Queen's Club in the National Finals where in 1970 she lost to Susan Minford of Ireland who was to win the event. In the following year Elaine reached the Final and lost to Michele Tyler of England.

Also 1971 Elaine Won the U18 Scottish Grasscourt Singles, and the Doubles in 1970 and 1971.The Scottish Hardcourt Ladies Doubles with SEL Moodie as partner a shared result with JM Erskine and VA Hutcheon.

Elaine played at Hamilton Club and was in the team when the Club won the First Division. She also was selected for the County Team for the Inter-County Championships from 1974 - 1980

1972 Elaine Robb shakes hands with Ken Rosewall after the BP International Fellowship Coaching, Aberdeen

KENNETH REVIE

Ken played at Bishopbriggs at first then moved to Broomhill. He won the U15 West of Scotland Singles in 1968. He followed this by winning the U18 Singles four times 1971-1974 and the U18 Doubles in 1971 and 1974 and the U18 Mixed Doubles thrice 1972-1974.

In 1971 Ken won the Nestlé Scottish Schools Tournament and he went on to the National Finals at Queen's Club which he won 6/1 6/2 against Martin Smith of England.

In 1974 Ken was the first Scot to win the British Junior U18 title and followed this with the British U21 title in 1977.

West of Scotland Senior wins were numerous and potentially record breaking. Ken was another player whose peak years fell at the time of the Red Hackle Years. There were four Singles wins 1984/86/88/89; six Doubles (five with partner Ian Allan and one with Russell Howat) 1984-87 1989 and 1991; seven Mixed Doubles between 1980 and 1989 (four with SEL Moodie and three with S Mair).

During the years 1978 to 1983 there was the Qualifying for the Open Singles and Doubles and the event was called the West of Scotland Shield. It took the shape of a championship played the week before the Open event and four players/couples qualified. At this time Ken won the Singles four times 1979-1982. Taken with his other four wins he would have equalled CV Baxter's record of eight wins. In the Doubles he won the Qualifying twice and would have then had eight wins to be second only to CV Baxter with his ten wins. The Mixed Doubles remained Open and seldom did visitors play. With his seven wins second position, shared with Ian Walker, is still short of CV Baxter's eleven consecutive wins.

At Scottish Events on Grass he won U15 Singles 1968/69/71; U18 Singles 1972/74 and Doubles 1971/72/ 74; U21 Ken won the Singles 1974/77 and the Doubles in 1976. Senior events on grass were Men's Singles 1977, Mixed Doubles 1981 and Men's Doubles in 1982.

At Scottish events on Hardcourts Ken was the winner of U18 Singles 1973, Men's Singles 1975 and 1983, Doubles in 1975 and 1979, Mixed Doubles 1975.

Scottish Indoor successes were U18 Singles 1972/73; U18 Doubles 1972/73and Men's Singles 1974 quite a catalogue!

Scottish National Championship Singles Winner 1984 and 1989 and Doubles five times in 1985/86/88/89/ 91 all with IJ Allan as his partner.

Ken was a member of the team every year in that great Broomhill run of fourteen wins in fifteen years in the Scottish Cup.

From 1972 until 1989 and 1991 Ken was a member of the County Team playing in the Inter-County Grasscourt Championship Week several of them as Captain

Ken is the most capped player for Scotland with a count of 44.

JOSIE BEELEY

Josie's tennis officiating career began in 1977 when Bearsden L.T.C. celebrated its 90th anniversary and decided to hold an Invitation Tournament to mark the event. Josie happened to be Club Tournament Convenor that year and found herself organising the event. It was so successful that it was repeated the following year. That event continues to be the major one day event in the north of the city and is now in its 27th year. In 1989 Bearsden LTC decided to hold one of the then new format "Volkswagen Ratings Tournaments" and Josie learned that she had been nominated as referee. thanks to the guidance and help of John Blane, the event was not only an outstanding success in 1991 it was awarded the SLTA Tournament of the Year Award. The 14th event (now LTA Summer Series) was played August 2003.

Shortly thereafter, she began to be asked to referee events elsewhere, the first of which was the Four Nations event in the SLTA centenary year at Newlands in 1995. Since then she has refereed numerous local, National and International events both in Scotland and elsewhere in the UK. These have included WSLTA Junior, Senior and Veterans Championships (the WSLTA 2002 Veterans Millennium Championships were awarded the Tennis Scotland 2002 Tournament of the Year Award), Ayrshire Junior Championships, LTA Junior and Senior Winter County Cup, LTA Clay Court events, LTA County, Regional and Grand Prix Challenges, National Club League matches, LTA County Week at Cheltenham and Edgebaston, Scottish National Championships, Scottish Junior, Senior and Veterans Open Indoor Championships, LTA Men's and Ladies over-35 Inter County Championships at Eastbourne, European Maccabi Games and British National Police Championships.

In addition to refereeing Josie is also an umpire who frequently appears on court at local and national events. She has officiated at Wimbledon since 1991 and has appeared on Centre Court several times. Highlight of her Wimbledon career was being a member of the Ladies Finals line team in 1996 when Steffi Graff beat Arantxa Sanchez-Vicario. In 1999 she featured on the back page of the Wimbledon programme being the line judge just behind Tim Henman when the photgraph was taken on Centre Court in 1998.

Josie is also a keen tennis player and regularly plays in WSLTA league matches for the Glasgow University Staff LTC as well as competing in Veterans Tournaments.

*Josie Beeley, at Wimbledon on the new
No. 1 Court still being constructed*

CLIVE THOMSON

Clive first became involved in Tennis Administration when he joined the committee of Clarkston Tennis Club in 1966. After serving as Captain of the club in 1970 he and a number of fellow members moved to Whitecraigs Lawn Tennis and Sports Club. After a number of years on the committee he became President of the Whitecraigs club in 1978.

Clive represented the Clarkston Club on the committee of the West of Scotland Lawn Tennis Association and continued to serve on the committee when he moved to Whitecraigs. He was elected as President of The West of Scotland LTA and represented them on the council of the Scottish Lawn Tennis Association. Clive served as President of the Scottish LTA in 1985 and 1986 and represented them on the Council of the Lawn Tennis Association.

After serving on a number of LTA committees Clive was elected Chairman of the International and Professional Tennis Divisional Board in 2000 and served as Chairman for 3 years. For the past 6 years Clive has served as a member of The Committee of Management of The Wimbledon Championships. He began his second term on the LTA main Board in 2000 and continues in 2003 as the President's nominee on the Main Board. In December 2002 he was elected as a Vice President of the Lawn Tennis Association and was elected as The Honorary Vice President of the Whitecraigs club in November 2002. He is West of Scotland President in 2004.

ROSS MATHESON

Born and bred in the south side of Glasgow in 1970 and stabled out of Whitecraigs Lawn Tennis Club I spent a huge amount of my youth annoying keen adult team players to "give me a knock". It is a rumour that members dived into hedges when they saw me arrive at the club. I was keen and lived and breathed the sport.

There were great people that assisted me in my development, my Mum and Dad were a huge support in these early times and they patiently guided my development under the watchful eye of Bill Moss. I could not have asked for a better coach and 20 years later I was still hanging on each and every word. There were no indoor courts and many winters were spent on the outdoor courts practicing the lessons that were learnt at my weekly lesson with Bill.

I was incredibly committed and ambitious with the only goal to play at Wimbledon. The Borg and McEnroe era inspired me. It would be over 15 years later before I faced one of them and competed at Wimbledon on the first of several occasions. To walk onto a court during Wimbledon and achieve a boyhood dream was a wonderful achievement for me and all those who had helped in my sporting career.

I spent 5 years in America at two separate universities before I was ready to give the tour a shot and with next to no money I battled my way around the world for six years. I was 24 before I played my first professional event and loved the challenge and competition. Playing all around the world and achieving a career high ATP singles ranking of 232 was a good achievement from a wee boy who had a dream.

There was one indoor court in Glasgow when I was a junior and it needed to be prepared with sawdust as the surface actually sweated. The scene in Scotland is now unrecognizable with plenty of coaches and world-class practice facilities. The sport has evolved.

Life is to be lived looking forward and understood looking back. There were some real mistakes that I made that could have been avoided with better advice and support and I truly feel for the professionals that are giving it their best shot at the moment.

The skills that I have learnt in professional sport have been invaluable in the business world and in my on going professional career. I have returned to my roots, met a great Glasgow girl, got married and brought our wee boy Max into the world. Who knows, he may be up at Whitecraigs soon!!

JOHN STEVENSON

John was co-opted on to the West Junior Committee in 1989 having assisted at the previous season's Junior Tournament. Following the untimely death of West of Scotland stalwart Irene MacKay he was voted on to the full Committee where he soon became Junior Convenor. As Director of the Junior Tournament at Craigholme School playing fields, the event won the SLTA Tournament of the Year in both 1992 and 1994. He was elected as Vice President of the Association in 1993 but on the retiral of Norman Floyd in 1994 was asked to become Honorary Secretary and Treasurer. John continued in this role until early 2003 when he was appointed as a full-time Executive Director of the new incorporated company Tennis West of Scotland and is now based in the County Office at the David Lloyd Club in Renfrew.

John served as the SLTA Convenor of Training and Selection for 4 years before being elected as President in 2000. When that Association incorporated in early 2001 he continued as President of Tennis Scotland until 2002. He has been an LTA Council Member since 1999.

John continues to play regularly at Strathgryffe Tennis & Squash Club. He served as President of Elderslie LTC from 1975-1980 and thereafter became Secretary until the club merged with Bridge of Weir to become Strathgryffe in 1991.

He is an active Referee Officiating at many of Scotland's premier events and has refereed his very popular Paisley & District Tournament since 1983.

DOROTHY BROWN

Mrs Dorothy Brown has served tennis well in the West of Scotland being on the WSLTA Committee for many years as well as currently being Secretary of the West of Scotland Junior Leagues and the Junior Tournament.

All the League results cards are sent to her involving over 500 matches and then she collates the individual results for the player ratings - quite a task.

Dorothy has been a member of Clarkston Lawn Tennis Club for more than 55 years and has served in many capacities in the Club during that time including Treasurer 1974-78, Secretary 1980-81 and Junior Match Secretary since 1979 and is still serving in that capacity.

Having served as Tennis Captain in 1978 she was elected as an Honorary Member of the Club in 1985 and has been Honorary Captain of the Club since 1995.

March 2003 - Mrs Dorothy Brown with her husband and the Scottish Award for Service to Tennis

In 2003 Dorothy was awarded the Honorary Vice Presidents Award at the Tennis Scotland Awards Dinner in recognition of voluntary services to tennis in Scotland. A similar award has recently been made by the Lawn Tennis Association at a ceremony in London.

HEATHER LOCKHART

Heather writes :-

"West of Scotland tennis is, and has been for me, synonymous with a number of events and places. It therefore seems appropriate, in the West's Centenary year, to record a few examples, the statistics can be found elsewhere!

I remember -

hitting against the practice board at Titwood LTC (which I still do on the rare occasion) and Billy Gillespie's coaching;

my first ever tournament match aged 9, at the West Junior Open at Anniesland against Mary Lavery;

participating at the Tea Cup at Inverclyde, Largs (under Mrs Mackay's watchful supervision - "no, I really don't know where the boys are!");

Johnny McKenzie's green flash shoes - he'll understand!;

debating with Grant Kerr as to who would get to play on the left for Junior League matches for Newlands (he became enlightened in the end!);

a road trip to Northumberland for the Junior County Cup with Mrs Matheson and some notable blondes (Katie Fulton, Carolyn Morgan, Ainslie McLellan et al!) and Mr M's Jag;

West Squad coaching with Sheila Moodie at the old indoor court at Scotstoun complete with puddles as the roof leaked;

partnering Lorna Browne for the first time at Senior County Week- and hardly hitting a ball as instructed - and enjoying some memorable County Weeks thereafter with "Big Cap" Christie and the rest of the West team (and eating lots of jammy doughnuts!).

I remember - spectating and playing at the West Senior Open (as a spectator, when an irate Ken Revie gave my little brother into trouble for playing in the stands whilst his match was in progress;

as a player, partnering Malky Watt to a Mixed title!);

Newlands winning the Scottish Cup after Marjory Love and Elena Baltacha saved match points.

There is no doubt that the above and many other opportunities would not have been possible were it not for the hard work and dedication of a whole host of people, mainly indeed volunteers, some of whom are mentioned above. On behalf of my contemporaries, I thank them and the Association for all that they have done over the years and wish the Association every success in the future."

Heather has recalled the above but has not mentioned her achievements which are considerable. Starting out as a Junior with the U12 in 1984, U14 in 1986, U16 in 1987 and 1988 and U18 in 1988/89/90. She also won the Doubles three times one of which was with her sister Abbe. She won the Scottish U18 in 1987/89/90.

Heather Lockhart 2001 Ladies Singles

Moving into Senior ranks Heather has won the Ladies Singles five times equalling Winnie Mason and just three less than that other Heather (Macfarlane). There is time yet to equal that record. The Doubles record is much nearer achievement, already with seven wins she just needs one more to equal Clara Black's record of eight wins achieved in 1961 (during the Red Hackle years when there was a qualifying Doubles SEL Moodie would have equalled Mrs Black's record). The 1998 win was with her mother Christine as her partner. Heather has won the Mixed Doubles four times.

Heather has played for Scotland and has played tournaments further afield and continues her high standard of play.

MALCOLM WATT

Malcolm started playing with a tennis ball in his grandfather's garden. Dr Miller, his grandfather, took him in hand and his tennis improved.

He played his first tournament at 11 years old - the West of Scotland Junior and he won the U12 event. His tennis continued to improve and Malcolm played in many tournaments and was awarded the Wilkinson Sword the SLTA Award after his successes in tournaments at Bell's, West of Scotland, Dunfermline and the Scottish at U14. He played in tournaments at Solihull, Worthing, Eastbourne and in 1983 Malcolm won the Scottish Nestlé Cup and went on to the International Finals at Queen's Club in London and was presented to H.R.H. the Duchess of Kent

Malcolm recollects a Doubles match partnered by Blane Dodds against David Felgate and Vitas Gerulitis which was very close the West pair losing 6/4 6/7 4/6. Another match was in the Scottish National League playing three sets against Miles McLagan.

As a Senior he won the Scottish Indoor Singles in 1990 and the Hardcourt Singles in 1992 and the Scottish University Singles 4 years in a row. Four Nations events were played in all there were 15 National Caps.

West of Scotland Championships have seen Malcolm have many successes including six Singles five Doubles and four Mixed Doubles as well as other appearances in the Finals.

Malcolm Watt meets the Duchess of Kent, 1983

DAVID BREWER

Born in 1985, David attended school at Belmont House, Glasgow and Leys School, Cambridge. David's early tennis was played at Whitecraigs Lawn Tennis & Sports Club, Glasgow where his first coach was John Howie. David Ison at Cambridge was his next coach and his present coach is Colin Beecher.

Brief Career Highlights

Won British 12 and under national championships and other age group titles then he competed in various ITF junior tournaments reaching semi-final at Winchester. He played in boys singles at Wimbledon in 2001.

In 2002 he competed in highest level of ITF junior events, reached the semi-final of Inka Bowl Quarter-final of Malta Cup, and won the tournament of Salsomaggiore. David competed in junior events at both the French Open and Wimbledon reaching the last 16 and also played in US Open Junior Event. By the year end he achieved Junior World Ranking of 38.

In 2003 David competed in Australian Open Junior Event and won the prestigious Banana Bowl Tournament. He reached the Quarter- final of European Junior Tournament and competed again in Wimbledon Junior Event. Playing in various ATP Future Tournaments, he reached his highest Junior World Ranking of No. 8.

ALAN MACKIN

Born in 1981, Alan attended Glasgow Academy until June 1997 when he joined L.T.A. squad at Bath University. His tennis was played at Whitecraigs Lawn Tennis & Sports Club, Glasgow where his first coach was John Howie. In 1995 Alan worked with Spanish coach, Master de Palmer whilst based for a time in Mallorca. Then from 1996 until 1998 he was coached by Simon Jones based at Bath University.

1998-2002: Member of squad, based in Monte Carlo managed by Ronnie Leitgeb who coached Thomas Muster, the Austrian player much admired by Alan for his achievements in recovering from serious injury to become World No.1 and winner of the French Open in 1995.

2003: Coached by Peter Mletzko, an Austrian based in Klagenfurt.

Brief Career Highlights

1993: Awarded scholarship by the Lawn Tennis Association as part of the Rover Junior Tennis Initiative.

1995: Won vital singles match against Navaho of Spain to set up success for Great Britain in the final of the Del Sol Cup, the European Team Championships for boys aged 14 and under. G.B. defeated Spain 3-2 in the final.

Won his match as member of the first British Team to win the NTT World Championship in Japan for boy's aged 14 and under. G.B. defeated Germany 3-0 in the final.

1997: Member of the British 16 and under team, which won the Jean Borotra Cup.

Won first ITF Junior World Ranking Tournament in Corfu, Greece.

1998-99: Competes in first ATP Futures Tournaments and achieves a world ranking of 616.

Reaches the quarter-final of the 1999 junior singles event at Wimbledon losing in three sets to David Nalbandian who goes on to reach the Men's final in 2002.

2000:   Reaches quarter-finals of ATP Future Tournaments in Slovenia, Eastbourne and Newcastle.

Selected for the Great Britain Davis Cup Squad v Czech Republic.

2001:   Competes in Satellite Circuits. Reaches semi-final of Futures event in Edinburgh.

Plays in first ATP Challenger Tournament in Tampere, Finland.

2002:   Starts the year at home, reaching the semi-final of Futures tournament in Glasgow.

Competes in Challenger Tournaments in Surbiton, Bristol, Finland & Russia.

Plays in Mens singles at Wimbledon losing to Jarkks Nieminen,world ranked no. 50 from Finland.

Year end Champions' Race ranking Position of 285.

2003:   Selected for Great Britain Davis Cup Team v Australia. Plays first singles tie losing to Mark Philippoussis 3-6, 3-6, 3-6.

Competes at Wimbledon losing in opening round to Flavio Saretta of Brazil, world ranked no.49.

Champions' Race Ranking Position- 229

JAMIE BAKER

Jamie had his first tennis racket at the age of 4 and even at such an early age he always said he was going to be a tennis player.

He played short tennis for a few months before moving on to a full size court. He was playing tournaments by the time he was 7. By 12 he was one of Britain's top players and was one of two players picked to play at the Orange Bowl Under 12 Tournament in Miami.

At age 13 he had to move south to maximize his tennis development.

At 14 he was Britain's top player in his age group and represented Great Britain on several occasions.

A major knee injury then resulted in 12 months out of tennis but undeterred Jamie returned again to be amongst the top 6 players in his age group in Britain by the time he was 16.

In 2003 his ITF World Junior ranking has risen from 505 to 18 and he is currently sitting at 23. This has allowed Jamie direct entry to the Junior Grand Slams and already his dream of playing at Wimbledon has been realised. Also in 2003 Jamie was in France leading the British U18 team in the European Championship Finals. He went on to compete in the British National Junior Championships before heading to the US Open. He then competed mainly in Senior Tournaments in order to start on his journey up the senior ATP rankings and also played in the Junior Grand Slams in his last year as a junior.

THE PURPLE PATCH

"The mind was there but the feet wouldn't go"
Elva Allan

There are occasions when the ball is out of reach but on the whole the Veterans are a hardy, fit group of people. Since the early 1980s this aspect of the sport has considerably developed. As the years go by and the players are moving up the age range more and more competitions are needed.

There is a comprehensive Veterans League and Cup Programme in the West of Scotland (see chapter on Leagues). In the year 2000 an Open Indoor West of Scotland Championship was inaugurated which has proved most popular.

The West of Scotland is a good example of the competitive spirit and our teams playing in the British Inter-County Championships in 2003 were :-

A Culloch, JT Wood, WJ Moss, JB Wilson & W Simpson at Inverclyde

Men's 45	Division 2B		Women's 40	Division 4A
Men's 55	Division 2A		Women's 50	Division 1 (S)
Men's 60	Division 1 (Runners-up)		Women's 60	Division 2B
Men's 65	Division 1		Women's 65	Division 1
Men's 70	Division 2A (Runners-up)			

In the years 2000 and 2001 the Ladies 50 team won Division 1 and in 2001 the Men's 65 team won Division 1. These teams were given special awards by both West of Scotland and Tennis Scotland.

Many of the Veterans take part in tournaments far and wide and there have been many successes. There is an exodus to the Veteran's Championships of Great Britain (played at Wimbledon) where the roll of honour is considerable.

1997 Scottish Team for the Four Nations International at Sundays Well Boating and Tennis Club Cork. 15 in photograph from West of Scotland.
Back row L-R - Ian Banner, John Coulter, Jimmy Wilson, Myra Hunter, Frank Paul, Jan Collins, George Copeland, Eileen Drummond, Graeme Downes, Lindsay McKendrick, Billy Simpson. Seated L-R - Sheila Moodie, Jet Morton, Christine Lockhart, Frances Taylor, Janette Coulter, Elizabeth Beeby, Elva Allan, Mina Brady. (Not in photo - Billy Gillespie, Jimmy Wood, Allan Black.)

2001 Scottish Veteran Indoor Championship at
Scotstoun - Finalists in Mixed Doubles
Jim & Lesley McGowan and Janette & John
Coulter

2001 Scottish Veterans Championships - Bridge of Allan

Veterans Tennis Championships of Great Britain - Singles

1990	WC Gillespie	M55 R/u		1986	Mrs FVM Taylor	L40 R/u
1993	AD Culloch	M60 W		1996	Miss MJ Love	L45 R/u
1994/5	JT Wood	M60 W		1997	Miss MJ Love	L45 W
1999/00/01	JT Wood	M65 W		1993	Mrs FVM Taylor	L50 R/u
1998/99	Mrs C Lockhart	L50 W				
2000	Miss MJ Love	L50 W				
2001	Miss MJ Love	L50 R/u				
2002	Mrs C Lockhart	L55 R/u				

West of Scotland Ladies 50 Team
2001 GB Division 1 Intercounty Champions.
L-R Christine Lockhart, Sheila Moodie, Marjory Love (Cap),
Janette Coulter

2001 Inter-County Ladies 50 Division 1 Champions
Tennis Scotland Award
L-R Eileen Mills, Sheila Moodie, Christine Lockhart,
Marjory Love

2002 West of Scotland Veterans Spring Knock Out - Winners Whitecraigs

2002 West of Scotland Indoor Championships

Doubles

1991	HS Matheson & (RA James)	M45 W	1986	Mrs FVM Taylor & (Mrs D Hunter)	L40 W
1992	HS Matheson & (RA James)	M45 R/u	1988	Mrs FVM Taylor & (Mrs MacPherson)	L40Ru
1999	G Copeland & HS Matheson	M55 W	1991/3	Mrs FVM Taylor & (Miss J Boothman)	L40 W
1996/97	JT Wood & (KF Buswell)	M60 R/u	1996	Mrs FVM Taylor & (Miss J Boothman)	L50 W
1999/01	JT Wood & (KF Buswell)	M65 W	1998	Mrs FVM Taylor & (Mrs B Norman)	L50 W
2000	JT Wood & (KF Buswell)	M65 R/u	2000/1/2	Mrs FVM Taylor & (Mrs D Hill)	L50 W
2001/2/3	Mrs J Coulter & (Mrs F Thomas)	L60 W			

Janette Coulter and her partner Felicity Thomas (Wales) are the holders of the British Ladies 60 Doubles on Grass, Hardcourt and Indoors.

The three Ladies who have won singles are all Captains of the British Team, Marjory Love of the 50 Team, Christine Lockhart of the 55 Team and Frances Taylor of the 60 Team. These teams play abroad in the World Team Championships.

Mens Division 1 (65) Inter County Champions 2001 - L-R W Simpson, P Leonard, W Gillespie, C Baker, F Murray, J Coulter

2003 British Grasscourt Champions Age 60 Ladies Doubles - Mrs Janette Coulter (Whitecraigs) & Mrs Felicity Thomas (Wales)

*West of Scotland Veterans Open
Indoors November 2003
Terry Smyth, Vic Stratta, Eric Dalgetty,
Keith Haig, Esther Haig, Keith
Berkley
Seated - Lesley McGowan, Eileen
Drummon, Alison Murchie, Marjorie
Love*

1948

 ## 𝓛awn 𝓣ennis 𝓒oaching 𝓛essons

MAY BE HAD ON WEST OF SCOTLAND COURTS, INDIVIDUALLY AND BY FOUR
PLAYERS, AT ANY TIME.

LECTURES and DEMONSTRATIONS can be given to groups of players.

FEE: £1 1s. 0d. per hour.   (No vacancies for Fridays or Saturdays).

Apply through your Club Secretaries or direct to—
DONALD MacPHAIL, Senr., Stuckgowan Lodge,
Arrochar, Tarbet, Loch Lomond.

MEMORABLE MOMENTS

Over the years there have been many occasions when an event has been outstanding and worthy of recording.

1884 RECORD OF MATCHES

From the foundation of the Club at Hamilton on 26th March 1884 progress to matchplay was speedy!

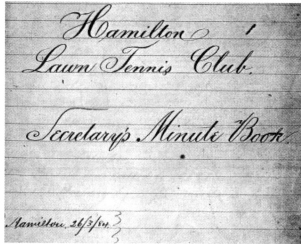

HAMILTON CUP 1886

Hamilton Lawn Tennis Club Tournament for which there was a silver chalice cup for the Ladies Singles was taking place from 1886. By 1891 Miss May Mitchell had won it for the third year running and as was the custom in those far off days May Mitchell won the cup outright.

In the 1990s the cup was for sale at an auction in New Zealand. The purchaser thought it had come from Hamilton New Zealand and on investigation it was discovered to have come from Scotland. It was then offered for sale to the Hamilton Club who duly purchased it.

Poloc Garden Party 1906

POLOC GARDEN PARTY

These featured in June of each year and photograph formally taken. Tennis was played before an audience of members and guests. The Minute of 24 May 1897 records that "Mrs Kennedy agreed to purvey the Garden Party on June 19th at 1/3 per head. It was agreed to have a Brass Band. It was agreed that gentlemen's tickets be 2/6 and ladies 1/6.

CORONATION MATCH 18th JULY 1911 GEORGE V

The Paisley Lawn Tennis Club have a minute of 6th June 1911 referring to the composition of the team which would give the impression that the Paisley and the Edinburgh branches of the MacRobert family were involved with the organisation of the match. The photograph of this match along with the newspaper report in the Paisley Daily Express of Wednesday 19th July gives the details.
The MacRobert family were and are solicitors and lawyers in Glasgow and Edinburgh

In 1937 the Coronation of GEORGE IV took place on 12th May. There were three matches played against the East of Scotland at that time though there is no indication that they were specially arranged : -

1st May	Mixed Doubles at Paisley	East won 10 matches to 6
15th May	Ladies Doubles at Edinburgh	West won 6 matches to 3
22nd May	Men's Doubles at Edinburgh	East won 6 matches to 0

In 1953 the Coronation of ELIZABETH II took place on 2nd June no signifcance was given to the West v East and the results were as follows : -

2nd May	Mixed Doubles at Pollokshields	match drawn 8 matches each.
23rd May	Ladies Doubles at Pollokshields	East won 6 matches to 3
23rd May	Men's Doubles at Craiglockhart	East won 6 matches to 3

18th July 1911
GA Patterson, JMN Sykes, R Welsh, H Cook, HA Fuller
WR Cook, AM MacKay, A Wylie Jr, AM MacRobert, JH Johnston, AW McGregor, JD Dallas

LAWN TENNIS.

PAISLEY (ASSISTED) V. EAST OF SCOTLAND.

This game, postponed from Coronation week owing to inclement weather, was brought off successfully yesterday afternoon at the Thornly Park Courts. The East of Scotland team was a strong one, including ex-Scottish Champion Morrell Mackay and A. Wallace M'Gregor, but the Paisley side was strengthened by the inclusion of ex-West Champions J. N. M. Sykes and George A. Patterson and Alex. Wylie, jun., a prominent figure in the West of Scotland League Championship team. The weather conditions were favourable, and the spectators, who were numerous, greatly enjoyed the match. Paisley at the end of the first set enjoyed a 2-1 lead, but at the end of the second round there was an equality in matches, but a two-set lead in the East's favour. This gave a tinge of keen play to the third round, where the East further improved their lead, and won by one match. The feature of the closing play was the stiff fight that Sykes and Patterson had to put up to overcome the opposition of the third Edinburgh couple—Dallas and M'Robert. Details:—

FIRST ROUND.

J. N. M. Sykes and George A. Patterson (Paisley) beat Robin Welsh and H. A. Fuller (East of Scotland)- 4-6, 6-4, 3-6.

Alexander Wylie, jun , and Jack Johnstone (Paisley) lost to A. Morrice MacKay and A. Wallace M'Gregor (East of Scotland)—3-6, 0-6.

W. R. Cook and H. Cook (Paisley) beat A M. M'Robert and J. D. Dallas (East of Scotland)—6-1, 6-3.

	Matches.	Sets.	Games.
Paisley,	2	4	33
East of Scotland,	1	3	53

SECOND ROUND.

W. R. Cook and H. Ocok (Paisley) lost to Robin Welsh and H. A. Fuller (East of Scotland)—2-6, 4-6.

Alex. Wylie, jun., and J. Johnstone (Paisley) beat J. D. Dallas and A. M'Robert (East of Scotland)—6-1, 5-7, 6-4.

A. Morrice MacKay and A. Wallace M'Gregor (East of Scotland) beat J. N. M. Sykes and George A. Paterson (Paisley)—7-5, 8-6.

	Matches.	Sets.	Games.
Paisley,	3	6	65
East of Scotland,	3	8	71

THIRD ROUND.

W. R. Cook and H. Ocok (Paisley) lost to A. Morrice MacKay and A. Wallace M'Gregor (East of Scotland) 5-7, 4-6.

Alex. Wylie, jun., and J. Johnstone (Paisley) lost to Robin Welsh and H. A. Fuller (East of Scotland)——2-6, 5-7.

J. N. M. Sykes and George A. Patterson (Paisley) beat J. D. Dallas and A. M. M'Robert (East of Scotland)—8-6, 3 6, 6-3.

	Matches.	Sets.	Games.
East of Scotland	5	13	112
Paisley,	4	8	100

VICTORY COMPETITION 1919

The Leagues did not recommence until 1920 and for 1919 A Victory Competition took place. Brass Shields mounted on wood were given to the winning clubs. Hamilton LTC have two of them one for the Ladies and one for the Men. No other club has so far mentioned them.

SUZANNE LENGLEN PLAYS AT HAMPDEN 1927

Mlle Suzanne Lenglen, the world famous tennis player, came to Glasgow to play an exhibition match at Hampden Park. This match, and other matches throughout the country, was promoted by Mr CB Cochrane. It was played on Tuesday 12th July 1927.

The Glasgow Herald reports that:-
"Accompanied by her mother, Suzanne wore a pretty beige frock and a dark blue sports blazer, and carried a heavy squirrel fur coat in her arm, was met at Central Station as she stepped from the London train by Mr CB Cochrane the promoter of the match, and presented with a bouquet of red roses. She then proceeded to the Central Station Hotel, where she will stay during her short visit to the city."

L-R - Karel Kozeluh, Evelyn Dewhurst, Suzanne, CB Cochran, the promoter, Vivien Glasspool, Dora Koring and Howard Kinsey.

The matches started at 6.30pm. The cost of entry was 2/- for the ground tickets and for the stand 7/6 up to half a guinea (10/6) and there were about eight thousand there to watch. The tennis court was wooden covered in a green cloth and was laid out on the pitch nearer the stand side.

The Glasgow Herald reports:- *"The progress of the matches was announced after every point by the umpire, Mr DL Craig, whose voice was carried to the most distant parts of the enclosure by amplifiers. The weather was favourable except for a fleeting shower which came on when the last match was in progress."* The umpire of 2004 would certainly not have chaired three consecutive matches!

Suzanne plays Evelyn Dewhurst before a crowd of over 8,000 at the Queen's Park Football Club at Hampden Park, Glasgow on 12th July.

There was a Gent's Singles to open the programme between Karl Kozeluh (from Prague) and Howard Kinsey (America) which Kinsey won 4/6 7/5 6/2.

Suzanne played Mrs Evelyn Dewhurst (a former Champion of Ceylon) which Suzanne won 6/2 6/0 in just twenty minutes, showing the superiority of her play.

The evening concluded with a Mixed Doubles between Suzanne and Karl Kozeluh and Evelyn Dewhurst and Howard Kinsey. This was a much closer encounter and Suzanne and Karl won 0/4 3/6 6/1.

POTTED HISTORY 1928

Andrew Clark Esq
Ryl Park View, Portland Park,
Hamilton

Greenhall, Mch
16 Nov 28.

Dear Sir,

Hamilton Lawn Tennis Club

I have yours of the 14th inst: Oh my if I only had you here for an hour I cd yarn about the old Club tell you wd be quite tired hearing me. Well in the spring of 1884 I got Sir H. S. Keith to go with me to Col. Clark-Forrest anent forming a Tennis Club & he went whole heartedly into the project, so that a meeting of all interested was held in the Commercial Hotel on 26 Mch 1884 presided over by Col Clark-Forrest & it was resolved to form a Club Col Clark Forrest was elected President, D. G. Kemp, Vice P. A. J. Joyce Hon Secy & your humble servant Match Secy & W.Al Dunnett Treasurer, the members of Comtee as far as I rememb. were, Sir H S. Keith, Melville Mitchell, Robin, Castlehill, Barrie Bothwell, & Wiseman, Jervial Jeweler. There were 76 members the first year at a guinea for Gentlemen

Gentlemen, & 10/6 for ladies

On the 30th Apl I sent out Circulars for the opening wh. took place on 3 May which was duly performed by Col Clark Forrest & his three daughters — thereafter the Club went ahead in full form. The first match we played on 3 July agt the Y. M. C. Ass. on the 8 in W. Coatbridge on 16th v Polock & 1st L.R.V. on 3d Augt. & the returns were all duly played thereafter. We did not loose a single one of these matches.

These matches were all played on grass courts. In 1885 we entered into a lease of the ground with the Duke & then made 4 ash Courts. In 1886 we joined the Tennis League. We had a very strong team in. Kemp & Shanks, Gordon Mitchell & Forgie, Young & Wiseman, Melville Mitchell & ~~Brown~~. Farrest. The 2d eight we had Dunnett, Miss Thorburn. Willie Ross, two Robins Tom Wiseman, Tom A. Dykes, London Clark as time went on we got Adam, McIntosh Hugh McLachlan, Robt Willie Robertson to join. In the year 1888 we got took the League Championship

M

In 1886 the Club started the Lanarkshire Tournament wh. was played first on (University) 23, 24, & 25 Sep. Jackson was Champion & Miss Jessie Forrest was Lady Champion. The Misses Forrest took the doubles – Miss Jessie took the Championship two years running & then Maggie Rose took it – she was a great player both in driving & volleying – next year Miss May Mitchell came to the front & she was a powerful player in driving & placing – Steel of Ednr. took the Champ. one year & Kemp another –

As far as the Club was concerned I have to mention that we had a great & grand ladies team wh. in all my term with the Club, they never lost a match they consisted of Misses Jessie & Annie Forrest, Miss Forrest & Miss Williams, Miss Maggie Rose & Miss Robin, Miss Clark & Miss Anderson. I remb at their request I went with them to Partickhill when they met their strong ladies team & won by 10 to 2. How proud I was of them!

I am sorry to say nearly all those fine old players are dead, but many happy times we all had together.

I am so pleased to hear that the Club is going on in the old ground yet. is truly a lovely spot — out of the way & yet so near.

If there is anything else you wish to know about hesitate to write me & I will do my best to answer. If there is any time you are passing this way be sure & call me up. I can show you two fine Photos of the Tournaments

Sincerely yours

Geo Young

TENNIS 1932

DL Craig who was a West of Scotland Champion became a coach and had his own brand of tennis racquet. His comments make interesting reading! Has anything really changed or should the point be considered that if the top team needs a substitute then that substitute needs the practise to be able to cope and it goes all the way to the fifth team. The modern coaching approach is different is it not?

TENNIS

No. 1 of a series by D. L. Craig.

THE weather prophets are all in agreement regarding the prospects of a good summer, so let's hope they are right and that we will have lots of good tennis weather.

I cannot help but think that if the average tennis player would just put a little more thought behind their shots, their game would be greatly improved and with that their enjoyment in playing the game.

Don't be ready to blame your partner, the racket, the balls, the court, in fact anything and everything but yourself when you are playing badly; just take a thought to yourself and you'll find, nine times out of ten, that the fault is with the wielder of the racket who is not concentrating sufficiently.

Tennis without concentration is quite hopeless, besides taking away from your partner's and opponent's pleasure. One point I have never heard cleared up is why the poorer players in a club who play perhaps once a week, and then with neither concentration nor enthusiasm, consider the team players selfish because they are not over anxious to play with them.

The team players have put in a lot of hard work to improve their game, they have gone to the Club earlier and stayed later than other members simply because of their enthusiasm and wish to improve, and, after having done that, it is hardly likely that they are going to burst themselves going round the Club playing with the poorer players who just can't be bothered.

It seems to me a selfish thought on the part of the poorer players to expect the team players to play them when they are not prepared to do their bit by working hard to improve their game.

Don't forget, if you are a beginner or have been playing without concentration or enthusiasm, that the moment you show real keenness to improve, the team players, as it is all to their benefit to improve the Club standard, will be the first to help and encourage.

Choosing a new racket is what most players will be thinking about at this time of the year. For a lady, I would suggest a 12½ oz. to 13 oz. racket with, if anything, the weight in the handle, and for a man a 13½ oz. to 14 oz., evenly balanced or the weight inclined to be in the handle.

If you have been playing Badminton during the winter, don't attempt to buy a new tennis racket until you have handled your old one enough to become quite accustomed to its weight.

Make up your mind what you wish to pay, then ask the assistant to put out four or five round about your price, the weight you require and size of handle. If you pick them up one at a time and play a few imaginary shots, you will be sure to like the feel of one so choose that one. To see and try a dozen or more rackets is only to get confused and buy one which in the end you will not be quite satisfied was the best of the large selection you saw.

The quickest method of improving one's game is by practising against a wall or Driving Board, and every Club should have the necessary space should be equipped with the latter. At the same time a Driving Board will be useless unless you are particular to play each shot as it should be played, correct foot-work being absolutely necessary.

I have gone through Messrs. Lumley's stock of Rackets, and one could not wish for a better selection, including a specially selected model of my own which is strung 1st quality tracey gut.

1932 TENNIS RACKETS

The following is a complete list of our 1932 range :—

RACKETS SPECIALLY MADE FOR LUMLEYS'.

The "R.R.20," 4-ply Beech and Ash, Beech outside, Leather Grip	55/-
The "Caledonia," 3-ply Ash and Beech, Ash outside, Rubber Grip	47/6
The "Varsity," 3-ply, Ash with coloured centre ply, Rubber Grip	47/6
The "Inner Court," 3-ply Beech and Ash, Beech outside	45/-
The "Scottish Champion Special," 3-ply, 2 Beech and 1 Ash	42/-
The "Hardcourt," Rent Ash, rolled frame, protected head, Leather Grip	42/-
The "Scottish Champion," 3-ply frame, 2 Ash and 1 Beech	37/6
The "Gold Medal," Ash with Green Inlay	32/6
The "Vantage," 3-ply frame, 2 Beech and 1 Ash	32/6
The "Standard," Rent Ash, rolled frame, blue slips under handle plates	27/6
The "Tournament," 2-ply Beech, Rubber Grip	25/-
The "International," Rent Ash, rolled frame	25/-
The "Liberton," Rent Ash, inside bevel, shoulder face-plates	21/-
The "Ace," 2-ply Ash, inlaid throat	18/6
The "Special Club," Rent Ash, rolled frame	14/6
The "Club," Rent Ash, inside bevel	10/6

RACKETS BY FAMOUS MAKERS.

Hazell's "Topspin"	75/-	Austin's "Blue Spot"	67/6
,, "Super Speed"	72/6	,, "Austin"	63/-
Dunlop's "Maxpli"	75/-	Ayres' "Davis Cup"	67/6
,, "De Luxe"	57/6	,, "New Wimbledon"	42/-
,, "Blue Flash"	42/-	Gray's "Super Blue"	67/6
Slazengers' "Queen's Tournament"	70/-	,, "Light Blue"	65/-
,, "Doherty"	60/-	,, "Cambridge"	42/-
,, "Meteor"	42/-	Sykes' "Prefectus"	65/-
Cobbett's "D. L. Craig"	63/-	Wisden's "Valkyrie"	67/6
,, "Ailza"	45/-	,, "New Wisden"	63/-

SOME NEW SUMMER LINES

IN the Golf Department a few new lines have been added. The most important of these is the Mark Seymour Silver Arrow Golf Club. We use in these an extremely attractive face inlaid with Ivorine in various colours, and we fit with Chromium Plated True Temper shaft and best Mark Seymour grip. The club sells at 21/- and is really a masterpiece. For those players who wish true temper shafts but who do not want to pay top price, we have brought out a special line to sell at 16/6. They are all made and in every way extremely good value.

A great difficulty amongst men players is to find something to take the place of ordinary braces. A belt is quite good, but the restriction caused by it is apt to become uncomfortable. To those players, the "Martin" Sports Braces should make a special appeal. They are made with spring wire threaded with a stout tape to prevent undue stretching. They are extremely comfortable and allow perfect freedom of the body when swinging. The price of them is 4/6.

Few Golfers nowadays do not carry an umbrella on the course. In the past, however, the price of a real Golf Umbrella has been rather high. We have been able to secure a very special line of 27½ inch umbrellas, with double ribs and covered with a stout cloth in two colour combinations, the price of this most attractive line is 8/6.

In the Tennis Department, there are several new lines worthy of a brief description. This season we offer a ball which should have a universal appeal on account of its price and its extremely durable qualities. This is the Spencer Moulton Tennis Ball, made by the well-known firm of rubber manufacturers of that name, and on test it is equal to any and superior to most other balls on the market. The price to the public is 13/6 per dozen and to Clubs 12/- per dozen.

The well-known Dunlop Sports Company are marketing two particularly attractive tennis shoes, one for ladies and one for gent.'s. They are made with canvas uppers and reinforced toe caps and finest quality black crepe rubber soles. They have been designed particularly to stand the hard wear and tear on hard courts. The price is 5/11 for ladies and 6/11 for gent.'s.

Although the bulk of our toy business is done during the winter months, there is always a ready sale for any new lines, and we are now taking delivery of a number of attractive items which our buyers purchased at the B.I.F.

Every parent knows the keen interest taken by their children in gardening, and a very pleasing series of garden rollers for children are made in England. When unfilled they are very light, but have been arranged so that they can be filled with either sand or water. The weight when so filled varies from 25 lbs. to 40 lbs., and the three sizes sell respectively at 8/11, 10/6 and 12/-.

Another line of interest to the young gardener is "Garden Joys." This is an attractive box containing six small pots, six packets of real seeds, a trowel and a watering-can, and costs only 2/-.

The Little Dressmaker sets will surely appeal to those little girls who are fond of needlework. Sufficient material is enclosed to make a number of very pretty and dainty frocks for their dolls. The sets are complete with every requisite, and there are four sizes ranging in price from 2/6 to 10/6.

Most little boys are imbued with a martial spirit and the "Jollyboy" machine gun will make universal appeal. This gun fires rolls of explosive caps in a most realistic and fascinating manner. It is strongly made and only costs 2/6.

Two new dolls are worthy of mention. First, the Beach Baby Doll, which, at 4/-, is a very attractive number. The doll is dressed in Beach Pyjamas, with a large sun hat, and colourings have been carefully designed. The other is the Birthday Doll. This very pretty English made doll costs 6/6, and each doll has a lucky stone necklace of the particular month in which the owner's birthday falls.

INTERNATIONALE LAWN TENNIS CLUB DE FRANCE v WEST OF SCOTLAND LTA

At Pollokshields Wednesday 12th July 1933

J Borotra was one of the Four Musketeers that famous group which were successful in the Davis Cup for France from 1927 to 1932.

In the Singles J Borotra played and won against Dr JB Fulton (Newlands); A Gentien played and lost to RR Finlay (Newlands). In the exhibition match A Gentien played with Archie McVie (Pollokshields) against J Borotra and Jack Hill (Newlands)

J Borotra

BROOMHILL 21st APRIL 1934

Shorts for tennis. Miss J Jamieson and Miss Winnie Mason gave the new fashion a "leg up" when with Mr McVie and Dr JB Fulton they palyed an exhibition game at the opening of Broomhill Courts. The opening ceremony was performed jointly by Lieut-Colonel McAndrew, MP for Partick and Mrs McAndrew.

WORLD WAR II 1939-1945

Hamilton LTC courts are covered over to provide a dance floor for troops.

Many clubs were open and allowed their members serving in the Armed Forces to play free of charge when home on leave.

The Leagues were suspended. A Charity League was run for clubs organised from the Glasgow University.

Balls were in short supply and rationing of them was in force for some time afterwards. Drumchapel minute of 20th April 1945 :-

The optimism of being able to survive on 20 is incredible!

Minutes of Meeting of.
General Committee of The
Paisley Lawn Tennis Club.
Held at The Club House,
on Tuesday, the 6th June 1911
at 8.30 oclock

It was decided to ask three men from
other Clubs to assist in the match against
Mr. MacRoberts Edinburgh Team.

COACHES COURSE 1950

Vaughan Owen ran a Coaching Course at Partick in November 1950.

An early coaching course by Vaughn Gwen (Partick), autumn 1950

1951 PROFESSIONAL TENNIS AT PAISLEY ICERINK

Juniors keenly watch the play.

West of Scotland juniors watching the professionals at Paisley Ice Rink. Front row L-R Anne Walker, Joan Thomson (Greenock), Cathy King (Western)

13 APRIL 1954 THE CORPORATION OF THE CITY OF GLASGOW

A RECEPTION on the occasion of the Jubilee of the WEST OF SCOTLAND LAWN TENNIS ASSOCIATION was given in the City Chambers Glasgow.

The Reception of Guests by the Lord Provost and Magistrates was in the Satinwood Salon from 7.30 till 8pm. The Guests then moved to the Banqueting Hall where the speakers were The Rt. Hon. The Lord Provost Thomas A. Kerr Esq., J.P. and D.N.Graham, Esq President, West of Scotland Lawn Tennis Association.

There followed Dancing in the Banqueting Hall till 12 Midnight with John McCormack's Orchestra. The Programme itemised all the dances from Quicksteps to Modern Waltzes and from the Gay Gordons and the Eightsome Reel. There was an alternative in the Council Hall of Vocal Music from 8.30 till 10.30pm. This was provided by Janette Sclanders Soprano, Agnes Duncan Contralto, C Archer Mitchell Entertainer, Matthew Nisbet Bass-Baritone and Sybil Tait, L.R.A.M., A.R.C.M. Accompanist. Refreshments were in the Upper Corridor till 11.30pm.

CANNES 1964

The Scots team leaving Turnhouse Airport for Cannes. L-R - Colin Baxter, Ann McAlpine, Harry Matheson, Joyce Barclay, George Kelly, Sheila Moodie, Jim Nicol and Frances MacLennan.

In February 1964 a team from Scotland were invited to Cannes to celebrate the 130th Anniversary of the first visit of Lord Brougham from Scotland who had been credited with having started the tourism to Cote d'Azur. This team of eight had five players from the West of Scotland. This visit to Cannes was hosted and paid for by the City of Cannes. There were representatives from Football, Golf, Yachting and Pipe Bands and Lord Provosts from Edinburgh Aberdeen and Perth, Quite an event!

There were Receptions and Parades and of course the spoting events. The Tennis matches played were Singles, Doubles and Mixed Doubles and the Scots won 11 matches to 3.

INDOOR TENNIS 1960s

Indoor tennis had become available at Glasgow Corporation Schools Games Halls at Nethercraigs, Scotstoun, Lochend and Liddlesdale. The West of Scotland had team practice time for Seniors and the Junior County Club and many clubs took advantage of being able to book time on a weekly or fortnightly basis. The surface was tarmac and, while not ideal, provided regular guaranteed tennis throughout the winter and the cost was 15/- per hour.

DIAMOND JUBILEE 1964

A Dance was held in the Marlborough Shawlands on 4th September 1964 to celebrate this occasion. One hundred and fifty-five were present and a profit of £31:6:0 was made.

MAUREEN CONNOLLY TROPHY 1995

This Trophy is played for between Great Britain and America for Ladies Under 21 teams. It is played alternately in Great Britain and America. It was played at Scotstoun in 1995.

It is supported by the Maureen Connolly Brinker Foundation to encourage young Players.

Anne Jones (British NPC)
taking coaching for local youngsters

Sally Smythe, Chauffeuse

Maureen Connolly Trophy, Scotstoun -
Rob Hardie instructing the ball girls

2004 CENTENARY CELEBRATIONS

The Centenary is being celebrated in several ways some of which have been at the planning stage for about three years.

There is an Exhibition "100 Years of Tennis In the West of Scotland" in the Peoples Palace Museum in Glasgow Green which runs from the 7th May until the 19th August. This fascinating exhibition celebrates the game, the people and the places associated with it over the past century. Photographs, memorabilia, trophies and costumes bring alive this popular sport.

A book on the History of the Association is also being published. It also has the title "100 Years of Tennis in the West of Scotland". This is a record of people places and events in our 100 years of existence.

Both the Exhibition and the Book have been supported by the Heritage Lottery Fund.

The Junior and Senior Championships too will celebrate the event.

In July there is planned a Match against the All England Club at Wimbledon and on 8th August at Strathgryffe Lawn Tennis Club there will be a Mixed Doubles Tournament at which there will be a Couple from every Club in the Association taking part.

Our Birthday is of course on 3rd of November and this special year will end with a Civic Reception followed by a Dinner in the City Chambers on 12th November. Tickets for the Dinner can be purchased from West of Scotland County Office.

6 May 2004, Opening of Exhibition in Peoples Palace
L-R - Elizabeth Stevenson (in costume), Myra Hunter, Exhibition Organiser, John Stevenson, West of Scotland County Tennis Executive, Fiona Hayes, Curator of Peoples Palace & Dave

PRESIDENTS

1904	AJ Smellie	Pollokshields		1958	CA Snell	Gartocharn
1905	AJ Smellie	Pollokshields		1959	JC Wall	Pollokshields
1906	GA Paterson	Partick		1960	JC Poole	Bellahouston
1907	JG Laing	Bothwell		1961	JG Steele	Hamilton
1908	A Buchanan	Bellahouston		1962	JG Rutherglen	Newlands
1909	JB Paterson	Partickhill		1963	JF Hunter	Broomhill
1910	JNM Sykes	Partick		1964	Mrs LB Stevenson	Hamilton
1911	GB Primrose	Titwood		1965	AG Thomson	Newlands
1912	R Paul	Mount Vernon		1966	JD Budge	Poloc
1913	WJ Hill	Partick		1967	Dr SC Freelander	Titwood
1914	AG McNaughton	Bearsden		1968	J Blain	Bellahouston
				1969	WC Gillespie	Newlands
1919	AL McKillop	Hamilton		1970	RS Allan	Cambuslang
1920	WB Barr	Partickhill		1971	JE McAlpine	Bellahouston
1921	K Buchanan	Thorntonhall		1972	Miss DR McNair	Western
1922	R Grieve	Hamilton		1973	KB Gray	Newlands
1923	HC Wright	Newlands		1974	T Brown	Thorn Park
1924	RE Boyd	Bearsden		1975	RS Paterson	Clarkston
1925	TC Caldwell	Dowanhill		1976	A Wotherspoon	Hamilton
1926	DW McLennan	Paisley		1977	BW Watson	Eaglesham
1927	T Scott	Titwood		1978	RJ Jenkins	Giffnock
1928	PR Moffat	Pollokshields		1979	JS Sinclair	Thorn Park
1929	JG Patrick	Partickhill		1980	CM Thomson	Whitecraigs
1930	JG Harvey	Partick		1981	GAB Holmes	Westerton
1931	BA Moulding	Titwood		1982	Mrs I McKay	Stepps
1932	J Dykes	Bearsden		1983	J Watson	Eaglesham
1933	AC Stokes	Cartha		1984	J Walker	Uplawmoor
1934	RB White	Thorntonhall		1985	DG Russell	Hamilton
1935	RG Thompson	Queens Park		1986	DTC Penny	Thorn Park
1936	RF Braid	Pollokshields		1987	T Rae	Weir Recreation
1937	RW Brown	Partick		1988	Dr CM Kesson	Dowanhill
1938	RW Brown	Partick		1989	RP Whitesmith	Broomhill
1939	Dr FW Sandeman	Hamilton		1990	GB Kerr	Newlands
				1991	GB Kerr	Newlands
1946	Dr FW Sandeman	Hamilton		1992	Mrs S Sim	Poloc
1947	JC Marshall	Thorntonhall		1993	JC Bell	Clarkston
1948	WF Fulton	Newlands		1994	Dr JG Beeley	Bearsden
1949	RA Lightbody	Cartha		1995	Dr JG Beeley	Bearsden
1950	W Reid	Ferguslie		1996	DW Marshall	Broomhill
1951	W Reid	Ferguslie		1997	DW Marshall	Broomhill
1952	H Herbert	Western		1998	Mrs AR Robertson	Titwood
1953	W Drummond	Langside Hill Church		1999	Mrs AR Robertson	Titwood
1954	DN Graham	Hillpark		2000	J Lavery	Stepps
1955	IS Stewart	Bellahouston		2001	J Lavery	Stepps
1956	Dr TJR Miller	Craighelen		2002	WB Allan	Next Generation
1957	JB Wilson	Cardonald		2003	WB Allan	Next Generation

HON. SECRETARIES & TREASURERS

1904 - 1910	John T. Rankin
1911 - 1914	L. Seymour Graham
1918	James B. Paterson (interim)
1919 - 1929	John W. Snodgrass
1930 - 1946	John G. Patrick
1947 - 1962	Aikman G. Thomson
1963 - 1966	Robert W. Muir
1967 - 1986	John Y. Crawford
1987 - 1994	Norman G. Floyd
1994 -	John A.E. Stevenson

WEST OF SCOTLAND LEAGUE COMPETITION

FIRST DIVISION WINNERS
PREMIER DIVISION from 1992

	MEN	LADIES		MEN	LADIES
1905	Pollokshields	No Contest	1960	Newlands	
1906	Pollokshields	Pollokshields	1961	Newlands	Pollokshields
1907	Pollokshields	Pollokshields	1962	Newlands	
1908	Pollokshields	Pollokshields	1963	Newlands	Pollokshields
1909	Pollokshields	Pollokshields	1964	Newlands	Newlands
1910	Pollokshields	Pollokshields	1965	Titwood	Newlands
1911	Pollokshields	Partick	1966	Titwood	Clarkston
1912	Titwood	Bellahouston	1967	Titwood	Western
1913	Titwood	Newlands	1968	Western	Cambuslang
1914	Partick	Partick	1969	Newlands	Craighelen
1915-1919 No Contests		No Contests	1970		Western
1920	Partick	Partick	1971	Western	Cambuslang
1921	Pollokshields	Partick	1972	Newlands	Clarkston
1922	Pollokshields	Partick	1973	Western	Elderslie
1923	Partick	Partick	1974	Western	Elderslie
1924	Partick	Titwood	1975	Western	Elderslie
1925	Newlands	Partick	1976	Western	Hamilton
1926	Newlands	Newlands	1977	Broomhill	Whitecraigs
1927	Partick	Newlands	1978	Broomhill	
1928	Newlands	Newlands	1979	Broomhill	Hamilton
1929	Pollokshields	Newlands	1980	Broomhill	Broomhill
1930	Newlands	Partick	1981	Broomhill	
1931	Newlands	Pollokshields	1982	Broomhill	Hamilton
1932	Newlands	Pollokshields	1983	Broomhill	Broomhill
1933	Pollokshields	Pollokshields	1984	Broomhill	Broomhill
1934	Pollokshields	Pollokshields	1985	Western	Broomhill
1935	Pollokshields	Pollokshields	1986	Newlands	Whitecraigs
1936	Pollokshields	Pollokshields	1987	Broomhill	Broomhill
1937	Pollokshields	Partick	1988	Broomhill	Newlands
1938	Pollokshields	Kelvinside	1989	Newlands	Broomhill
1939	Pollokshields	Partick	1990	Newlands	Whitecraigs
1940-1946 No Contests		No Contests	1991	Broomhill	Whitecraigs
1947	Western	Kelvinside	1992	Broomhill	Broomhill
1948	Newlands	Pollokshields	1993	Broomhill	Newlands
1949	Newlands	Pollokshields	1994	Newlands	Broomhill
1950	Newlands	Pollokshields	1995	Newlands	Newlands
1951	Pollokshields	Pollokshields	1996	Newlands	Newlands
1952	Pollokshields	Pollokshields	1997	Strathgryffe	Newlands
1953	Pollokshields	Pollokshields	1998	Giffnock	Newlands
1954	Pollokshields	Newlands	1999	Giffnock	Newlands
1955	Hamilton	Pollokshields	2000	Whitecraigs	Newlands
1956		Pollokshields	2001	Giffnock	Newlands
1957			2002	Newlands	Newlands
1958	Newlands	Pollokshields	2003	Newlands	Newlands

WEST OF SCOTLAND JUNIOR LEAGUE COMPETITION MIXED DOUBLES

FIRST DIVISION WINNERS

1937	Newlands	1972	Hamilton
1938	Woodend	1973	Thorn Park
1939	Pollokshields	1974	Thorn Park
1940 -1946 No Contests		1975	
1947	Woodend	1976	Thorn Park
1948	Woodend	1977	
1949	Woodend	1978	Whitecraigs
1950	Newlands	1979	Whitecraigs
1951	Uddingston	1980	Whitecraigs
1952	Hillpark	1981	Whitecraigs
1953	Hillpark	1982	D1a Thorn Park D1b Giffnock
1954	Newlands	1983	D1a Broomhill D1b Whitecraigs
1955	Titwood	1984	D1a Broomhill D1b Whitecraigs
1956		1985	D1a Helensburgh D1b Giffnock
1957		1986	D1a Helensburgh D1b Giffnock
1958	Titwood	1987	D1a Helensburgh D1b Newlands
1959	Woodend	1988	Newlands
1960		1989	Newlands
1961	Stepps	1990	Newlands
1962	Titwood	1991	Newlands
1963	Newlands	1992	No results
1964	Whitecraigs	1993	No results
1965	Clarkston	1994	Strathgryffe
1966	Hillpark	1995	Strathgryffe
1967	Giffnock	1996	Helensburgh
1968	Newlands	1997	Strathgryffe
1969	Clarkston	1998	Strathgryffe
1970		1999	Strathgryffe
1971	Springboig	2000	Rutherglen

NB from 1982 - 1987 the leagues were a & b, a being north of the Clyde and b being south of the Clyde.

JUNIOR CLYDESDALE CUP

From 2001 the Junior Mixed Doubles changed to a knock out competition and renamed

2001	Thorn Park
2002	Thorn Park
2003	Thorn Park

WEST OF SCOTLAND JUNIOR LEAGUE COMPETITION

In the OPEN UNDER 12 age group girls and boys played in the same teams and in any combination. This was equality in that being so young there was deemed to be little difference in playing ability and since there were noticeably fewer girls in many clubs it allowed for say one girl and three boys to be in the same team. However when W.S.L.T.A. joined the National Junior Club Leagues this was not allowed.

	UNDER 16		UNDER 12	
	GIRLS	BOYS	OPEN	GIRLS
1992	Strathgryffe	Helensburgh		
1993	Strathgryffe	Whitecraigs		
1994	Helensburgh	Newlands	Bearsden	Woodend
1995	Helensburgh	Giffnock	Broomhill	Titwood
1996	Helensburgh	Bearsden	Broomhill	Newlands
1997	Helensburgh	Giffnock	Titwood	Whitecraigs
1998	David Lloyd	Giffnock	Giffnock	DavidLloyd
1999	David Lloyd	David Lloyd	Drumchapel	Thorn Park
2000	Whitecraigs	Giffnock	Thorn Park	Newlands

NATIONAL JUNIOR CLUB LEAGUES

	GIRLS U17	BOYS U17	GIRLS U 13	BOYS U13	GIRLS U 11	BOYS U 11
2001	Strathgryffe	Whitecraigs	Thorn Park	Giffnock	Thorn Park	Thorn Park
2002	Whitecraigs	Whitecraigs	ThornPark	Giffnock	Mount Vernon	Giffnock
2003	Thorn Park	Thorn Park	Thorn Park	Giffnock	Thorn Park	Thorn Park

SENIOR CALCUTTA CUP

Cup Presented by Hamilton Lawn Tennis Club
The Trophy is of Indian design and was donated by George Paterson, Calcutta.

The Cup is for Men's teams of affiliated clubs excluding the Premier Divison Clubs. Originally prior to the formation of the Premier Divison it excluded teams from the First Division.

1907	Pollokshields II	1961	Bellahouston
1908	Pollokshields II	1962	Paisley
1909	Pollokshields II	1963	Poloc
1910	Pollokshields II	1964	Hamilton
1911	Pollokshields II	1965	Hillpark
1912	Cambuslang	1966	Bellahouston
1913	Titwood II	1967	Broomhill
1914	Pollokshields II	1968	Poloc
1915-19	No contests	1969	Hamilton
1920	Partick II	1970	Hamilton
1921	Uddingston	1971	Craighelen LTC
1922	Ardgowan	1972	Craighelen LTC
1923	Hamilton	1973	Thorn Park
1924	Partick II	1974	Wishaw
1925	Pollokshields II	1975	Hamilton
1926	Springboig	1976	Mount Vernon
1927	Pollokshields II	1977	Springwells
1928	Kelvinside	1978	Whitecraigs
1929	Kelvinside	1979	East Kilbride
1930	Glasgow HSFP's	1980	Giffnock
1931	Kirkhill	1981	Western II
1932	Rutherglen	1982	Westermains
1933	Titwood	1983	Drumchapel
1934	Clarkston	1984	Craighelen
1935	Cathcart	1985	Craighelen
1936	Rutherglen	1986	Ardgowan
1937	Clarkston	1987	Ardgowan
1938	Paisley	1988	Milngavie & Bearsden
1939	Clarkston	1989	Burnside
1940-46	No contests	1990	Mount Vernon
1947	Kingswood	1991	Hamilton
1948	Newlands II	1992	Ardgowan
1949	Hillpark	1993	Strathgryffe
1950	Hillpark	1994	David Lloyd Renfrew
1951	Woodend	1995	David Lloyd Renfrew
1952	Pollokshields II	1996	David Lloyd Renfrew
1953	Pollokshields II	1997	Giffnock II
1954	The Glasgow University	1998	Milngavie & Bearsden
1955	Newlands II	1999	Milngavie & Bearsden
1956	Titwood	2000	Milngavie & Bearsden
1957	Paisley	2001	Milngavie
1958	Paisley	2002	Hamilton

JUNIOR CALCUTTA CUP

This competition is open to Men's teams from affiliated clubs except teams in the Premier to 4th Divisions.

Year	Winner	Year	Winner
1931	Millbrae	1971	East Kilbride
1932	Hallside	1972	Busby
1933	Drumpellier	1973	Westermains
1934	Hallside	1974	Kirktonhill
1935	Hallside	1975	Weir Recreation
1936	Hallside	1976	Garrowhill
1937	Greenock High School Former Pupils	1977	East Kilbride
1938	Whitecraigs	1978	Clarkston
1939	Finalists Whitecraigs/Templeton	1979	Kilmacolm
1940-1946	No Competition	1980	Burnside
1947	Elderslie	1981	Queens Park
1948	Glasgow Corporation Gas Dept	1982	Craighelen II
1949	Elderslie	1983	Garrowhill
1950	Hillhead High School Former Pupils	1984	Kirkhill
1951	Clyde Paper	1985	Poloc II
1952	Clyde Paper	1986	Mount Vernon II
1953	Hillington Estate	1987	Oban
1954	Thorn Park	1988	Thorn Park
1955	Renfrew	1989	Burnside II
1956	Thorn Park	1990	Mount Vernon II
1957	Partickhill	1991	Hamilton II
1958	Partickhill	1992	Broomhill II
1959	Civil Service Riddrie	1993	Broomhill II
1960	Civil Service Riddrie	1994	Hamilton III
1961	Ferguslie	1995	Partickhill
1962	Singer	1996	Titwood
1963	Lenzie	1997	Clarkston
1964	Ralston	1998	Ardgowan
1965	Hillpark II	1999	Ardgowan
1966	Rolls Royce Lanarkshire	2000	Craighelen
1967	Busby	2001	Rutherglen
1968	Whifflet	2002	Rutherglen
1969	Whifflet	2003	Mount Vernon II
1970	Elderslie		

CLYDESDALE CUP

Mixed Doubles - First Division

Cup Presented by
Clydesdale Lawn Tennis Club 1934

The First Division of this cup consists of 16 clubs who have the best aggregate in the Leagues

1920	Titwood	1965	Western
1921	Pollokshields	1966	Ardgowan
1922	Titwood	1967	Western
1923	Newlands	1968	Newlands
1924	Pollokshields	1969	Newlands
1925	Newlands	1970	Western
1926	Partick	1971	Hamilton
1927	Partick	1972	Hamilton
1928	Newlands	1973	Western
1929	Newlands	1974	Whitecraigs
1930	Not completed	1975	Elderslie
1931	Newlands	1976	Western
1932	Pollokshields	1977	Western
1933	Partick	1978	Elderslie
1934	Pollokshields A C	1979	Broomhill
1935	Pollokshields A C	1980	Broomhill
1936	Pollokshields A C	1981	Elderslie
1937	Pollokshields A C	1982	Elderslie
1938	Newlands LTC	1983	Broomhill
1939	Pollokshields A C	1984	Broomhill
1940-46	No Contests	1985	Broomhill
1947	Pollokshields A C	1986	Giffnock
1948	Pollokshields A C	1987	Newlands
1949	Pollokshields A C	1988	Dowanhill
1950	Newlands LTC	1989	Broomhill
1951	Pollokshields LTC	1990	Newlands
1952	Pollokshields LTC	1991	Broomhill
1953	Pollokshields LTC	1992	Broomhill
1954	Pollokshields LTC	1993	Newlands
1955	Newlands LTC	1994	Westermains
1956	Pollokshields LTC	1995	Strathgryffe
1957	Craighelen	1996	Newlands
1958	Newlands	1997	Strathgryffe
1959	Pollokshields	1998	Giffnock
1960	Hamilton	1999	Giffnock
1961	Pollokshields	2000	Newlands
1962	Pollokshields	2001	Newlands
1963	Newlands	2002	Giffnock
1964	Newlands	2003	Newlands

CLYDESDALE CUP

Mixed Doubles - Second Division

Cup Presented by
Clydesdale Lawn Tennis Club 1934

The Second Division of the cup consists of the clubs not in the first 16.

1920	Dalmuir	1965	Elderslie LTC
1921	Cambuslang	1966	Cambuslang LTC
1922	Renfrew	1967	Drumchapel LTC
1923	Dalmuir	1968	Cambuslang LTC
1924	Burnside	1969	Broomhill LTC
1925	Kirkhill	1970	Fort Matilda LTC
1926	Thorntonhall	1971	Giffnock LTC
1927	Not Completed	1972	Giffnock LTC
1928	Woodend	1973	Wishaw LTC
1929	Hamilton	1974	Ardgowan LTC
1930	Bridge of Weir	1975	Cambuslang LTC
1931	Drumchapel	1976	Ferguslie LTC
1932	Cathcart	1977	Bearsden LTC
1933	Fort Matilda	1978	Milngavie & Bearsden LTC
1934	Cathcart LTC	1979	East Kilbride LTC
1935	Clarkston LTC	1980	Clarkston LTC
1936	Queen's ParkLTC	1981	Uddingston LTC
1937	Drumchapel LTC	1982	Westermains LTC
1938	Western LTC	1983	Helensburgh LTC
1939	Bridge of Weir LTC	1984	Uddingston LTC
1940-46	No contests	1985	Mount Vernon LTC
1947	Queen's Park LTC	1986	Mount Vernon LTC
1948	Broomhill LTC	1987	Lenzie LTC
1949	Muirend & Busby LTC	1988	Thorn Park LTC
1950	Kirktonfield LTC	1989	Uddingston LTC
1951	Cardonald LTC	1990	Kilmacolm LTC
1952	Scottish Gas Board LTC	1991	Uddingston
1953	Dowanhill LTC	1992	Mount Vernon
1954	Alexandria LTC	1993	Mount Vernon
1955	Stepps LTC	1994	Mount Vernon
1956	Titwood LTC	1995	Mount Vernon
1957	Public Parks LTA	1996	Bearsden LTC
1958	Partickhill LTA	1997	Mount Vernon
1959	Elderslie LTC	1998	Ardgowan
1960	Broomhill LTC	1999	East Kilbride LTC
1961	Paisley LTC	2000	Lenzie
1962	Ferguslie LTC	2001	Ardgowan
1963	Ferguslie LTC	2002	Milngavie
1964	Lenzie LTC	2003	Busby

Dunlop West of Scotland Senior League Positions on 27/10/03

MEN

PREMIER DIVISION	P	W	D	L	WO	PTS
Newlands	10	9	0	0	-1	84
Giffnock	10	7	0	2	-1	74
Whitecraigs	10	6	0	3	-1	58
Western	10	4	0	6	0	43
Strathgryffe	10	2	0	8	0	24
Hamilton	10	0	0	9	-1	13

Play off: Mount Vernon beat Strathgryffe 7-2

DIVISION 1	P	W	D	L	WO	PTS
David Lloyd	10	10	0	0	0	90
Mount Vernon	10	8	0	2	0	82
Helensburgh	10	5	1	4	0	59
Newlands 2	10	5	0	5	0	52
Giffnock 2	10	2	1	7	0	40
Strathgryffe 2	10	0	0	10	0	7

Play off: Milngavie beat Giffnock 2 5-4

DIVISION 2	P	W	D	L	WO	PTS
Western 2	8	8	0	0	0	74
Milngavie	8	7	0	1	0	67
Ardgowan	8	6	0	2	0	61
Broomhill	8	4	1	3	0	51
Bearsden	8	4	0	4	0	37
Whitecraigs 2	8	3	0	5	0	36
Hamilton 2	8	1	1	6	0	30
Clarkston	8	1	0	7	0	23
Fort Matilda	8	1	0	7	0	17

DIVISION 3	P	W	D	L	WO	PTS
Titwood	8	7	1	0	0	65
Thorn Park	8	6	1	1	0	64
Dowanhill	8	6	0	2	0	59
Weir Recreation	8	3	2	2	1	50
Clarkston 2	8	4	1	3	0	40
Craighelen	8	0	1	6	1	36
Newlands 3	8	2	1	4	-1	27
Strathgryffe 3	8	0	1	6	-1	19
Hillhead HSFP	8	1	0	5	-2	11

DIVISION 4A	P	W	D	L	WO	PTS
Rutherglen	8	8	0	0	0	69
David Lloyd 2	8	5	1	2	0	58
Helensburgh 2	8	4	0	4	0	51
Milngavie 2	8	4	1	3	0	49
Broomhill 2	8	4	0	4	0	42
Giffnock 3	8	3	0	5	0	38
Clarkston 3	8	1	0	6	1	29
Uddingston	8	2	0	6	0	28
Busby	8	3	0	4	-1	27

DIVISION 4B	P	W	D	L	WO	PTS
Woodend	8	8	0	0	0	78
Western 3	8	6	0	1	1	72
Whitecraigs 3	8	5	1	2	0	57
Thorn Park 2	8	5	1	2	0	54
East Kilbride	8	4	0	4	0	45
Dowanhill 2	8	2	1	5	0	36
David Lloyd 3	8	2	1	5	0	32
Strathgryffe 4	8	0	0	7	1	17
Strathaven	8	0	0	6	-2	-1

DIVISION 5A	P	W	D	L	WO	PTS
Newlands 4	8	7	0	1	0	64
Giffnock 4	8	7	0	1	0	62
Lenzie	8	6	0	2	0	56
Esporta Glasgow	8	4	1	3	0	49
Drumchapel	8	2	1	4	1	44
Cardross	8	3	2	3	0	41
David Lloyd 4	8	2	1	5	0	32
Hamilton 3	8	1	1	6	0	22
Kilmacolm	8	0	0	7	-1	21

DIVISION 5B	P	W	D	L	WO	PTS
Mount Vernon 2	7	7	0	0	0	73
Esporta Hamilton	7	6	0	1	0	59
Bishopton	7	3	0	3	1	45
Springwells	7	3	0	3	1	41
Titwood 2	7	2	0	4	1	35
Craighelen 2	7	3	0	3	-1	28
Weir Recreation 2	7	1	0	5	-1	16
Dowanhill 3	7	0	0	6	-1	2
Fort Matilda 2	Match results void					

WOMEN

PREMIER DIVISION	P	W	D	L	WO	PTS
Newlands	10	8	0	2	0	83
Clarkston	10	6	1	3	0	64
Whitecraigs	10	5	2	3	0	59
Strathgryffe	10	5	0	5	0	58
David Lloyd	10	4	1	5	0	49
Western	10	0	0	10	0	17

Play off: David Lloyd beat Giffnock 9-0

DIVISION 1	P	W	D	L	WO	PTS
Broomhill	10	9	0	1	0	85
Giffnock	10	8	0	2	0	67
Bearsden	10	5	0	5	0	63
Thorn Park	10	4	0	6	0	51
Craighelen	10	3	0	7	0	40
Helensburgh	10	1	0	9	0	24

Play off: Craighelen beat Strathgryffe 2 6-3

DIVISION 2	P	W	D	L	WO	PTS
David Lloyd 2	8	6	2	0	0	59
Strathgryffe 2	8	4	2	2	0	53
Uddingston	8	5	1	2	0	50
Kilmacolm	8	3	1	4	0	46
Woodend	8	3	2	3	0	43
Lenzie	8	3	2	3	0	42
East Kilbride	8	3	0	5	0	39
Western 2	8	2	2	4	0	39
Whitecraigs 2	8	0	2	6	0	25

DIVISION 3	P	W	D	L	WO	PTS
Thorn Park 2	8	7	0	1	0	65
Titwood	8	6	1	1	0	62
Strathgryffe 3	8	5	1	2	0	59
Fort Matilda	8	5	0	3	0	55
Mount Vernon	8	4	0	4	0	45
Bearsden 2	8	3	0	5	0	40
Oban	8	2	2	3	0	36
Milngavie	8	2	0	6	0	27
Newlands 2	8	0	0	8	0	7

DIVISION 4A	P	W	D	L	WO	PTS
Hamilton	8	7	1	0	0	71
Craighelen 2	8	6	0	1	1	65
Clarkston 2	8	5	1	2	0	58
Helensburgh 2	8	5	0	3	0	48
Titwood 2	8	4	0	4	0	44
David Lloyd 3	8	3	1	4	0	36
Western 3	8	2	0	6	0	36
Giffnock 2	8	1	1	6	0	29
Cambuslang	8	0	0	7	-1	6

DIVISION 4B	P	W	D	L	WO	PTS
Bishopton	8	6	1	0	1	70
Esporta Hamilton	8	5	1	2	0	52
Dowanhill	8	5	1	1	-1	51
Poloc	8	4	1	3	0	50
Kirktonhill	8	2	1	4	1	48
Uplawmoor	8	4	1	3	0	47
Helensburgh 3	8	4	0	4	0	44
Rutherglen	8	1	0	7	0	24
Weir Recreation	8	0	0	7	-1	2

DIVISION 5A	P	W	D	L	WO	PTS
Whitecraigs 3	8	6	0	2	0	63
Fort Matilda 2	8	6	0	2	0	54
Hillhead HSFP	8	6	0	2	0	54
Esporta Glasgow	8	4	1	3	0	52
Giffnock 3	8	4	0	4	0	48
Clarkston 3	8	5	0	3	0	38
Bearsden 3	8	2	0	6	0	34
Mount Vernon 2	8	1	1	6	0	28
Thorn Park 3	8	1	0	7	0	25

DIVISION 5B	P	W	D	L	WO	PTS
Hillhead HSFP 2	8	5	1	2	0	56
Busby	8	5	2	1	0	55
Woodend	8	5	1	2	0	54
Newlands 3	8	4	1	3	0	49
Strathgryffe 4	8	4	1	3	0	47
Broomhill 2	8	2	3	3	0	46
Whitecraigs 4	8	4	1	3	0	44
Stepps	8	1	0	7	0	25
Esporta Hamilton 2	8	1	0	7	0	20

Dunlop West of Scotland Senior League Positions on 27/10/03

MEN

DIVISION 6A

	P	W	D	L	WO	PTS
Kirkhill	8	8	0	0	0	77
Next Gen West End	8	7	0	1	0	67
Whitecraigs 4	8	4	1	3	0	46
Springwells 2	8	4	0	4	0	46
Giffnock 5	8	2	1	5	0	42
Western 4	8	3	2	3	0	41
Mount Vernon 3	8	2	0	6	0	29
Milngavie 3	8	2	0	6	0	27
Woodend 2	8	2	0	6	0	21

DIVISION 6B

	P	W	D	L	WO	PTS
GU Staff	8	7	0	1	0	70
Helensburgh 3	8	7	0	1	0	67
Giffnock 6	8	5	0	3	0	55
Hillhead HSFP 2	8	5	0	3	0	52
Arthurlee	8	4	0	4	0	42
Drumchapel 2	8	2	1	5	0	38
Clarkston 4	8	3	0	5	0	34
Bearsden 2	8	1	1	5	1	31
Cardross 2	8	0	0	7	-1	4

DIVISION 7A

	P	W	D	L	WO	PTS
Thorn Park 3	8	7	0	0	1	75
Uddingston 2	8	5	0	3	0	55
Ardgowan 2	8	5	0	3	0	54
Lenzie 2	8	6	0	2	0	50
Stepps	8	3	0	5	0	45
East Kilbride 2	8	4	0	4	0	37
Broomhill 3	8	2	0	6	0	26
Kirktonhill	8	2	0	5	-1	26
Hamilton 4	8	1	0	7	0	25

DIVISION 7B

	P	W	D	L	WO	PTS
Wishaw	8	7	0	1	0	71
Bishopbriggs	8	7	0	1	0	68
Hillhead HSFP 3	8	7	0	1	0	68
Bishopton 2	8	4	0	4	0	46
Giffnock 7	8	3	1	4	0	43
Next Gen West End	8	3	0	5	0	33
Whitecraigs 5	8	2	1	5	0	30
Uplawmoor	8	0	0	7	1	24
Fort Matilda 3	8	0	2	5	-1	10
Helensburgh 5	0	0	0	0	0	0

DIVISION 7C

	P	W	D	L	WO	PTS
Craighelen 3	9	8	0	1	0	88
Titwood 3	9	8	0	1	0	83
Westerton	9	7	1	1	0	69
Rutherglen	9	6	1	2	0	56
Strathgryffe 5	9	4	0	4	1	48
Helensburgh 4	9	3	0	6	0	42
Ardgowan 3	9	2	1	6	0	38
GU Staff 2	9	3	1	5	0	36
Mount Vernon 4	9	1	0	7	-1	17
Cambuslang	9	0	0	9	0	15

DIVISION 8A

	P	W	D	L	WO	PTS
Busby 2	7	7	0	0	0	63
David Lloyd 5	7	4	1	1	1	59
Esporta Glasgow 2	7	4	0	1	1/-1	44
Milngavie 4	7	3	1	3	0	42
Paisley	7	4	0	2	-1	32
Hillhead HSFP 4	7	2	0	5	0	30
Kilmacolm 2	7	1	0	6	0	18
Woodend 4	7	0	0	7	0	10
Weir Recreation 3	0	0	0	0	0	0

DIVISION 8B

	P	W	D	L	WO	PTS
Newlands 5	9	8	0	0	1	94
Esporta Glasgow 3	9	6	1	2	0	71
Lenzie 3	9	5	3	1	0	68
Thorn Park 4	9	6	1	2	0	68
Craighelen 4	9	4	0	5	0	46
Bishopbriggs 2	9	4	1	4	0	45
Woodend 3	9	3	0	6	0	43
Bearsden 3	9	4	0	4	-1	35
Kirkhilll 2	9	0	0	8	1	27
Hillpark	9	0	0	8	-1	1

WOMEN

DIVISION 6A

	P	W	D	L	WO	PTS
Next Gen West End	8	8	0	0	0	78
Milngavie 2	8	7	0	1	0	63
Helensburgh 4	8	5	1	2	0	56
Bishopton 2	8	4	0	4	0	47
Hillhead HSFP 3	8	2	3	3	0	39
Kilmacolm 3	8	1	1	6	0	35
Craighelen 4	8	1	1	5	1	31
Woodend 3	8	3	0	5	0	31
Strathaven	8	1	0	6	-1	13

DIVISION 6B

	P	W	D	L	WO	PTS
Kilmacolm 2	7	4	1	1	1	56
Anchor	7	5	0	2	0	47
Craighelen 3	7	4	0	3	0	46
Bishopbriggs	7	5	0	2	0	46
Broomhill 3	7	3	1	3	0	41
Esporta Glasgow 2	7	2	0	5	0	28
Helensburgh 5	7	2	0	5	0	23
Cardross	7	1	0	5	-1	16
Cambuslang 2	0	0	0	0	0	0

DIVISION 7A

	P	W	D	L	WO	PTS
Uddingston 2	7	6	1	0	0	64
Hamilton 2	7	6	1	0	0	60
Titwood 3	7	5	0	2	0	47
GU Staff	7	3	0	3	1	44
Next Gen West End	7	3	0	4	0	43
Springwells	7	2	0	5	0	27
Poloc 2	7	1	0	6	0	17
Esporta Glasgow 3	7	0	0	6	-1	3

DIVISION 7B

	P	W	D	L	WO	PTS
Uplawmoor 2	7	6	0	1	0	61
Bearsden 4	7	6	1	0	0	55
Busby 2	7	5	0	2	0	50
Mount Vernon 3	7	3	1	3	0	42
David Lloyd 4	7	3	0	4	0	31
Esporta Hamilton 3	7	2	0	5	0	25
Bishopbriggs 2	7	0	0	6	1	22
Ardgowan	7	1	0	5	-1	18

DIVISION 8A

	P	W	D	L	WO	PTS
Lenzie 2	7	7	0	0	0	75
Hillhead HSFP 4	7	5	0	2	0	50
East Kilbride 2	7	4	0	3	0	44
David Lloyd 5	7	4	0	3	0	40
Milngavie 4	7	3	0	4	0	39
Craighelen 5	7	3	0	3	-1	28
Mount Vernon 4	7	1	0	5	-1	8
Kirkhill	7	0	0	7	0	7

DIVISION 8B

	P	W	D	L	WO	PTS
Giffnock 4	7	7	0	0	0	73
Bishopton 3	7	5	1	1	0	51
Whitecraigs 5	7	3	2	1	1	48
Milngavie 3	7	3	1	3	0	45
Westerton	7	3	0	3	-1	27
Fort Matilda 3	7	2	0	4	-1	17
Weir Recreation 2	7	0	0	7	0	15
Rutherglen 2	7	1	0	5	-1	11

DIVISION 8C

	P	W	D	L	WO	PTS
Paisley	7	6	0	1	0	58
Thorn Park 4	7	6	0	1	0	58
Western 4	7	5	1	1	0	53
GU Staff 2	7	4	0	3	0	41
Esporta Hamilton 2	7	2	2	3	0	36
Newlands 4	7	2	0	5	0	29
Woodend 4	7	0	1	6	0	18
Cardross 2	7	1	0	6	0	15

Dunlop West of Scotland National Junior Club League (NJCL) Positions on 27/10/03

BOYS 17 & Under

DIVISION 1

	P	W	D	L	WO	PTS
Thorn Park	6	6	0	0	0	38
Strathgryffe	6	2	2	2	0	29
Mount Vernon	6	3	0	3	0	27
Clarkston	6	2	2	2	0	23
Rutherglen	6	2	0	3	1	18
Giffnock	6	1	1	4	0	15
Whitecraigs	6	0	3	2	-1	14

DIVISION 2A

	P	W	D	L	WO	PTS
Western	7	7	0	0	0	52
Newlands	7	6	0	1	0	51
Bishopbriggs	7	5	0	2	0	33
Thorn Park 2	7	2	1	3	1	32
Bishopton	7	2	2	3	0	24
Kirktonhill	7	1	2	3	-1	11
Clarkston 3	7	0	1	6	0	11
Woodend	7	1	0	6	0	9
Giffnock 3	Match results void					

DIVISION 2B

	P	W	D	L	WO	PTS
Lenzie	7	5	1	0	-1	41
Clarkston 2	7	5	2	0	0	39
Helensburgh	7	2	1	3	1	32
Drumchapel	7	4	2	0	-1	31
Titwood	7	2	2	2	1	29
Strathgryffe	7	1	0	6	0	15
Giffnock 2	7	1	0	4	-2	6
Fort Matilda	7	0	0	5	-2	3

DIVISION 3A

	P	W	D	L	WO	PTS
Craighelen	5	5	0	0	0	35
Milngavie	5	4	0	1	0	28
Cardross	5	2	0	2	-1	17
Busby	5	2	0	2	-1	14
Bearsden	5	1	0	4	0	8
Thorn Park 3	5	0	0	5	0	6

DIVISION 3B

	P	W	D	L	WO	PTS
Ardgowan	8	6	0	1	1	48
Uddingston	8	6	1	1	0	48
David Lloyd Renfre	8	5	1	1	-1	39
Uplawmoor	8	5	0	2	-1	33
Whitecraigs 2	8	2	1	4	-1	23
East Kilbride	8	1	1	5	1	20
Hillhead HSFP	8	3	0	3	-2	17
Bishopbriggs 2	8	1	0	7	0	17
Strathgryffe 3	8	1	0	6	-1	12

DIVISION 4

	P	W	D	L	WO	PTS
Western 2	5	4	0	0	1	38
Craighelen 2	5	3	1	1	0	21
Rutherglen 2	5	2	1	2	0	20
Kilmacolm	5	2	0	2	-1	20
Milngavie 2	5	2	0	3	0	15
Hamilton	5	0	0	5	0	7
Mount Vernon 2	Match results void					
Giffnock 4	Match results void					
Esporta Glasgow	Match results void					

BOYS 13 & Under

DIVISION 1

	P	W	D	L	WO	PTS
Giffnock	5	4	1	0	0	31
Newlands	5	3	0	2	0	21
Rutherglen	5	1	1	2	1	20
Strathgryffe	5	1	1	3	0	19
Thorn Park	5	2	1	1	-1	16
Giffnock 2	5	0	0	3	-2	-1
Lenzie	0	0	0	0	0	0

DIVISION 2A

	P	W	D	L	WO	PTS
Western	7	6	1	0	0	48
Kilmacolm	7	5	0	1	1	40
Whitecraigs 2	7	4	0	2	1	36
Milngavie 2	7	3	0	4	0	26
Craighelen	7	3	0	2	-2	24
Clarkston	7	2	1	4	0	20
Thorn Park 2	7	2	0	5	0	16
Giffnock 3	7	0	0	7	0	6
Cardross	Match results void					

DIVISION 2B

	P	W	D	L	WO	PTS
Milngavie	7	7	0	0	0	51
Helensburgh	7	6	0	1	0	41
Whitecraigs	7	5	0	2	0	40
Weir Recreation	7	4	0	3	0	31
Woodend	7	3	0	4	0	25
Rutherglen 2	7	2	0	5	0	21
Mount Vernon	7	1	0	6	0	13
Strathgryffe 2	7	0	0	7	0	2
Ardgowan	Match results void					

DIVISION 3A

	P	W	D	L	WO	PTS
Hamilton	5	4	1	0	0	33
Newlands 2	5	4	0	1	0	31
Kirkhill	5	2	1	2	0	21
East Kilbride	5	1	1	3	0	12
Bearsden 2	5	1	0	4	0	12
Drumchapel	5	1	1	3	0	11
David Lloyd Ren.	Match results void					

DIVISION 3B

	P	W	D	L	WO	PTS
Uddingston	5	3	1	1	0	28
Bearsden	5	4	0	1	0	26
Hillhead HSFP	5	3	1	1	0	23
Bishopton	5	2	0	3	0	23
Titwood	5	1	0	4	0	11
Woodend 2	5	1	0	4	0	9
Kirktonhill	Match results void					
Busby	Match results void					

Dunlop West of Scotland National Junior Club League (NJCL) Positions on 27/10/03

GIRLS 17 & Under

DIVISION 1

	P	W	D	L	WO	PTS
Thorn Park	5	5	0	0	0	40
Thorn Park 2	5	3	0	1	1	29
Kilmacolm	5	3	0	2	0	21
Strathgryffe	5	2	0	2	-1	12
Bearsden	5	1	0	4	0	9
Newlands	5	0	0	5	0	7
Whitecraigs	0	0	0	0	0	0

DIVISION 2A

	P	W	D	L	WO	PTS
Whitecraigs 2	4	4	0	0	0	28
Woodend	4	3	0	1	0	26
Titwood	4	1	1	2	0	11
Newlands	4	0	2	2	0	10
Clarkston	4	0	1	3	0	7
Rutherglen	Match results void					

DIVISION 2B

	P	W	D	L	WO	PTS
Helensburgh	4	4	0	0	0	32
David Lloyd Ren.	4	3	0	1	0	21
Bishopton	4	2	0	2	0	15
Thorn Park 3	4	1	0	3	0	12
Strathgryffe 2	4	0	0	4	0	0
Giffnock	Match results void					

DIVISION 3

	P	W	D	L	WO	PTS
Milngavie	4	3	1	0	0	23
East Kilbride	4	2	0	2	0	17
Ardgowan	4	2	1	0	-1	14
Woodend 2	4	0	1	2	1	11
Bearsden 2	4	0	1	3	0	11

GIRLS 13 & Under

DIVISION 1

	P	W	D	L	WO	PTS
Thorn Park	6	6	0	0	0	44
Whitecraigs	6	4	1	1	0	33
Newlands	6	4	0	2	0	26
Woodend	6	1	1	3	1	22
Whitecraigs 2	6	2	1	3	0	20
Helensburgh	6	0	2	4	0	15
Mount Vernon	6	0	1	4	-1	6

DIVISION 2A

	P	W	D	L	WO	PTS
Thorn Park 2	6	5	1	0	0	41
Bearsden	6	4	1	1	0	32
Western	6	3	1	2	0	24
Kilmacolm	6	3	1	2	0	23
Titwood	6	2	0	3	-1	14
Strathgryffe	6	1	0	4	-1	9
Milngavie	6	0	0	6	0	8
Bishopton	Match results void					
Esporta Glasgow	Match results void					

DIVISION 2B

	P	W	D	L	WO	PTS
Thorn Park 3	5	4	0	1	0	28
Craighelen	5	2	0	2	1	28
Newlands 2	5	4	0	0	-1	25
Est Kilbride	5	2	0	3	0	14
Milngavie 2	5	2	0	3	0	12
Rutherglen	5	0	0	5	0	9
Hillhead HSFP	Match results void					

BOYS 11 & Under

DIVISION 1

	P	W	D	L	WO	PTS
Thorn Park	6	5	0	0	1	43
Newlands	6	5	0	1	0	38
Whitecraigs	6	3	1	2	0	31
Giffnock	6	3	1	1	-1	24
Bearsden	6	2	0	4	0	20
Milngavie	6	1	0	5	0	5
Helensburgh	6	0	0	6	0	4

DIVISION 2A

	P	W	D	L	WO	PTS
Western	6	6	0	0	0	47
Strathgryffe	6	5	0	1	0	33
Thorn Park 2	6	4	0	2	0	33
Rutherglen	6	0	2	3	1	17
Clarkston	6	0	1	5	0	12
Bearsden	6	1	1	3	-1	9
Kilmacolm	6	1	0	3	-2	3

DIVISION 2B

	P	W	D	L	WO	PTS
Woodend	6	6	0	0	0	43
Whitecraigs 2	6	5	0	1	0	40
Bishopton	6	3	0	2	1	29
East Kilbride	6	1	0	5	0	13
Craighelen	6	2	0	3	-1	12
Milngavie 2	6	1	0	4	-1	10
Kirkhill	6	1	0	4	-1	7

DIVISION 3

	P	W	D	L	WO	PTS
Newlands 2	5	4	1	0	0	30
Thorn Park 3	5	3	1	1	0	28
Titwood	5	1	0	3	-1	11
David Lloyd Ren.	5	2	0	1	-2	11
Milngavie 3	5	0	0	4	1	11
Ardgowan	5	1	0	2	-2	1
Western 2	Match results void					

GIRLS 11 & Under

DIVISION 1

	P	W	D	L	WO	PTS
Thorn Park	4	4	0	0	0	27
Newlands	4	3	0	1	0	18
Whitecraigs	4	2	0	2	0	17
Helensburgh	4	1	0	3	1	15
Kilmacolm	4	0	0	4	0	3
Mount Vernon	Match results void					

DIVISION 2

	P	W	D	L	WO	PTS
East Kilbride	4	4	0	0	0	26
Giffnock	4	1	1	1	1	20
Bearsden	4	1	2	1	0	16
Milngavie	4	0	0	3	-1	4
Titwood	4	0	1	1	-2	0

DIVISION 3

	P	W	D	L	WO	PTS
Western	4	1	0	1	2	24
Craighelen	4	3	0	1	0	23
David Lloyd Ren.	4	3	0	0	-1	18
Strathgryffe	4	1	0	2	-1	7
Milngavie 2	4	0	0	4	0	1

DUNLOP

TAKE CONTROL • GET DUNLOP

Dunlop West of Scotland Senior Spring / Winter League Positions on 27/10/03

SPRING SINGLES LEAGUES

MEN

Premier Division

Premier Division	P	W	D	L	WO	PTS
Newlands	5	5	0	0	0	14
Giffnock	5	3	0	1	1	10
Milngavie	5	2	0	3	0	7
Western	5	2	0	2	-1	5
Mount Vernon	5	2	0	3	0	5
Strathgryffe	5	0	0	5	0	2

Division 1

Division 1						
Whitecraigs	4	4	0	0	0	10
Thorn Park	4	3	0	1	0	7
Ardgowan	4	1	0	2	1	6
Giffnock 2	4	1	0	3	0	5
Dowanhill	4	0	0	3	-1	-1
Esporta Hamilton	0	0	0	0	0	0

Division 2

Division 2						
Rutherglen	4	3	0	0	1	12
Western 2	4	3	0	0	-1	6
Craighelen	4	1	0	2	1	5
Weir Recreation	3	0	0	3	0	2
Uddingston	3	0	0	2	-1	-2

Division 3

Division 3						
Broomhill	5	5	0	0	0	13
Titwood	5	3	0	1	1	12
Milngavie 2	5	2	0	2	1	8
Esporta Glasgow	5	1	0	3	1	8
Thorn Park 2	5	0	0	4	-1	0
Busby	5	1	0	2	-2	-2

WOMEN

Premier Division

Premier Division						
Newlands	5	5	0	0	0	12
Bearsden	5	3	0	1	1	11
Whitecraigs	5	2	0	3	0	6
Thorn Park	5	1	0	4	0	5
Western	5	0	0	3	1/-1	4
Strathgryffe	5	2	0	2	-1	3

Division 1

Division 1						
Uddingston	4	4	0	0	0	10
Clarkston	4	2	0	1	1	8
Mount Vernon	4	1	0	3	0	4
Giffnock	4	0	0	4	0	4
Craighelen	4	2	0	1	-1	2

Division 2

Division 2						
Thorn Park 2	4	4	0	0	0	11
Broomhill	4	3	0	1	0	10
Esporta Glasgow	4	1	0	3	0	4
Esporta Hamilton	4	1	0	3	0	3
Giffnock 2	4	1	0	3	0	2

2002 / 03 WINTER LEAGUES

SUNDAY AFTERNOON LEAGUES

Division 1

Division 1	P	W	D	L	WO	Pts
Bearsden	5	4	1	0	0	42
East Kilbride	5	3	0	2	0	33
Uddingston	5	2	1	2	0	30
Woodend	5	3	0	2	0	24
Western	5	1	0	3	-1	13
Clarkston	5	0	0	4	-1	6
Mount Vernon	Match results void					

Division 2

Division 2						
Hamilton	5	5	0	0	0	47
Milngavie	5	3	0	2	0	33
Titwood	5	3	0	2	0	30
Helensburgh	5	3	0	2	0	28
David Lloyd Ren.	5	1	0	4	0	16
Craighelen	5	0	0	5	0	11
Busby	Match results void					
Esporta Hamilton	Match results void					

Division 3A

Division 3A						
Next Gen West End	5	5	0	0	0	46
Bearsden 2	5	2	0	1	2	42
Milngavie 2	5	2	0	3	0	24
Broomhill	5	2	0	3	0	21
Woodend 2	5	1	0	2	1/-1	18
Cardross	5	0	0	3	-2	0
Giffnock	Match results void					

Division 3B

Division 3B						
Whitecraigs	6	5	0	1	0	53
Thorn Park	6	5	0	1	0	46
Rutherglen	6	4	0	2	0	40
Mount Vernon 2	6	3	0	3	0	36
Helensburgh 2	6	1	1	4	0	27
Hillhead HSFP	6	2	1	3	0	26
East Kilbride 2	6	0	0	6	0	3
Giffnock 2	Match results void					

MONDAY EVENING LEAGUES

Division 1

Division 1		W	D	L	WO	Pts
Clarkston	6	4	0	0	2	51
Mount Vernon	6	3	1	1	1	45
Woodend	6	2	1	3	0	33
Strathgryffe	6	3	1	1	-1	32
Broomhill	6	1	1	2	-2	16
Giffnock	6	2	0	2	-2	16
Titwood	6	0	0	6	0	6

Division 2

Division 2						
Thorn Park	6	4	0	0	2	60
Lenzie	6	5	0	1	0	49
Kilmacolm	6	4	0	1	-1	37
Strathgryffe 2	6	3	0	2	-1	30
Mount Vernon 2	6	2	0	4	0	25
Woodend 2	6	1	0	5	0	12
Bearsden	6	0	0	6	0	8
Busby	Match results void					

Dunlop West of Scotland Vets' League Positions on 27/10/03

VET WOMEN

DIVISION 1

	P	W	D	L	WO	PTS
Whitecraigs	5	4	1	0	0	25
Bearsden	5	4	1	0	0	25
Thorn Park	5	2	1	2	0	14
Helensburgh	5	0	3	2	0	10
Western	5	0	2	3	0	9
Clarkston	5	0	2	3	0	7

DIVISION 2A

	P	W	D	L	WO	PTS
David Lloyd Ren.	5	4	0	1	0	21
Giffnock	5	3	2	0	0	19
Craighelen	5	2	2	1	0	16
Strathgryffe 2	5	1	2	2	0	15
Thorn Park 2	5	1	1	3	0	13
Bishopton	5	0	1	4	0	6

DIVISION 2B

	P	W	D	L	WO	PTS
Fort Matilda	5	3	1	1	0	20
Whitecraigs 2	5	2	2	1	0	18
Strathgryffe	5	2	2	1	0	18
Kilmacolm	5	2	1	2	0	14
Titwood	5	1	2	2	0	13
Cambuslang	5	1	0	4	0	7

DIVISION 3A

	P	W	D	L	WO	PTS
Woodend	5	4	1	0	0	24
Titwood 2	5	2	2	1	0	18
Uplawmoor	5	1	2	2	0	15
Newlands	5	1	3	1	0	14
Lenzie	5	0	3	2	0	10
Clarkston 2	5	1	1	3	0	9

DIVISION 3B

	P	W	D	L	WO	PTS
Bearsden 2	5	4	0	0	1	29
Milngavie	5	3	1	1	0	19
Poloc	5	2	1	2	0	15
Stepps	5	1	2	2	0	13
Craighelen 2	5	2	0	3	0	12
East Kilbride	5	0	0	4	-1	0

DIVISION 4A

	P	W	D	L	WO	PTS
Mount Vernon	5	4	0	1	0	22
Hamilton	5	2	1	1	1	19
Helensburgh 2	5	3	0	0	1/-1	19
Uplawmoor 2	5	1	1	3	0	12
Hillhead HSFP	5	2	0	2	-1	10
Anchor	5	0	0	5	0	2

DIVISION 4B

	P	W	D	L	WO	PTS
Whitecraigs 3	5	3	2	0	0	24
Esporta Hamilton	5	4	1	0	0	22
Giffnock 2	5	3	1	1	0	21
Bishopton 2	5	2	0	3	0	12
Milngavie 2	5	0	1	4	0	6
Helensburgh 3	5	0	1	4	0	5

DIVISION 5A

	P	W	D	L	WO	PTS
Busby	5	4	0	1	0	25
Whitecraigs 4	5	2	2	1	0	17
Fort Matilda 2	5	2	0	3	0	14
Bearsden 3	5	2	1	2	0	13
Broomhill	5	2	1	2	0	13
GU Staff	5	1	0	4	0	8

VET MEN

DIVISION 1

	P	W	D	L	WO	PTS
Strathgryffe	5	2	2	0	1	22
Whitecraigs	5	3	2	0	0	20
Hamilton	5	3	1	1	0	20
Dowanhill	5	1	1	2	1	18
Clarkston	5	0	0	5	0	5
Milngavie	5	1	0	2	-2	1

DIVISION 2A

	P	W	D	L	WO	PTS
Helensburgh	5	5	0	0	0	29
Bearsden	5	2	1	2	0	16
Hamilton 2	5	3	0	1	-1	13
Newlands	5	1	0	2	1/-1	10
Craighelen	5	0	2	3	0	8
Uddingston	5	0	1	3	-1	2

DIVISION 2B

	P	W	D	L	WO	PTS
Mount Vernon	5	4	0	0	1	24
David Lloyd Ren.	5	2	2	1	0	16
Giffnock	5	2	1	2	0	14
Strathgryffe 2	5	1	1	3	0	12
Weir Recreation	5	0	1	3	1	12
Thorn Park	5	1	1	1	-2	6

DIVISION 3A

	P	W	D	L	WO	PTS
Thorn Park 2	4	4	0	0	0	18
Whitecraigs 2	4	3	0	1	0	17
Clarkston 2	4	1	1	2	0	11
Giffnock 2	4	0	2	2	0	8
GU Staff	4	0	1	3	0	6
David Lloyd Ren.2	Match results void					

DIVISION 3B

	P	W	D	L	WO	PTS
Broomhill	5	1	4	0	0	18
Busby	5	1	4	0	0	18
Helensburgh 2	5	2	3	0	0	18
Titwood	5	1	3	1	0	16
Bishopton	5	1	1	3	0	11
Milngavie 2	5	1	1	3	0	9

DIVISION 4A

	P	W	D	L	WO	PTS
Esporta Glasgow	4	4	0	0	0	23
Lenzie	4	3	0	1	0	16
Hamilton 3	4	1	0	2	1	12
Whitecraigs 3	3	0	0	3	0	3
Fort Matilda	3	0	0	2	-1	-2

DIVISION 4B

	P	W	D	L	WO	PTS
Hillhead HSFP	3	2	1	0	0	13
Giffnock 3	3	2	1	0	0	12
Craighelen 2	3	1	0	2	0	9
Next Gen West End	3	0	0	3	0	2
Woodend	0	0	0	0	0	

DIVISION 5

	P	W	D	L	WO	PTS
Hillhead HSFP 2	2	2	0	0	0	11
Bearsden 2	2	1	0	1	0	6
Mount Vernon 2	2	0	0	2	0	1
Kirktonhill	Match results void					

Dunlop West of Scotland Vets' League Positions on 27/10/03

VET WOMEN

DIVISION 5B

Esporta Hamilton 2	5	3	0	1	1	21
Woodend 2	5	4	0	0	-1	19
Helensburgh 4	5	1	2	2	0	12
Rutherglen	5	1	1	3	0	10
Weir Recreation	5	1	1	3	0	10
Hillhead HSFP 2	5	1	0	2	-2	5

DIVISION 6A

Uddingston	5	4	0	0	1	29
Kirktonhill	5	4	0	1	0	24
Thorn Park 3	5	3	0	2	0	17
Busby 2	5	2	0	3	0	10
Bishopton 3	5	0	1	3	-1	4
Bishopbriggs 2	5	0	1	4	0	4

DIVISION 6B

Giffnock 3	4	3	1	0	0	19
Esporta Glasgow	4	2	1	1	0	16
Bishopbriggs	4	1	2	1	0	14
Strathaven	4	1	1	2	0	8
Kirktonhill 2	4	0	1	3	0	3
Cardross	0	0	0	0	0	

DIVISION 7A

Craighelen 3	5	3	2	0	0	24
Next Gen West End	5	3	1	1	0	21
Fort Matilda 3	5	0	2	1	2	18
Milngavie 3	5	2	2	1	0	16
Woodend 3	5	1	1	2	-1	8
Cardross 2	5	0	0	4	-1	-1

DIVISION 7B

David Lloyd Ren. 2	5	5	0	0	0	30
Titwood 3	5	3	1	1	0	21
Mount Vernon 2	5	3	1	1	0	19
Uddingston 2	5	2	0	3	0	11
Esporta Hamilton 3	5	1	0	4	0	5
Newlands 2	5	0	0	5	0	4

NATIONAL JUNIOR CLUB LEAGUE TEAMS PER COUNTY

2003

COUNTY	11 & under		13 & under		15 & under		17 & under		Per County		
	boys	girls	boys	girls	boys	girls	boys	girls	Boys	Girls	Total
Avon	9	4	8	3	7	4	5	3	29	14	43
Bedfordshire	5	-	6	-	6	6	5	-	22	6	28
Berkshire		4								4	4
Buckinghamshire											
Cambridgeshire	13	5	10	8	12	3	7	6	42	22	64
Channel Islands	4	3	4	4	6	3	4	3	18	13	31
Cheshire	18	11	23	14	22	11	18	11	81	47	128
Cornwall	10	4	11	4	7	2	7	2	35	12	47
Cumbria	7	3	7	5	8	1	4	1	26	10	36
Derbyshire	7	1	5	2	6	2	7	1	25	6	31
Devon	9	3	12	5	9	4	2	4	32	16	48
Dorset	7	3	6	5	4	-	3	3	20	11	31
Durham & Cleveland Northumberland	14	8	10	7	9	4	6	4	39	23	62
Essex	5	4	8	3	8	4	10	5	31	16	47
Gloucestershire	10	4	15	4	19	7	7	5	51	20	71
Hampshire & Isle of Wight	13	5	13	6	11	5	6	5	43	21	64
Hereford & Worcester											
Hertfordshire	18	7	15	13	14	10	12	4	59	34	93

NATIONAL JUNIOR CLUB LEAGUE
TEAMS PER COUNTY

COUNTY	11 & under		13 & under		15 & under		17 & under		Per County		
	boys	girls	boys	girls	boys	girls	boys	girls	Boys	Girls	Total
Kent											
Lancashire	12	6	15	10	13	10	13	7	53	33	86
Leicestershire	13	8	18	10	12	9	9	3	52	30	82
Lincolnshire	11	6	12	5	7	3	6	5	36	19	55
Middlesex	48	12	52	23	55	25	32	13	187	73	260
Norfolk	4	2	4	5	6	3	1	1	15	11	26
Northamptonshire	6	4	3	4	6	3	5	4	20	15	35
Northumberland	* see Durham & Cleveland		-	-	-	-	-	-	-	-	-
Nottinghamshire	6	4	3	4	6	3	5	4	20	15	35
Oxfordshire	4	3	6	3	14	5	7	0	31	11	42
Scotland (East)	7	8	6	6	6	5	5	3	24	22	46
Scotland (North)	3	-	6	3	3	3	3	3	15	9	24
Scotland (South)	9	3	8	4	3	3	3	3	23	13	36
Scotland (West)*	32	19	41	25	-	-	51	27	124	71	195
Shropshire	9	3	9	3	8	4	9	4	35	14	49
Somerset	12	5	8	6	6	2	1	2	27	15	42
Staffordshire	9	2	13	9	12	4	8	3	41	18	59
Suffolk	9	6	9	5	9	4	6	2	33	17	50
Surrey	30.	16	36	18	29	21	20	14	115	69	184
Sussex	16	4	21	10	12	-	10	5	59	19	78

NATIONAL JUNIOR CLUB LEAGUE
TEAMS PER COUNTY

COUNTY	11 & under		13 & under		15 & under		17 & under		Per County		
	boys	girls	boys	girls	boys	girls	boys	girls	Boys	Girls	Total
Wales (North)	3	3	4	3	3	3	3	3	13	12	25
Wales (South)	14	9	17	14	19	10	13	8	63	41	104
Warwickshire	33	11	32	12	32	14	24	9	121	46	167
Wiltshire	17	7	13	7	8	6	10	5	48	25	73
Yorkshire	16	9	14	5	7	7	6	2	43	23	66
TOTAL (approx.)											

N.B. The West of Scotland has the second highest number of teams entered in these Leagues. The West has not yet entered the 15 & under age group and if this age group were discounted for Milledsex then the West of Scotland would have the highest entry in Great Britain.

The West of Scotland Lawn Tennis Association.

Season 1954

INTER-CLUB LEAGUE COMPETITION.

WOMEN

1st DIVISION.

	No.	Won	Drn.	W.O.	Lost	Sets Won	Sets Lost	Pts.
Pollokshields	6	6	0	0	0	46	8	12
Craighelen	6	4	0	1	1	39	15	10
Newlands	6	3	1	0	2	34	20	7
Western	6	3	1	0	2	27	27	7
Paisley	6	2	0	0	4	17	37	4
Ardgowan	6	1	0	0	5	19	35	2
Kelvinside	6	0	0	0	6	7	47	0
	42	19	2	1	20	189	189	42

2nd DIVISION.

	No.	Won	Drn.	W.O.	Lost	Sets Won	Sets Lost	Pts.
Kingswood	7	6	0	0	1	44	18	12
Partickhill	7	5	1	0	1	42	20	11
Kenmure	7	4	1	0	2	36	26	9
Bearsden	7	3	1	0	3	31	32	7
Downahill	7	3	0	0	4	30	33	6
Pollokshields II.	7	3	0	0	4	25	38	6
Western II.	7	2	0	0	5	32	30	4
Giffnock	7	0	1	0	6	10	53	1
	56	26	4	0	26	250	250	56

3rd DIVISION.

	No.	Won	Drn.	W.O.	Lost	Sets Won	Sets Lost	Pts.
Lenzie	9	8	1	0	0	56	25	17
Fort Matilda	9	7	1	0	1	51	30	15
Muirend and Busby	9	6	0	0	3	43	38	12
Queen's Park	9	4	2	0	3	47	34	10
Bellahouston	9	5	0	0	4	40	39	10
Cambuslang	9	4	0	0	5	42	39	8
Clarkston	9	4	0	0	5	38	42	8
Poloc	9	3	0	6	6	36	45	6
Rutherglen	9	2	0	0	7	32	49	4
Newlands II.	9	0	0	0	9	17	61	0
	90	43	4	0	43	402	402	90

4th DIVISION.

	No.	Won	Drn.	W.O.	Lost	Sets Won	Sets Lost	Pts.
Cardonald	9	7	2	0	0	64	17	16
Alexandria	9	7	1	0	1	52	29	15
Cartha	9	6	0	0	3	45	36	12
Mount Vernon	9	4	2	0	3	45	36	10
Hamilton	9	5	0	0	4	44	37	10
Stepps	9	5	0	0	4	43	36	10
Hillpark	9	4	0	0	5	37	44	8
Ralston	9	3	1	0	5	32	47	7
Yarrow	9	1	0	0	8	23	54	2
Titwood	9	0	0	0	9	16	65	0
	90	42	6	0	42	401	401	90

5th DIVISION.

	No.	Won	Drn.	W.O.	Lost	Sets Won	Sets Lost	Pts.
Helensburgh	9	9	0	0	0	60	21	18
Burnside	9	8	0	0	1	55	26	16
Craighelen II.	9	5	2	0	2	52	29	12
Broomhill	9	5	1	0	3	43	38	11
Hillhead H.S.F.P.	9	5	0	0	4	47	34	10
Kilmacolm	9	3	0	1	5	36	45	8
Ardgowan II.	9	2	2	0	5	30	51	6
Drumchapel	9	2	0	0	7	29	52	4
Springboig	9	2	0	0	7	25	56	4
University	9	0	1	0	8	28	53	1
	90	41	6	1	42	405	405	90

6th DIVISION.

	No.	Won	Drn.	W.O.	Lost	Sets Won	Sets Lost	Pts.
Public Parks	9	9	0	0	0	60	21	18
Langside Hill C.	9	7	0	0	2	56	25	14
Scottish Gas Board	9	7	0	0	2	55	26	14
Springwells	9	6	0	0	3	48	31	12
Elderslie	9	5	1	0	3	50	31	11
Woodend	9	4	0	0	5	39	42	8
Kelvindale	9	3	1	0	5	38	43	7
Weir	9	1	1	0	7	25	56	3
Giffnock II.	9	1	0	0	8	16	62	2
Greenock H.S.F.P.	9	0	1	0	8	15	65	1
	90	43	4	0	43	402	402	90

7th DIVISION.

	No.	Won	Drn.	W.O.	Lost	Sets Won	Sets Lost	Pts.
King's Park	9	7	0	1	1	53	28	16
Paisley II.	9	7	0	0	2	47	34	14
Uddingston	9	6	1	0	2	53	27	13
Sandhills	9	6	1	0	2	48	33	13
Whitecraigs	9	5	0	0	4	43	38	10
Ferguslie	9	3	1	0	5	37	44	7
Kirktonhill	9	3	1	0	5	32	49	7
Hamilton II.	9	2	2	0	5	40	41	6
Bearsden II.	9	1	2	0	6	31	50	4
Bridge of Weir	9	0	0	0	9	20	60	0
	90	40	8	1	41	404	404	90

8th DIVISION.

	No.	Won	Drn.	W.O.	Lost	Sets Won	Sets Lost	Pts.
Westerton	9	8	0	1	0	67	14	18
Millbrae	9	7	0	0	2	53	28	14
Partickhill II.	9	7	0	0	2	48	33	14
Cardonald II.	9	6	0	0	3	45	36	12
Kirkhill	9	5	0	0	4	48	33	10
Titwood II.	9	4	1	0	4	33	48	9
Ferguslie Mills	9	2	1	0	6	35	46	5
Scotstounhill	9	2	0	0	7	30	51	4
Hawthorn	9	1	0	1	7	29	52	4
Falcon	9	0	0	0	9	17	64	0
	90	42	2	2	44	405	405	90

9th DIVISION.

	No.	Won	Drn.	W.O.	Lost	Sets Won	Sets Lost	Pts.
Poloc II.	9	7	0	0	2	58	23	14
Possilpark	9	7	0	0	2	47	34	14
Hillington Est.	9	6	1	0	2	54	27	13
Johnston C.O.S.	9	6	1	0	2	51	30	13
Babcock and Wilcox	9	5	2	0	2	46	35	12
Rutherglen II.	9	3	2	0	4	40	41	8
Clarkston II.	9	3	0	0	6	41	40	6
Broomhill II.	9	3	0	0	6	31	50	6
Ralston II.	9	2	0	0	7	27	54	4
Erskine	9	0	0	0	9	10	71	0
	90	42	6	0	42	405	405	90

10th DIVISION.

	No.	Won	Drn.	W.O.	Lost	Sets Won	Sets Lost	Pts.
Kingswood II.	9	8	0	0	1	61	20	16
Port Glasgow	9	8	0	0	1	60	21	16
Kenmure II.	9	6	2	0	1	52	29	14
Rankin Park	9	4	1	0	4	45	36	9
Bellahouston II.	9	4	1	0	4	35	46	9
Thorn Park	9	2	3	0	4	31	50	7
Hillhead H.S.F.P. II.	9	3	0	0	6	36	45	6
Hillhead	9	3	0	0	6	35	46	6
Lenzie II.	9	2	1	0	6	30	51	5
Cathcart O.P.C.	9	0	2	0	7	20	61	2
	90	40	10	0	40	405	405	90

11th DIVISION.

	No.	Won	Drn.	W.O.	Lost	Sets Won	Sets Lost	Pts.
Renfrew	9	8	1	0	0	60	21	17
Stephen Rec.	9	8	0	0	1	57	24	16
Barclay Curle	9	7	0	0	2	58	23	14
Mearns	9	6	0	0	3	56	25	12
Templeton	9	5	0	0	4	42	39	10
Cartha II.	9	3	0	0	6	34	47	6
Milngavie	9	3	0	0	6	29	52	6
Uddingston II.	9	2	1	0	6	25	56	5
Hillpark II.	9	2	0	0	7	28	53	4
Ferguslie II.	9	0	0	0	9	16	65	0
	90	44	2	0	44	405	405	90

12th DIVISION.

	No.	Won	Drn.	W.O.	Lost	Sets Won	Sets Lost	Pts.
Anchor	9	9	0	0	0	60	21	18
Yarrow II.	9	7	0	1	1	64	17	16
Albion Motors	9	6	0	1	2	57	24	14
Langside Hill Church II.	9	5	1	0	3	42	39	11
Whitecraigs II.	9	5	0	0	4	46	35	10
Coats. Staff Cl.	9	2	1	2	4	42	39	9
Fort Matilda II.	9	1	0	1	7	33	48	4
Drumchapel II.	9	1	0	1	7	32	49	4
Kirtonfield	9	1	0	0	8	21	60	2
Drumpellier	9	1	0	0	8	8	73	2
	90	38	2	6	44	405	405	90

WOMEN—(continued) 1954

13th DIVISION.

	No.	Won	Drn.	W.O.	Lost	Sets Won	Sets Lost	Pts.
Muirend and Busby II.	10	8	0	1	1	70	20	18
Singer	10	8	0	0	2	60	30	16
Glenfield	10	7	1	0	2	47	43	15
Johnston C.O.S. II.	10	5	0	1	4	60	30	12
Springboig II.	10	6	0	0	4	47	43	12
Clyde Paper	10	6	0	0	4	41	48	12
Old Kilpatrick	10	3	1	0	6	44	46	7
Woodend II.	10	3	0	0	7	34	56	6
Cambuslang II.	10	2	0	0	8	33	57	4
Millbrae II.	10	2	0	0	8	31	58	4
Eaglesham	10	2	0	0	8	27	63	4
	110	52	2	2	54	494	494	110

14th DIVISION.

	No.	Won	Drn.	W.O.	Lost	Sets Won	Sets Lost	Pts.
Elderslie II.	9	9	0	0	0	59	22	18
Stepps II.	9	8	0	0	1	69	12	16
Kirkintilloch M.W.	9	6	1	0	2	58	23	13
Port Glasgow II.	9	5	1	0	3	41	37	11
Sandyhills II.	9	5	0	0	4	41	40	10
Garrowhill	9	4	0	0	5	35	43	8
Walsco	9	2	2	0	5	34	47	6
King's Park II.	9	3	0	0	6	29	52	6
Greenock H.S.F.P. II.	9	1	0	0	8	21	60	2
Cathcart O.P.C. II.	9	0	0	0	9	15	66	0
	90	43	4	0	43	402	402	90

15th DIVISION.

	No.	Won	Drn.	W.O.	Lost	Sets Won	Sets Lost	Pts.
Burnside II.	8	8	0	0	0	65	7	16
Dowanhill II.	8	7	0	0	1	61	11	14
Halfway	8	6	0	0	2	39	33	12
India of Inchinnan	8	4	0	0	4	36	36	8
Pressed Steel	8	3	1	0	4	34	38	7
Hyndland School F.P.	8	2	2	0	4	29	43	6
Stephen Rec. II.	8	1	1	1	5	32	40	5
Victoria Drive F.P.	8	2	0	0	6	22	50	4
Mt. Vernon II.	8	0	0	0	8	6	66	0
	72	33	4	1	34	324	324	72

16th DIVISION.

	No.	Won	Drn.	W.O.	Lost	Sets Won	Sets Lost	Pts.
Brookfield	10	9	0	0	1	76	14	18
Cardross	10	8	1	0	1	59	31	17
Renfrew II.	10	6	1	0	3	54	36	13
Kirktonhill II.	10	6	1	0	3	49	41	13
Killermont	10	4	0	1	5	50	40	10*
Civil Service	10	5	0	0	5	50	40	10*
Templeton II.	10	4	1	0	5	40	50	9
Rankin Pk. II.	10	3	0	1	6	41	49	8
Ruchill Ch.	10	4	0	0	6	38	52	8
Clyde Paper II.	10	1	0	1	8	31	59	4
Pressed Steel II.	10	0	0	0	10	7	83	0
	110	50	4	3	53	495	495	110

* Killermont 441 games against 378.
Civil Service 437 games against 401.

MEN 1954

1st DIVISION.

	No.	Won	Drn.	W.O.	Lost	Sets Won	Sets Lost	Pts.
Newlands	6	5	0	0	1	40	14	10
Pollokshields	6	4	0	0	2	37	17	8
Giffnock	6	4	0	0	2	30	24	8
Western	6	3	0	0	3	31	23	6
Titwood	6	3	0	0	3	24	30	6
Hillpark	6	2	0	0	4	22	32	4
Woodend	6	0	0	0	6	5	49	0
	42	21	0	1	21	189	189	42

2nd DIVISON.

	No.	Won	Drn.	W.O.	Lost	Sets Won	Sets Lost	Pts
Hamilton	6	5	0	0	1	33	21	10
Rutherglen	6	3	1	0	2	30	24	7
Criaghelen	6	2	2	0	2	29	25	6
Pollokshields II.	6	3	0	0	3	28	26	6
Bellahouston	6	2	1	0	3	23	31	5
Kingswood	6	2	1	0	3	22	32	5
Paisley	6	1	1	0	4	24	30	3
	42	18	6	0	18	189	189	42

3rd DIVISION.

	No.	Won	Drn.	W.O.	Lost	Sets Won	Sets Lost	Pts.
Cardonald	8	6	0	0	2	50	22	12
Poloc	8	6	0	0	2	46	26	12
Alexandria	8	6	0	0	2	42	30	12
Western II.	8	6	0	0	2	41	31	12
Kenmure	8	3	0	0	5	34	38	6
Ardgowan	8	3	0	0	5	29	43	6
Newlands II.	8	2	0	0	6	31	41	4
Queen's Park	8	2	0	0	6	28	44	4
Clarkston	8	2	0	0	6	23	49	4
	72	36	0	0	36	324	324	72

4th DIVISION.

	No.	Won	Drn.	W.O.	Lost	Sets Won	Sets Lost	Pts.
Dowanhill	8	6	0	1	1	57	15	14
Cartha	8	7	0	0	1	55	17	14
Springboig	8	6	0	0	2	45	27	12
Falcon	8	4	0	1	3	40	32	10
Bearsden	8	4	0	0	4	33	39	8
Titwood II.	8	3	0	0	5	34	38	6
Greenock H.S.F.P.	8	2	0	0	6	21	51	4
Kelvinside	8	1	0	0	7	20	52	2
Giffnock II.	8	1	0	0	7	19	53	2
	72	34	0	2	36	324	324	72

5th DIVISION.

	No.	Won	Drn.	W.O.	Lost	Sets Won	Sets Lost	Pts.
Whitecraigs	8	7	1	0	0	50	22	15
Elderslie	8	6	0	0	2	47	25	12
Public Parks	8	5	0	0	3	43	29	10
Stepps	8	4	1	0	3	43	29	9
Anchor	8	3	1	0	4	42	30	9
Rutherglen II.	8	3	1	0	4	30	42	7
Kingswood II.	8	2	2	0	4	34	38	6
Drumchapel	8	2	0	0	6	24	48	4
Bridge of Weir	8	0	0	0	8	11	61	0
	72	33	6	0	33	324	324	72

6th DIVISION.

	No.	Won	Drn.	W.O.	Lost	Sets Won	Sets Lost	Pts.
Broomhill	8	8	0	0	0	56	16	16
Burnside	8	7	0	0	1	54	18	14
Port Glasgow	8	6	0	0	2	51	21	12
Cardonald II.	8	5	0	0	3	38	34	10
Langside Hill Church	8	4	0	0	4	33	39	8
Muirend and Busby	8	3	0	0	5	32	40	6
Hawthorn	8	1	1	0	6	23	49	3
Lenzie	8	1	0	0	7	10	62	2
Kelvindale	8	0	1	0	7	27	45	1
	72	35	2	0	35	324	324	72

7th DIVISION.

	No.	Won	Drn.	W.O.	Lost	Sets Won	Sets Lost	Pts.
Bellahouston II.	8	7	0	0	1	55	17	14
Cambuslang	8	6	0	0	2	42	30	12
Mount Vernon	8	5	1	0	2	41	31	11
Millbrae	8	4	2	0	2	44	28	10
Scottish Gas Board	8	3	3	0	2	44	28	9
Clyde Paper	8	3	1	0	4	28	44	7
Clarkston II.	8	2	1	0	5	33	39	5
Ferguslie	8	1	2	0	5	28	44	4
Partickhill	8	0	0	0	8	9	63	0
	72	31	10	0	31	324	324	72

8th DIVISION.

	No.	Won	Drn.	W.O.	Lost	Sets Won	Sets Lost	Pts.
Coats' Staff Club	8	7	0	0	1	57	15	14
Hamilton II.	8	6	0	1	1	53	19	14
Hillhead H.S.F.P.	8	5	0	0	3	40	32	10
Ardgowan II.	8	4	1	0	3	40	32	9
Renfrew	8	3	1	0	4	32	40	7
Ralston	8	2	3	0	3	29	43	7
Uddingston	8	3	0	0	5	34	38	6
Thorntonhall	8	1	1	0	6	24	48	3
Eaglesham	8	1	0	0	7	15	57	2
	72	32	6	1	33	324	324	72

MEN 1954

12th DIVISION.

	No.	Won	Drn.	W.O.	Lost	Sets Won	Sets Lost	Pts.
Poloc II.	9	8	0	1	0	65	16	18
Erskine	9	6	1	0	2	49	32	13
Old Kilpatrick	9	6	0	0	3	52	29	12
Springboig II.	9	6	0	0	3	46	35	12
Rankin Park	9	4	2	0	3	44	37	10
Drumchapel II.	9	4	1	0	4	43	38	9
Halfway	9	3	1	0	5	41	40	7
Stephen Rec.	9	2	1	0	6	32	49	5
Kirkhill	9	2	0	0	7	29	52	4
Mechans	9	0	0	0	9	4	77	0
	90	41	6	1	42	405	405	90

13th DIVISION.

	No.	Won	Drn.	W.O.	Lost	Sets Won	Sets Lost	Pts.
Templeton	10	7	0	2	1	74	16	18
Albion Motors	10	7	0	1	2	61	29	16
Muirend and Busby II.	10	7	0	0	3	52	38	14*
Alexandria II.	10	7	0	0	3	52	38	14*
Scottish Gas Board II.	10	2	1	2	5	49	41	9
Hawthorn II.	10	2	2	1	5	40	50	8
Langside Hill Church II.	10	3	1	0	6	45	45	7
Ferguslie II.	10	3	1	0	6	41	49	7
Anchor II.	10	3	1	0	6	31	59	7
Hillhead H.S.F.P. II.	10	1	0	2	7	31	59	6
Greenock H.S.F.P. II.	10	2	0	0	8	19	71	4
	110	44	6	8	52	495	495	110

* Muirend and Busby II. 466 games against 386.
Alexandria II. 450 games against 386.

17th DIVISION.

	No.	Won	Drn.	W.O.	Lost	Sets Won	Sets Lost	Pts.
Ferguslie Mills	9	9	0	0	0	73	8	18
Cambuslang II.	9	7	0	0	2	56	25	14
King's Park II.	9	7	0	0	2	48	33	14
Pressed Steel	9	6	0	0	3	56	25	12
Hallside	9	5	0	0	4	45	36	10
Walsco	9	5	0	0	4	43	38	10
Albion Motors II.	9	3	0	0	6	33	48	6
Rankin Park II.	9	2	0	0	7	23	58	4
Halfway II.	9	1	0	0	8	25	56	2
Brown and Polson II.	9	0	0	0	9	3	78	0
	90	45	0	0	45	405	405	90

18th DIVISION.

	No.	Won	Drn.	W.O.	Lost	Sets Won	Sets Lost	Ots.
Kirkintilloch M.W. II.	8	7	0	1	0	57	15	16
Kirktonhill II.	8	6	0	0	2	45	27	12
Templeton II.	8	4	1	1	2	56	16	11
Civil Service	8	5	0	2		49	23	11
Ruchill Ch.	8	4	0	0	4	38	34	8
Clyde Paper II.	8	3	0	0	5	24	48	6
Killermont	8	3	0	0	5	22	50	6
Fort Matilda II.	8	1	0	0	7	24	48	2
Pressed Steel II.	8	0	0	0	8	9	63	0
	72	33	2	2	35	324	324	72

JUNIOR MIXED DOUBLES. 1954

1st DIVISION.

	No.	Won	Drn.	W.O.	Lost	Sets Won	Sets Lost	Pts.
Newlands	7	7	0	0	0	53	10	14
Hillpark	7	5	0	0	2	45	18	10
Titwood	7	5	0	0	2	44	19	10
Alexandria	7	4	0	0	3	31	32	8
Kirkhill	7	3	0	0	4	25	38	6
Drumchapel	7	0	0	2	5	19	44	4
Uddingston	7	1	0	0	6	20	43	2
Clarkston	7	1	0	0	6	15	48	2
	56	26	0	2	28	252	252	56

2nd DIVISION.

	No.	Won	Drn.	W.O.	Lost	Sets Won	Sets Lost	Pts.
Partickhill	6	6	0	0	0	44	10	12
Giffnock	6	4	0	1	1	42	12	10
Stepps	6	3	0	0	3	30	24	6
Whitecraigs	6	1	0	2	3	28	26	6
Pollokshields	5	2	0	0	3	19	26	4
Woodend	5	1	0	0	4	13	32	2
Burnside	6	0	0	0	6	4	50	0
	40	17	0	3	20	180	180	40

3rd DIVISION.

	No.	Won	Drn.	W.O.	Lost	Sets Won	Sets Lost	Pts.
Broomhill	6	5	0	1	1	46	8	12
Westerton	6	3	1	1	1	39	15	9
Hamilton	6	3	1	1	1	37	17	9
Rutherglen	6	1	0	2	3	31	23	6
Lenzie	6	1	0	1	4	21	33	4
Mearns	6	0	0	1	5	15	39	2
Cambuslang	6	0	0	0	6	0	54	0*
	42	13	2	7	20	189	189	42

* Cambuslang unable to raise a Team.

4th DIVISION.

	No.	Won	Drn.	W.O.	Lost	Sets Won	Sets Lost	Pts.
Cardonald	7	6	0	1	0	54	9	14
Muirend and Busby	7	5	1	0	1	45	18	11
Thorn Park	7	5	1	0	1	43	20	11
Sandyhills	7	3	0	1	3	38	25	8
Woodend II.	7	3	0	0	4	23	40	6
Hawthorn	7	1	0	1	5	22	41	4
Springboig	7	0	0	1	6	24	39	2
Poloc	7	0	0	0	7	3	60	0
	56	23	2	4	27	252	252	56

Results of Matches played during Season 1954 in which Teams representing the West of Scotland Lawn Tennis Association took part.

(1). INTER-ASSOCIATION REPRESENTATIVE MATCHES.

LADIES' DOUBLES.

WEST *v.* EAST at Craiglockhart, on 22nd May, 1954.
Match cancelled due to rain.

WEST *v.* MIDLANDS, at Dundee, on 3rd July, 1954.   Match abandoned due to rain.

WEST *v.* CENTRAL at Pollokshields, on 7th August, 1954.
West won by 9 rubbers, 18 sets, 116 games to 0 rubbers, 1 set, 43 games.

WEST *v.* AYRSHIRE, at Pollokshields, on 14th August, 1954.   Match cancelled.

"UNDER 21."

WEST *v.* EAST, at Cardonald, on 11th September, 1954.
West won by 5 rubbers, 10 sets, 77 games to 1 rubber, 2 sets, 59 games.

MEN'S DOUBLES.

WEST *v.* EAST, at Pollokshields, on 22nd May, 1954.   Match cancelled due to rain.

WEST *v.* MIDLANDS, at Pollokshields, on 3rd July, 1954.
West won by 5 rubbers, 10 sets, 68 games to 0 rubbers, 1 set, 35 games.

WEST *v.* AYRSHIRE, at Ayr, on 10th July, 1954.
West won by 9 rubbers, 12 sets to 0 rubbers, 1 set.

WEST *v.* CENTRAL, at Grangemouth, on 7th August, 1954.
West won by 9 rubbers, 18 sets, 115 games to 0 rubbers, 2 sets, 51 games.

"UNDER 21."

WEST *v.* EAST, at Craiglockhart, on 11th September, 1954.   Match abandoned due to rain.

MIXED DOUBLES.

WEST *v.* EAST, at Craiglockhart, on 1st May, 1954.
West won by 9 rubbers, 21 sets, 197 games to 7 rubbers, 16 sets, 173 games.

DOUBLES MATCH.

WEST *v.* ULSTER, at Belfast, on 11th September, 1954.

Ladies' Doubles.	West won by 2 rubbers, 4 sets, 36 games to 0 rubbers, 2 sets, 27 games.
Men's Doubles.	West won by 2 rubbers, 4 sets, 34 games to 0 rubbers, 2 sets, 30 games.
Mixed Doubles.	West won by 4 rubbers, 8 sets, 59 games to 0 rubbers, 1 set, 38 games.
Total.	West won by 8 rubbers, 16 sets, 129 games to 0 rubbers, 5 sets, 95 games.

(2). INTER-COUNTY CHAMPIONSHIPS ON HARD COURTS. (SINGLES).

WEST *v.* CUMBERLAND, at Carlisle, on 3rd October, 1953.
West won by 12 rubbers, 24 sets, to 0 rubbers, 0 sets.

WEST *v.* YORKSHIRE, at Huddersfield, on 10th October, 1953.
West won by 7 rubbers, 16 sets to 5 rubbers, 12 sets.

WEST *v.* CHESHIRE, at Wallasey, on 24th October, 1953.
West lost by 6 rubbers 15 sets to 6 rubbers, 16 sets.

(3). INTER-COUNTY CHAMPIONSHIPS ON GRASS. (DOUBLES).

These matches were played during the week commencing 19th July, 1954. Teams representing the Scottish Western Counties Lawn Tennis Association (which includes this Association), took part in the Competitions, the Ladies' Team playing at Folkestone in Group III. and the Men's Team at Scarborough in Group II. Both teams were successful in gaining second place in their respective Groups, and will be promoted to the next higher Group for 1955.

Results of Ladies' Matches :—West of Scotland beat Gloucestershire, 5 rubbers, 11 sets, 104 games to 4 rubbers, 9 sets, 93 games ; lost to South Wales, 4 rubbers, 12 sets, 112 games to 5 rubbers, 11 sets, 99 games ; lost to East of Scotland, 3 rubbers, 8 sets, 111 games to 6 rubbers, 14 sets, 138 games ; beat Berkshire, 9 rubbers, 18 sets, 121 games to 0 rubbers, 3 sets, 69 games ; beat Dorset, 8 rubbers, 16 sets, 119 games to 1 rubber, 4 sets, 76 games ;   The Team consisted of Mrs. L. S. Black (Pollokshields), Miss K. A. Gillespie (Newlands), Mrs. J. B. Harvey (Craighelen) Captain, Mrs. K. Horne (Dulwich), Miss H. M. Macfarlane (Craighelen), Miss C. Dunglison (Bridge of Allan) and Miss I. S. Vallance (Pollokshields).

Results of Men's Matches :—West of Scotland lost to Yorkshire, 3 rubbers, 8 sets 98 games to 6 rubbers, 12 sets, 111 games lost to Essex, 4 rubbers, 10 sets, 101 games to 5 rubbers, 10 sets, 103 games ; beat Gloucestershire, 7 rubbers, 15 sets, 122 games to 2 rubbers, 6 sets, 95 games ; beat Cheshire, 7 rubbers, 15 sets, 130 games to 2 rubbers, 6 sets, 106 games ; beat Derbyshire, 8 rubbers, 16 sets, 123 games to 1 rubber, 4 sets, 67 games.   The Team consisted of C. V. Baxter (Titwood), T. Boyd (Giffnock), I. M. Campbell (Pollokshields), W. C. Gillespie (Newlands), R. G. Harris (Titwood), I. Loudon (Titwood), J. G. Rutherglen (Newlands) and J. B. Wilson (Pollokshields).   Dr. J. B. Fulton (Chapel Allarton) acted as non-playing Captain.

SCOTTISH CUP COMPETITION (West of Scotland Section). 1954
WOMEN.

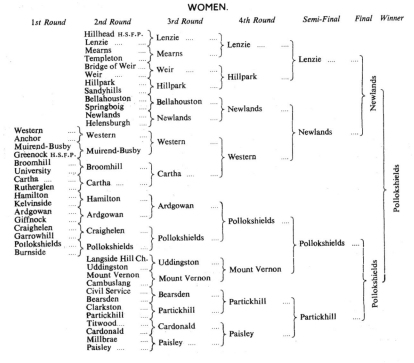

1st Round	2nd Round	3rd Round	4th Round	Semi-Final	Final	Winner

Hillhead H.S.F.P.
Lenzie — Lenzie — Lenzie — Lenzie — Lenzie — Newlands — Pollokshields
Mearns — Mearns
Templeton
Bridge of Weir — Weir — Hillpark
Weir
Hillpark — Hillpark
Sandyhills
Bellahouston — Bellahouston — Newlands — Newlands
Springboig
Newlands — Newlands
Helensburgh

Western — Western — Western — Western
Anchor
Muirend-Busby — Muirend-Busby
Greenock H.S.F.P.
Broomhill — Broomhill — Cartha
University
Cartha — Cartha
Rutherglen
Hamilton — Hamilton — Ardgowan — Pollokshields — Pollokshields — Pollokshields
Kelvinside
Ardgowan — Ardgowan
Giffnock
Craighelen — Craighelen — Pollokshields
Garrowhill
Pollokshields — Pollokshields
Burnside

Langside Hill Ch. — Uddingston — Mount Vernon
Uddingston
Mount Vernon — Mount Vernon
Cambuslang
Civil Service — Bearsden — Partickhill — Partickhill
Bearsden
Clarkston — Partickhill
Partickhill
Titwood — Cardonald — Paisley
Cardonald
Millbrae — Paisley
Paisley

SECOND STAGE RESULTS.

First Round—Pollokshields (West) beat Girvan (Ayrshire).
Second Round—Pollokshields (West) beat Hawick (Borders).
Semi-Final—Pollokshields (West) beat Bridge of Allan (Central).
Final—Pollokshields (West) beat Murrayfield (East).

SCOTTISH CUP COMPETITION (West of Scotland Section). 1954
MEN.

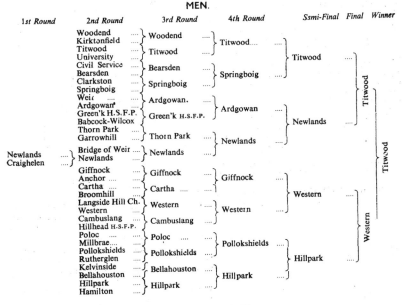

1st Round	2nd Round	3rd Round	4th Round	Ssmi-Final	Final	Winner

Woodend — Woodend — Titwood — Titwood — Titwood — Titwood
Kirktonfield
Titwood — Titwood
University
Civil Service — Bearsden — Springboig
Bearsden
Clarkston — Springboig
Springboig
Weir — Ardgowan — Ardgowan — Newlands
Ardgowan
Green'k H.S.F.P. — Green'k H.S.F.P.
Babcock-Wilcox
Thorn Park — Thorn Park — Newlands
Garrowhill

Newlands — Bridge of Weir — Newlands
Craighelen — Newlands

Giffnock — Giffnock — Giffnock — Western
Anchor
Cartha — Cartha
Broomhill
Langside Hill Ch. — Western — Western
Western
Cambuslang — Cambuslang
Hillhead H.S.F.P.
Poloc — Poloc — Pollokshields — Hillpark
Millbrae
Pollokshields — Pollokshields
Rutherglen
Kelvinside — Bellahouston — Hillpark
Bellahouston
Hillpark — Hillpark
Hamilton

SECOND STAGE.

First Round—Titwood (West)—Bye.
Second Round—Titwood (West) beat Darvel (Ayrshire).
Semi-Final—Titwood (West) beat Dumfries (South-West).
Final—Titwood (West) beat Murrayfield (East).

CALCUTTA CUP. 1954

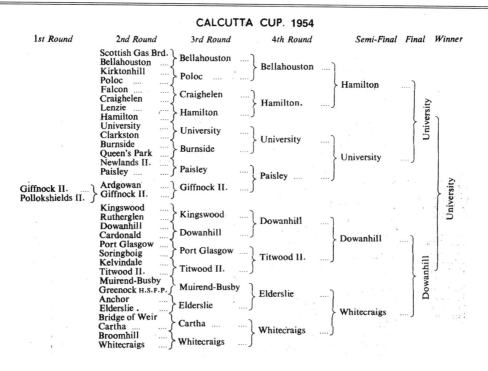

JUNIOR CALCUTTA CUP. 1954

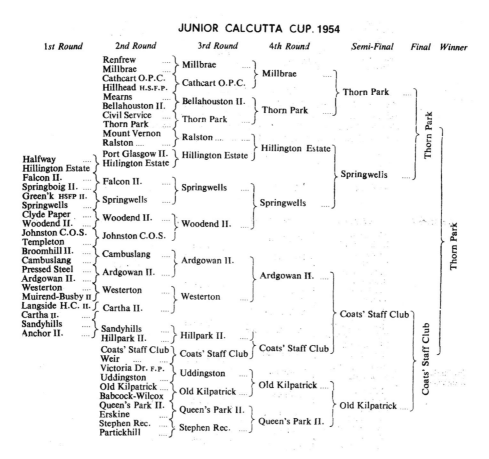

MIXED DOUBLES—First Division. 1954

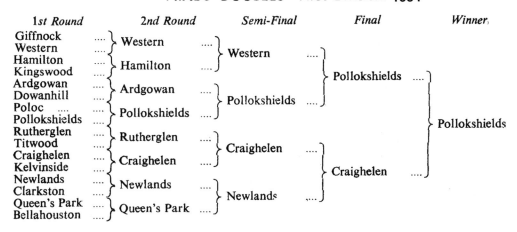

Second Division. 1954

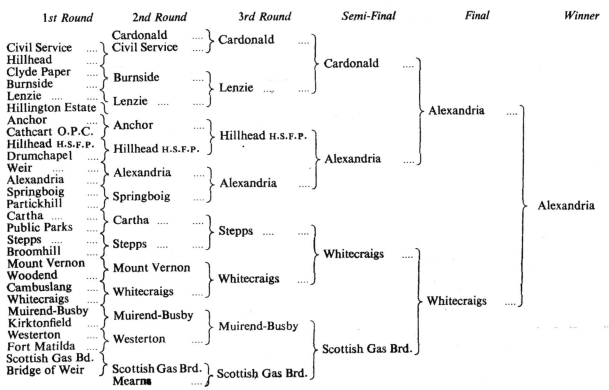

LADIES SINGLES CHAMPIONSHIP - OPEN

Instituted 1886

Challenge Cup Presented by Mr. Keith Buchanan.

1886	Miss Jane Meikle		1957	Miss H.M. Macfarlane	Craighelen
1887	Miss J. McKenzie		1958	Miss E.A. Walker	Ayr
1888	Miss Rose		1959	Miss F.V.M. Maclennan	Newlands
1889	Miss Playfair		1960	Miss A.G. McAlpine	Bellahouston
1890	Miss Ferguson		1961	Miss A.G. McAlpine	Bellahouston
1891	Miss Jones	London	1962	Miss J.S. Barclay	Kircaldy
1892	No Contest		1963	Mrs. E.A. Paul	Darvel
1893	Miss Watson		1964	Miss F.V.M. MacLennan	Glasgow University
1894	Miss G.F. Hardie		1965	Miss A.G. McAlpine	Bellahouston
1895-1910	No Contest		1966	Miss A.G. McAlpine	Bellahouston
1911	Mrs. Robin Welsh	East of Scot.	1967	Miss K. Harter	USA
1912	Miss M.M. Fergus		1968	Miss S.E.L. Moodie	Stepps
1913	Miss M.R.H. Stewart		1969	Mrs. C.A. Matheson	Hillpark
1914	Miss E. Abercrombie		1970	Miss M. Guzman	Equador
1915-1918	No Contest		1971	Miss Jane O'Hara	Canada
1919	Miss M.R.H. Stewart		1972	Miss M. Tesch	Australia
1920	Miss M. Thom	Gleneagles	1973	Miss M. Tesch	Australia
1921	Miss M.R.H. Stewart		1974	Miss D. Fromholtz	Australia
1922	Mrs. D.J. Richardson		1975	Mrs. J.S. Hume	Whitecraigs
1923	Miss P. Hengler	Partick	1976	Abandoned	
1924	Mrs. Keith Buchanan	Helensburgh	1977	Mrs. A. Jones	England
1925	Miss M. Thom	Gleneagles	1978	Miss C. Murphy	USA
1926	Miss J.C. Rankine	Newlands	1979	Miss S Leo	Australia
1927	Miss J. Riddick	Central District	1980	Miss Sue Saliba	Australia
1928	Miss J.C. Rankine	Newlands	1981	Miss L. Gordon	S. Africa
1929	Miss J.C. Rankine	Newlands	1982	Miss B. Randall	Australia
1930	Miss W.A. Mason	Pollokshields	1983	Miss Rene Mentz	S. Africa
1931	Miss G.R. Sterry	London	1984	Miss J.M. Erskine	Dunblane
1932	Miss W.A. Mason	Pollokshields	1985	Miss J.M. Erskine	Dunblane
1933	Miss W.A. Mason	Pollokshields	1986	Miss M.J. Love	Elderslie
1934	Miss W.A. Mason	Pollokshields	1987	Miss S.T.G. Mair	Colinton
1935	Miss J. Hartigan	Australia	1988	Miss S.T.G. Mair	Colinton
1936	Miss W.A. Mason	Pollokshields	1989	Miss S.T.G. Mair	Colinton
1937	Miss L. Anderson	Pollokshields	1990	Miss H. Lockhart	Newlands
1938	Mrs J.B. Fulton	Guisborough	1991	Miss M. Mair	Colinton
1939	Mrs P. Smith	Clarkston	1992	Miss J. Walker	Newlands
1940 -1946	No Contest		1993	Miss D. Forrest	Broomhill
1947	Mrs. W.M. Simmers	Kelvinside	1994	Miss N. Burns	Whitecraigs
1948	Miss H.M. Macfarlane	Craighelen	1995	Miss N. Burns	Whitecraigs
1949	Mrs. L.S. Black	Pollokshields	1996	Miss D. Forrest	Newlands
1950	Miss H.M. Macfarlane	Craighelen	1997	Miss H. Lockhart	Newlands
1951	Miss H.M. Macfarlane	Craighelen	1998	Miss H. Lockhart	Newlands
1952	Miss I.S. Vallance	Pollokshields	1999	Miss N. Burns	David Lloyd
1953	Miss H.M. Macfarlane	Craighelen	2000	Miss M. Whitelaw	Prestwick & Sym.
1954	Miss H.M. Macfarlane	Craighelen	2001	Miss H Lockhart	Newlands
1955	Miss H.M. Macfarlane	Craighelen	2002	Mrs. R. Owen	Clarkston
1956	Miss H.M. Macfarlane	Craighelen	2003	Miss H Lockhart	Newlands

MEN'S SINGLES CHAMPIONSHIP

Instituted 1886

Challenge Cup Presented by Pollokshields Athletic club in 1898

The Original Challenge Cup was Presented by Slazenger and won outright by J.H. Neil in 1897 who presented it to Pollokshields Athletic Club in January 1951, and it was then Presented to W.S.L.T.A. and is in use as the Trophy for the most successful Club in the Championships.

Confined to players in the West of Scotland Counties from 1886 to 1929, and thereafter open to all comers

1886	L. Maclachlan	Glasgow University	1927	E. Rayner	Pollokshields
1887	G.S. Jackson	Glasgow University	1928	A.W. Hill	Newlands
1888	J.B. Gray		1929	A.W. Hill	Newlands
1889	G.S. Jackson	Glasgow University	1930	A.W. Hill	Newlands
1890	G.S. Jackson	Glasgow University	1931	A.W. Hill	Newlands
1891	T.L. Hendry	Langside	1932	A.W. Hill	Newlands
1892	T.L. Hendry	Langside	1933	D. MacPhail, Jr	Pollokshields
1893	A.W. Scott	Partickhill	1934	D. MacPhail, Jr	Pollokshields
1894	F.J. Barker	Glasgow University	1935	C.E. Malfroy	New Zealand
1895	J.H. Neil	Pollokshields	1936	D. MacPhail, Jr	Pollokshields
1896	J.H. Neil	Pollokshields	1937	D. MacPhail, Jr	Pollokshields
1897	J.H. Neil	Pollokshields	1938	L. Shaffi	London
1898	J.H. Neil	Pollokshields	1939	E.H. Taylor	Pollokshields
1899	T.L. Hendry	Langside	1940 - 1946 No Contest		
1900	R. Baird		1947	R. Barr	Pollokshields
1901	R. Baird		1948	R.G. Harris	St. Andrews University
1902	J.H. Neil	Pollokshields	1949	D. McPhail, Jr	Pollokshields
1903	R. Baird		1950	J.G. Rutherglen	Newlands
1904	R. Baird		1951	J.M. Mehta	India
1905	R. Baird		1952	J.G. Rutherglen	Newlands
1906	J.T. Butters	Pollokshields	1953	C.V. Baxter	Titwood
1907	J.T. Butters	Pollokshields	1954	C.V. Baxter	Titwood
1908	G.A. Paterson	Partick	1955	J.B. Wilson	Cardonald
1909	A.M'D. Chalmers		1956	C.V. Baxter	Titwood
1910	J.T. Butters	Pollokshields	1957	C.V. Baxter	Titwood
1911	H.E.B. Neilson		1958	C.V. Baxter	Titwood
1912	R. Baird		1959	C.V. Baxter	Titwood
1913	A. Fraser		1960	C.V. Baxter	Titwood
1914	A. Fraser		1961	K.B. Gray	Newlands
1915 - 1918 No Contest			1962	Ian M. Campbell	Cape Province SA
1919	L.F. Davin		1963	C.V. Baxter	Titwood
1920	A. Blair	Pollokshields	1964	G.B. Kerr	Newlands
1921	A. Blair	Pollokshields	1965	W.C. Gillespie	Newlands
1922	A. Blair	Pollokshields	1966	H.S. Matheson	Hillpark
1923	E. Rayner	Pollokshields	1967	T. Addison	Australia
1924	D.L. Craig	Partick	1968	H.S. Matheson	Hillpark
1925	E. Rayner	Pollokshields	1969	D.A. Lloyd	England
1926	E. Rayner	Pollokshields	1970	D.A. Lloyd	England

1971	D.A. Lloyd	England	1988	K.M. Revie	Broomhill
1972	J.G. Clifton	Queen's Club	1989	K.M. Revie	Broomhill
1973	F.D. McMillan	South Africa	1990	R. Matheson	Whitecraigs
1974	J. Yuill	South Africa	1991	B. Dodds	Broomhill
1975	D. Joubert	South Africa	1992	M. Watt	Newlands
1976	Abandoned		1993	M. Watt	Newlands
1977	D.A. Lloyd	England	1994	M. Watt	Newlands
1978	A. Jarrett	England	1995	M. Watt	Newlands
1979	F.D. McMillan	South Africa	1996	M. Watt	Newlands
1980	A. Jarrett	England	1997	M. McGill	Giffnock
1981	C. Miller	Australia	1998	M. Watt	Newlands
1982	P. Kronk	Australia	1999	A. MacDonald	Thistle
1983	B. Mottram	England	2000	A. MacDonald	Thistle
1984	K.M. Revie	Broomhill	2001	J. Gray	Next Generation West End
1985	I..J. Allan	Broomhill	2002	A. MacDonald	Next Generation Newhaven
1986	K.M. Revie	Broomhill	2003	J Gray	Newlands
1987	C.J. McGill	Colinton			

MEN'S SINGLES OPEN

1930 and afterwards this Event merged with West Men's Singles

1886	A Thomson	1900	AJ Rowan / CRD Pritchett tied
1887	JG Horn	1901	R Baird
1888	ANJ Storey	1902	———
1889	AA Thomson	1903	R Baird
1890	EB Fuller	1904	———
1891	A Thomson	1905	to 1921 no contest
1892	JH Conyers	1922	A Blair
1893	HL Fleming	1923	E Rayner
1894	HE Cladecott	1924	HEB Neilson
1895	FJ Barker	1925	E Rayner
1896	RM Watson	1926	WAR Collins
1897	AJ Rowan	1927	AW Hill
1898	JM Buist	1928	E Rayner
1899	AJ Rowan	1929	E Rayner

LADIES' DOUBLES CHAMPIONSHIP - OPEN

Instituted 1892

Challenge Cups presented by the late Mr J. Dykes and Mr J. McQueen

The Cups were originally for Veteran Mens Doubles and with the Donors' consent changed to Ladies Doubles in 1930

1892	Miss B. Watson	Miss Playfair	1954	Miss K.A. Gillespie	Mrs. L.S. Black
1893	No Contest		1955	Mrs. L. Dick	Miss H.M. Macfarlane
1894	Miss Watson	Miss G.F. Hardie	1956	Mrs. L. Dick	Miss H.M. Macfarlane
1895-1907 No Contest			1957	Mrs. L. Dick	Miss H.M. Macfarlane
1908	Miss Stewart	Miss Highet	1958	Miss E.A. Walker	Miss M.L. Walker
1909	Miss B. Smellie	Miss E. Smellie	1959	Miss C.E. Dungliston	Mrs. L.S. Black
1910	Miss B. Smellie	Miss E. Smellie	1960	Miss C.E. Dungliston	Mrs. L.S. Black
1911	Miss M.M. Fergus	Miss Donaldson	1961	Miss C.E. Dungliston	Mrs. L.S. Black
1912	Miss M.M. Fergus	Miss Donaldson	1962	Miss C.E. Dungliston	Miss B.J. McCallum
1913	Miss B. Pratt	Miss E. Pratt	1963	Miss C.E. Dungliston	Miss M. Ferguson
1914	Miss B. Pratt	Miss E. Pratt	1964	Miss F.V. Maclennan	Mrs. F.A.S. Paul
1915-1918 No Contest			1965	Miss A.G. McAlpine	Miss B.J. Mc Callum
1919	Miss M.R.Ferguson	Miss H.M. Stanley	1966	Miss A.G. McAlpine	Mrs. R. Livingstone
1920	Mrs. Keith Buchanan	Miss A.B. Macdonald	1967	Miss K.M. Harter	Mrs. E.A. Paul
1921	Mrs. Keith Buchanan	Miss A.B. Macdonald	1968	Miss S.E.L. Moodie	Mrs. E.A. Paul
1922	Miss M. Morton	Miss P. Morton	1969	Mrs C. Matheson	Mrs. B. Livingstone
1925	Mrs. Keith Buchanan	Mrs. Murray	1970	Miss E. Armstrong	Miss G. Armstrong
1923	Mrs. Keith Buchanan	Miss A.B. Macdonald	1971	Miss B. Walsh	Miss M. Greenwood
1924	Mrs. Keith Buchanan	Miss A.B. Macdonald	1972	Miss P. Cody	Miss B. Vircoe
1926	Miss P. Hengler	Miss J.C. Rankine	1973	Miss M. Tesch	Miss C. Matison
1927	Hon. Mrs. Corbett	Miss N.B. Grimmond	1974	Miss D. Fromholtz	Miss J. Dimond shared
1928	Miss J.C.Rankine	Miss M. Langmuir		Mrs. P. Gregg	Mrs. C. Matheson
1929	Miss J.C.Rankine	Miss M. Langmuir	1975	Mrs. J. Hume	Mrs. C. Matheson
1930	Miss M. Langmuir	Miss A.E. Middleton	1976	Abandoned	
1931	Miss J.C.Rankine	Miss M. Langmuir	1977	Miss C. Harrison	Miss J. Durie
1932	Miss W.A. Mason	Miss J.A. Jamieson	1978	Miss P. Bailey	Miss K. Gulley
1933	Miss W.A. Mason	Miss J.A. Jamieson	1979	Miss A. Coe	Miss L. Charles
1934	Miss W.A. Mason	Miss J.A. Jamieson	1980	Miss S. Saliba	Miss L. Charles
1935	Mrs. Robertson	Miss J. Hartigan	1981	Miss B. Mould	Miss L. Gordon
1936	Miss W.A. Mason	Miss J.A. Jamieson	1982	Miss E. Mintner	Miss B. Randall
1937	Mrs. R. Harvey	Miss M Thomson	1983	Miss R. Mentz	Miss M. Reinach
1938	Miss C.H. Butters	Miss M. Thomson	1984	Miss M.J. Love	Miss S.E.L. Moodie
1939	Miss C.H. Butters	Miss M. Thomson	1985	Miss J.M. Erskine	Miss I. Stadele
1940-1946 No Contest			1986	Miss A. Smith	Miss I. Smith
1947	Mrs. W.M. Simmers	Miss M.S. Allan	1987	Miss S.T.G. Mair	Miss L.J. Reid
1948	Mrs. L.S. Black	Miss M. Thomson	1988	Miss K. Harrison	Miss M. Mair
1949	Mrs. L.S. Black	Miss M. Thomson	1989	Miss S.T.G. Mair	Mrs. J. Murray
1950	Mrs. R. Harvey	Miss H.M. Macfarlane	1990	Miss H. Lockhart	Miss L. Browne
1951	Mrs. W.M. Simmers	Miss I.S. Vallance	1991	Miss K. Ross	Miss E. Adams
1952	Miss H.M. Macfarlane	Miss I.S. Vallance	1992	Miss K. Ross	Miss J. Walker
1953	Mrs. L. Dick	Mrs. H. Proudfoot	1993	Miss L. Adams	Miss D. Forrest

1994	Miss N. Burns	Miss J. Walker	1999	Mrs. A. Brown	Miss N. Burns
1995	Miss E. Adams	Miss K. Fulton	2000	Miss H. Lockhart	Miss E. Stevenson
1996	Miss D. Forrest	Mrs. J. Oliphant	2001	Miss H. Lockhart	Mrs. R. Owen
1997	Miss H. Lockhart	Miss R. Orsi	2002	Miss H. Lockhart	Mrs. R. Owen
1998	Miss H. Lockhart	Mrs. C. Lockhart	2003	Miss H Lockhart	Mrs J Oliphant

Single & Married names of Ladies

Miss Craig	Mrs. Keith Buchanan	Miss E.A. Walker	Mrs. F.A.S. Paul
Hon. Mrs. Corbett	Lady Rowallan	Miss B.J. McCallum	Mrs. R. Livingstone
Miss G. Sterry	Mrs. W.M. Simmers	Miss J.S. Barclay	Mrs. J.S. Hume
Miss C.H. Butters	Mrs. L.S. Black	Miss J.M. Erskine	Mrs. J.M. Murray
Miss KA Gillespie	Mrs. KA Dingwall	Miss J Walker	Mrs J. Oliphant
Miss R. Orsi	Mrs. R. Owen		
Miss L. Anderson	Mrs. L. Dick		

MEN'S DOUBLES CHAMPIONSHIPS - OPEN

Instituted 1886

Challenge Cups presented by Mr. Stanley N. Doust

1886	W.W. Chamberlain	A.N.J. Storey	1932	J.T. Hill	A.W. Hill
1887	R.M. Watson	J.H. Conyers	1933	Dr. J.B. Fulton	R.R. Finlay
1888	H.G. Nadin	G.S. Jackson	1934	Dr. J.B. Fulton	R.R. Finlay
1889	H.G. Nadin	G.S. Jackson	1935	A.C. Stedman	C.E. Malfroy
1890	H.G. Nadin	G.S. Jackson	1936	W.R. Finlay	B. Butters
1891	H.G. Nadin	H.E. Caldecott	1937	D. MacPhail Jr	B. Butters
1892	R.M. Watson	J.H. Conyers	1938	R.A. Gray	L. Shaffi
1893	H.L. Fleming	C.J. Glenny	1939	J.A. Robertson	A.G.M. Keir
1894	R.M. Watson	H.E. Caldecott	1940-1946 No Contests		
1895	A.W. Scott	W.F. McEwan	1947	J.F. Morton	R. Morton
1896	R.M. Watson	J.M. Buist	1948	J.F. Morton	R. Morton
1897	A.J. Rowan	G.L. Findlay shared	1949	J.B. Wilson	A.B. Murray
	T.L. Hendry	S.M. "Ash"	1950	A.T. McDowall	R.G. Harris
1898	J.N.M. Sykes	A.W. Scott	1951	A.D.L.Hunter	C.V. Baxter
1899	J.H. Neil	J.G. Couper	1952	I.M. Campbell	C.V. Baxter
1900	A.J. Rowan	C.R.D. Pritchett	1953	I.M. Campbell	C.V. Baxter
1901	J.H. Neil	J.G. Couper	1954	I.M. Campbell	C.V. Baxter
1902	J.H. Neil	G.A. Paterson	1955	J.B. Wilson	R.G. Harris
1903	—		1956	J.B. Wilson	R.G. Harris
1904	R. Baird	G.A. Patersons	1957	C.V. Baxter	M.A. Macdonald
1905	J.T. Butters	A.J. Smellie	1958	T. Boyd	K.B. Gray
1906	J.T. Butters	A.J. Smellie	1959	K.B. Gray	C.V. Baxter
1907	J.T. Butters	A.J. Smellie	1960	C.V. Baxter	J.T. Wood
1908	J.N.M. Sykes	G.A. Paterson	1961	J.R. Maguire	C.V. Baxter
1909	A. Wylie	J. Fraser	1962	J.R. Maguire	C.V. Baxter
1910	J.N.M. Sykes	G.A. Paterson	1963	J.R. Maguire	C.V. Baxter
1911	Rev R.B. Irons	G.A. Paterson	1964	J.R. McAlpine	W.C. Gillespie
1912	R. Baird	G.A. Paterson	1965	H. Roulston	J.K. McNeillage
1913	Rev R.B. Irons	A. Fraser	1966	H.S. Matheson	F.N. Thomson
1914	J. Hamilton	J. Mathie Jr	1967	T. Addison	V. Israel
1915-1918 No Contest			1968	D.C. Braid	I. Walker
1919	Rev R.B. Irons	L.F. Davin	1969	G. Copland	D.A. Lloyd
1920	J.N.M. Sykes	H.E.B Neilson	1970	G.T. Downes	H.S. Matheson
1921	A. Blair	D.L. Craig	1971	G. Thomson	J.F. Manderson
1922	A. Blair	D.L. Craig	1972	G. Thomson	D.A. Lloyd
1923	D.L. Craig	H.L. Steel	1973	F.D. McMillan	M.J. Farrell
1924	J. van Ende	C.E.W. Jones	1974	G. Perkins	J. Yuill shared
1925	A. Bray	E. Rayner		N. Callaghan	R. Garey
1926	W.A.R. Collins	I.G. Collins	1975	E. Ewert	C. Kachel
1927	W.A.R. Collins	I.G .Collins	1976	Abandoned	
1928	J.T. Hill	A.W. Hill	1977	R. Taylor	D.A. Lloyd
1929	J.T. Hill	A.W. Hill	1978	G. Attiker	J. Thanin
1930	J.T. Hill	A.W. Hill	1979	G. Masters	F.D. McMillan
1931	J.T. Hill	A.W. Hill	1980	R.A.J. Hewitt	F.D. McMillan

1981	P. Dent	J. Alexander		1993	C. McKnight	M. Watt
1982	F.D. McMillan	C.J. Mottram		1994	G. Bell	R. Terras
1983	F.D. McMillan	C.J. Mottram		1995	C. McKnight	M. Watt
1984	R.W. Howat	K.M. Revie		1996	M. Watt	R. Terras
1985	K.M. Revie	I.J. Allan		1997	J. Gray	M. Hendry
1986	K.M. Revie	I.J. Allan		1998	J. Barnett	A. Macdonald
1987	K.M. Revie	I.J. Allan		1999	C. McKnight&	M. Watt
1988	G. Bell	J.F. Howie		2000	A. MacDonald	G. Smith
1989	K.M. Revie	I.J. Allan		2001	A. MacDonald	G. Smith
1990	R. Terras	M. Watt		2002	A. MacDonald	S. McGuckin
1991	K.M. Revie	I.J. Allan		2003	J Gray	R Terras
1992	G. Bell	K. Wood				

MIXED DOUBLES CHAMPIONSHIP OPEN

Instituted 1886

Challenge Cups presented by Messrs A. G. Spalding & Bros Ltd.

1886	W.W. Chamberlain	Miss J. Meikle		1947	B. Fulton	Mrs. H.M. Simmers
1887	J.G. Horn	Miss J. McKenzie		1948	R. Barr	Mrs. L.S. Black
1888	R.M. Watson	Miss B. McLellan		1949	B. Fulton	Mrs. H.M. Simmers
1889	A. Thomson	Miss Robertson		1950	B. Fulton	Mrs. H.M. Simmers
1890	E.B. Fuller	Miss Playfair		1951	Abandoned	
1891	A.A. Thomson	Miss Jones		1952	J.G. Rutherglen	Mrs. D.H. Dick
1892	H.E Caldecott	Partner		1953	I.M. Campbell	Miss I.S. Vallance
1893	A.W. Scott	Miss Robertson		1954	I.M. Campbell	Miss I.S. Vallance
1894	J.N.M. Sykes	Miss B. Smellie		1955	C.V. Baxter	Miss H.M. Macfarlane
1895-1904	No Contests			1956	C.V. Baxter	Miss H.M. Macfarlane
1905	R. Baird	Miss Robertson		1957	C.V. Baxter	Miss H.M. Macfarlane
1906	A.J. Smellie	Miss B. Smellie		1958	C.V. Baxter	Miss E.A. Walker
1907	A.J. Smellie	Miss B. Smellie		1959	C.V. Baxter	Miss A.V. Paterson
1908	A.McD. Chalmers	Miss Stewart		1960	C.V. Baxter	Miss A.V.Paterson
1909	G.A. Paterson	Miss Cooke Gray		1961	C.V. Baxter	Miss J.S. Barclay
1910	A.J. Smellie	Miss B. Smellie		1962	C.V. Baxter	Miss J.S. Barclay
1911	R.H. Brand	Mrs. R. Welsh		1963	C.V. Baxter	Miss W.M. Shaw
1912	W.D. Bayne	Miss M.M. Fergus		1964	C.V. Baxter	Miss W.M. Shaw
1913	A. Fraser	Miss B. Pratt		1965	C.V. Baxter	Miss B.J. McCallum
1914	A. Fraser	Miss B. Pratt		1966	W.C. Gillespie	Miss A.G. McAlpine
1915-1918	No Contest			1967	R. Keldie	Miss K.M. Harter
1919	J. Mathie Jr.	Miss E. Hendry		1968	H.S.Matheson	Miss S.E.L. Moodie
1920	H.E.B. Neilson	Miss A.B. Macdonald		1969	D.A. Lloyd	Miss S.E.L. Moodie
1921	D.L. Craig	Mrs. Keith Buchanan		1970	D.A. Lloyd	Miss M. Guzman
1922	D.L. Craig	Mrs. Keith Buchanan		1971	I. Walker	Miss G. Armstrong
1923	D.L. Craig	Mrs. Keith Buchanan		1972	I. Walker	Miss M.J. Love
1924	D.L. Craig	Mrs. Keith Buchanan		1973	I. Walker	Miss M.J. Love
1925	D.L. Craig	Mrs. Keith Buchanan		1974	I. Walker	Miss M.J. Love shared
1926	R.F. Scovell	Hon Mrs. G. Corbett			T. Bardsley	Mrs. S. Bardsley
1927	W.A.R. Collins	Miss N.B. Grimmond		1975	I. Walker	Miss M.J. Love
1928	A.W. Hill	Miss J.C. Rankine		1976	Abandoned	
1929	A.W. Hill	Miss J.C. Rankine		1977	J.F. Howie	Miss J. Erskine
1930	J.T. Hill	Miss W.A. Mason		1978	I. Walker	Miss M.J. Love
1931	J.T. Hill	Miss W.A. Mason		1979	I. Walker	Miss M.J. Love
1932	J.T. Hill	Miss W.A. Mason		1980	K.M. Revie	Miss S.E.L. Moodie
1933	A. McVie	Miss J.B. Dunn		1981	K.M. Revie	Miss S.E.L. Moodie
1934	D. MacPhail Jr.	Miss W.A. Mason		1982	K.M. Revie	Miss S.E.L. Moodie
1935	I.G. Collins	Lady Rowallan		1983	A. Lackie	Miss J. Erskine
1936	D. MacPhail Jr.	Miss W.A. Mason		1984	K.M. Revie	Miss S.E.L. Moodie
1937	B. Butters Jr.	Miss M. McEwan shared		1985	H. Shields	Miss I Stadele shared
	A.S. Gilchrist	Miss J.A. Jamieson			I.J. Allan	Miss J. Erskine
1938	J.T.Hill	Mrs. J.B. Fulton		1986	I.J. Allan	Miss J. Erskine
1939	N.C. McKenzie	Miss M. Thomson		1987	K.M. Revie	Miss S. Mair
1940-1946	No Contest			1988	K.M. Revie	Miss S. Mair

1989	K.M. Revie	Miss S. Mair		1997	R. Terras	Miss H. Lockhart
1990	M. Watt	Miss H. Lockhart		1998	M. Watt	Miss E. Stevenson
1991	E.R. McGinn	Miss M. Mair		1999	M. Watt	Miss E. Stevenson
1992	B. Dodds	Miss D. Forrest		2000	A. MacDonald	Miss V. Jigajinni
1993	O. Hadden	Miss E. Smith		2001	S. Hurst	Miss H. Lockhart
1994	A. Smith	Miss J. Walker		2002	A. MacDonald	Miss H. Lockhart
1995	C. McKnight	Miss N. Burns		2003	S McGuckin	Mrs R Owen
1996	M. Watt	Miss D. Forrest				

LADIES DOUBLES HANDICAP - OPEN

In 1925 there were 88 couples entered in this event. As there are no other programmes available for years prior to 1947 provision has not been made for those years.

1947				
1948				
1949				
1950				
1951				
1952	Mrs ML Beverage	Cambuslang	Miss MV Carnie	Cambuslang
1953	Miss AKL Gibson	Cartha	Miss N Adams	Cartha
1954	Miss SM Walker	Uddingston	M McGhie	Uddingston
1955	Mrs V Crabb	Whitecraigs	Miss BME Tweedie	Whitecraigs
1956	Miss PJ Horn	Newlands	Miss E Grieve	Newlands
1957	Mrs LP Anderson	Hamilton	Miss F Gillies	Hamilton
1958	Miss FVM MacLennan	Newlands	Miss HM McVie	Kirkhill
1959	Mrs AL Paterson	Queen's Park	Miss M Walker	Queen's Park
1960	Miss DD Graham	Springboig	Miss E Milloy	Springboig
1961	Miss A Hepburn	King's Park	Miss MB Russell	King's Park	Shared
	Mrs PMC Miller	Craighelen	Miss Morgan	Craighelen
1962	Miss E Buttar	Arthurlie	Miss J Brown	Arthurlie
1963	Miss J McGregor	Cowan Park	Miss H McGregor	Cowan Park
1964	Miss ND Provan	Titwood	Miss J McNeil	Titwood
1965				

MEN'S DOUBLES HANDICAP - OPEN

In 1925 there were 99 couples entered in this event. As there are no other programmes available for years prior to 1947 provision has not been made for these years

1947				
1948				
1949				
1950				
1951				
1952	J Henderson	Shotts Ironworks	JCM Summers	Strathaven
1953	W Kilpatrick	Thorn Park	GS Morrison	Thorn Park
1954	A Campbell	Hillington	J Cant	Hillington
1955	DC Moir	Thorn Park	AJC Smith	Thorn Park
1956	AN Coppell	Newlands	GB Kerr	Newlands
1957	J Eelloo	Public Parks	T McQuillan	Public Parks
1958	IR Young	Titwood	RH Thomson	Titwood
1959	R Russell	Springboig	A Meikle	Springboig
1960	SG Black	Kirkhill	KW Walker	Kirkhill
1961	KB McAlpine	Bellahouston	JE Thomson	Rutherglen
1962	TM Russell	Kirkintilloch M.W.	AM Russell	Kirkintilloch M.W.
1963	EW Harding	Lenzie	WS McLay	Lenzie
1964	S McCann	Dowanhill	T Mair	Dowanhill

MIXED DOUBLES HANDICAP - OPEN

In 1925 there were 94 couples entered for this event. As there are no other programmes available for years prior to 1947 provision has not been made for those years.

1947				
1948				
1949				
1850				
1951				
1952	KB Gray	Newlands	Miss ME Davidson	Newlands
1953	WA Brand	Ardrossan	Mrs A Munro	Ardrossan
1954	GS Anderson	Bellahouston	Miss I Brown	Bellahouston
1955	C Coley	Mount Vernon	Mrs V Coley	Mount Vernon
1956	GI Whiteman	Uddingston	Miss Boyd	Uddingston
1957	J Philip	Hamilton	Mrs I Philip	Hamilton
1958	IR Young	Titwood	Miss M Lindsay	Titwood
1959	R Randall	Millbrae	Mrs I Mackay	Millbrae
1960	A Galloway	Pollokshields	Miss I Galloway	Pollokshields
1961	E Cunningham	Poloc	Miss A Smith	Poloc
1962	Event not held			
1963	Event not held			
1964	P Kerr	Busby	Miss M McNeil	Busby
1965				

WEST OF SCOTLAND SHIELD (LADIES SINGLES)

Instituted 1937

Challenge Shield presented by Mr G.B. Primrose.

Confined to players who are members of Clubs affiliated to W.S.L.T.A. and who have never reached the Final Round of the Women's Singles (Handicaps excepted) in any Open Tournament, and who have never previously won this Event.

1937	Mrs P Smith (Clarkston)		1958	Miss BM McKean (Paisley)
1938	Miss MD Black (Giffnock)		1959	Miss HM McVie (Kirkhill)
1939	Mrs MF Craig (Bellahouston)		1960	Miss HE Simpson (Cambuslang)
1940-1946	No competitions		1961	Miss MB Russell (King's Park)
1947	Miss EM Wilson (Glasgow University)		1962	Miss MM MacDonald (Woodend)
1948	Miss MSC McHattie (Hamilton)		1963	Miss JH Walters (Hillpark)
1949	Miss MA Stewart (Muirend)		1964	Miss AEM Sinclair (Western)
1950			1965	Miss I Hunter (Hamilton)
1951	Miss JJ Hunter (Muirend & Busby)		1966	Miss P Veitch (Hamilton)
1952	Miss CC Gordon (Dowanhill)		1967	Miss JGM Brown (Hamilton)
1953	Mrs WW MacKenzie (Dowanhill)		1968	Miss ECL Robb (Hamilton)
1954	Miss CS McTavish (Ardgowan)		1969	Miss E Tweedie (Wishaw)
1955	Miss CB King (Western)		1970	Miss EA Simpson (Whitecraigs)
1956	Miss SA Easton (Kingswood)		1971	MIss E McIntosh (Queen's Park)
1957	Miss KE Mann (Western)		1972	Miss IV Thomson (Broomhill)

PLATE EVENT

Confined to players eliminated in their first match scheduled to be played of the Ladies Singles Challenge Cup.

1973	Mrs C Lockhart (Newlands)		1976	Abandoned
1974	Miss J Paul (Thorn Park)			
1975	Miss C Newton (NZ)			

QUALIFYING EVENT for the Open Singles

1977	Miss ECL Robb	Hamilton		1982	Miss MJ Love	Elderslie
1978	Miss MJ Love	Elderslie		1983	Miss J Erskine	Broomhill
1979	Miss MJ Love	Elderslie		1984	Miss J Erskine	Broomhill
1980	Miss MJ Love	Elderslie		1985	-	
1981	Miss MJ Love	Elderslie		1986	-	

PLATE EVENT

1987	-		1990	Not played	
1988	-		1991	E Williamson	Burnside
1989	-				

WEST OF SCOTLAND SHIELD (MEN'S SINGLES)

Instituted 1936

Challenge Shield presented by Mr G.B. Primrose

Confined to players who are members of clubs affiliated to W.S.L.T.A. and who have never reached the Final round of the Men's Singles (Handicap excepted) in any Open Tournament, and who have never previously won this Event.

Year	Name	Club		Year	Name	Club
1936	JB McAlpine			1958	JI Smith	Craighelen
1937	D Watson			1959	WB Allardice	Kingswood
1938	T Boyd	Giffnock		1960	J Eelloo	Western
1939	NK Smith	Pollokshields		1961	S Donaldson	Broomhill
1940-1946	No Contests			1962	I McCulloch	Hamilton
1947	AH Young	Newlands		1963	JM McKenzie	Burnside
1948	JA Elder	Kingswood		1964	WB Gibson	Westerton
1949	HJ Wyld	Hillpark		1965	R Randall	Westerton
1950	R Munro			1966	A Wilson	Hillpark
1951	IKE Milligan			1967	IM Bill	Wishaw
1952	CE Russell	Hillpark		1968	JB Duncan	
1953	BB MacDonald	Hillington		1969	MT McKnight	Newlands
1954	R Fraser	Scottish Gas Board		1970	D Woodhouse	Springwells
1955	WT Holnes	Renfrew		1971	AA Hutton	Elderslie
1956	RD Richmond	Kingswood		1972	M Shrigley	Thorn Park
1957	GB Kerr	Newlands				

PLATE EVENT
Confined to players eliminated in their first match scheduled to be played of the Men's Singles Challenge Cup

Year	Name	Club		Year	Name	Club
1973	AT Sibbald	Dowanhill		1975	D Woodhouse	Springwells
1974	WC Gillespie	Newlands		1976	Abandoned	

QUALIFYING EVENT for the Open Singles
Year	Name	Club		Year	Name	Club
1977	G Suyderhoud	S. Africa		1982	KM Revie	Broomhill
1978	I Walker	Western		1983	R Scott	
1979	KM Revie	Broomhill		1984	KM Revie	Broomhill
1980	KM Revie	Broomhill		1985	-	
1981	KM Revie	Broomhill		1986	-	

PLATE EVENT
Year	Name	Club		Year	Name	Club
1987	G McAinsh	Giffnock		1990	J Ridley	
1988	-			1991	C Jaap	Weir Recreation
1989	GB Kerr Jr.	Newlands				

CHANGED TO MEN'S OVER 35 EVENT
Year	Name	Club		Year	Name	Club
1992	G Reid	Whitecraigs		1998	D McKay	Strathgryffe
1993	C Hanbidge	Giffnock		1999	DA Brown	Strathgryffe
1994	C Hanbidge/G Reid Shared			2000	JS Mackechnie	Newlands
1995	C Hanbidge	Giffnock		2001	R Terras	Newlands
1996	G McAinsh	Giffnock		2002	I MacAulay	Newlands
1997	DW Morrison	Strathgryffe		2003	R Terras	Newlands

LADIES' SHIELD DOUBLES

Instituted 1966

Cups presented by Messrs JB and K McAlpine

Confined to players who are members of clubs affiliated to the W.S.L.T.A. and who have never reached the final round in any Open Tournament and who have never previously won this Event.

1966	Miss MR Wright	Hamilton	Miss IC Hunter	Hamilton
1967	Mrs S Frame	Cambuslang	Mrs HE Allan	Cambuslang
1968	Mrs S Fraser		Miss H Burleigh	
1969	Miss R McChesney	Rutherglen	Miss M McConnell	Rutherglen

PLATE EVENT
Confined to players eliminated in their first Match scheduled to be played of the Ladies Doubles

1970	Miss R McChesney	Rutherglen	Miss M McConnell	Rutherglen
1971	Mrs EH McKenzie	Hillpark	Mrs B Watt	Hillpark
1972	Mrs HE Allan	Cambuslang	Miss E N Winning	Cambuslang
1973	Miss S Arnott	Australia	Miss M Arnott	Australia
1974	Miss M Paterson	Broomhill	Mrs BW Hunter	Broomhill
1975	Miss C Newton	New Zealand	Mrs E Severin	Whitecraigs
1976	Abandoned			

QUALIFYING EVENT for the OPEN DOUBLES

1977	Miss SEL Moodie	Stepps	Mrs EA Paul	Elderslie
1978	Miss E Armstrong	Kilmacolm	Miss G Armstrong	Kilmacolm
1979	Miss MJ Love	Elderslie	Miss SEL Moodie	Hamilton
1980	Miss MJ Love	Elderslie	Miss SEL Moodie	Hamilton
1981	Miss MJ Love	Elderslie	Miss SEL Moodie	Hamilton
1982	Miss MJ Love	Elderslie	Miss SEL Moodie	Hamilton
1983	Miss L Browne	Whitecraigs	Miss J Erskine	Broomhill
1984	Miss MJ Love	Elderslie	Miss SEL Moodie	Hamilton

1985 - 1999   No Competition

SHIELD PLATE

Confined to players eliminated in their first Match scheduled to be played of the Ladies Doubles.

2000	Mrs K Gairns	Fort Matilda	Mrs J Gribben	Cambuslang
2001	Ms J Haslam	David Lloyd	Mrs M Shahmir	David Lloyd
2002	Mrs M Boyd	Busby	Miss M Gow	Clarkston
2003	Mrs S Fraser	Killearn	Mrs K McColl	Killearn

GENTLEMEN'S CONFINED DOUBLES SHIELD

Instituted 1966

Cups presented by Messrs. J.B. and K. McAlpine

Confined to players who are members of Clubs affiliated to the W.S.L.T.A. and who have never reached the final round in any Open Tournament, and who have never previously won this Event.

1966	DC Miller	Hillpark	GC Fulton	Hillpark
1967	AM Smith	Wishaw	IM Bill	Wishaw
1968	JB Duncan		AE Tankel	
1969	A Brown		I McKenzie	
1970	A A Hutton	Elderslie	JI Crawford	Elderslie
1971	DJ Scatchard		S McKellar	
1972	AA Burnett		AR McDougall	

PLATE EVENT
Confined to players eliminated in their first Match scheduled to be played of the Men's Doubles Challenge Cup

1973	J McKenzie		NR Paterson	
1974	RW Howat		E McGregor	
1975	J McKenzie	Newlands	GH Reid	Newlands
1976	Abandoned			
1977	J MacKenzie		A Gibson	

QUALIFYING EVENT for the Open Doubles

1978	JF Howie	GH Crosbie	1982	KM Revie	R Howat
1979	DJ Watt	KM Revie	1983	I MacAulay	J Fraser
1980	KM Revie	JF Howie	1984	R W Howat	KM Revie
1981	GH Reid	GH Crosbie			

1985 - 1992 No Competition

SHIELD EVENT

1993	G Robertson	A Summers	
1994	P Anderson	D Shaw	Westermains
1995	S Clarke	R Mackintosh	Giffnock
1996	N McLean Busby	G Smith	Kilmarnock
1997	J Singh	J Singh	Newlands
1998	C Russell	A Sandilands	Hamilton

PLATE EVENT
Confined to players eliminated in their first Match scheduled to be played in the Men's Doubles Challenge Cup

1999	A Cameron	P Waterfield	
2000	D Culshaw	G McAinsh	
2001	B Fox	R Fox	Rutherglen
2002	B Fox	R Fox	Rutherglen
2003	G McAinsh	N McKenzie	Giffnock

WEST OF SCOTLAND VETERANS OPEN INDOOR CHAMPIONSHIPS

Instituted 2000

	WINNER		RUNNER UP	

LADIES 40 SINGLES

2000	Miss A Murchie	Blackhall	Mrs E Haig	Mount Vernon
2001	Miss A Murchie	Blackhall	Mrs M Stewart	Thorn Park
2002	Miss A Murchie	Blackhall	Mrs L Baker	David Lloyd
2003	Miss MJ Love	Newlands	Miss A Murchie	Blackhall

LADIES 55 SINGLES

2000	Mrs C Lockhart	Newlands	Mrs L McGowan	Craighelen
2001	Mrs E Drummond	Craighelen	Mrs L McGowan	Craighelen
2002	Mrs E Drummond	Craighelen	Mrs E Lindsay	Western
2003	Mrs E Drummond	Craighelen	Mrs E Lindsay	Western

LADIES' 40 DOUBLES

2000	Mrs E Haig	Miss A Murchie	Mrs M Boyd	Miss M Gow
2001	Mrs E Haig	Miss A Murchie	Mrs L McCracken	Mrs E Percival
2002	Mrs E Haig	Miss A Murchie	Mrs M Stewart	Mrs A Smillie
2003	Mrs E Haig	Miss A Murchie	Mrs E Christie	Mrs M Hayworth

LADIES' 55 DOUBLES

2000	Mrs E Mills	Miss SEL Moodie	Mrs S Rowand	Mrs I Stewart
2001	Mrs E Drummond	Mrs L McGowan	Mrs S Rowand	Mrs I Stewart
2002	Mrs S Rowand	Mrs I Stewart	Mrs E Drummond	Mrs E Lindsay
2003	Mrs E Drummond	Mrs L McGowan	Mrs S Rowand	Mrs I Stewart

WEST OF SCOTLAND VETERANS OPEN INDOOR CHAMPIONSHIPS

Instituted 2000

	WINNER		RUNNER UP	

MEN 40 SINGLES

2000	E Dalgetty	Mount Vernon	K Haig	Mount Vernon
2001	E Dalgetty	Mount Vernon	K Haig	Mount Vernon
2002	R Terras	Newlands	K Haig	Mount Vernon
2003	K Haig	Mount Vernon	D Lamont	Broomhill

MEN 55 SINGLES

2000	A Nicol	Linlithgow	GB Kerr	Newlands
2001	RT Smyth	Strathgryffe	S Walker	Broomhill
2002	L McKendrick	Weir Recreation	R Whitesmith	Broomhill
2003	K Berkley	Thistle	S Walker	Broomhill

MENS' 40 DOUBLES

2000	E Dalgetty	K Haig	J Armstrong	R Newlands
2001	E Dalgetty	K Haig	G Crosbie	R Prentice
2002	C Handbidge	R Terras	E Dalgetty	K Haig
2003	E Dalgetty	K Haig	H Shields	J Wilson

MEN'S 55 DOUBLES

2000	HS Matheson	A Nicol	GB Kerr	L McKendrick
2001	JI Crawford	AA Hutton	JG Beeley	S Walker
2002	L McKendrick	P Leonard	R Whitesmith	S Walker
2003	T Smyth	V Stratta	K Berkley	J Noble

BULLETIN CUP   1952

This Cup was awarded to the winning Ladies Club in the West of Scotland section of the Scottish Cup. Originally only one Club team went forward to the Scottish section and since the proportion of West Clubs entering was much larger than those from other Districts there followed that there were firstly four teams and presently five teams going forward. Because the programme of matches is now so crowded with Spring Singles, Leagues, Scottish Cup and National League the West Section is no longer played to a conclusion. The last year of this Competition 1987.

1952	Pollokshields	1970	Cambuslang
1953	Pollokshields	1971	Cambuslang
1954	Pollokshields	1972	Western
1955	Pollokshields	1973	Elderslie
1956	Pollokshields	1974	Western*
1957	Pollokshields	1975	Whitecraigs
1958	Pollokshields	1976	Elderslie
1959	Western	1977	Whitecraigs
1960	Pollokshields	1978	Elderslie
1961	Pollokshields	1979	Hamilton
1962	Pollokshields	1980	Elderslie
1963	Newlands	1981	Elderslie
1964	Newlands	1982	Hamilton
1965	Newlands	1983	Broomhill
1966	Newlands	1984	Broomhill
1967	Newlands	1985	Broomhill
1968	Newlands	1986	Broomhill
1969	Newlands	1987	Whitecraigs*

* Other West teams won the Scottish Cup. See Scottish Cup for details.

ROWAN CUP 1930

The Rowan Cup was awarded to the winning Gentlemen's Club in the West of Scotland section of the Scottish Cup. Originally only one team went forward to the Scottish section. Probably about 1974 the West had four teams who went forward to the National rounds and from 1994 five teams. Because the programme of matches is now so crowded with Spring Singles, Leagues, Scottish Cup, and National League the West section is no longer played to a conclusion. The last year of this competition was 1987.

1930	Newlands	1962	Pollokshields
1931	Newlands	1963	Newlands
1932	Newlands	1964	Newlands
1933	Pollokshields	1965	Titwood
1934	Newlands	1966	Titwood
1935	Pollokshields	1967	Western
1936	Pollokshields	1968	Western
1937	Pollokshields	1969	Newlands
1938	Pollokshields	1970	Whitecraigs
1939	Pollokshields	1971	Whitecraigs
1940-45	No Competition	1972	Newlands
1946	Pollokshields	1973	Newlands
1947	Newlands	1974	Whitecraigs*
1948	Pollokshields	1975	Western*
1949	Newlands	1976	Western
1950	Newlands	1977	Western
1951	Pollokshields	1978	Broomhill
1952	Western	1979	Broomhill
1953	Pollokshields	1980	Broomhill
1954	Titwood	1981	Broomhill
1955	Pollokshields	1982	Broomhill
1956	Newlands	1983	Broomhill
1957	Newlands	1984	Broomhill
1958	Newlands	1985	Broomhill
1959	Titwood	1986	Broomhill
1960	Newlands	1987	Broomhill
1961	Newlands		

* Other West Teams won the Scottish Cup. See Scotish Cup for details.

SCOTTISH CUP

The "Scottish Cup" was instituted in 1896 for Men and 1924 for the Ladies and the following are the successes for West of Scotland Clubs.

MEN

1899	Pollokshields	1972	Newlands
1903	Pollokshields	1974	Western
1904	Pollokshields	1975	Newlands
1908	Pollokshields	1976	Western
1909	Pollokshields	1977	Western
1911	Pollokshields	1978	Western
1913	Pollokshields	1979	Broomhill
1914	Partick	1980	Broomhill
1915-1918	No Competition	1981	Broomhill
1919	Partick	1982	Broomhill
1920	Partick	1983	Broomhill
1922	Pollokshields	1984	Broomhill
1927	Newlands	1985	Broomhill
1929	Newlands	1986	Broomhill
1930	Newlands	1987	Broomhill
1931	Newlands	1989	Broomhill
1932	Newlands	1990	Broomhill
1933	Pollokshields	1991	Broomhill
1934	Newlands	1992	Broomhill
1940-1945	No Competition	1993	Broomhill
1946	Pollokshields	1994	David LLoyd
1947	Newlands	1995	Newlands
1949	Newlands	1997	Newlands
1952	Western	1998	Newlands
1953	Pollokshields	1999	Giffnock
1954	Titwood	2001	No Competition
1960	Newlands	2002	Newlands
1961	Newlands	2003	Newlands
1965	Titwood		

LADIES

1929	Newlands	1964	Newlands
1931	Pollokshields	1966	Newlands
1932	Pollokshields	1969	Newlands
1935	Pollokshields	1974	Elderslie
1936	Pollokshields	1976	Elderslie
1940-1945	No Competition	1977	Whitecraigs
1952	Pollokshields	1980	Elderslie
1954	Pollokshields	1983	Broomhill
1956	Pollokshields	1987	Newlands
1957	Pollokshields	1997	Newlands
1960	Pollokshields	1998	Newlands
1961	Pollokshields	2001	No Competition

West of Scotland Junior Tennis Champions

SINGLES

	BOYS U/18	GIRLS U/18	BOYS U/16	GIRLS U/16	BOYS U/15	GIRLS U/15	BOYS U/14	GIRLS U/14	BOYS U/12	GIRLS U/12	BOYS U/10	GIRLS U/10
1919	J Watson Black	Dorothy Mitchell										
1920	M C Ferguson	Hilda Rosser										
1921	John B Fulton	Marjorie Langmuir										
1922	John T Hill	Grace S Barclay										
1923	Arthur W Hill	Helen M Barr										
1924	Arthur W Hill	Jean T Butters										
1925	Gordon Watson	E Borthwick										
1926	Robert R Findlay	M McAdam										
1927	EH Taylor	W Mason										
1928	D McPhail	W Mason										
1929	JF Hay	J Macintyre										
1930	RO Frame	J Macintyre										
1931	HL Macmillan	CH Butters										
1932	JM Sayers	CH Butters										
1933	RA Simpson	KAS Nicol										
1934	DS Service	HR Knight										
1935	RTG Stirling	M Sutherland										
1936	RG Lawson	J Richard										
1937	Alexander Cross	L Anderson										
1938	WM Gilmour	MA Stewart										
1939	Wm J Blackadder	JHM Preston										
1940	JA Elder											
1941	No Competition	No Competition										
1942	No Competition	No Competition										
1943	No Competition	No Competition										
1944	No Competition	No Competition										
1945	No Competition	No Competition										
1946	Colin V Baxter	Isobel Vallance										
1947	Colin V Baxter	Isobel Vallance										
1948	Colin V Baxter	MM Innes										
1949	Jack D Somervill	JM Wilson										
1950	WK McCandlish	KA Gillespie										
1951	Kenneth B Gray	EA Walker										
1952	J Cowie	ML Walker										
1953	JD Lillie	ML Walker										
1954	AG McNeilage	CB King			G Copeland	Norma J Forbes						
1955	R Seaton	IB Miller			R McAlpine	EH Baird						
1956	GB Kerr	IC Webster			Brian Young	MM McDonald						
1957	R McAlpine	ES Holmes			Ronald B Low	A McAlpine						
1958	AS Black	EH Baird			David C McVie	FVM MacLennan						
1959	Tommy Walker	FVM MacLennan			M DeFelice	SEL Moodie						
1960	TC MacNair	AG McAlpine			WM Currie	L D MacLennan						
1961	AS Nicol	SEL Moodie			Graham Young	WM Shaw						

West of Scotland Junior Tennis Champions

SINGLES

Year	BOYS U/18	GIRLS U/18	BOYS U/16	GIRLS U/16	BOYS U/15	GIRLS U/15	BOYS U/14	GIRLS U/14	BOYS U/12	GIRLS U/12	BOYS U/10	GIRLS U/10
1962	N Thompson	SEL Moodie			G W Jack	HF Morton						
1963	WM Currie	WM Shaw			I Kirkwood	M J Love						
1964	JD Edmond	WM Shaw			M D Paul	J Bell						
1965	IA Kirkwood	VJ MacLennan			RB Kerr	J Bell						
1966	IA Kirkwood	M J Love			J H Moore	J Bell						
1967	NR Paterson	M J Love			AL Miller	R Allan						
1968	S Robertson	R Allan			KM Revie	ECL Robb						
1969	AL Miller	E Tweedie			D A Hutchison	MAF Andrew						
1970	CM Duthie	R Allan			GC Robson	C Shaw						
1971	KM Revie	ECL Robb			R W Howat	M F Dutch						
1972	KM Revie	R Pullar			EJ Riley	J E Paul						
1973	KM Revie	LA Johnson			KH Walker	K Glancy						
1974	KM Revie	AJ Graham			R Caldwell	JM Erskine						
1975	EJ Riley	J ErsKine			R Caldwell	C Wilson						
1976	KH Walker	J Erskine			R Stadele	V Hutcheon						
1977	A McNab	V Hutcheon							C Stewart	I Stadele		
1978	A Galbraith	V Hutcheon							S Wilson	J Ross		
1979	A Lackie	M Crawford							I McKinley	S Mair		
1980	R Stadele	P Hendry							G Bell	J Kinloch		
1981	I Allan	L Browne							M Watt	M Mair		
1982	J Fraser	L Browne	S Wilson	A Fraioli			G Bell	M Mair	P Mair	J Hunter		
1983	I MacAuley	I Stadele	G Low	M Armstrong			M Watt	G Anderson	G Stadele	J Hunter		
1984	B Dodds	J Hutchison	G Bell	E Adams			R Matheson	V Lakin	A Low	H Lockhart		
1985	A Wright	K Christie	M Watt	E Adams			A Douglas	J Walker	K Duffy	J Shaw		
1986	G Bell	K Ross	R Matheson	L Clark			A Low	H Lockhart	J Soutar	N Sills		
1987	J Woodall	E Adams	M Cranstoun	H Lockhart			J Fairhurst	J Shaw	C McKnight	C Anderson		
1988	M Cranstoun	H Lockhart	J Fairhurst	H Lockhart			C McKnight	N Ledingham	G Darlington	J Taylor		
1989	M Cranstoun	H Lockhart	J Fairhurst	J Shaw			J Barnett	C Anderson	G Darlington	J Taylor		
1990	A Low	H Lockhart	J Barnett	E Smith			B McColl	J Taylor	B McColl	A McGarthland		
1991	J Barnett	E Smith	J Barnett	N Burns			B McColl	Y Hutton	M Gilmour	L Reilly		
1992	T Smith	E Smith	S McGuckin	J Duncan			A MacDonald	L Reilly	A Mackin	K Paterson		
1993	O Hadden	N Burns	R McDonald	N Payne			A Mackechnie	L Reilly	T Ogilvie	M Brown		
1994	S McGuckin	L Reilly	A MacDonald	L Reilly			M Hendry	M Brown	N McPhee	L Drennan	J Murray	K McRae
1995	A MacDonald	EL Stevenson	A MacDonald	S McFadyen			R Maxfield	M Brown	S Milne	K McRae	D Culshaw	F Hendry
1996	M Gilmour	C Lavery	G Smith	S McFadyen			R Allan	L Drennan	D Culshaw	N Slater	O Abdul-Mannan	K McAloon
1997	A Mackechnie	K Paterson	R Maxfield	S McFadyen			B McNeil	N Slater	D Brewer	J Stevenson	O Abdul-Mannan	N Allan
1998	R Maxfield	F Gordon	J Lints	L Gibson			J Baker	V Jigajinni	G Watson	H Graham	G MacDonald	P Pretswell
1999	R Allan	G Bickerstaff	R Allan	J Stevenson			G Murray	J Stevenson	R Grant	S Roy	S Nicholls	P Pretswell
2000	R Allan	M Whitelaw	D McCall	M Whitelaw			S Smyth	H Graham	R MacLeod	C Steel	G Weanie	C Steel
2001	B McNeil	S Norris	N Koronka	S Norris			A Conroy	K McAloon	S Birrell	C Steel	J Drummond	S Lister
2002	G Neil	S Norris	G Neil	S Roy			C Gee	C Steel	G Weanie	C Steel	C McNaught	C McVay
2003	D Thatcher	S Roy	R Dalgetty	C Steel				C Steel	W Collins	S Lister	B Halsman	Z Drummond

West of Scotland Junior Tennis Champions

DOUBLES

	BOYS U/18 DOUBLES	GIRLS U/18 DOUBLES	MIXED U/18 DOUBLES	BOYS U/14 DOUBLES	GIRLS U/14 DOUBLES	LAFFERTY CUP
1919						
1920						
1921						
1922						
1923						
1924						
1925						
1926						
1927						
1928						
1929						
1930						
1931						
1932						
1933						
1934						
1935						
1936	B Fulton & RG Lawson					
1937	GB MacFarlane & R Morton					
1938	JC Nicol & J Oliver					
1939	W Blackadder Jr. & AB Murray					
1940	CWR Andrew & AB Murray	D Donn & B Halcrow	IW White & Miss CM Kirk			
1941	No Competition	No Competition	No Competition			
1942	No Competition	No Competition	No Competition			
1943	No Competition	No Competition	No Competition			
1944	No Competition	No Competition	No Competition			
1945	No Competition	No Competition	No Competition			
1946	CV Baxter & G Ferrari	S Litton & I Vallance	J Baird & Miss I Vallance			
1947	CV Baxter & AR MacWilliam	S Litton & I Vallance	CV Baxter & Miss I Vallance			
1948	CV Baxter & N Henderson	M Innes & K Peel	CV Baxter & Miss MM Innes			
1949	N Neil & J Vallance	EI Dunlop & MA Martin	WC Gillespie & Miss KA Gillespie			
1950	HM Lang & WK McCandlish	KA Gillespie & JM Wilson	WC Gillespie & Miss KA Gillespie			
1951	M McMillan & AE Tankel	EA Walker & ML Walker	KB Gray & Miss ME Davidson			
1952	JC Clark & CM Colquhoun	MI Harvey & ML Walker	HC Hendry & Miss ML Walker			
1953	RT Lang & AG McNeilage	CB King & ML Walker	HC Hendry & Miss ML Walker			
1954	RT Lang & AT McNeilage	CB King & KCB Taylor	JD Lillie & Miss IB Miller			
1955	AN Coppell & GB Kerr	IB Miller & SA Miller	GT Downes & Miss IB Miller			
1956	AN Coppell & GB Kerr	SA Butters & JB Nimmo	GB Kerr & Miss NJ Forbes			
1957	I Davidson & AP Summers	M Ferguson & ES Holmes	DD Bell & Miss NJ Forbes			
1958	AS Black & GE Mason	FVM MacLennan & HM McVie	R McAlpine & Miss EH Baird			
1959	S Russell & T Walker	EA Lennox & MM McDonald	RB Low & Miss FVM MacLennan			
1960	DM Davidson & HS Matheson	EA Lennox & A McAlpine	HS Matheson & Miss HM McVie			
1961	WM Currie & N Thompson	HF Morton & WM Shaw	N Thompson & Miss WM Shaw			

West of Scotland Junior Tennis Champions

DOUBLES

Year	BOYS U/18 DOUBLES	GIRLS U/18 DOUBLES	MIXED U/18 DOUBLES	BOYS U/14 DOUBLES	GIRLS U/14 DOUBLES	LAFFERTY GROUP TROPHY
1962	DC Baird & I Walker	HF Morton & WM Shaw	DC Baird & Miss HF Morton			
1963	DC Baird & WM Currie	HF Morton & WM Shaw	WM Currie & Miss WM Shaw			
1964	IGM Cowper & JD Edmond	HF Morton & WM Shaw	JD Edmond & Miss WM Shaw			
1965	I Kirkwood & G Notman	JH Jamieson & VJ MacLennan	IA Kirkwood & Miss MJ Love			
1966	IC Conway & AC Wilson	E Armstrong & G Armstrong	No Competition			
1967	WE Dickson & NR Paterson	MJ Love & C Montgomery	NR Paterson & Miss MJ Love			
1968	LA Findlay & JH Moore	K Murray & N Murray	JS Robertson & Miss J Grant			
1969	CM Duthie & JH Moore	R Allan & ECL Robb	JH Moore & Miss ET Turnbull			
1970	CM Duthie & CF Simpson	R Allan & ECL Robb	CM Duthie & Miss SCH Smith			
1971	EM Anderson & KM Revie	A Douglas & ECL Robb	EM Anderson & Miss ECL Robb			
1972	KM Revie & DF Williamson	MAF Andrew & RL Pullar	KM Revie & Miss IM Cowper			
1973	G Robson & J Williams	MF Dutch & LA Johnston	KM Revie & Miss IM Cowper			
1974	RW Howat & KM Revie	A Forgie & T Sutherland	KM Revie & Miss J Paul			
1975	EJ Riley &K Walker	J Erskine & E Walker	A Chisholm & Miss J Erskine			
1976	A Chisholm & K Walker	J Erskine & E Walker	A Chisholm & Miss J Erskine			
1977	A Galbraith & R Stadele	J Cramond & V Hutcheon	E Dalgetty & Miss V Hutcheon			
1978	A Galbraith & R Stadele	M Bain & V Hutcheon	R Stadele & Miss V Hutcheon			
1979	A Lackie & R Stadele	L Boyd & J Leach	A Lackie & Miss L Reid			
1980	I Allan & A Lumsden	L Boyd & J Leach	I Allan & Miss J Leach			
1981	I Allan & I MacAuley	L Browne & J Hosie	I Allan & Miss I Stadele			
1982	J Fraser & D Holmes	L Browne & I Stadele	I MacAuley & Miss I Stadele	G Bell & M Watt	M Mair & L Ryan	Broomhill
1983	A Bell & G Bell	M Armstrong & I Stadele	I MacAuley & Miss I Stadele	M Watt & K Wood	A Lockhart & H Lockhart	Giffnock
1984	G Bell & S Wilson	R Adam & S Dickson	G Bell & Miss M Armstrong	G Stadele & K Wood	A Lockhart & H Lockhart	Ayr
1985	G Bell & A Wright	R Adam & M Armstrong	J Woodall & Miss K Ross	M Cranstoun & A Smith	L Clark & J Walker	Ayr
1986	G Bell & J Woodall	E Adams & K Ross	J Woodall & Miss K Ross	J Ledvinka & E Rodger	K Fulton & F Sharp	Giffnock
1987	A Cooper & J Woodall	E Adams & A Lockhart	G Alston & Miss E Adams	K Duffy & G Soutar	K Fulton & C Morgan	Newlands
1988	M Cranstoun & A Smith	A Lockhart & H Lockhart	A Low & Miss H Lockhart	C McKnight & G Soutar	N Ledingham & N Sills	Newlands
1989	E McGinn & A Smith	H Lockhart & J Walker	M Cranstoun & Miss J Walker	I Boyd & C McKnight	M Barclay & Y Hutton	Whitecraigs
1990	G Alston & G Kerr	H Lockhart & A Reid	A Low & Miss H Lockhart	O Hadden & R Sandilands	L Morley & J Taylor	Newlands
1991	R Sharpe & T Smith	D Forrest & L Smith	C McKnight & Miss J Shaw	Gordon Smith & B Thompson	M Barclay & Y Hutton	Whitecraigs
1992	C McKnight & T Smith	L Reilly & EL Stevenson	C McKnight & Miss Y Hutton	M Gilmour & A MacDonald	K Hunter & L Paterson	Thistle
1993	C McKnight & S Watt	N Burns & E Smith	C McKnight & Miss N Burns	M Gilmour & A MacDonald	J Colston & L Reilly	Thistle
1994	R McDonald & S McGuckin	L Reilly & EL Stevenson	S McGuckin & Miss Y Hutton	R MacAulay & A Mackin	M Brown & K Paterson	Thistle
1995	M Gilmour & A MacDonald	R Orsi & EL Stevenson	Gregor Smith & Miss F Drennan	J Gray & M Hendry	M Brown & K Paterson	David Lloyd Renfrew
1996	S Jiqaiinni & B Saunders	P Downes & S McFadyen	J Gray & Miss P Downes	A Hawke & N McPhee	F Gordon & K Paterson	David Lloyd Renfrew
1997	M Gilmour & A MacDonald	F Gordon & K Paterson	A Mackechnie &Miss J Fulton	R Allan & S Milne	F Hendry & V Jiqaiinni	David Lloyd Renfrew
1998	R Allan & A Mackechnie	J Fulton & K Thomson	A Mackechnie & Miss J Fulton	D Kinnaird & D McCall	K McRae & J Stevenson	David Lloyd Renfrew
1999	R Allan & M Hendry	G Bickerstaff & L McCambridge	R Allan & Miss S Norris	D Barnes & G Watson	A Allan & J Ronnie	Strathgryffe
2000	R Allan & R Maxfield	J Ronnie & M Whitelaw	R Maxfield & Miss M Whitelaw	D Barnes & G Watson	H Graham & S Norris	Thorn Park
2001	No Competition	No Competition	No Competition	No Competition	No Competition	
2002	D Kinnaird & G Thomson	H Graham & S Norris	No Competition	J Steel & G Weanie	J Drummond & P Pretswell	Thorn Park
2003	D Barnes & R Dalgetty	H Graham & S Norris	D Barnes & Miss S Norris	G Ewing & S Nicholls	J Bell & K Hamilton	Thorn Park

SCOTTISH JUNIOR INTER-COUNTY CUP "THE TEA CUP"

There are four teams one each from North of Scotland, South of Scotland, East of Scotland and West of Scotland.

Each County is represented by a team of four boys and four girls..

1966 North	1979 West	1991 West
1967 East	1980 West	1992 North
1968 East	1981 North	1993 West
1969 West	1982 West	1994 North
1970 West	1983 West	1995 West
1971 West	1983 West	1996 West
1972 West	1984 West	1997 West
1973 East	1985 North	1998 North
1974 West	1986 East	1999 North
1975 West	1987 North	2000 North
1976 West	1988 North	2001 West
1977 West	1988 North	2002 North
1978 West	1989 North	

SCOTTISH INTER-DISTRICT CHAMPIONSHIPS

	Under 11 & 13	Under 15 & 17	Venue
1993	West	-	Glen almond
1994	North East	West	Kilgraston
1995	East	-	Kilgraston
1996	Central	-	Kilgraston
1997	Midlands	North East	Kilgraston
1998	East	East	Kilgraston
1999	West	-	Kilgraston
2000	Midlands	West	Kilgraston
2001	Midlands	West	Kilgraston
2002	West	West	Kilgraston
2003	West	West	Kilgraston

INTER-COUNTY GRASS COURT CHAMPIONSHIPS (County Week)

"The Lawn Tennis Association Inter-Club Challenge Cup was replaced in 1895 by the Inter-County Challenge Cup, the forerunner of County Week. In 1906 Scotland was divided into two "counties" East & West, the West included Ayrshire, South West & Stirling. "Fifty Years of Lawn Tennis In Scotland" deals with the early years. The Competition was recast in 1925 with leagues replacing "the Cup", the counties were divided into eight groups of of six teams, with the appropriate group for each county being determined on merit"
From "Tennis in Scotland" 100 years of the Scottish Lawn Tennis Association by George Robertson

1961 Men Rest Of Scotland renamed North of Scotland
1962 North of Scotland Ladies
1963 South of Scotland Men and Ladies

LADIES

Year	Venue	Pos	Players
1931	Peebles	3	Miss M Langmuir, Miss Barr, Miss JB Dunn, Miss W Mason, Miss JC Rankine, Miss Thomson, Miss J Weir
1932	Newcastle	2	Miss M Langmuir (C), Mrs Campbell, Miss JB Dunn, Miss Hardy, Mrs Hill,, Miss JC Rankine, Miss AE Middleton, Mrs AAF Peel, Mrs Turnbull, Miss JC Turnbull.
1933	Scarborough		Jeanette Weir (C), May Thomson, Clara Butters, Jessie Riddick, Annie Brown, Jean Jamieson, Janet Harvey
1934	Southend	3	Mrs JB Harvey(C), Miss CH Butters, Miss B Beaton, Miss JC Ceasar, Miss M Harvey, Miss G Manson, Miss M Thomson.
1935	Felixtow	4	Miss J Weir (C), Miss CH Butters, Miss B Beaton, Miss JC Ceasar, Miss WA Mason, Miss PS Morton, Miss K Rooney, Miss M Thomson,
1936	Cheltenham	5	Mrs Harvey, Miss C Butters, Miss Thomson, Miss Gillespie, Miss Rooney, Miss Hamilton
1937	Rhos on Sea	6	
1938	Ross on Wye	6	Mrs J Harvey, Miss M Thomson, Miss CH Butters, Miss C Rooney, Mrs AAF Peel, Miss C Callander, Miss L Anderson, Mrs JB Jones
1939	Bognor Regis	5	
1946	Zoned		Mrs C Black, Miss L Anderson, Miss M Thomson, Mrs C Dobson, Mrs McKay, Miss H Muir
1947	Malvern	5	
1948	Hunstanton	6	Mrs J Harvey(C), Mrs C Black, Miss H Macfarlane, Miss I Vallance, Misss M Allan Miss IM Clark, Mrs Lesley-Carter
1949	Shrewsbury	5	Mrs J Harvey(C), Mrs C Black, Miss H Macfarlane, Miss I Vallance, Misss M Allan Miss EM Wilson, Mrs Lesley-Carter
1950	Bognor Regis	5	Mrs J Harvey(C), Mrs C Black, Miss H Macfarlane, Miss I Vallance, Miss M Allan, Mrs L Perpoli, Miss JS Reid
1951	Alvestoke	4	Mrs J Harvey(C), Mrs C Black, Miss H Macfarlane, Miss I Vallance, Miss M Allan, Mrs DLDick, Mrs L Perpoli
1952	Budleigh Salterton	3	Mrs J Harvey(C), Mrs C Black, Miss H Macfarlane, Miss I Vallance, Miss M Allan, Miss GS Horne
1953	Budleigh Salterton	3	Mrs J Harvey(C), Mrs C Black, Miss H Macfarlane, Mrs L Dick, Mrs Baird, Miss I Vallance, Miss KA Gillespie
1954	Folkstone	3	Mrs J Harvey(C), Mrs C Black, Miss H Macfarlane, Miss I Vallance, Miss KA Gillespie, Mrs K Horne, Miss CE Dungliston, Miss KH Horne
1955	Scarborough	2	Mrs J Harvey(C), Mrs C Black, Miss H Macfarlane, Miss KA Gillespie, Miss M Bell, Mrs L Dick, M Harvey, Mrs K Horne
1956	Bournemouth	2	Mrs J Harvey (C), Mrs C Black, Miss H Macfarlane, Miss KA Gillespie, Miss M Walker, Miss A Walker, Miss K Horne, Mrs L Dick.

1957	Exmouth	3	Mrs C Black(C), Mrs L Dick, Miss C Dungliston, Miss K Gillespie, Miss M Harvey, Miss H Macfarlane, Miss A Walker, Miss M Walker.
1958	Scarborough	2	Mrs C Black(C), Mrs A Baird, Miss M Bell, Miss C Dungliston, Miss M Ferguson, Miss K Gillespie, Mrs K Horne, Miss A Walker
1959	Ilkley	3	Mrs C Black(C), Mrs IM Baird, Miss C Dungliston, Miss M Ferguson, Mrs GS Horne, Miss FVM MacLennan, Miss IB Miller, Miss M Steuart-Corry
1960	Budleigh Saltertnn	4	Mrs C Black(C), Miss C Dungliston, Miss M Ferguson, Miss A G Mc Alpine, Miss BJ McCallum, Miss FVM Maclennan, Miss IB Miller, Miss A Walker.
1961	Ilkley	4	Mrs C Black(C), Miss EH Baird, Miss CE Dungliston, Miss MB Fergusson, Miss A G McAlpine, Miss BJ McCallum, Mrs E Mackenzie, Miss IB Miller
1962	Bournemouth	4	Mrs C Black(C), Miss CE Dungliston, Miss MB Fergusson, Miss A GMcAlpine, Mrs K McCready, Miss FVM MacLennan, Miss SEL Moodie, Miss W M Shaw
1963	Frinton	3	Mrs C Black(NPC), Miss CE Dungliston, Miss M Fergusson, Miss AG McAlpine, Miss FVM MacLennan, Mrs EA Paul, Miss SEL Moodie, Miss WM Shaw
1964	Cromer	2	Mrs C Black(NPC), Miss M Ferguson, Miss AG McAlpine, Miss BJ McCallum, Miss FVM MacLennan, Mrs EA Paul, Miss SEL Moodie, Miss WM Shaw
1965	Bournemouth	2	Mrs C Black(NPC), Miss M Fergusson, Miss AG McAlpine, Miss BJ McCallum, Miss FVM MacLennan, Mrs EA Paul, Miss SEL Moodie, Miss WM Shaw
1966	Eastbourne	1	Mrs C Black(NPC), Miss MJ Love, Miss AG McAlpine, Miss BJ McCallum, Miss FVM MacLennan, Miss V McaLennan, Miss SEL Moodie, Mrs EA Paul, Miss WM Shaw
1967	Cromer	2	Mrs C Black(NPC), Miss B Livingston, Miss MJ Love, Miss FVM MacLennan, Miss V MacLennan, Mrs CA Matheson, Miss SEL Moodie, Mrs EA Paul, Miss WM Shaw.
1968	Eastbourne	1	Mrs C Black(C), Miss MJ Love, Miss FVM MacLennan, Miss V McaLennan, Miss H McVie, Miss SEL Moodie, Mrs EA Paul, Miss WM Shaw, Miss E Winning.
1969	Cromer	2	Mrs C Black(C) Mrs HE Allan, Mrs BJ Livingstone, Miss MJ Love,Miss V MacLennan, Miss SEL Moodie, Mrs EA Paul, Miss WM Shaw, Miss EN Winning.
1970	Eastbourne	1	Mrs C Black(NPC), Miss R Allan, Miss MJ Love,Miss V MacLennan, Miss SEL Moodie, Mrs EA Paul, Miss WM Shaw, Miss M Woodcock.
1971	Cromer	2	Mrs C Black(NPC), Miss R Allan, Mrs A Barrow, Mrs BJ Livingstone, Mrs C Lockhart, Miss MJ Love, Miss SEL Moodie, Mrs EA Paul, Miss WM Shaw,
1972	Eastbourne	1	Mrs C Black(NPC), Miss R Allan, Mrs BJ Livingstone, Miss MJ Love, Miss V MacLennan, Miss SEL Moodie, Mrs EA Paul, Miss WM Shaw, Miss S Smith.
1973	Cromer	2	Mrs EA Paul(C), Miss R Allan, Mrs A Barrow, Mrs BJ Livingstone, Mrs C Lockhart, Miss MJ Love, Miss SEL Moodie, Miss WM Shaw,
1974	Eastbourne	1(Ru)	Mrs EA Paul(C), Mrs WM Wooldridge, Mrs FVM Taylor, Mrs CA Matheson, Miss MJ Love, Miss SEL Moodie,Miss R Allan, Miss ECL Robb
1975	Eastbourne	1	Mrs EA Paul(C), Miss R Allan, Mrs AG Barrow, Miss MJ Love, Miss SEL Moodie, Miss S Smith, Mrs FVM Taylor, Mrs WM Wooldridge
1976	Eastbourne	1	Mrs EA Paul(C), Mrs V Lloyd, Miss MJ Love, Miss SEL Moodie, Miss ECL Robb, Miss E Simpson, Mrs FVM Taylor, Mrs WM Wooldridge
1977	Eastbourne	1	Mrs EA Paul(C), Mrs AG Barrow, Miss MJ Love, Miss SEL Moodie, Miss ECL Robb, Mrs FVM Taylor, Mrs WM Wooldridge
1978	Eastbourne	1	Mrs WM Wooldridge(C)
1979	Cheltenham	2	Miss MJ Love(C), Miss SEL Moodie, Miss L Boyd, Miss M Crawford, Miss ECL Robb, Miss C Lindsay, Miss E Tweedlie, Miss M Stevenson
1980	Worthing	3	Miss MJ Love(C), Miss SEL Moodie, Miss L Boyd, Miss J Leach, Mis R Harvie, Miss M Crawford, Miss ECL Robb, Miss C Lindsay.
1981	Cambridge	4	Miss MJ Love(C), Miss SEL Moodie, Miss L Browne, Miss L Boyd, Miss J Leach, Mis R Harvie, Miss I Stadele.

1982	Worthing	4	Miss SEL Moodie(C), Miss MJ Love, Miss L Browne, Miss L Boyd, Miss J Hosie, Miss I Stadele, Miss C Wilson, Miss M Crawford
1983	Exmouth	5	Miss SEL Moodie(C), Miss MJ Love, Miss L Browne, Miss L Boyd, Miss J Hosie, Miss I Stadele, Miss L Wall, Miss C Wilson
1984	Worthing	5	Miss SEL Moodie(C), Miss MJ Love, Miss L Browne, Miss M Crawford, Miss J Hosie, Miss A Lavery, Miss C Wilson
1985	Exmouth	4	Miss SEL Moodie(C) Miss MJ Love, Miss A Lavery, Miss E Ure, Miss L Brown, Miss J Hosie, Miss L Wall
1986	Exmouth	4	Miss SEL Moodie(C), Miss H Lockhart, Miss A Lockhart, Miss L Browne, Miss A Lavery, Miss E Ure, Miss L Clark
1987	Exmouth	5	Mrs J Howie, Miss A Lavery, Miss E Ure, Miss L Brown, Miss L Clark, Miss A Lockhart, Miss H Lockhart,
1988	Frinton	6	Miss L Browne, Miss L Clark, Mrs J Howie, Miss A Lockhart, Miss H Lockhart, Miss A Lavery, Miss M Lavery, Miss E Ure
1989	Exmouth	5	Miss L Browne, Miss L Boyd, Miss A Lockhart, Miss H Lockhart, Miss A Lavery, Miss M Lavery, Mrs C Windmill.
1990	Worthing	5	Miss L Browne, Miss H Lockhart, Miss A Lavery, Miss M Lavery, Miss K Fulton, Mrs C Windmill, Miss S Anderson, Mrs J Howie.
1991	Exmouth	5	Miss L Browne, Miss A Lockhart, Miss H Lockhart, Miss A Lavery, Miss M Lavery, Miss C Towers, Miss N Burns, Mrs J Howie.
1992	Worthing	5	Miss MJ Love, Mrs J Howie, Mrs A Brown, Miss H Lockhart, L Browne, C Morgan, K Fulton, S Mitchell.
1993	Oxford	6	Mrs E Christie(NPC)Miss MJ Love, Mrs A Brown, Miss N Burns, K Fulton, Mrs J Howie, Miss Y Hutton, Miss H Lockhart.
1994	Poole	5	Mrs E Christie(NPC) Miss MJ Love, Miss H Lockhart, Mrs A Lavery, Mrs M Lavery, Miss N Burns, K Fulton, Miss R Orsi.
1995	Cheltenham	5	Mrs E Christie(NPC),Abbe Brown Miss H Lockhart Miss MJ Love, Miss N Burns, Miss R Orsi, Miss V Reid, Miss E Stevenson, Miss M Stevenson.
1996	Exmouth	6	Mrs A Brown(C) & Miss H Lockhart(C), Miss M Barclay, Miss E Stevenson, Miss N Burns, Miss C Lavery, Miss R Orsi.
1997	Purley	5	Mrs Anna Brown(C) & Miss Heather Lockhart(C) Mlss N Burns, Miss K Fulton, Miss F Gordon, Miss C Lavery, Miss R Orsi, Miss E Stevenson.
1998	Worthing	6	Mrs E Christie(NPC) Mrs A Brown, Miss N Burns, Miss Y Hutton, Miss E Stevenson, Miss C Lavery, Miss H Lockhart, Miss R Orsi.
1999	Worthing	5	Mrs E Christie(NPC), Mrs A Brown, Miss N Burns, Miss J Dickson, Miss C Lavery, Miss H Lockhart, Mrs L Middleton, Miss R Orsi, Miss E Stevenson.
2000	Ilkley	5	Mrs E Christie(NPC), Mrs A Brown, Miss N Burns, Miss C Lavery, Miss H Lockhart, Mrss R Orsi, Miss E Stevenson
2001	Cromer	6	Mrs E Christie(NPC), Mrs A Brown, Miss N Burns, Miss H Lockhart, Miss R Orsi, Miss E Stevenson, Miss S Norris, Miss H Graham
2002	Ilkley	5	Mrs E Christie(NPC), Mrs A Brown, Miss N Burns, Miss H Graham, Miss H Lockhart, Miss M McKenzie, Miss S Norris, Miss E Stevenson,
2003	Cheltenham	5	Mrs E Christie(NPC), Miss N Allan, Miss N Burns, Miss H Graham, Miss H Lockhart, Miss S Norris, Mrs R Owen, Miss E Stevenson

INTER-COUNTY GRASS COURT CHAMPIONSHIPS (County Week)

GENTLEMEN

1933	Hythe	2	W Buchanan(C), B.Butters(J),RR.Finlay, WF Fulton, A McVie, DT.McVie, JHA.Watson
1934	Scarborough	3	JT Hill(C), RW Blakey, W Fulton, D MacPhail Jr, A McVie, DT McVie, EH Taylor.
1935	Paignton	3	A McVie(C), AS Gilchrist, D MacPhail Jr, DT McVie, EH Taylor, D Watson, JHA Watson.
1936	Bexhill	4	A McVie, EA Taylor, D MacPhailJr, CR Marks, DT McVie, D Watson,
1937	Paignton	5	JA Robertson, AGM Keir, B Butters jr, JT Hill, D MacPhailjr, Dr JB Fulton
1938	Bournemouth	4	JT Hill, B Buttersjr, AGM Keir, JA Robertson, JB Fulton EH Taylor
1939	Angmering-on- Sea	5	JW Bell, B Butters, JT Hill, R Lawson, PB Macfarlane, NC Mackenzie, D MacPhail
1946	Newcastle		JT Hill, AGM Keir, AJT McDowall, W Reid, R Lawson, B Fulton.
1947	Folkstone	4	Dr JB Fulton(C), T Boyd, B Fulton, JG Rutherglen and 3
1948	Bedford	4	Dr JB Fulton(C), T Boyd, B Fulton, AB Murray, WJ Reid, JG Rutherglen, NK Smith, JHA Watson.
1949	Cambridge	4	Dr JB Fulton(C), JG Rutherglen,, B Fulton, T Boyd, WJ Reid, AH Young, AB Murray, CV Baxter.
1950	Ilkley	4	Dr JB Fulton(C), JG Rutherglen, AB Murray, T Boyd, JB Wilson, I Campbell, WJ Reid.
1951	Paignton	3	Dr JB Fulton(C), JG Rutherglen, CV Baxter B Fulton, T Boyd, IM Campbell, A Murray, JB Wilson
1952	Exeter	3	Dr JB Fulton,(C), JG Rutherglen, CV Baxter B Fulton, T Boyd, M McDonald, JB Wilson, A McNeilage, WC Gillespie
1953	Folkstone	3	DrJB Fulton(C), CV Baxter, IM Campbell, T Boyd, JB Wilson, JG Rutherglen, IT Louden, R Smith
1954	Scarborough	2	Dr JB Fulton(NPC), CV Baxter IM Campbell, JB Wilson, RG Harris, JG Rutherglen, WC Gillespie, T Boyd, IT Louden
1955	Eastbourne	1	Dr JB Fulton(NPC),CV Baxter, IM Campbell, JB Wilson, T Boyd, JG Rutherglen, WC Gillespie, M Macdonald
1956	Budleigh Salterton	2	Dr JB Fulton(NPC),CV Baxter, JB Wilson, WC Gillespie, MD Macdonald, T Boyd A McNeilage, JG Rutherglen,
1957	Cromer	3	Dr JB Fulton(NPC), CV Baxter, T Boyd, JB Wilson, JG Rutherglen, KB Gray, WC Gillespie, A McNeilage
1958	Southsea	2	Dr JB Fulton(NPC), CV Baxter, TA Boyd, WC Gillespie, KB Gray, AG McNeilage, JG Rutherglen, JB Wilson
1959	Minehead	3	Dr JB Fulton(NPC),CV Baxter, MA Macdonald, WC Gillespie, KB Gray, JG Rutherglen JB Wilson, JT Wood
1960	Exmouth	2	CV Baxter, JT Wood, JG Rutherglen, JB Wilson, KB Gray, AG McNeilage, DD Bell, AD Culloch
1961	Scarborough	3	Dr JB Fulton(NPC), CV Baxter, KB Gray, JG Rutherglen, WC Gillespie, AD Culloch JB Wilson, DDBell, JT Wood
1962	Frinton	3	Dr JB Fulton (NPC), CV Baxter, IM Campbell, WC Gillespie, KB Gray, HS Matheson, JR Coulter, GT Downes, JB Wilson
1963	Southsea	2	Dr JB Fulton(NPC), CV Baxter, HS Matheson, WC Gillespie, GT Downes, RB ow, GB Kerr, KB Gray,,AD Culloch
1964	Frinton	3	Dr JB Fulton(NPC),CV Baxter, HS Matheson WC Gillespie, GB Kerr, JR McAlpine, FN Thompson, JB Wilson, T McNair
1965	Budleigh Salterton	2	Dr JB Fulton(NPC),CV Baxter, HS Matheson, FN Thompson, GB Kerr, I Walker, T Walker, WC Gillespie, AD Culloch
1966	Minehead	3	WC Gillespie(C), CV Baxter, GB Hendry, TC Macnair, HS Matheson, FN Thompson, I Walker, T Walker.
1967	Frinton	2	WC Gillespie(C), HS Matheson, KB Gray, I Walker, T Walker, GB Kerr, FN Thompson, M Hall, N Paterson.

1968	Cromer	2	WC Gillespie(C) ,HS Matheson, I Walker, GT Downes, KB Gray GB Kerr, FN Thompson, G Copeland
1969	Minehead	3	WC Gillespie(C), HS Matheson, GT Downes, I Walker, GB Kerr, FN Thompson, J McKenzie,KB Gray.
1970	Southsea	2	KB Gray(NPC), HS Matheson, G Copeland, I Walker, T Walker, GT Downes FN Thompson, WC Gillespie, GB Kerr.
1971	Malvern	3	KB Gray(NPC), HS Matheson FN Thompson, GT Downes, I Walker, WC Gillespie, G Copeland, H Drummond.
1972	Southsea	2	KB Gray(NPC), HS Matheson, WC Gillespie, G Copeland, GT Downes, I Walker, T Walker, K Revie, R Howat
1973	Frinton	3	WC. Gillespie(C), GT.Downes, R.Howat, HS. Matheson, K. Revie, FN. Thompson, I. Walker
1974	Ilkley	3	KB Gray (NPC), IC Conway, WC Gillespie, GT Downes, JF Howie, HS Matheson, N Paterson, K Revie, I Walker
1975	Frinton	2	HS Matheson, IC Conway, G Crosbie, GT Downes, WC GillespieJF Howie, N Paterson, K Revie, I Walker
1976	Frinton	3	HS Matheson, IC Conway, G Crosbie, GT Downes, WC GillespieJF Howie, K Revie, I Walker
1977	Southsea	3	HS Matheson, G Crosbie, R Howat, J Howie, N Paterson, K. Revie, I Walker.
1978	Ilkley	2	HS Matheson, G Crosbie, R Howat, J Howie, J Markson, K. Revie, I Walker.
1979	Bournmouth	3	HS Matheson, A Galbraith, R Howat, N Paterson, K. Revie, R Stadele,I Walker.
1980	Cromer	3	HS Matheson, A Galbraith, R Howat, J Howie, N Paterson, G Reid, K. Revie, I Walker.
1981		3	G Crosbie, E Dalgetty, A Galbraith, R Howat, J Howie, G Reid, K. Revie, I Walker.
1982	Bournmouth	4	K Revie (C), I Allan, D Anderson, A Galbraith, E Dalgetty, R Howatt, A Lackie.
1983	Southsea	3	K Revie (C), I Allan, A Galbraith, E Dalgetty, J Howie, R Howatt, M Kilday, A Lackie.
1984	Felixstow	2	K Revie (C), I Allan, A Galbraith, J Howie, R Howatt, A Lackie, I MacAulay
1985	Cambridge	3	K Revie (C), I Allan, A Galbraith, J Howie, M Kilday, A Lackie, R Howatt.
1986	Cromer	2	KB Gray (NPC), R Howatt.
1987	Southsea	2	K Revie, J Howie, I Allan, R Howat, J Macaulay, B Dodds, R Terras, R Martin.
1988	Hunstanton	3	K McCready(NPC) I Allan, J Howie, I Macaulay, R Martin, R Matheson, K Revie, R Terras.
1989	Worthing	2	I Allan, B Dodds, J Howie, R Matheson, K Revie, A Simcox, M Watt.
1990	Cromer	3	I Allan, G Alston, G Bell, J Howie, R Martin, R Matheson, R Terras, M Watt
1991	Cambridge	2	I Allan, G Bell, B Dodds, K Revie, R Matheson, R Terras, MWatt
1992	Southsea	2	J Howie, M Watt, G Alston, G Bell, B Dodds, I Campbell, A Smith R Terras.
1993	Cambridge	3	K McCready(NPC)M Watt, C McKnight, G Bell, R Terras, I Campbell, A Smith, I Macaulay.
1994	Cromer	4	G Reid(C) M Watt, C McKnight,G Bell, R Terras, T Smith, G Alston, A Smith.
1995	Cambridge	3	G Reid (C) M Watt, C McKnight, G Bell, R Terras, I Campbell, T Smith, K Spencer.
1996	Hunstanton	3	WJ Moss(NPC) R Matheson, M Watt, C McKnight, G Bell, R Terras, G Alston, D Morrison.
1997	Bude	3	WJ Moss(NPC) R Matheson, M Watt, C McKnight, J Gray, G Bell, D Morrison, P Lavery.
1998	Cambridge	4	HS Matheson(NPC) J Gray, R Terras, M Watt, A Ralston, G Alston, JG Bell, G Smith.
1999	Felixstow	5	HS Matheson (NPC) J Gray, C McKnight, R Terras, M Watt, R Maxfield, A Ralston, G Smith.
2000	Cambridge	5	HS Matheson (NPC) J Gray, C McKnight, R Terras, M Watt, R Maxfield, G Smith, R Allan
2001	Beckenham	6	HS Matheson (NPC) J Gray, C McKnight, R Terras, M Watt, G Smith, R Allan, C Taylor
2002	Cambridge	6	HS Matheson (NPC) J Gray, C McKnight, R Terras, M Watt, D Culshaw, A Ralston C Taylor
2003	Nottingham	6	HS Matheson (NPC) J Gray, C McKnight, R Terras, M Watt, D Culshaw, C Taylor, G Thomson.

Results of Matches played during Season 1933, in which Teams representing the
West of Scotland Lawn Tennis Association took part.

(1) INTER-ASSOCIATION REPRESENTATIVE MATCHES. 1933

29th April.   Mixed Doubles *v.* East of Scotland at Glasgow (Pollokshields).   West of Scotland won by 9 matches to 7.
6th May.   Ladies' Doubles *v.* East of Scotland at Edinburgh.   West of Scotland won by 5 matches to 4.
13th May.   Men's Doubles *v.* Central Districts at Falkirk.   West of Scotland won by 6 matches to 0.
13th May.   Ladies' Doubles *v.* Central Districts at Glasgow (Titwood).   West of Scotland won by 8 matches to 1.
20th May.   Men's Doubles *v.* East of Scotland at Edinburgh.   West of Scotland won by 6 matches to 3.
10th June.   Men's Doubles (2nd League) *v.* East of Scotland at Glasgow (Hillhead High School F.P.).   West of Scotland won by 6 matches to 3.
17th June.   Ladies', Men's, and Mixed Doubles *v.* Glasgow Public Parks at Hillpark.   West of Scotland won by 11 matches to 1.
5th August.   Ladies' Doubles *v.* Ayrshire at Ayr.   West of Scotland won by 9 matches to 0.
5th August.   Men's Doubles *v.* Midland Counties at Dundee.   West of Scotland won by 3 matches to 2.
12th August.   Men's Doubles *v.* Ayrshire at Elderslie.   West of Scotland won by 9 matches to 0.
12th August.   Ladies' Doubles *v.* Midland Counties at Glasgow (Dowanhill).   West of Scotland won by 8 matches to 0.

(2) INTER-COUNTY CUP COMPETITIONS.

The matches in the Inter-County Championships on Grass were played during the week commencing 24th July.   Teams representing West of Scotland took part in the competitions, the Ladies' Doubles Team playing at Scarborough in Group II. of the Ladies' Competition and the Men's Doubles Team at Hythe in Group II. of the Men's Competition.

Results of Ladies' Doubles Matches.—West of Scotland lost to Kent by 4 matches to 5, 9 sets to 11, 97 games to 103 ; lost to Essex by 3 matches to 6, 9 sets to 14, 97 games to 123 ; lost to Nottinghamshire by 2 matches to 7, 7 sets to 14, 83 games to 110 ; lost to East of Scotland by 1 match to 8, 4 sets to 17, 79 games to 128 ; lost to Yorkshire by 2 matches to 7, 7 sets to 14, 52 games to 92.   West of Scotland were represented by Miss C. H. Butters (Pollokshields), Miss J. B. Dunn (Pollokshields), Miss J. A. Jamieson (Pollokshields), Miss A. E. Middleton (Central Districts), Mrs. J. M'Laren (Central Districts), Miss M. Thomson (Partick), and Miss J. Weir (Newlands), *Captain.*

Results of Men's Doubles Matches.—West of Scotland lost to Essex by 3 matches to 6, 9 sets to 13, 96 games to 104 ; lost to Lancashire by 3 matches to 6, 8 sets to 13, 96 games to 107 ; lost to Somerset by 2 matches to 7, 6 sets to 14, 72 games to 107 ; lost to East of Scotland by 3 matches to 6, 8 sets to 14, 94 games to 105 ; lost to Northumberland by 4 matches to 5, 8 sets to 10, 80 games to 96.   West of Scotland were represented by W. Buchanan (Partick), *Captain*, B. Butters, jun. (Pollokshields), R. R. Finlay (Newlands), W. F. Fulton (Newlands), A. M'Vie (Pollokshields), D. T. M'Vie (Pollokshields), and J. H. A. Watson (Pollokshields).

Results of Matches played during Season 1934, in which Teams representing the
West of Scotland Lawn Tennis Association took part.

(1) INTER-ASSOCIATION REPRESENTATIVE MATCHES.

28th April.   Mixed Doubles *v.* East of Scotland at Edinburgh.   East of Scotland won by 10 matches to 6.
5th May.   Ladies' Doubles *v.* East of Scotland at Bearsden.   West of Scotland won by 6 matches to 3.
16th June.   Men's Doubles (2nd League) *v.* East of Scotland at Edinburgh.   East of Scotland won by 6 matches to 3
23rd June.   Ladies', Men's and Mixed Doubles *v.* Glasgow Public Parks, at Newlands Park.   West of Scotland won by 11 matches to 1.
30th June.   Ladies' Doubles *v.* Central Districts at Falkirk.   West of Scotland won by 9 matches to 0.
30th June.   Men's Doubles *v.* Central Districts at Glasgow (Partick).   West of Scotland wom by 7 matches to 2.
4th August.   Ladies' Doubles *v.* Ayrshire at Elderslie.   West of Scotland won by 9 matches to 0.
4th August.   Men's Doubles *v.* Midland Counties at Glasgow (Dowanhill).   West of Scotland won by 9 matches to 0.
10th August.   Men's Doubles *v.* Scottish Welfare Association at Thorntonhall.   West of Scotland won by 4 matches to 3.
11th August.   Men's Doubles *v.* Ayrshire at Ayr.   West of Scotland won by 9 matches to 0
11th August.   Ladies' Doubles *v.* Midland Counties at Dundee.   West of Scotland won by 6 matches to 1.
25th August.   Men's Doubles *v.* North East of Scotland at Gleneagles.   West of Scotland won by 5 matches to 3.

The Men's Doubles match against East of Scotland fixed for 19th May was cancelled owing to rain.

(2) INTER-COUNTY CUP COMPETITIONS.

The matches in the Inter-County Championships on Grass were played during the week commencing 23rd July. Teams representing West of Scotland took part in the competitions, the Ladies' Doubles Team playing at Westcliff-on-Sea in Group III. of the Ladies' Competition and the Men's Doubles Team at Scarborough in Group III. of the Men's Competition.

Results of Ladies' Doubles Matches.—West of Scotland lost to Somerset by 0 matches to 9, 0 sets to 18, 25 games to 109 ; lost to Leicestershire by 2 matches to 7, 5 sets to 15, 74 games to 114 ; lost to Suffolk by 1 match to 8, 4 sets to 17, 68 games to 114 ; lost to Cheshire by 0 matches to 9, 2 sets to 18, 38 games to 117 ; lost to Kent by 1 match to 8, 2 sets to 17, 47 games to 112.   West of Scotland were represented by Miss B. Beaton (Newlands), Miss C. H. Butters (Pollokshields), Miss J. C. Caesar (Newlands), Miss M. Harvey (Central Districts), Mrs. J. B. Harvey (Pollokshields), Captain, Miss G. Manson (Partick), and Miss M. Thomson (Partick).

Results of Men's Doubles Matches.—West of Scotland lost to Staffordshire by 1 match to 8, 2 sets to 17, 67 games to 117 ; lost to Leicestershire by 2 matches to 7, 6 sets to 15, 83 games to 114 ; beat Northumberland by 7 matches to 2, 16 sets to 8, 118 games to 95 ; beat Worcestershire by 5 matches to 4, 10 sets to 11, 104 games to 103 ; lost to Durham by 1 match to 8, 5 sets to 16, 86 games to 122.   West of Scotland were represented by R. W. Blakey (Springboig), W. Fulton (Newlands), J. T. Hill (Newlands), Captain, D. McPhail, Jr. (Pollokshields), A. McVie (Pollokshields), D. T. McVie (Pollokshields), and E. H. Taylor (Springboig).

Results of Matches played during Season 1935, in which Teams representing the West of Scotland Lawn Tennis Association took part.

(1) INTER-ASSOCIATION REPRESENTATIVE MATCHES.

4th May.   Ladies' Doubles *v.* East of Scotland at Edinburgh. West of Scotland won by 5 matches to 4.
4th May.   Men's Doubles *v.* East of Scotland at Glasgow (Partick). West of Scotland won by 5 matches to 3.
25th May.   Mixed Doubles *v.* East of Scotland at Glasgow (Pollokshields). West of Scotland won by 9 matches to 7.
9th June.   Ladies', Men's and Mixed Doubles *v.* Glasgow Public Parks at Newlands Public Park. West of Scotland won by 9 matches to 3.
15th June. Men's Doubles (2nd League) *v.* East of Scotland at Glasgow (Clarkston). West of Scotland won by 5 matches to 3.
22nd June. Men's Doubles *v.* Ayrshire at Elderslie. West of Scotland won by 6 matches to 0.
22nd June. Ladies' Doubles *v.* Ayrshire at Troon. West of Scotland won by 6 matches to 3.
29th June. Ladies' Doubles *v.* Central Districts at Glasgow (Poloc). West of Scotland won by 6 matches to 3.
29th June. Men's Doubles *v.* Central Districts at Dunblane. West of Scotland won by 9 matches to 0.

The Ladies' and Men's Doubles matches against the Midland Counties fixed for 6th July were cancelled owing to the difficulty in raising a team. The Men's Doubles match against the North East of Scotland fixed for August 10th was cancelled owing to rain.

(2) INTER-COUNTY CUP COMPETITIONS.

The matches in the Inter-County Championships on Grass were played during the week commencing 22nd July. Teams representing West of Scotland took part in the Competitions, the Ladies' Doubles Team playing at Felixstowe in Group IV. of the Ladies' Competition and the Men's Doubles Team at Paignton in Group III. of the Men's Competition.

Results of Ladies' Doubles Matches.—West of Scotland lost to Durham by 2 matches to 7, 7 sets to 14, 72 games to 102 ; lost to Norfolk by 3 matches to 6, 6 sets to 14, 65 games to 99 ; beat Lincolnshire by 6 matches to 3, 12 sets to 7, 89 games to 82 ; lost to Suffolk by 4 matches to 5, 8 sets to 12, 77 games to 89 ; lost to Derbyshire by 3 matches to 6, 6 sets to 12, 69 games to 93. West of Scotland were represented by Miss B. Beaton (Newlands), Miss C. H. Butters (Pollokshields), Miss J. C. Caesar (Newlands), Miss W. A. Mason (Pollokshields), Miss P. S. Morton (Pollokshields), Miss K. Rooney (Hamilton), Miss M. Thomson (Partick), and Miss J. Weir (Newlands) Capt.

Results of Men's Doubles Matches.—West of Scotland beat Devonshire by 5 matches to 4, 10 sets to 10, 98 games to 95 ; lost to Leicestershire by 3 matches to 6, 8 sets to 13, 92 games to 116 ; lost to Derbyshire by 2 matches to 7, 6 sets to 15, 78 games to 114 ; lost to Nottinghamshire by 2 matches to 7, 6 sets to 14, 69 games to 104 ; lost to Hampshire by 2 matches to 7, 7 sets to 15, 89 games to 120. West of Scotland were represented by A. S. Gilchrist (Pollokshields), D. McPhail, Jr. (Pollokshields), A. McVie (Pollokshields), Captain, D. T. McVie (Pollokshields), E. H. Taylor (Springboig), D. Watson (Titwood). and J. H. A. Watson (Pollokshields).

Results of Matches played during 1937, in which Teams representing West of Scotland Association took part.

(1). INTER-ASSOCIATION REPRESENTATIVE MATCHES.

1st May.   Mixed Doubles *v.* East of Scotland at Paisley. West of Scotland lost by 6 matches to 10.
15th May.   Ladies' Doubles *v.* East of Scotland at Edinburgh. West of Scotland won by 6 matches to 3.
22nd May.   Men's Doubles *v.* East of Scotland at Edinburgh. West of Scotland lost by 0 matches to 6.
12th June. Men's Doubles (2nd League) *v.* East of Scotland at Glasgow (Clarkston). West of Scotland lost by 1 match to 5.
19th June. Ladies', Men's and Mixed Doubles *v.* Glasgow Public Parks at Hillpark. West of Scotland won by 9 matches to 3.
26th June. Men's Doubles *v.* Ayrshire at Ardrossan. West of Scotland won by 5 matches to 3.
26th June. Ladies' Doubles *v.* Ayrshire at Elderslie. West of Scotland won by 7 matches to 2.
3rd July.   Men's Doubles *v.* Central Districts at Dollar. West of Scotland won by 5 matches to 1.
3rd July.   Ladies' Doubles *v.* Central Districts. This match was not played owing to rain.
10th July. Men's Doubles *v.* Midlands at Dundee. West of Scotland lost by 3 matches to 5.
10th July. Ladies' Doubles *v.* Midlands at Glasgow (Partick). West of Scotland won by 6 matches to 0.
21st Aug.   Men's Doubles *v.* North East at Gleneagles. West of Scotland won by 6 matches to 3.

(2). INTER-COUNTY CUP COMPETITIONS.

The Matches of the Inter-County Championships on Grass were played during the week commencing 19th July. Teams representing West of Scotland took part in the Competitions, the Ladies' Doubles Team playing at Vale of Clwyd in Group VI. of the Ladies' Competition and the Men's Doubles Team at Paignton in Group V. of the Men's Competition.

Results of Ladies' Doubles Matches. West of Scotland beat Shropshire by 7 matches to 2, 15 sets to 9, 131 games to 107 ; beat Oxfordshire by 5 matches to 4, 12 sets to 9, 119 games to 101 ; lost to Bedfordshire by 2 matches to 7, 4 sets to 14, 59 games to 103 ; lost to Cambridgeshire by 4 matches to 5, 12 sets to 12, 130 games to 122; lost to Northamptonshire by 1 match to 8, 3 sets to 16, 56 games to 113. West of Scotland were represented by Miss E. A. R. Anderson (Lenzie), Miss B. Beaton (Newlands), Miss A. H. G. Gillespie (Pollokshields), Mrs. R. Harvey (Pollokshields) Captain, Miss McEwen (New Galloway), Miss M. Rooney (Hamilton), Miss J. Thomson (Giffnock), and Miss M. Thomson (Partick).

Results of Men's Doubles Matches. West of Scotland beat Devonshire by 5 matches to 4, 12 sets to 9, 96 games to 87 ; beat Buckinghamshire by 9 matches to 0, 18 sets to 3, 128 games to 76 ; beat Bedfordshire by 9 matches to 0, 18 sets to 1, 127 games to 73 ; beat Gloucestershire by 7 matches to 2, 16 sets to 7, 122 games to 79 ; beat Berkshire by 6 matches to 3, 12 sets to 6, 90 games to 63.. West of Scotland were represented by B. Butters, Jr. (Chiswick Park), J. B. Fulton (Middlesbrough), J. T. Hill, Jr., (Newlands), A. G. M. Keir (Partick), D. McPhail, Jr. (Pollokshields), J. A. Robertson (Newlands) and E. H. Taylor (Pollokshields).

Results of Matches played during 1938, in which Teams representing
West of Scotland Association took part.

(1) INTER-ASSOCIATION REPRESENTATIVE MATCHES.

7th May.   Mixed Doubles *v.* East of Scotland at Edinburgh. West of Scotland lost by 5 matches to 11.

21st May.   Men's Doubles *v.* East of Scotland at Glasgow (Titwood). Unfinished.

21st May.   Ladies' Doubles *v.* East of Scotland at Glasgow (Bearsden). West of Scotland lost by 1 match to 5.

11th June. Men's Doubles (2nd League) *v.* East of Scotland at Edinburgh. West of Scotland won by 8 matches to 1.

18th June. Ladies', Men's and Mixed Doubles *v.* Glasgow Public Parks at Newlands Park. West of Scotland won by 6 matches to 6, 15 sets to 13.

25th June. Men's Doubles *v.* Ayrshire at Ardeer. West of Scotland won by 5 matches to 1.

25th June. Ladies' Doubles *v.* Ayrshire at Elderslie. West of Scotland won by 6 matches to 0.

2nd July.   Men's Doubles *v.* Central Districts at Glasgow (Whitecraigs). West of Scotland won by 7 matches to 2.

2nd July.   Ladies' Doubles *v.* Central Districts at Stirling. West of Scotland lost by 4 matches to 5.

9th July.   Men's Doubles *v.* Midlands at Glasgow (Partick). West of Scotland won by 9 matches to 0.

9th July.   Ladies' Doubles *v.* Midlands at Dundee. Unplayed.

13th Aug.   Men's Doubles *v.* The Railway Athletic Association at Glasgow (King's Park). West of Scotland won by 6 matches to 3.

20th Aug.   Men's Doubles *v.* North-East at Gleneagles. West of Scotland won by 7 matches to 1.

(2). INTER-COUNTY CUP COMPETITIONS.

The Matches of the Inter-County Championships on Grass were played during the week commencing 19th July. Teams representing the West of Scotland took part in the Competitions, the Ladies' Doubles Team playing at Ross-on-Wye in Group VI. of the Ladies' Competition and the Men's Doubles Team at Bournemouth in Group IV. of the Men's Competition.

Results of Ladies' Doubles Matches. West of Scotland beat South Wales by 8 matches to 1, 17 sets to 2, 110 games to 60 ; beat Hertfordshire by 9 matches to 0, 18 sets to 0, 109 games to 27 ; beat North Wales by 7 matches to 2, 15 sets to 5, 106 games to 81 ; beat Cambridgeshire by 6 matches to 3, 13 sets to 7, 111 games to 93 ; lost to Derbyshire by 3 matches to 5, 9 sets to 13, 106 games to 111. West of Scotland were represented by Miss L. Anderson (Pollokshields), Miss C. H. Butters (Pollokshields), Miss C. Callander (Larbert), Mrs. J. B. Jones (Larbert), Mrs. R. Harvey (Pollokshields), Captain, Mrs. A. A. F. Peel (Newlands), Miss C. Rooney (Hamilton) and Miss M. Thomson (Partick).

Results of Men's Doubles Matches. West of Scotland beat Devonshire by 7 matches to 2, 15 sets to 7, 118 games to 87 ; lost to Northamptonshire by 3 matches to 6, 11 sets to 14, 110 games to 118 ; lost to Hampshire by 4 matches to 5, 11 sets to 12, 107 games to 104 ; lost to Wiltshire by 1 match to 8, 4 sets to 17, 81 games to 116 ; lost to Hertfordshire by 4 matches to 5, 10 sets to 11, 96 games to 103. West of Scotland were represented by B. Butters, Jr. (Chiswick Park), J. B. Fulton (Guisborough), J. T. Hill (Newlands), A. G. M. Keir (Partick), J. A. Robertson (Newlands), and E. H. Taylor (Pollokshields). J. C. Marshall (Thorntonhall) acted as non-playing Captain.

Results of Matches played during 1939, in which Teams representing
West of Scotland Lawn Tennis Association took part.

(1). INTER-ASSOCIATION REPRESENTATIVE MATCHES.

6th May.   Ladies' Doubles *v.* East of Scotland at Edinburgh. West of Scotland lost by 1 match to 5.

            Men's Doubles *v.* East of Scotland at Glasgow (Titwood). West of Scotland won by 5 matches to 4

20th May.   Mixed Doubles *v.* East of Scotland—Match cancelled.

10th June. Men's Doubles (2nd League) *v.* East of Scotland at Glasgow (Thorntonhall). West of Scotland won by 4 matches to 2.

17th June. Ladies', Men's and Mixed Doubles *v.* Glasgow Public Parks at Cartha. West of Scotland won by 9 matches to 3.

24th June. Ladies' Doubles *v.* Ayrshire at Largs. West of Scotland won by 6 matches to 0.

            Men's Doubles *v.* Ayrshire at Paisley. West of Scotland won by 5 matches to 4.

1st July.   Ladies' Doubles *v.* Central Districts at Glasgow (Clarkston). West of Scotland won by 7 matches to 2.

            Men's Doubles *v.* Central Districts at Grangemouth. West of Scotland won by 5 matches to 1.

8th July.   Ladies' Doubles *v.* Midlands at Glasgow (Partick).—Match cancelled.

            Men's Doubles *v.* Midlands at Dundee. West of Scotland lost by 3 matches to 6.

19th August. Men's Doubles *v.* North East at Gleneagles. West of Scotland won by 5 matches to 1.

26th August. Men's Doubles *v.* Railways Athletic Association at Glasgow (Pollokshields)—Match cancelled.

(2). INTER-COUNTY CUP COMPETITIONS.

The Matches of the Inter-County Championships on Grass were played during the week commencing 24th July. Teams representing the Scottish Western Counties Lawn Tennis Association (which includes this Association) took part in the Competitions, the Ladies' Doubles Team playing at Bognor in Group V. of the Ladies' Competition and the Men's Doubles Team at Angmering-on-Sea in Group V. of the Men's Competition.

Results of Ladies' Doubles Matches. West of Scotland lost to Buckinghamshire by 0 matches to 9, 1 set to 18, 55 games to 118 ; beat Bedfordshire by 5 matches to 4, 12 sets to 10, 115 games to 107 ; beat Norfolk by 5 matches to 4, 12 sets to 9, 110 games to 101 ; beat Derbyshire by 6 matches to 3, 12 sets to 9, 105 games to 100 ; lost to Lincolnshire by 4 matches to 5, 11 sets to 12, 118 games to 130. The team consisted of Miss C. H. Butters (Pollokshields), Mrs. J. W. Bell (Clarkston), Miss C. Callander (Central), Mrs. R. Harvey (Partick) Captain, Mrs. A. A. F. Peel (Newlands), Miss K. Rooney (Hamilton), Mrs. P. Smith (Clarkston), Miss M. Thomson (Partick).

Results of Men's Doubles Matches. West of Scotland beat Bedfordshire by 7 matches to 2, 16 sets to 5, 115 games to 79 ; beat Oxfordshire by 5 matches to 4, 14 sets to 10, 112 games to 105 ; beat Northumberland by 7 matches to 2, 15 sets to 8, 124 games to 109 ; beat Devon by 7 matches to 2, 14 sets to 6, 114 games to 86 ; beat Dorset by 7 matches to 2, 14 sets to 4, 109 games to 69. The team consisted of J. W. Bell (Clarkston), B. Butters (Chiswick Park), J. T. Hill (Newlands), R. Lawson (Pollokshields), P. B. Macfarlane (Clarkston), N. C. Mackenzie (Kelvinside), D. MacPhail (Pollokshields).

Results of Matches played during 1947 in which Teams representing the West of Scotland Lawn Tennis Association took part.

(1). INTER-ASSOCIATION REPRESENTATIVE MATCHES.

LADIES' DOUBLES.

WEST *v.* AYRSHIRE, at Whitecraigs.
 West won by 5 matches 10 sets 75 games to 1 match 3 sets 39 games.
WEST *v.* CENTRAL DISTRICTS, at Bonnybridge.
 West won by 6 matches 14 sets 110 games to 3 matches 8 sets 91 games.
WEST *v.* EAST, at Western.
 West lost by 4 matches 10 sets 109 games to 5 matches 10 sets 116 games.
WEST *v.* MIDLANDS, at Perth.
 West won by 6 matches 13 sets 104 games to 3 matches 10 sets 93 games.

MEN'S DOUBLES.

WEST *v.* AYRSHIRE, at Ardeer.
 West won by 5 matches 12 sets 109 games to 4 matches 10 sets 110 games.
WEST *v.* CENTRAL DISTRICTS, at Giffnock.
 West won by 8 matches 16 sets to 1 match 4 sets.
WEST *v.* EAST, at Waverley.
 West lost by 1 match 5 sets 73 games to 7 matches 15 sets 110 games.
WEST *v.* MIDLANDS, at Kelvinside.
 West lost by 3 matches 8 sets 94 games to 5 matches 12 sets 103 games.

(2). INTER-COUNTY CUP COMPETITION ON GRASS.

 The Ladies' Team playing in Group V. at Malvern won 1 match and lost 4 matches and drop to Group VI.
 The Men's Team playing in Group IV. at Folkestone won 2 matches and lost 3 matches and remain in Group IV.

Results of Matches played during 1948 in which Teams representing the West of Scotland Lawn Tennis Association took part.

(1). INTER-ASSOCIATION REPRESENTATIVE MATCHES.

LADIES' DOUBLES.

WEST *v.* AYRSHIRE, at Ardeer, on 15th May, 1948.
 West won by 9 matches 18 sets 112 games to 0 matches 1 set 24 games.
WEST *v.* EAST, at Waverley, on 5th June, 1948.
 West lost by 2 matches 6 sets 71 games to 7 matches 14 sets 107 games.
WEST *v.* CENTRAL, at Weir Recreation Club, on 12th June, 1948.
 West won by 6 matches 14 sets 103 games to 3 matches 7 sets 79 games.
WEST *v.* MIDLANDS—Match cancelled.

MEN'S DOUBLES.

WEST *v.* AYRSHIRE, at Western on 15th May, 1948.
 West won by 7 matches 16 sets 110 games to 2 matches 5 sets 69 games.
WEST *v.* EAST, at Newlands, on 5th June, 1948.
 Rain stopped play.
WEST *v.* CENTRAL, at Livilands, on 12th June, 1948.
 West won by 8 matches 16 sets 106 games to 1 match 2 sets 51 games.
WEST *v.* MIDLANDS—Match cancelled.

MIXED DOUBLES.

WEST *v.* EAST, at Craiglockhart, on 8th May, 1948.
 West lost by 5 matches 13 sets 167 games to 11 matches 26 sets 232 games.

(2). INTER-COUNTY CHAMPIONSHIPS ON GRASS.

 These matches were played during the week commencing 19th July, 1948. Teams representing the Scottish Western Counties Lawn Tennis Association (which includes this Association) took part in the Competitions, the Ladies' Doubles Team playing at Hunstanton in Group VI. and the Men's Doubles Team at Bedford in Group IV.

 Results of Ladies' Doubles Matches : West of Scotland lost to Shropshire, 4 matches to 5, 10 sets to 10, 91 games to 92 ; lost to South Wales, 3 matches to 6, 7 sets to 14, 73 games to 104 ; beat Cambridgeshire, 9 matches to 0, 18 sets to 1, 115 games to 49 ; Berkshire scratched. The team consisted of Miss M. S. Allan (Pollokshields), Mrs. L. S. Black (Pollokshields), Mrs. L. Carter (Ardgowan), Miss I. M. Clark (Paisley), Mrs. J. B. Harvey (Craighelen), Captain, Miss H. M. MacFarlane (Craighelen), and Miss I. S. Vallance (Pollokshields).

 Results of Men's Doubles Matches : West of Scotland beat Cheshire, 8 matches to 1, 16 sets to 9, 141 games to 121 ; lost to Hertfordshire, 2 matches to 7, 5 sets to 15, 86 games to 115 ; beat Northamptonshire, 5 matches to 4, 11 sets to 8, 98 games to 93 ; beat Oxfordshire, 9 matches to 0, 18 sets to 3, 120 games to 59 ; lost to Bedfordshire, 4 matches to 5, 9 sets to 13, 102 games to 114. The team consisted of T. Boyd (Giffnock), B. Fulton (Newlands), J. B. Fulton (Chapel Allarton), Captain, A. B. Murray (Pollokshields), W. J. Reid (Western), J. G. Rutherglen (Newlands), N. K. Smith (Pollokshields) and J. H. A. Watson (Pollokshields).

Results of Matches played during 1949 in which Teams representing the West of Scotland Lawn Tennis Association took part.

(1) INTER-ASSOCIATION REPRESENTATIVE MATCHES.

LADIES' DOUBLES.

WEST v. AYRSHIRE, at Pollokshields, on 14th May, 1949.
West won by 6 matches, 12 sets, 76 games to 0 matches, 1 set, 16 games.
WEST v. CENTRAL, at Bridge of Allan, on 28th May, 1949.
West won by 5 matches, 11 sets, 93 games to 2 matches, 6 sets, 63 games.
WEST v. EAST, at Pollokshields, on 4th June, 1949.
West lost by 1 match, 5 sets, 64 games to 5 matches, 10 sets, 83 games.
WEST v. MIDLANDS, at Pollokshields, on 2nd July, 1949.
West lost by 2 matches, 6 sets, 71 games to 5 matches, 10 sets, 84 games.

MEN'S DOUBLES.

WEST v. AYRSHIRE, at DARVEL, on 14th May, 1949.
Match abandoned owing to weather.
WEST v. CENTRAL, at Pollokshields, on 28th May, 1949.
West won by 6 matches, 15 sets, 118 games to 3 matches, 8 sets, 90 games.
WEST v. EAST, at Edinburgh, on 4th June, 1949.
West lost by 1 match, 4 sets, 54 games to 5 matches, 11 sets, 79 games.
WEST v. MIDLANDS, at Dundee, on 2nd July, 1949.
West won by 5 matches, 12 sets, 115 games to 4 matches, 9 sets, 104 games.

MIXED DOUBLES.

WEST v. EAST, at Pollokshields, on 7th May, 1949.
West won by 10 matches, 24 sets, 200 games to 6 matches, 18 sets, 198 games.

DOUBLES MATCH v. ULSTER LAWN TENNIS ASSOCIATION.

Ladies, West, won by	....	....	3 matches	6 sets	40 games	to	0 matches	1 set	27 games
Men, West, lost by	....	....	1 match	2 sets	30 games	to	2 matches	4 sets	34 games
Mixed, West, won by	....	....	3 matches	8 sets	80 games	to	3 matches	7 sets	70 games
Total	:...	....	7 matches	16 sets	150 games		5 matches	12 sets	131 games

(2). INTER-COUNTY CHAMPIONSHIPS ON GRASS.

These matches were played during the week commencing 18th July, 1949. Teams representing the Scottish Western Counties Lawn Tennis Association (which includes this Association) took part in the Competitions, the Ladies' Doubles Team playing at Shrewsbury in Group VI. and the Men's Doubles Team at Cambridge in Group IV.

Results of Ladies' Doubles Matches: West of Scotland beat Lincolnshire, 6 matches, 13 sets, 121 games to 3 matches, 9 sets, 103 games; beat Northamptonshire, 5 matches, 13 sets, 110 games to 4 matches, 8 sets, 92 games; beat Northumberland, 8 matches, 16 sets, 102 games to 1 match, 2 sets, 54 games; beat Westmorland, 9 matches, 18 sets, 108 games to 0 matches, 0 sets, 25 games. The team consisted of Miss M. S. Allan (Pollokshields), Mrs. L. S. Black (Pollokshields), Mrs. L. Carter (Ardgowan), Mrs. R. Harvey (Craighelen) *Captain*, Miss H. M. Macfarlane (Craighelen), Miss M. E. M. Wilson (Pollokshields), and Miss I. S. Vallance (Pollokshields).

Results of Men's Doubles Matches: West of Scotland beat Northamptonshire, 5 matches, 12 sets, 121 games to 4 matches, 11 sets, 106 games; lost to Cambridge, 4 matches, 10 sets 99 games, to 5 matches, 12 sets, 113 games; lost to Somerset, 2 matches, 7 sets, 95 games to 7 matches, 15 sets, 125 games; beat Suffolk, 6 matches, 12 sets, 86 games to 3 matches, 7 sets, 75 games; beat Durham, 5 matches, 11 sets, 113 games to 4 matches, 10 sets, 103 games. The team consisted of C. V. Baxter (Titwood), T. Boyd (Giffnock), B. Fulton (Newlands), J. B. Fulton (Chapel Allarton), *Captain*, A. B. Murray (Pollokshields), W. J. Reid (Western), J. G. Rutherglen (Newlands), and A. H. Young (Newlands).

Results of Matches played during Season 1950 in which Teams representing the West of Scotland Lawn Tennis Association took part.

(1). INTER-ASSOCIATION REPRESENTATIVE MATCHES.

LADIES' DOUBLES.

WEST *v.* CENTRAL, at Pollokshields, on 29th April, 1950.
    West won by 8 rubbers, 17 sets, 110 games to 0 rubbers, 1 set, 61 games.
WEST *v.* AYRSHIRE, at Ayr, on 13th May, 1950.
    West won by 9 rubbers, 18 sets, 117 games to 0 rubbers, 1 set, 55 games.
WEST *v.* EAST, at Westhall, on 27th May, 1950.
    West lost by 1 rubber, 4 sets, 65 games to 8 rubbers, 16 sets, 108 games.
WEST *v.* MIDLANDS, at Dundee, on 1st July, 1950.
    West won by 6 rubbers, 13 sets, 108 games to 3 rubbers, 7 sets, 91 games.

MEN'S DOUBLES.

WEST *v.* CENTRAL, at Ochilview, on 29th April, 1950.
    West won by 8 rubbers, 17 sets, 117 games to 1 rubber, 3 sets, 69 games.
WEST *v.* AYRSHIRE, at Pollokshields, on 13th May, 1950.
    West won by 5 rubbers, 13 sets, 122 games to 3 rubbers, 7 sets, 97 games.
WEST *v.* EAST, at Pollokshields, on 27th May, 1950.
    West lost by 3 rubbers, 7 sets, 94 games to 5 rubbers, 13 sets, 118 games.
WEST *v.* MIDLANDS, at Pollokshields, on 1st July, 1950.
    West won by 9 rubbers, 18 sets, 123 games to 0 rubbers, 3 sets, 77 games.

MIXED DOUBLES.

WEST *v.* EAST, at Craiglockhart, on 6th May, 1950.
    West lost by 4 rubbers, 11 sets, 148 games to 12 rubbers, 27 sets, 207 games.

DOUBLES MATCH *v.* ULSTER LAWN TENNIS ASSOCIATION.
Played at Belfast Boat Club, on 3rd June, 1950.

Ladies.   West won by 3 rubbers, 6 sets, 43 games to 0 rubbers, 1 set, 32 games.
Men.   West won by 2 rubbers, 4 sets, 36 games to 1 rubber, 2 sets, 31 games.
Mixed.   West won by 6 rubbers, 12 sets, 89 games to 0 rubbers, 3 sets, 66 games.
    TOTAL : 11 rubbers, 22 sets, 168 games to 1 rubber, 6 sets, 129 games.

(2). INTER-COUNTY CHAMPIONSHIPS ON GRASS.

These matches were played during the week commencing 24th July, 1950. Teams representing the Scottish Western Counties Lawn Tennis Association (which includes this Association), took part in the Competitions, the Ladies' Doubles Team playing at Middleton-on-Sea in Group V., and the Men's Doubles Team at Ilkley, in Group IV.

Both teams were successful in gaining promotion to the next higher Group.

Results of Ladies Doubles' Matches : West of Scotland beat Shropshire, 7 rubbers, 16 sets, 133 games to 2 rubbers, 6 sets, 97 games ; beat Worcestershire, 7 rubbers, 16 sets, 126 games to 2 rubbers, 7 sets, 98 games ; beat Bedfordshire, 8 rubbers, 17 sets, 122 games to 1 rubber, 3 sets, 74 games ; beat Durham, 8 rubbers, 17 sets, 109 games to 1 rubber, 3 sets, 64 games ; beat Northamptonshire, 5 rubbers, 12 sets, 109 games to 4 rubbers, 10 sets, 105 games   The team consisted of Miss M. S. Allan (Pollokshields), Mrs. L. S. Black (Pollokshields), Mrs. R. Harvey (Craighelen), *Captain*, Mrs. G. S. Horne (Pollokshields), Miss H. M. Macfarlane (Craighelen), Mrs. I. Perpoli (Western) and Miss I. S. Vallance (Pollokshields).

Results of Men's Doubles Matches : West of Scotland beat Cheshire, 5 rubbers, 11 sets, 116 games to 4 rubbers, 10 sets, 114 games ; lost to Bedfordshire, 4 rubbers, 10 sets, 117 games to 5 rubbers, 10 sets, 116 games ; beat Somerset, 7 rubbers, 16 sets, 119 games to 2 rubbers, 5 sets, 81 games ; beat Staffordshire, 5 rubbers, 12 sets, 107 games to 4 rubbers, 10 sets, 107 games ; beat Oxfordshire, 6 rubbers, 15 sets, 121 games to 3 rubbers, 7 sets, 86 games.   The team consisted of T. Boyd (Giffnock), I. Campbell (Pollokshields), J. B. Fulton (Chapel Allarton), *Captain*, A. B. Murray (Pollokshields), W. Reid (Western), J. G. Rutherglen (Newlands), and J. B. Wilson (Cardonald).

Results of Matches played during Season 1951 in which Teams representing the West of Scotland Lawn Tennis Association took part.

(1). INTER-ASSOCIATION REPRESENTATIVE MATCHES.

WOMEN'S DOUBLES.

WEST *v.* CENTRAL at Grangemouth on 19th May, 1951.
West won by 9 rubbers, 13 sets, 113 games to 0 rubbers, 1 set, 43 games.
WEST *v.* EAST at Pollokshields on 26th May, 1951.
West won by 5 rubbers, 12 sets, 97 games to 4 rubbers, 9 sets, 92 games.
WEST *v.* AYRSHIRE—not played.
WEST *v.* MIDLANDS at Pollokshields on 7th July, 1951.
West won by 7 rubbers, 15 sets, 102 games to 1 rubber, 3 sets, 48 games.

"UNDER 21."

WEST *v.* EAST at Craiglockhart on 15th September, 1951.
West won by 7 rubbers, 15 sets, 110 games to 2 rubbers, 7 sets, 77 games.

MEN'S DOUBLES.

WEST *v.* CENTRAL at Pollokshields on 19th May, 1951.
West won by 9 rubbers, 18 sets, 111 games to O rubbers, 1 set, 42 games.
WEST *v.* EAST at Craiglockhart on 14th July, 1951.
West lost by 4 rubbers, 11 sets, 99 games to 5 rubbers, 11 sets, 102 games.
WEST *v.* AYRSHIRE—not played.
WEST *v.* MIDLANDS at Broughty Ferry on 7th July, 1951.
West won by 5 rubbers, 10 sets, 85 games to 1 rubber, 5 sets, 64 games.

"UNDER 21."

WEST *v.* EAST at Western L.T.C. on 15th September, 1951.
West won by 8 rubbers, 16 sets, 113 games to 1 rubber, 3 sets, 55 games.

MIXED DOUBLES.

WEST *v.* EAST at Pollokshields on 5th May, 1951.
West 8 rubbers, 18 sets, 181 games. ⎫
East 8 rubbers, 21 sets, 192 games. ⎬ Match drawn.

DOUBLES MATCH *v.* ULSTER LAWN TENNIS ASSOCIATION.

Played at Pollokshields on 1st September, 1951.
Women. West won by 2 rubbers, 4 sets, 30 games to 0 rubbers, 1 set, 19 games.
Men. West won by 2 rubbers, 4 sets, 31 games to 0 rubbers, 0 sets, 20 games.
Mixed. West won by 3 rubbers, 6 sets, 51 games to 1 rubber, 3 sets, 27 games.
TOTAL. 7 rubbers, 14 sets, 112 games to 1 rubber, 4 sets, 66 games.

(2). INTER-COUNTY CHAMPIONSHIP ON GRASS.

These matches were played during the week commencing 23rd July, 1951. Teams representing the Scottish Western Counties Lawn Tennis Association (which includes this Association) took part in the Competitions, the Women's Doubles Team playing at Alverstoke in Group IV., and the Men's Doubles Team at Paignton, in Group III.

The Women's Team were successful in gaining promotion to Group III. and the Men's Team remain in Group III. having missed promotion by a narrow margin.

Results of Women's Doubles Matches ; West of Scotland lost to Dorset, 4 rubbers, 9 sets, 88 games to 5 rubbers, 10 sets, 93 games ; beat South Wales, 7 rubbers, 14 sets, 99 games to 2 rubbers, 5 sets, 65 games ; beat Northants., 7 rubbers, 15 sets, 108 games to 2 rubbers, 4 sets, 78 games ; beat Somerset 7 rubbers, 14 sets, 103 games to 2 rubbers, 4 sets, 56 games ; beat Essex, 5 rubbers, 11 sets, 94 games to 4 rubbers, 10 sets, 102 games. The team consisted of Miss M. S. Allan (Pollokshields), Mrs. L. S. Black (Pollokshields), Mrs. D. Dick (Pollokshields), Mrs. J. B. Harvey (Craighelen), *Captain*, Miss H. M. Macfarlane (Craighelen), Mrs. I. Perpoli (Western) and Miss I. S. Vallance (Pollokshields).

Results of Men's Doubles Matches ; West of Scotland beat Bedfordshire 6 rubbers, 14 sets, 128 games to 3 rubbers, 6 sets, 98 games ; lost to Northants., 3 rubbers, 10 sets, 107 games to 6 rubbers, 14 sets, 129 games ; lost to East of Scotland, 3 rubbers, 10 sets, 116 games to 6 rubbers, 13 sets, 127 games ; beat Cambridgeshire, 6 rubbers, 14 sets, 132 games to 3 rubbers, 9 sets, 105 games ; beat Hampshire, 6 rubbers, 13 sets, 127 games to 3 rubbers, 11 sets, 124 games. The team consisted of C. V. Baxter (Titwood), T. Boyd (Giffnock), I. Campbell (Pollokshields), B. Fulton (Newlands), J. B. Fulton (Chapel Allarton), *Captain*, A. B. Murray (Pollokshields), J. G. Rutherglen (Newlands) and J. B. Wilson (Cardonald).

Results of Matches played during Season 1952 in which Teams representing the West of Scotland Lawn Tennis Association took part.

(1). INTER-ASSOCIATION REPRESENTATIVE MATCHES.

WOMEN'S DOUBLES.

WEST *v.* CENTRAL, at Pollokshields, on 17th May, 1952.
West won by 8 rubbers, 16 sets, 106 games to 1 rubber, 3 sets, 51 games.

WEST *v.* EAST, at Craiglockhart, on 24th May, 1952.
West lost by 4 rubbers, 9 sets, 93 games to 5 rubbers, 11 sets, 95 games.

WEST *v.* MIDLANDS, at Dundee, on 5th July, 1952.
West won by 5 rubbers, 10 sets, 94 games to 3 rubbers, 7 sets, 77 games.

WEST *v.* AYRSHIRE, at Pollokshields, on 12th July, 1952.
West won by 5 rubbers, 11 sets, 90 games to 2 rubbers, 6 sets, 66 games.

UNDER 21.

WEST *v.* EAST, at Newlands, on 13th September, 1952.
West won by 6 rubbers, 14 sets, 106 games to 2 rubbers, 5 sets, 77 games.

MEN'S DOUBLES.

WEST *v.* CENTRAL, at Bonnybridge, on 17th May, 1952.
West won by 6 rubbers, 12 sets, 85 games to 0 rubbers, 3 sets, 47 games.

WEST *v.* EAST, at Pollokshields, on 24th May, 1952.
West won Singles by 4 rubbers, 9 sets, 79 games to 2 rubbers, 7 sets 66 games.
West lost Doubles by 1 rubber, 4 sets, 41 games to 2 rubbers, 4 sets, 38 games.
West won Match by 5 rubbers, 13 sets, 120 games to 4 rubbers, 11 sets, 104 games.

WEST *v.* MIDLANDS, at Pollokshields, on 5th July, 1952.
West won by 8 rubbers, 17 sets, 129 games to 1 rubber, 5 sets, 87 games.

WEST *v.* AYRSHIRE, at Darvel, on 12th July, 1952.
West lost by 4 rubbers, 10 sets, 94 games to 5 rubbers, 11 sets, 98 games.

UNDER 21.

WEST *v.* EAST, at Craiglockhart, on 13th September, 1952.
West won Singles by 4 rubbers, 9 sets, 67 games to 2 rubbers, 4 sets, 54 games.
West drew Doubles by 1 rubber, 4 sets, 48 games to 1 rubber 4 sets, 42 games.
West won match by 5 rubbers, 13 sets, 115 games to 3 rubbers, 8 sets, 96 games.

MIXED DOUBLES.

WEST *v.* EAST, at Craiglockhart, on 3rd May, 1952.
West 8 rubbers, 18 sets, 188 games ; East 8 rubbers, 19 sets, 184 games.   Match drawn.

DOUBLES MATCH *v.* ULSTER LAWN TENNIS ASSOCIATION.   In Belfast on 21st June, 1952.   Rain stopped play.

(2). INTER-COUNTY CHAMPIONSHIPS ON HARD COURTS (SINGLES).

West beat Cumberland at Giffnock, on 13th October, 1951, by 12 rubbers to 0 rubbers.
West lost to Yorkshire at Huddersfield, on 27th October, 1951, by 4 rubbers to 8 rubbers.
The Team consisted of C. V. Baxter (Titwood), I. Campbell (Pollokshields), R. Morton (Giffnock), A. B. Murray (Pollokshields), J. G. Rutherglen (Newlands) and J. B. Wilson (Pollokshields).

(3). INTER-COUNTY CHAMPIONSHIPS ON GRASS (DOUBLES).

These matches were played during the week commencing 21st July, 1952.   Teams representing the Scottish Western Counties Lawn Tennis Association (which includes this Association) took part in the Competitions, the Women's Team playing at Budleigh Salterton in Group III., and the Men's Team at Minehead in Group III.   Both Teams remain in Group III.

Results of Women's Matches : West of Scotland lost to Essex, 3 rubbers, 8 sets, 91 games to 6 rubbers, 13 sets, 112 games ; lost to Lancashire, 4 rubbers, 8 sets, 90 games to 5 rubbers, 12 sets, 106 games ; beat Devon, 6 rubbers, 12 sets, 98 games to 3 rubbers, 7 sets, 85 games ; beat Buckinghamshire, 5 rubbers, 12 sets, 115 games to 4 rubbers, 10 sets, 112 games ; lost to Staffordshire, 4 rubbers, 8 sets, 80 games to 5 rubbers, 11 sets, 90 games.   The Team consisted of Miss M. S. Allan (Pollokshields), Mrs. I. M. Baird (Pollokshields), Mrs. L. S. Black (Pollokshields), Mrs. D. Dick (Pollokshields), Mrs. J. B. Harvey (Craighelen) *Captain*, Mrs. G. S. Horne (Pollokshields), Miss H. M. Macfarlane (Craighelen), and Miss I. S. Vallance (Pollokshields).

Results of Men's Matches.   West of Scotland lost to Gloucestershire, 3 rubbers, 6 sets 66 games to 6 rubbers, 12 sets, 93 games ; beat East of Scotland, 6 rubbers, 15 sets, 130 games to 3 rubbers, 7 sets, 94 games ; beat Berkshire 6 rubbers, 13 sets, 108 games to 3 rubbers, 8 sets, 86 games ; lost to Lancashire, 2 rubbers, 7 sets, 101 games to 7 rubbers, 15 sets, 124 games ; beat Hertfordshire, 8 rubbers, 16 sets, 137 games to 1 rubber, 6 sets, 103 games.   The Team consisted of C. V. Baxter (Titwood), T. Boyd (Giffnock), I. Campbell (Pollokshields), B. Fulton (Newlands), J. B. Fulton (Chapel Allarton) *Captain*, W. J. Reid (Western), J. G. Rutherglen (Newlands) and J. B. Wilson (Pollokshields).

Results of Matches played during Season 1953 in which Teams representing the West of Scotland Lawn Tennis Association took part.

(1). **INTER-ASSOCIATION REPRESENTATIVE MATCHES.**
WOMEN'S DOUBLES.
WEST *v.* CENTRAL, at Laurelhill, on 9th May, 1953.
   West won by 8 rubbers, 16 sets, 108 games to 1 rubber, 3 sets, 58 games.
WEST *v.* EAST, at Pollokshields, on 23rd May, 1953.
   West lost by 3 rubbers, 8 sets, 97 games to 6 rubbers, 12 sets, 107 games.
WEST *v.* AYRSHIRE, at Troon, on 20th June, 1953.
   West won by 6 rubbers, 12 sets, 80 games to 0 rubbers, 0 sets, 27 games.
WEST *v.* MIDLANDS, at Kelvinside, on 12th September, 1953.
   West won by 7 rubbers, 15 sets, 109 games to 2 rubbers, 4 sets, 66 games.
"UNDER 21."
WEST *v.* EAST, at Craiglockhart, on 12th September, 1953.
   West won by 7 rubbers, 15 sets, 104 games to 2 rubbers, 4 sets, 73 games.
MEN'S DOUBLES.
WEST *v.* CENTRAL, at Pollokshields, on 9th May, 1953.
   West won Singles by 6 rubbers, 12 sets, 78 games to 0 rubbers, 0 sets, 32 games.
   West won Doubles by 3 rubbers, 6 sets, 36 games to 0 rubbers, 0 sets, 17 games.
   West won Match by 9 rubbers, 18 sets, 114 games to 0 rubbers, 0 sets, 49 games.
WEST *v.* EAST, at Craiglockhart, on 23rd May. 1953.
   West lost Singles by 2 rubbers, 5 sets, 42 games to 4 rubbers, 8 sets, 65 games.
   West lost Doubles by 1 rubbers, 2 sets, 26 games to 2 rubbers, 5 sets, 37 games.
   West lost Match by 3 rubbers, 7 sets, 68 games to 6 rubbers, 13 sets, 102 games.
WEST *v.* AYRSHIRE, at Pollokshields, on 11th July, 1953.
   West won by 6 rubbers, 12 sets, 88 games to 0 rubbers, 3 sets, 61 games.
WEST *v.* MIDLANDS, at Dundee, on 12th September, 1953.
   West lost by 3 rubber, 11 sets, 118 games to 5 rubbers, 13 sets, 118 games.
"UNDER 21."
WEST *v.* EAST, at Whitecraigs, on 12th September, 1953.
   West won Singles by 5 rubbers, 10 sets, 72 games to 1 rubber, 4 sets, 58 games.
   West won Doubles by 3 rubbers, 6 sets, 46 games to 0 rubbers, 1 set, 33 games.
   West won Match by 8 rubbers, 16 sets, 118 games to 1 rubber, 5 sets, 91 games.
MIXED DOUBLES.
WEST *v.* EAST, at Pollokshields, on 2nd May, 1953.
   West 8 rubbers, 19 sets, 183 games }
   East 8 rubbers, 17 sets, 168 games } Match drawn.
DOUBLES MATCH *v.* ULSTER LAWN TENNIS ASSOCIATION.
   At Pollokshields, on 5th September, 1953. Rain stopped play.

(2). **INTER-COUNTY CHAMPIONSHIPS ON HARD COURTS. (SINGLES).**
   West beat Cumberland at Carlisle, on 4th October, 1952, by 12 rubbers to 0 rubbers.
   West beat Yorkshire at Pollokshields, on 11th October, 1952, by 8 rubbers to 4 rubbers.
   West beat Northamptonshire, at Pollokshields, on 25th October, 1952, by 8 rubbers to 4 rubbers.
   West lost to Middlesex at Birmingham, on 27th March, 1953, by 0 rubbers to 12 rubbers in the Semi-Final.

(3). **INTER-COUNTY CHAMPIONSHIPS ON GRASS. (DOUBLES).**
   These matches were played during the week commencing 20th July, 1953. Teams representing the Scottish Western Counties Lawn Tennis Association (which includes this Association), took part in the Competitions, the Women's Team playing at Budleigh Salterton in Group III, and the Men's Team at Folkestone in Group III. The Women's Team gained third place and remain in Group III. The Men's Team were successful in gaining first place and will be promoted to Group II.

   Results of Women's Matches :—West of Scotland lost to Hertfordshire, 4 rubbers, 10 sets, 93 games to 5 rubbers, 10 sets, 92 games ; lost to Nottinghamshire, 2 rubbers, 7 sets, 90 games to 7 rubbers, 14 sets, 101 games ; beat Cheshire, 6 rubbers, 13 sets, 121 games to 3 rubbers, 9 sets, 106 games ; beat Buckinghamshire, 5 rubbers, 11 sets, 113 games to 4 rubbers, 9 sets, 99 games ; beat Berkshire, 6 rubbers, 12 sets, 91 games to 3 rubbers, 7 sets, 82 games ; The Team consisted of Mrs. I. M. Baird (Pollokshields), Mrs. L. S. Black (Pollokshields), Mrs. D. Dick (Pollokshields), Miss K. A. Gillespie (Newlands), Mrs. J. B. Harvey (Craighelen), Captain, Miss H M. Macfarlane (Craighelen), and Miss L. S. Vallance (Pollokshields).

   Results of Men's Matches : West of Scotland beat Cambridgeshire, 5 rubbers, 12 sets, 101 games to 4 rubbers, 11 sets, 115 games ; lost to Cheshire, 2 rubbers, 6 sets, 75 games to 7 rubbers, 14 sets, 110 games ; beat Leicestershire, 6 rubbers, 12 sets, 107 games to 3 rubbers, 10 sets, 100 games ; beat Hertfordshire, 6 rubbers, 13 sets, 117 games to 3 rubbers, 8 sets, 90 games : beat Hampshire, 7 rubbers, 15 sets, 114 games to 2 rubbers, 5 sets, 75 games. The team consisted of C. V. Baxter (Titwood), T. Boyd (Giffnock), I. M. Campbell (Pollokshields), J. B. Fulton (Chapel Allarton), Captain, (I. Loudon (Titwood), J. G. Rutherglen (Newlands), R. Smith (Western) and J. B. Wilson (Pollokshields).

Results of Matches played during Season 1954 in which Teams representing the West of Scotland Lawn Tennis Association took part.

(1). INTER-ASSOCIATION REPRESENTATIVE MATCHES.

LADIES' DOUBLES.

WEST *v.* EAST at Craiglockhart, on 22nd May, 1954.
    Match cancelled due to rain.

WEST *v.* MIDLANDS, at Dundee, on 3rd July, 1954.   Match abandoned due to rain.

WEST *v.* CENTRAL at Pollokshields, on 7th August, 1954.
    West won by 9 rubbers, 18 sets, 116 games to 0 rubbers, 1 set, 43 games.

WEST *v.* AYRSHIRE, at Pollokshields, on 14th August, 1954.   Match cancelled.

"UNDER 21."

WEST *v.* EAST, at Cardonald, on 11th September, 1954.
    West won by 5 rubbers, 10 sets, 77 games to 1 rubber, 2 sets, 59 games.

MEN'S DOUBLES.

WEST *v.* EAST, at Pollokshields, on 22nd May, 1954.   Match cancelled due to rain.

WEST *v.* MIDLANDS, at Pollokshields, on 3rd July, 1954.
    West won by 5 rubbers, 10 sets, 68 games to 0 rubbers, 1 set, 35 games.

WEST *v.* AYRSHIRE, at Ayr, on 10th July, 1954.
    West won by 9 rubbers, 12 sets to 0 rubbers, 1 set.

WEST *v.* CENTRAL, at Grangemouth, on 7th August, 1954.
    West won by 9 rubbers, 18 sets, 115 games to 0 rubbers, 2 sets, 51 games.

"UNDER 21."

WEST *v.* EAST, at Craiglockhart, on 11th September, 1954.   Match abandoned due to rain.

MIXED DOUBLES.

WEST *v.* EAST, at Craiglockhart, on 1st May, 1954.
    West won by 9 rubbers, 21 sets, 197 games to 7 rubbers, 16 sets, 173 games.

DOUBLES MATCH.

WEST *v.* ULSTER, at Belfast, on 11th September, 1954.
    Ladies' Doubles.   West won by 2 rubbers, 4 sets, 36 games to 0 rubbers, 2 sets, 27 games.
    Men's Doubles.   West won by 2 rubbers, 4 sets, 34 games to 0 rubbers, 2 sets, 30 games.
    Mixed Doubles.   West won by 4 rubbers, 8 sets, 59 games to 0 rubbers, 1 set, 38 games.
        Total.   West won by 8 rubbers, 16 sets, 129 games to 0 rubbers, 5 sets, 95 games.

(2). INTER-COUNTY CHAMPIONSHIPS ON HARD COURTS. (SINGLES).

WEST *v.* CUMBERLAND, at Carlisle, on 3rd October, 1953.
    West won by 12 rubbers, 24 sets, to 0 rubbers, 0 sets.

WEST *v.* YORKSHIRE, at Huddersfield, on 10th October, 1953.
    West won by 7 rubbers, 16 sets to 5 rubbers, 12 sets.

WEST *v.* CHESHIRE, at Wallasey, on 24th October, 1953.
    West lost by 6 rubbers 15 sets to 6 rubbers, 16 sets.

(3). INTER-COUNTY CHAMPIONSHIPS ON GRASS. (DOUBLES).

These matches were played during the week commencing 19th July, 1954. Teams representing the Scottish Western Counties Lawn Tennis Association (which includes this Association), took part in the Competitions, the Ladies' Team playing at Folkestone in Group III. and the Men's Team at Scarborough in Group II. Both teams were successful in gaining second place in their respective Groups, and will be promoted to the next higher Group for 1955.

Results of Ladies' Matches :—West of Scotland beat Gloucestershire, 5 rubbers, 11 sets, 104 games to 4 rubbers, 9 sets, 93 games ; lost to South Wales, 4 rubbers, 12 sets, 112 games to 5 rubbers, 11 sets, 99 games ; lost to East of Scotland, 3 rubbers, 8 sets, 111 games to 6 rubbers, 14 sets, 138 games ; beat Berkshire, 9 rubbers, 18 sets, 121 games to 0 rubbers, 3 sets, 69 games ; beat Dorset, 8 rubbers, 16 sets, 119 games to 1 rubber, 4 sets, 76 games ; The Team consisted of Mrs. L. S. Black (Pollokshields), Miss K. A. Gillespie (Newlands), Mrs. J. B. Harvey (Craighelen) Captain, Mrs. K. Horne (Dulwich), Miss H. M. Macfarlane (Craighelen), Miss C. Dunglison (Bridge of Allan) and Miss I. S. Vallance (Pollokshields).

Results of Men's Matches :—West of Scotland lost to Yorkshire, 3 rubbers, 8 sets 98 games to 6 rubbers, 12 sets, 111 games lost to Essex, 4 rubbers, 10 sets, 101 games to 5 rubbers, 10 sets, 103 games ; beat Gloucestershire, 7 rubbers, 15 sets, 122 games to 2 rubbers, 6 sets, 95 games ; beat Cheshire, 7 rubbers, 15 sets, 130 games to 2 rubbers, 6 sets, 106 games ; beat Derbyshire, 8 rubbers, 16 sets, 123 games to 1 rubber, 4 sets, 67 games. The Team consisted of C. V. Baxter (Titwood), T. Boyd (Giffnock), I. M. Campbell (Pollokshields), W. C. Gillespie (Newlands), R. G. Harris (Titwood), I. Loudon (Titwood), J. G. Rutherglen (Newlands) and J. B. Wilson (Pollokshields). Dr. J. B. Fulton (Chapel Allarton) acted as non-playing Captain.

Results of Matches played during Season 1955 in which Teams representing the West of Scotland Lawn Tennis Association took part.

(1). INTER-ASSOCIATION REPRESENTATIVE MATCHES.

LADIES' DOUBLES.

WEST *v.* CENTRAL at I.C.I., Grangemouth, on 7th May, 1955.
 West won by 7 rubbers, 14 sets, 96 games to 0 rubbers, 2 sets, 51 games.

WEST *v.* EAST, at Pollokshields, on 21st May, 1955.
 West won by 5 rubbers, 12 sets, 100 games to 4 rubbers, 8 sets, 76 games.

WEST *v.* MIDLANDS, at Pollokshields, on 2nd July, 1955.
 Match cancelled.

WEST *v.* AYRSHIRE at Ayr, on 9th July, 1955.
 West won by 9 rubbers, 18 sets, 117 games to 0 rubbers, 3 sets, 61 games.

"UNDER 21."

WEST *v.* EAST, at Craiglockhart, on 10th September, 1955.
 West lost by 3 rubbers, 6 sets, 63 games to 3 rubbers, 7 sets, 64 games.

MEN'S DOUBLES.

WEST *v.* CENTRAL, at Thorn Park, on 7th May, 1955.
 West won by 6 rubbers. 12 sets, 89 games to 0 rubbers, 1 set, 49 games.

WEST *v.* EAST, at Craig lockhart, on 21st May, 1955.
 Match abandoned due to rain.

WEST *v.* MIDLANDS, at Dundee, on 2nd July, 1955.
 Match cancelled.

WEST *v.* AYRSHIRE, at Pollokshields, on 9th July, 1955.
 West won by 5 rubbers, 10 sets, 86 games to 1 rubber, 5 sets, 68 games.

"UNDER 21."

WEST *v.* EAST, at Whitecraigs, on 10th September, 1955.
 West won by 5 rubbers, 12 sets, 107 games to 4 rubbers, 10 sets, 103 games.

MIXED DOUBLES.

WEST *v.* EAST, at Meikleriggs, on 30th April, 1955.
 West, 8 rubbers, 22 sets, 208 games—East, 8 rubbers, 18 sets, 177 games.   Match drawn.

(2). INTER-COUNTY CHAMPIONSHIPS ON HARD COURTS, 1954-55. (SINGLES).

WEST *v.* CUMBERLAND, at Carlisle, on 25th September, 1954.
 West won by 11 rubbers, 23 sets, 154 games to 1 rubber, 3 sets, 70 games.

WEST *v.* YORKSHIRE, at Poloc, on 9th October, 1954.
 West won by 4 rubbers, 9 sets, 79 games to 2 rubbers, 7 sets, 61 games.

WEST *v.* LANCASHIRE, at Cardonald, Pollokshields and Newlands, on 19th March, 1955.
 West won by 8 rubbers, 16 sets, 145 games to 4 rubbers, 12 sets, 139 games.

WEST *v.* WARWICKSHIRE, at Birmingham, on 25th March, 1955.
 West lost by 0 rubbers, 1 set, 35 games to 6 rubbers, 12 sets, 75 games.

(3). INTER-COUNTY CHAMPIONSHIPS ON GRASS, 1955. (DOUBLES).

These matches were played during the week commencing 18th July, 1955.   Teams representing the Scottish Western Counties Lawn Tennis Association (which includes this Association), took part in the Competitions, the Ladies' Team playing at Scarborough in Group II. and the Men's Team at Eastbourne in Group I.   The Ladies' Team gained third place and missed promotion by a narrow margin.   The Men's Team did not win any of their Matches.

Results of Ladies' Matches :—West of Scotland lost to Hertfordshire, 4 rubbers, 10 sets, 96 games to 5 rubbers, 10 sets, 90 games; lost to Yorkshire, 2 rubbers, 5 sets, 77 games to 7 rubbers, 15 sets, 106 games ; beat Sussex, 5 rubbers, 11 sets, 91 games to 4 rubbers, 9 sets, 93 games ; beat East of Scotland, 6 rubbers, 13 sets, 106 games to 3 rubbers, 7 sets, 76 games; beat Wiltshire, 7 rubbers, 14 sets, 103 games to 2 rubbers, 5 sets, 66 games. The Team consisted of Miss M. B. Bell (Pollokshields), Mrs. L. S. Black (Pollokshields), Mrs. D. H. Dick (Pollokshields), Miss K. A. Gillespie (Newlands), Mrs. J. B. Harvey (Craighelen), *Captain*, Miss M. I. Harvey (Craighelen), Mrs. G. S. Horne (Dulwich) and Miss H. M. Macfarlane (Craighelen).

Results of Men's Matches :—West of Scotland lost to Surrey, 2 rubbers, 4 sets, 69 games to 7 rubbers, 14 sets, 103 games ; lost to Essex, 2 rubbers, 6 sets, 106 games to 7 rubbers, 16 sets, 131 games ; lost to Warwickshire, 2 rubbers, 6 sets, 93 games to 7 rubbers, 15 sets, 127 games ; lost to Lancashire, 2 rubbers, 7 sets, 106 games to 7 rubbers, 14 sets, 122 games ; lost to Middlesex, 2 rubbers, 6 sets, 102 games to 7 rubbers, 15 sets, 135 games.   The Team consisted of C. V. Baxter (Titwood) , T. Boyd (Giffnock), I. M. Campbell (Pollokshields), W. C. Gillespie (Newlands), M. A. MacDonald (Pollokshields), J.G. Rutherglen (Newlands), and J. B. Wilson (Pollokshields).   R. G. Harris (Polllokshields), was unable to take part and Dr. J. B. Fulton (Chapel Allerton) acted as non-playing Captain.

Results of Matches played during the Season 1958 in which Teams representing the West of Scotland Lawn Tennis Association took part.

(1). INTER-ASSOCIATION REPRESENTATIVE MATCHES.

LADIES' DOUBLES.

West *v*. East at Craiglockhart, on 17th May. 1958.
   West won by 5 rubbers, 11 sets, 104 games to 4 rubbers, 9 sets, 104 games.
West *v*. Ayrshire, at Pressed Steel, Linwood, on 28th June, 1958.
   West won by 5 rubbers, 11 sets 95 games to 4 rubbers, 9 sets, 91 games.
West *v*. Midlands, at Broughty Ferry, on 5th July, 1958.
   West won by 6 rubbers, 12 sets, 97 games to 3 rubbers, 8 sets, 89 games.
West *v*. Central—unplayed.

"UNDER 21."

West *v*. East, at Partickhill, on 6th September, 1958.   Match cancelled due to rain.

"18 and UNDER."

West *v*. Midlands, at Ferguslie, on 30th August, 1958.
   West won by 7 rubbers, 16 sets, 106 games to 0 rubbers, 2 sets, 43 games.

MEN'S DOUBLES.

West *v*. East, at Pollokshields, on 17th May, 1958.
West won by 5 rubbers, 12 sets, 131 games to 4 rubbers, 10 sets, 119 games.
West *v*. Ayrshire, at Troon, on 28th June, 1958.
   West won by 5 rubbers, 10 sets, 78 games to 1 rubber, 3 sets, 59 games.
West *v*. Midlands, at Pollokshields, on 5th July, 1958.
   West won by 6 rubbers, 13 sets, 109 games to 2 rubbers, 6 sets, 79 games.
West *v*. Central—unplayed.

"UNDER 21."

West *v* Central, at Westerton, on 2nd August, 1958.
   West lost by 4 rubbers, 9 sts, 80 games to 5 rubbers, 11 sets, 86 games.
West *v*. East, at Craiglockhart, on 6th September, 1958.   Match cancelled due to rain.

"18 and UNDER."

West *v*. Midlands, at Broughty Ferry Games Club, on 30th August, 1958.
   West won by 5 rubbers, 11 sets, 71 games to 0 rubbers, 1 set, 31 games.

MIXED DOUBLES.

West *v*. East, at Craiglockhart, on 3rd May, 1958.
   West lost by 5 rubbers, 12 sets, 160 games to 10 rubbers, 22 sets, 186 games.

(2). INTER-COUNTY CHAMPIONSHIPS ON GRASS. (DOUBLES).

These matches were played during the week commencing 21st July, 1958. Teams representing the Scottish Western Counties Lawn Tennis Association (which includes this Association) took part in the Competitions, the Ladies' Team playing at Scarborough in Group II. and the Men's Team at Southsea in Group II. Both Teams finished in fifth place and will play in Group III. in 1959.

Results of Ladies' Matches: West of Scotland beat Sussex, 5 rubbers, 10 sets, 88 games to 4 rubbers, 10 sets, 90 games; beat East of Scotland 5 rubbers, 11 sets, 110 games to 4 rubbers, 11 sets, 106 games; lost to Middlesex, 3 rubbers, 7 sets 89 games to 6 rubbers, 14 sets, 117 games; lost to Nottinghamshire, 4 rubbers, 9 sets, 84 games to 5 rubbers, 10 sets 89 games; lost to Devon, 3 rubbers, 8 sets, 80 games to 6 rubbers, 14 sets, 119 games.   The Team consisted of Mrs. I. M Baird (Pollokshields), Miss M. B. Bell (Pollokshields), Mrs. L. S. Black (Pollokshields), Captain, Miss C. E. Dunglison (Pollokshields), Miss M. Ferguson (Ardgowan), Miss K. A. Gillespie (Newlands), Mrs. G. S. Horne (Dulwich) and Miss E A. Walker (Ayr).

Results of Men's Matches :—West of Scotland lost to Warwickshire, 3 rubbers, 7 sets, 87 games to 6 rubbers, 12 sets 110 games; lost to Gloucestershire, 0 rubbers, 5 sets, 90 games to 9 rubbers, 18 sets, 133 games; lost to Kent, 4 rubbers 12 sets, 126 games to 5 rubbers, 14 sets, 139 games; lost to Derbyshire, 3 rubbers, 6 sets, 89 games to 6 rubbers, 12 sets 101 games; the match against Nottinghamshire who finished in sixth place was not played due to rain.   The Team consisted of C. V. Baxter (Titwood), T. Boyd (Newlands), W. C. Gillespie (Newlands), K. B. Gray (Newlands), A. G. McNeilage (Hillpark), J. G. Rutherglen (Newlands), and J. B. Wilson (Cardonald). Dr. J. B. Fulton (Chapel Allarton) acted as non-playing Captain.

Results of Matches played during the Season 1959 in which Teams representing the West of Scotland Lawn Tennis Association took part.

(1). INTER-ASSOCIATION REPRESENTATIVE MATCHES.

LADIES' DOUBLES.

West v. Central at Castings, Falkirk, on 9th May, 1959.
 West won by 7 rubbers, 15 sets, 117 games to 2 rubbers, 5 sets, 83 games.

West v. East at Pollokshields, on 16th May, 1959.
 West lost by 4 rubbers 8 sets, 75 games to 5 rubbers, 11 sets, 85 games.

West v. Ayrshire, at Ardeer, on 27th June, 1959.
 West won by 7 rubbers, 14 sets, 121 games to 2 rubbers, 6 sets, 62 games.

West v. Midlands, at Pollokshields, on 4th July, 1959.
 West lost by 4 rubbers, 8 sets, 91 games to 5 rubbers, 10 sets, 98 games.

West v. Perth and District, at Perth, on 22nd August. 1959.
 West won by 9 rubbers, 18 sets, 113 games to 0 rubbers, 1 set, 51 games.

" UNDER 21."

West v. East, at Craiglockhart, on 5th September, 1959.
 West won by 5 rubbers, 13 sets, 97 games to 2 rubbers, 5 sets, 60 games.

" 18 and UNDER."

West v. Midlands, at Broughty Ferry, on 29th August, 1959.
 West won by 6 rubbers, 13 sets, 111 games to 3 rubbers, 7 sets, 78 games.

MEN'S DOUBLES.

West v. Central, at Templeton, on 9th May, 1959.
 West won by 5 rubbers, 10 sets, 71 games to 1 rubber, 2 sets, 49 games.

West v. East, at Craiglockhart, on 16th May, 1959.
 West won by 5 rubbers, 13 sets, 122 games to 4 rubbers, 8 sets, 100 games.

West v. Ayrshire, at Pressed Steel, on 27th June, 1959.
 West won by 6 rubbers, 12 sets, 79 games to 0 rubbers, 0 sets, 38 games.

West v. Midlands, at Invergowrie, on 4th July, 1959.
 West won by 5 rubbers, 11 sets, 78 games to 1 rubber 4 sets, 53 games.

West v. Perth and District, at Scone, on 22nd August, 1959.
 West won by 5 rubbers, 11 sets, 85 games to 1 rubber, 4 sets, 60 games.

" UNDER 21."

West v. Central, at Livilands, on 1st August, 1959.
 West won by 6 rubbers, 12 sets, 101 games to 3 rubbers, 7 sets, 72 games.

West v. East, at Partickhill, on 5th September, 1959 (6 singles, 3 doubles).
 West won by 7 rubbers, 14 sets, 118 games to 2 rubbers, 6 sets, 90 games.

" 18 and UNDER."

West v. Midlands, at Pollokshields, on 29th August, 1959.
 West won by 7 rubbers, 16 sets, 104 games to 0 rubbers, 2 sets, 56 games.

MIXED DOUBLES.

West v. East, at Ferguslie, on 2nd May, 1959.

West lost by 6 rubbers, 17 sets, 197 games to 10 rubbers, 22 sets, 212 games.

(2). INTER-COUNTY CHAMPIONSHIPS ON HARD COURTS, 1958-59—(SINGLES).

At Pollokshields, on 20th September, 1958.

West lost to Yorkshire by 3 rubbers, 8 sets, 96 games to 9 rubbers, 20 sets, 142 games.

At Newcastle, on 4th October, 1958.

West beat Northumberland by 10 rubbers, 22 sets, 165 games to 2 rubbers, 7 sets, 111 games.

At Western on 11th October, 1958.

West lost to Durham by 6 rubbers, 14 sets, 144 games to 6 rubbers, 16 sets, 144 games

The following players took part:—C. V. Baxter (Titwood), G. Copeland (Hamilton), A. D. Culloch (Paisley), W. C. Gillespie (Newlands), K. B. Gray (Newlands), G. B. Kerr (Newlands), F. A. S. Paul (Darvel), J. G. Rutherglen (Newlands) J. B. Wilson (Cardonald).

(3). INTER-COUNTY CHAMPIONSHIPS ON GRASS, 1959—(DOUBLES).

These matches were played during the week commencing 20th July, 1959. Teams representing the Scottish Western Counties Lawn Tennis Association (which includes this Association), took part in the Competitions; the Ladies' Team playing at Ilkley in Group III., and the Men's Team at Minehead, in Group III. The Ladies did not win any of the 5 matches played and will play in Group IV. next year. The Men won 4 of the 5 matches played, taking second place, and will play in Group II. next year.

Results of Ladies' Matches:—West lost to Hertfordshire, 3 rubbers, 7 sets, 89 games to 6 rubbers, 13 sets 112 games; lost to Nottinghamshire, 1 rubber, 6 sets, 86 games to 8 rubbers, 16 sets, 125 games; lost to Staffordshire, 4 rubbers 9 sets, 102 games, to 5 rubbers, 12 sets, 114 games; lost to Berkshire, 3 rubbers, 10 sets, 103, games to 6 rubbers, 12 sets 116 games; lost to Wiltshire, 3 rubbers, 8 sets, 84 games to 6 rubbers, 13 sets, 101 games. The Team consisted of Mrs I. M. Baird (Pollokshields), Mrs. L. S. Black (Pollokshields), *Captain*, Miss C. E. Dunglison (Pollokshields), Miss M. Ferguson (Ardgowan), Mrs. G. S. Horne (Dulwich), Miss F. V. M. MacLennan (Newlands), Miss I. B. Miller (Pollokshields), Miss M. K. Steuart-Corry (Helensburgh).

Results of Men's Matches:—West beat Northamptonshire, 5 rubbers, 11 sets, 101 games to 4 rubbers, 9 sets, 97 game lost to Staffordshire, 4 rubbers, 11 sets, 125 games to 5 rubbers, 13 sets, 122 games; beat Durham, 6 rubbers, 15 sets 139 games to 3 rubbers, 8 sets, 115 games; beat Hampshire, 8 rubbers 17 sets, 140 games to 1 rubber, 4 sets, 109 games; beat Cheshire, 6 rubbers, 12 sets, 100 games to 3 rubbers, 7 sets, 87 games. The Team consisted of C. V. Baxter (Titwood); W. C. Gillespie (Newlands), K. B. Gray (Newlands), M. A. McDonald (Titwood), A. G. McNeilage (Hillpark), J. G. Rutherglen (Newlands), J. B. Wilson (Cardonald), J. Wood (Pollokshields), Dr. J. B. Fulton (Chapel Allerton) acted as non-playing Captain.

Results of Matches played during 1961 in which Teams representing the West of Scotland Lawn Tennis Association took part.

(1). INTER-ASSOCIATION REPRESENTATIVE MATCHES.

LADIES' DOUBLES.

West v. East at Pollokshields, on 20th May, 1961.
West lost by 4 rubbers, 9 sets, 94 games to 5 rubbers, 12 sets, 106 games.

West v. Central at Bridge of Allan, on 24th June, 1961.
West won by 9 rubbers, 18 sets, 120 games to 0 rubbers, 1 set, 47 games.

West v. Midlands at Rutherglen, on 1st July, 1961.
West won by 8 rubbers, 16 sets, 105 games to 1 rubber, 2 sets, 53 games.

West v. Ayrshire, at I.C.I., Ardeer, on 8th July, 1961.
West won by 6 rubbers, 12 sets, 79 games to 0 rubbers, 1 set, 37 games.

FRIENDLY MATCH.

West of Scotland L.T.A. v. Durham County L.T.A., at Partickhill on 11th June, 1961.
West won by 6 rubbers, 13 sets, 120 games to 3 rubbers, 8 sets, 102 games.

" UNDER 21."

West v. East, at Craiglockhart, on 16th September, 1961.
Match cancelled due to storm.

" 18 AND UNDER."

West v. Midlands, at Kinnoull, Perth, on 26th August, 1961.
West won by 7 rubbers, 16 sets, 128 games to 2 rubbers, 7 sets, 96 games.

MEN'S DOUBLES.

West v. East, at Craiglockhart, on 20th May, 1961.
West lost by 1 rubber, 5 sets, 95 games to 8 rubbers, 17 sets, 132 games.

West v. Central, at Pollokshields, on 24th June, 1961.
West won by 8 rubbers, 16 sets, 128 games to 1 rubber, 6 sets, 94 games.

West v. Midlands, at Dundee West End, on 1st July, 1961.
West won by 5 rubbers, 12 sets, 115 games to 4 rubbers 10 sets, 98 games.

West v. Ayrshire, at Pollokshields, on 8th July, 1961.
West won by 6 rubbers, 12 sets, 77 games to 0 rubbers, 1 set, 40 games.

FRIENDLY MATCH.

West of Scotland L.T.A. v. Civil Service L.T.A., at Pollokshields, on 10th September, 1961.
West won by 7 rubbers, 14 sets, 101 games to 2 rubbers, 5 sets, 75 games.

" UNDER 21."

West v. Central, at Stirling, on 5th August, 1961.
   West won by 6 rubbers, 12 sets, 83 games to 3 rubbers, 8 sets, 74 games.
West v. East at Poloc, on 16th September, 1961.
   West led by 4 rubbers to 2 rubbers when storm stopped play.

"18 AND UNDER."

West v. Midlands, at Kelvinside, on 26th August, 1961.
   Match cancelled due to rain.

MIXED DOUBLES.

West v. East at Ferguslie, on 6th May, 1961.
   West won by 10 rubbers, 24 sets, 202 games to 6 rubbers, 15 sets, 154 games.

(2). INTER-COUNTY CHAMPIONSHIPS ON GRASS (DOUBLES).

These matches were played during the week commencing 24th July, 1961. Teams representing the Scottish Western Counties Lawn Tennis Association (which includes this Association) took part, the Ladies' Team playing at Ilkley in Group IV., and the Men's Team at Scarborough, in Group III. The Ladies' Team won three of the five matches played taking third place and will play in Group IV. next year. The Men's Team won two of the five matches played, taking fourth place, and will play in Group III. next year.

Results of Ladies' Matches:—West of Scotland lost to Berkshire, 4 rubbers, 9 sets, 100 games to 5 rubbers, 11 sets, 101 games; beat Hertfordshire, 6 rubbers, 14 sets, 124 games to 3 rubbers, 11 sets, 113 games; beat Leicestershire, 5 rubbers, 11 sets, 102 games to 4 rubbers, 9 sets, 97 games; lost to Durham, 3 rubbers, 8 sets, 82 games to 6 rubbers 13 sets, 108 games; beat South Wales, 5 rubbers, 13 sets, 108 games to 4 rubbers, 8 sets, 94 games. The Team consisted of Mrs. L. S. Black (Pollokshields), Captain, Miss E. H. Baird (Hillpark,) Miss C. E. Dunglison (Pollokshields), Miss M. Ferguson (Ardgowan), Miss A. G. McAlpine (Bellahouston), Miss B. J. McCallum (Newlands), Mrs. E. Mackenzie (Partickhill), and Miss I. B. Miller (Pollokshields).

Results of Men's Matches:—West of Scotland lost to Staffordshire, 4 rubbers, 11 sets, 107 games to 5 rubbers, 12 sets 113 games; lost to North Wales, 3 rubbers, 8 sets, 87 games to 6 rubbers, 12 sets, 101 games; beat Worcestershire 5 rubbers, 12 sets, 115 games to 4 rubbers, 9 sets, 99 games; lost to Northamptonshire, 4 rubbers, 10 sets, 91 games to 5 rubbers, 10 sets, 100 games; beat Sussex, 6 rubbers, 14 sets, 120 games to 3 rubbers, 9 sets, 104 games. The Team consisted of C. V. Baxter (Titwood), D. D. Bell (Pollokshields), A. D. Culloch (Cardonald), W. C. Gillespie (Newlands) K. B. Gray (Newlands), J. G. Rutherglen (Newlands), J. B. Wilson (Cardonald), and J. T. Wood (Pollokshields). Dr. J. B. Fulton (Chapel Allerton) acted as non-playing captain.

(3). INTER-COUNTY CHAMPIONSHIPS ON HARD COURTS (SINGLES), 1960-61.

Preliminary Stage—

West of Scotland v. Northumberland, at Newcastle, on 24th September, 1960.
   West won by 8 rubbers, 18 sets, 168 games to 2 rubbers, 8 sets, 121 games.
West of Scotland v. Cumberland at Carlisle, on 1st October, 1960.
   West won by 11 rubbers, 22 sets, 143 games to 1 rubber, 2 sets, 57 games.
West of Scotland v. Durham, at Pollokshields, on 8th October, 1960.
   West won by 7 rubbers, 15 sets, 139 games to 5 rubbers, 12 sets, 124 games.

Intermediate Stage—

West of Scotland v. North Wales, at Wrexham, on 19th November, 1960.
   Drawn Match, 6 rubbers 15 sets, 144 games to 6 rubbers, 15 sets, 144 games.
   Replayed at Inverclyde, Largs, on 3rd December, 1960.
   West won by 6 rubbers, 15 sets, 139 games to 3 rubbers, 8 sets, 115 games.

Quarter-Final Stage—

West of Scotland v. Lancashire, at Inverclyde, Largs, on 25th February, 1961.
   West lost by 2 rubbers, 6 sets, 88 games to 10 rubbers, 22 sets, 154 games.

The following players took part:—C. V. Baxter (Titwood), 6; A. S. Black (Troon), 2; J. R. Coulter (Pollokshields) 2; A. D. Culloch (Cardonald) 5; G. T. Downes (Western), 1; W. C. Gillespie (Newlands) 3; K. B. Gray (Newlands), 6; J. G. Rutherglen (Newlands), 6; and J. B. Wilson (Cardonald), 5.

Results of Matches played during 1963 in which Teams representing the West of Scotland Lawn Tennis Association took part.

(1). INTER-ASSOCIATION REPRESENTATIVE MATCHES.
LADIES' DOUBLES.
West v. Central at Stirling, on 11th May, 1963.
  West won by 9 rubbers, 18 sets, 124 games, to 0 rubbers, 4 sets, 59 games.
West v. Midlands at Whitecraigs, on 29th June, 1963.
  West won by 7 rubbers, 14 sets, 98 games to 2 rubbers, 4 sets, 73 games.
West v. East. Rained off.

"UNDER 21."
West v. East, at Edinburgh, 7th September, 1963.
  East won by 5 rubbers, 13 sets, 111 games, to 4 rubbers, 10 sets, 104 games.

MEN'S DOUBLES.
West v. Central at Rutherglen, on 11th May, 1963.
  West won by 7 rubbers, 15 sets, 121 games to 2 rubbers, 7 sets, 83 games.
West v. East at Edinburgh, 18th May, 1963.
  West won by 7 rubbers, 16 sets, 127 games to 2 rubbers, 6 sets, 101 games.
West v. Midlands at Dundee, on 29th June, 1963.
  West won by 7 rubbers, 16 sets, 135 games to 2 rubbers, 5 sets, 79 games.
West v. Ayrshire at Pollokshields, on 7th September, 1963.
  West won by 8 rubbers, 16 sets, 105 games to 1 rubber, 3 sets, 57 games.

"UNDER 21."
West v. East at Pollokshields, on 7th September, 1963.
  West won by 4 rubbers, 9 sets, 69 games to 2 rubbers, 4 sets, 52 games.
West v. Central. Cancelled.
West v. East. Mixed Doubles. Senior. Rained off.

(2). INTER-COUNTY CHAMPIONSHIPS ON GRASS (DOUBLES).
These matches were played during the week commencing 22nd July, 1963. Teams representing the West of Scotland Lawn Tennis Association took part, the Ladies' Team playing at Frinton-on-Sea in Greoup 3, and the Men's Team at Southsea in Group 2. The Ladies' Team won five out of five matches played, taking First Place and will play in Group 2 next year. The Men's Team won One out of Five Matches played and will play in Group 3 next Year.

Results of Ladies' Matches:—West of Scotland beat Staffordshire 8 rubbers, 16 sets, 108 Games to 1 rubber, 3 sets, 68 games; beat Gloucestershire 5 rubbers, 13 sets, 108 games to 4 rubbers, 8 sets, 98 games; beat Cheshire 6 rubbers, 13 sets, 107 games to 3 rubbers, 9 sets, 97 games; beat Hampshire 6 rubbers, 13 sets, 117 games to 3 rubbers, 8 sets, 98 games; beat Nottinghamshire 7 rubbers, 15 sets, 107 games to 2 rubbers, 4 sets, 60 games.

The Team consisted of Mrs. L. S. Black (Bristol) Captain, Miss C. E. Dunglison, Miss M. Ferguson and Miss S. E. L. Moodie (Pollokshields), Miss A. G. McAlpine (Bellahouston), Miss F. V. MacLennan and Mrs. F. A. S. Paul (Newlands), Miss W. M. Shaw (Clarkston).

Results of Men's Matches:—West of Scotland lost to North Wales 4 rubbers, 10 sets, 121 games to 5 rubbers, 10 sets, 115 games; lost to Essex 1 rubber, 4 sets, 74 games to 8 rubbers, 17 sets, 117 games; lost to Kent 2 rubbers, 6 sets, 100 games to 7 rubbers, 14 sets, 123 games; beat Cheshire 5 rubbers, 11 sets, 114 games to 4 rubbers, 11 sets, 114 games; lost to Derbyshire 2 rubbers, 5 sets, 89 games to 7 rubbers, 16 sets, 131 games.

The Team consisted of C. V. Baxter (Titwood), A. D. Culloch (Cardonald), G. T. Downes (Pollokshields), W. C. Gillespie K. B. Gray, G. B. Kerr (Newlands), R. B. Low (Western), H. S. Matheson (Hillpark), Dr. J. B. Fulton (Chapel Allerton) acted as Non-Playing Captain.

(3). INTER-COUNTY CHAMPIONSHIPS ON HARD COURTS (SINGLES), 1961-63.
Preliminary Stage—
West of Scotland v. Cumberland at Carlisle, on 6th October, 1962.
  West won by 11 rubbers, 23 sets, 156 games to 1 rubber, 3 sets, 61 games.
West of Scotland v. Yorkshire at Paisley, on 29th September, 1962.
  West lost by 6 rubbers, 13 sets, 131 games to 6 rubbers, 14 sets, 136 games.
  Yorkshire won this Section.

The following players took part:—C. V. Baxter (Titwood), W. C. Gillespie (Newlands), R. B. Low (Western), H. Matheson (Hillpark), J. R. McAlpine (Bellahouston), T. C. MacNair (Poloc), J. B. Wilson (Cardonald), T. Walker (Western), J. G. Rutherglen (Newlands).

INTER-ASSOCIATION REPRESENTATIVE MATCHES.

LADIES

West v. East. Ladies at Helensburgh, 13/5/67.
>West won by 5 rubbers to 4 rubbers.

MEN

East v. West. Men at Edinburgh, 13/5/67. Rained off.

MIXED DOUBLES

West v. East. Mixed Doubles at Ferguslie, 30/4/67.
>East won by 9 rubbers to 7 rubbers.

West v. Ayrshire at Kingswood, 9/7/67.
>West won by 7 rubbers to 2 rubbers.

INTER-COUNTY CHAMPIONSHIPS ON GRASS (DOUBLES).

These matches were played during the week commencing 24th July, 1967. Teams representing the West of Scotland Lawn Tennis Association took part, the Ladies' Team playing at Cromer and the Men at Frinton. The Ladies' Team won 5 out of 5 matches in Group 2 and will play in Group 1 next year. The Men's Team won 2 out of 5 matches in Group 2 and will play in the same Group next year.

The Ladies' Team consisted of Mrs. L. S. Black (Bristol), captain, Mrs. R. J. Livingstone, Miss M. J. Love, Mrs. H. Matheson, Miss S. E. L. Moodie, Miss F. V. M. MacLennan, Miss V. J. MacLennan, Miss W. M. Shaw, Mrs. F. A. S. Paul.

The Men's Team consisted of W. C. Gillespie (captain), M. D. Hall, G. Kerr, H. S. Matheson, N. Paterson, N. Thompson, I. Walker and T. Walker.

INTER-COUNTY CHAMPIONSHIPS ON HARD COURTS, 1966-67.

MEN

Preliminary Stage.
>West of Scotland beat Northumberland at Paisley on 10/9/66.
>>11 rubbers to 1 rubber.

>West of Scotland beat East of Scotland at Edinburgh on 2/10/66.
>>7 rubbers to 5 rubbers.

>West of Scotland beat Cumberland at Carlisle on 8/10/66.
>>10 rubbers to 2 rubbers.

>West of Scotland lost to Lancashire at Largs on 12/11/66.
>>2 rubbers to 10 rubbers.

The following players took part:—W. C. Gillespie, H. S. Matheson, J. Mackenzie, T. C. McNair, N. Paterson, A. T. Sibbald, I. Walker, G. Copeland, N. Thompson.

LADIES

West of Scotland beat Cheshire at Western L.T.C. on 16/4/67.
>6 rubbers to 3 rubbers.

Semi-Final at Bournemouth on 23/9/67.
>West of Scotland lost to Surrey.
>>3 rubbers to 6 rubbers.

The following players took part:—Mrs. R. J. Livingstone, Miss M. J. Love, Mrs. H. S. Matheson, Miss S. E. L. Moodie, Miss F. V. M. MacLennan, Miss V. J. MacLennan, Mrs. F. A. S. Paul, Miss W. M. Shaw.

INTER-ASSOCIATION REPRESENTATIVE MATCHES.

LADIES

East v. West. At Craiglockhart, 11/5/68.
    West led by 3 rubbers to nil (abandoned).
West v. Central. At Stepps, 19/5/68.
    West won by 5 rubbers to 1 rubber.
West v. Ayrshire. At Cardonald, 7/7/68.
    West won by 5 rubbers to 1 rubber.

MEN

West v. East. At Craighelen, 11/5/68.
    West won by 5 rubbers to 3 rubbers.
Central v. West. At Dollar, 19/5/68.
    West won by 8 rubbers to nil.

INTER-COUNTY CHAMPIONSHIPS ON GRASS (DOUBLES).

These matches were played during the week commencing 22nd July, 1968. Teams representing the West of Scotland Lawn Tennis Association took part, the Ladies' Team playing at Eastbourne and the Men at Cromer. The Ladies' Team won 1 out of 5 matches in Group 1 and will play in Group 2 next year. The Men's Team won none out of 5 matches in Group 2 and will play in Group 3 next year.

The Ladies' Team consisted of Mrs. L. S. Black (Bristol), captain, Miss M. J. Love, Miss S. E. L. Moodie, Miss F. V. M. Maclennan, Miss V. J. Maclennan, Miss H. McVie, Mrs. F. A. S. Paul, Miss W. M. Shaw and Miss E. Winning.

The Men's Team consisted of W. C. Gillespie (captain), G. Copeland, G. T. Downes, K. B. Gray, G. B. Kerr, H. S. Matheson, F. N. Thompson and I. Walker.

INTER-COUNTY CHAMPIONSHIPS ON HARD COURTS, 1967-68.

MEN

Preliminary Stage.
    West of Scotland beat Northumberland at Newcastle on 10/9/67.
        11 rubbers to 1 rubber.
    West of Scotland beat Cumberland at Paisley on 17/9/67.
        12 rubbers to nil.
    West of Scotland beat East of Scotland at Craighelen on 8/10/67.
        11 rubbers to 1 rubber.
    West of Scotland lost to Warwickshire at Birmingham on 12/11/67.
        1 rubber to 11 rubbers.
The following players took part:—W. C. Gillespie, I. C. Conway, K. B. Gray, M. Hall, H. S. Matheson, J. Mackenzie, T. C. McNair, N. Paterson, F. N. Thompson and I. Walker.

LADIES

Quarter Final.
    West of Scotland lost to Yorkshire at Bradford on 28/4/68.
        1 rubber to 8 rubbers.
The following players took part:—Miss M. J. Love, Miss I. Hunter, Miss S. E. L. Moodie, Miss V. J. Maclennan, Mrs. F. A. S. Paul and Mrs. A. Smith.

INTER-ASSOCIATION REPRESENTATIVE MATCHES.

LADIES

West v. Central. At Falkirk, 18/5/69.
West won by 6 rubbers to 2 rubbers.

West v. Ayrshire. At Darvel, 29/6/69.
West led by 2 rubbers to 1 rubber (abandoned).

MEN

West v. Ayrshire. At Thorn Park, 29/6/69.
West won by 8 rubbers to nil.

West v. Central. At Lenzie, 18/5/69.
West won by 7 rubbers to 1 rubber.

INTER-COUNTY CHAMPIONSHIPS ON GRASS (DOUBLES).

These matches were played during the week commencing 21st July, 1969. Teams representing the West of Scotland Lawn Tennis Association took part, the Ladies' Team playing at Cromer and the Men at Minehead. The Ladies' Team won 4 out of 5 matches in Group 2 and will play in Group 1 next year. The Men's Team won 4 out of 5 matches in Group 3 and will play in Group 2 next year.

The Ladies' Team consisted of Mrs. L. S. Black (Bristol), captain, Mrs. R. S. Allan, Mrs. R. J. Livingstone, Miss M. J. Love, Miss S. E. L. Moodie, Miss V. J. Maclennan, Mrs. F. A. S. Paul, Miss W. M. Shaw and Miss E. Winning.

The Men's Team consisted of W. C. Gillespie (captain), G. T. Downes, K. B. Gray, G. B. Kerr, J. Mackenzie, H. S. Matheson, F. N. Thompson and I. Walker.

INTER-COUNTY CHAMPIONSHIPS ON HARD COURTS, 1968-69.

MEN

Preliminary Stage.

West of Scotland beat Northumberland at Glasgow on 29/9/68.
11 rubbers to 1 rubber.

West of Scotland beat Cumberland at Carlisle on 21/9/68.
9 rubbers to 1 rubber.

West of Scotland beat Westmorland at Glasgow on 6/10/68.
12 rubbers to nil.

West of Scotland lost to Nottingham at Nottingham on 10/11/68.
3 rubbers to 9 rubbers.

The following players took part:—W. C. Gillespie, G. Copeland, K. B. Gray, G. B. Kerr, H. S. Matheson, J. Mackenzie, F. N. Thompson and I. Walker.

LADIES

Preliminary Stage.

West of Scotland beat Cumberland at Keswick on 15/9/68.
9 rubbers to nil.

West of Scotland beat Durham at Broomhill on 28/9/68.
9 rubbers to nil.

West of Scotland beat Northumberland at Newcastle on 29/9/68.
9 rubbers to nil.

West of Scotland beat Nottingham at Nottingham on 3/11/68.
5 rubbers to 4 rubbers.

Quarter Final.

West of Scotland lost to Warwickshire at Glasgow on 20/4/69.
2 rubbers to 7 rubbers.

The following players took part:—Miss M. J. Love, Miss V. J. Maclennan, Miss H. McVie, Mrs. H. S. Matheson, Miss S. E. L. Moodie, Mrs. F. A. S. Paul, Mrs. A. Smith and Miss E. N. Winning.

INTER-ASSOCIATION REPRESENTATIVE MATCHES

LADIES

West v. East. At Craighelen, 9/5/71.
    West won by 6 rubbers to 2.

West v. Central. At Falkirk, 16/5/71.
    West won by 7 rubbers to 1.

West v. Ayrshire. Abandoned.

MEN

West v. Ayrshire. Abandoned.

West v. Central. At Hamilton, 16/5/71.
    West won by 6 rubbers to 2.

West v. East. At Edinburgh, 9/5/71.
    West drew with East, 4 rubbers each.

INTER-COUNTY CHAMPIONSHIPS ON GRASS (DOUBLES).

These matches were played during the week commencing 19th July. Teams representing the West of Scotland Tennis Association took part, the Ladies' Team playing at Cromer and the men at Malvern. The Ladies' Team won 4 out of 5 matches in Group 2 and will play in Group 1 next year. The Men's Team won 5 out of 5 matches in Group 3 and will play in Group 2 next year.

The Ladies' Team consisted of Mrs. L. S. Black (Bristol), captain, Miss R. Allan, Mrs. A. Barrow, Mrs. C. A. R. Lockhart, Miss M. J. Love, Miss S. E. L. Moodie, Miss V. J. MacLennan, Mrs. F. A. S. Paul and Miss W. M. Shaw.

The Men's Team consisted of G. Copeland, G. T. Downes, H. Drummond, W. C. Gillespie, M. Hier, H. S. Matheson, F. N. Thompson and I. Walker. K. B. Gray acted as non-playing captain.

INTER-COUNTY CHAMPIONSHIPS ON HARD COURTS, 1970-71.

MEN

Quarter Final.
    West of Scotland beat Nottinghamshire in Glasgow on 17/4/71.
        8 rubbers to 3 rubbers.

Semi-final.
    West of Scotland lost to Essex at Bournemouth on 18/9/71.
        2 rubbers to 10 rubbers.

Play-off for Third Place.
    West of Scotland lost to Yorkshire at Bournemouth on 19/9/71.
        4 rubbers to 8 rubbers.

The following players took part :—G. Copeland, G. T. Downes, H. Drummond, W. C. Gillespie, H. S. Matheson, F. N. Thompson and I. Walker.

LADIES

Preliminary Stage.
    West of Scotland beat Durham in Glasgow on 27/9/70.
        9 rubbers to 0 rubbers.

    West of Scotland beat Northumberland at Newcastle on 6/9/70.
        5 rubbers to 4 rubbers.

    West of Scotland beat Cumberland in Glasgow on 20/9/70.
        9 rubbers to nil.

Intermediate Stage.
    West of Scotland beat Cheshire in Manchester on 8/11/70.
        4 rubbers to 2 rubbers.

Quarter Final.
    West of Scotland lost to Yorkshire at Bradford on 17/4/71.
        1 rubber to 8 rubbers.

The following players took part :—Mrs. H. E. Allan, Miss R. Allan, Mrs. R. J. Livingstone, Miss M. J. Love, Mrs. H. S. Matheson, Miss S. E. L. Moodie, Mrs. J. Mackenzie, Miss V. J. MacLennan, Mrs. F. A. S. Paul, Miss E. Robb, Mrs. H. Robb, Mrs. M. P. Smith and Miss E. Tweedlie.

INTER-ASSOCIATION REPRESENTATIVE MATCHES

LADIES

West v. East. At Edinburgh, 14/5/72.
   West won by 5 rubbers to 3.

West. v. Central. At Clarkston, 21/5/72.
   West won by 7 rubbers to 1.

West v. Ayrshire. At Titwood, 2/7/72.
   West won by 6 rubbers to 1.

MEN

West v. Ayrshire. At Largs, 2/7/72.
   West won by 6 rubbers to 2.

West v. Central. At Bridge of Allan, 21/5/72.
   West won by 6 rubbers to 2.

West v. East. At Thorn Park, 14/5/72.
   West won by 6 rubbers to 2.

INTER-COUNTY CHAMPIONSHIPS ON GRASS (DOUBLES)

These matches were played during the week commencing 24th July. Teams representing the West of Scotland Tennis Association took part, the Ladies' Team playing at Eastbourne and the men at Southsea. The Ladies' Team lost all 5 matches in Group 1 and will play in Group 2 next year. The Men's Team won 1 out of 5 matches in Group 2 and will play in Group 3 next year.

The Ladies' Team consisted of Mrs. L. S. Black (Bristol), captain, Miss R. Allan, Mrs. R. J. Livingstone, Miss M. J. Love, Miss S. E. L. Moodie, Miss V. J. MacLennan, Mrs. F. A. S. Paul, Miss W. M. Shaw and Miss S. C. Smith.

The Men's Team consisted of G. Copeland, G. T. Downes, W. C. Gillespie, R. Howat, H. S. Matheson, K. Revie, I. Walker and T. Walker. K. B. Gray acted as non-playing captain.

INTER-COUNTY CHAMPIONSHIPS ON HARD COURTS, 1971-72.

MEN

Quarter Final.

West of Scotland lost to Lancashire in Glasgow on 15/4/72.
   3 rubbers to 9 rubbers.

The following players took part :—G. Copeland, H. Drummond, H. S. Matheson, K. Revie, F. N. Thompson and I. Walker.

LADIES

Preliminary Stage.

West of Scotland lost to Durham in Darlington on 18/9/71.
   4 rubbers to 5 rubbers.

West of Scotland beat Northumberland at Giffnock on 3/10/71.
   9 rubbers to nil.

West of Scotland beat Cumberland in Carlisle on 11/9/71.
   9 rubbers to nil.

The following players took part :—Mrs. C. A. R. Lockhart, Miss M. J. Love, Miss S. E. L. Moodie, Mrs. A. McGill, Mrs. E. Mackenzie, Mrs. F. A. S. Paul, Miss E. Robb, Mrs. M. P. Smith, Miss S. C. Smith, Miss E. Tweedlie and Miss E. N. Winning.

INTER-ASSOCIATION REPRESENTATIVE MATCHES

LADIES

West v. East. At Giffnock, 13/5/73.
    West won by 7 rubbers to 1 rubber.
West v. Central. At Bridge of Allan, 20/5/73.
    West won by 6 rubbers to 2 rubbers.
West v. Ayrshire. At Largs, 1/7/73.
    West won by 6 rubbers to 0.

MEN

West v. East. At Abercorn, 13/5/73.
    West won by 6 rubbers to 2 rubbers.
West v. Ayrshire. At Giffnock, 1/7/73.
    West won by 7 rubbers to 1 rubber.

INTER-COUNTY CHAMPIONSHIPS ON GRASS (DOUBLES)

These matches were played during the week commencing 23rd July. Teams representing the West of Scotland Lawn Tennis Association took part; the Ladies playing at Cromer and the men at Frinton. The Ladies' team won all 5 matches in Group 2 and will play in Group 1 next year.   The Men's team won 3 out of 5 matches in Group 3 and will play in Group 3 next year.

The Ladies' team consisted of Mrs F. A. S. Paul (Captain), Miss R. Allan, Mrs D. W. Barrow, Mrs R. J. Livingstone, Mrs. C. R. Lockhart, Miss M. J. Love, Miss S. E. L. Moodie and Mrs K. Woolridge.

The Men's team comsisted of W. C. Gillespie (Captain), G. T. Downes, R. Howat, J. Howie, H. S. Matheson, K. Revie, F. N. Thompson and I. Walker.

INTER-COUNTY CHAMPIONSHIPS ON HARD COURTS, 1972-73.

MEN

Preliminary Stage.
    West of Scotland beat Northumberland at Newlands on 24/9/72.
        11 rubbers to 1 rubber.
    West of Scotland lost to East in Edinburgh on 1/10/72.
        5 rubbers to 7 rubbers.

The following players took part:—G. Copeland, G. T. Downes, W. C. Gillespie, H. S. Matheson, K. Revie, F. N. Thompson, I. Walker and T. Walker.

LADIES

Preliminary Stage.
    West of Scotland beat Durham at Whitecraigs on 30/9/72.
        8 rubbers to 1 rubber.
    West of Scotland beat Northumberland at Newcastle on 1/10/72.
        8 rubbers to 1 rubber.

Intermediate Stage.
    West of Scotland beat Worcestershire at Stourbridge on 10/3/73.
        9 rubbers to nil.

Quarter Final.
    West of Scotland beat Yorkshire at Hillpark on 22/4/73.
        5 rubbers to 4 rubbers.

Semi-Final.
    West of Scotland beat Warwickshire at Bournemouth on 22/9/73.
        7 rubbers to 2 rubbers.

Final.
    West of Scotland lost to Middlesex at Bournemouth on 23/9/73.
        4 rubbers to 5 rubbers.

The following players took part:—Miss R. L. Allan, Mrs R. J. Livingstone, Mrs C. R. Lockhart, Miss M. J. Love, Mrs H. S. Matheson, Miss S. E. L. Moodie, Mrs F. A. S. Paul, Miss S. C. Smith, Miss M. Stevenson, Mrs R. Taylor and Mrs K. Woolridge. MISS ECL ROBB.

Results of Matches played during 1974, in which teams representing the West of Scotland Lawn Tennis Association took part

INTER-ASSOCIATION REPRESENTATIVE MATCHES

LADIES

West v. East. At Edinburgh, 12/5/74.
  West won by 5 rubbers to 3 rubbers.

West v. Central. At Hamilton, 19/5/74.
  West won by 8 rubbers to nil.

West v. Ayrshire. At Elderslie, 30/6/74.
  West won by 6 rubbers to 2 rubbers.

MEN

West v. East. At Giffnock, 12/5/74.
  West won by 8 rubbers to nil.

West v. Central. At Bridge of Allan, 19/5/75.
  West drew 4 rubbers each.

West v. Ayrshire. At Largs, 30/6/74.
  West won by 7 rubbers to 1 rubber.

INTER-COUNTY CHAMPIONSHIPS ON GRASS (DOUBLES)

These matches were played during the week commencing 22nd July.   Teams representing the West of Scotland Lawn Tennis Association took part, the Ladies playing at Eastbourne and the men at Ilkley, The Ladies' team won four out of five matches in Group 1, being runners-up in their group and will play in group 1 next year.   The men also won four out of five matches in Group 3 and, finishing as runners-up in their group, will play in group 2 next year.

The Ladies' team consisted of Mrs. F. A. S. Paul (Captain), Miss R. L. Allan, Miss M. J. Love, Mrs. H. S. Matheson, Miss S. E. L. Moodie, Miss E. Robb, Mrs. R. Taylor and Mrs. K. Woolridge.

The Men's team consisted of I. C. Conway, W. C. Gillespie, G. T. Downes, J. F. Howie, H. S. Matheson, N. Paterson, K. Revie and I. Walker.   K. B. Gray acted as non-playing captain.

INTER-COUNTY CHAMPIONSHIPS ON HARD COURTS, 1973-74

MEN

Preliminary Stage.

  West of Scotland beat Northumberland at Newcastle on 30/9/73.
    10 rubbers to 2 rubbers.

  West of Scotland beat East of Scotland in Glasgow on 7/10/73.
    11 rubbers to 1 rubber.

Play-off.

  West of Scotland beat Durham at Sunderland on 4/11/73.
    7 rubbers to 5 rubbers.

Intermediate Stage.

  West of Scotland beat Staffordshire at Whitecraigs on 6/4/74.
    7 rubbers to 5 rubbers.

Quarter-final.

  West of Scotland lost to Yorkshire in Sheffield on 21/4/74.
    2 rubbers to 10 rubbers.

The following players took part:—G. Copeland, I. C. Conway, R. Howat, J. F. Howie, H. S. Matheson, N. Paterson, K. Revie, and I. Walker.

LADIES

Quarter-Final.

  West of Scotland beat Lincolnshire at Whitecraigs on 6/4/74.
    9 rubbers to nil.

Semi-Final.

  West of Scotland beat Surrey at Bournemouth on 21/9/74.
    5 rubbers to 4.

Final.

  West of Scotland lost to Devon at Bournemouth on 22/9/74.
    4 rubbers to 5 rubbers.

The following players took part:—Miss R. L. Allan, Mrs. R. J. Livingstone, Miss M. J. Love, Mrs. H. S. Matheson, Miss S. E. L. Moodie, Mrs. F. A. S. Paul, Mrs. R. Taylor and Mrs. K. Woolridge.

BIBLIOGRAPHY

Regality Club / Rottenrow of Glasgow p77 (Mitchell Library)

Jamiesons Dictionary

The Ballie (Mitchell Library) 1880s

Quiz (Mitchell Library) 1880s

Pastime, A weekly record of Sports (Kenneth Ritchie Library) 1880s

Fifty Years of Lawn Tennis in Scotland, Edinburgh : Scottish Lawn Tennis Association / Morrison & Gibb Ltd. 1927

Jubilee Souvenir of the West of Scotland Tennis Championships, George B Primrose Coatbridge 1935

The West of Scotland Lawn Tennis Association Jubilee Souvenir 1904-1954, George B Primrose Glasgow 1954.

The Lawn Tennis Year,   pub Pelam Books 1971

Scottish Tennis, Edinburgh: Learmonth / Scottish Lawn Tennis Association

Centenary Books of

Bearsden 1887 - 1987

Poloc 1883 - 2003

Titwood 1890 - 1990

Minutes of The West of Scotland Lawn Tennis Association

Tennis in Scotland 100 Years of the Scottish Lawn Tennis Association 1895-1995 George Robertson / SLTA

Wimbledon The Official History of the Championships John Barrett: pub in assoc with The All England Lawn Tennis & Croquet Club 2001

2000 Wimbledon Compendium Allan Little : All England Lawn Tennis and Croquet Club

The Real James Herriot The Authorised Biography : Jim Wight, Penguin 1999

The Glasgow Herald / The Herald / Bulletin / Evening Times Newsquest Media Group

The Scottish Daily Record

Suzanne Lenglen (Tennis Idol of the Twenties) by Alan Little pub Wimbledon Lawn Tennis Museum 1988

MYRA HUNTER

Myra began playing tennis at the age of fourteen at Alexandra Park, played in the teams and in the West of Scotland League. In the 1960s & 1970s played at and for Springboig LTC where she was Club Champion nine times and was the first Lady President. She gained the Coaching Certificate.

When Springboig finally closed Myra became a member of Rutherglen LTC and in time President of the Club during which time she was responsible for the up-grading of the courts to all weather and the installation of floodlights.

Serving on the West of Scotland Committee in 1969 then again since 1993, Myra was responsible for the production of the Centenary Exhibition "100 Years of Tennis in the West of Scotland" at the People's Palace Museum, Glasgow Green.